Asa Keyes

**Genealogy**

Asa Keyes

**Genealogy**

ISBN/EAN: 9783337142063

Printed in Europe, USA, Canada, Australia, Japan

Cover: Foto ©ninafisch / pixelio.de

More available books at **www.hansebooks.com**

# GENEALOGY

# ROBERT KEYES

OF WATERTOWN, MASS.,

1633.

# SOLOMON KEYES

OF NEWBURY AND CHELMSFORD, MASS.,

1653.

AND THEIR DESCENDANTS:

ALSO,

## OTHERS OF THE NAME,

BY

## ASA KEYES.

—

BRATTLEBORO:
GEO. E. SELLECK, PRINTER.
1880.

# PREFACE.

After some years of study into the history of the Keyes family, in order to ascertain my own remote ancestry and connections, and without a thought of putting into print the result of my research, I yielded to the wishes of many of my name, and concluded to put the (at that time) scanty information I had gained, into a short, informal pamphlet. This may account for the want of consistent, artistic arrangement in the work, which, as I advanced and the field opened before me, I regretted, too late. But we do not expect from the pioneer, in new countries or new fields, what must of necessity belong to maturer knowledge and more complete development; and I am a pioneer in the Genealogy of the Keyes family.

In seeking my own ancestry, my first idea was to look for it in the line, at the head of which stood Robert of Watertown, and much material had been accumulated, and much advance made, before grave doubts arose in my mind (as to what has been assumed by many of those who have any knowledge of our Genealogy, namely) whether Solomon of Newbury and Chelmsford, was the son of Robert. Those doubts have not been, and probably cannot be, solved, at present. I feel sure that a relationship existed, and, until the mist enveloping their early history be cleared away, let us content ourselves, with having the Genealogy of their descendants. The records of later emigrants have been added, both to save the trouble of farther research in that direction in order to find the missing links in our own history, and because among them are names we might be proud to place beside our own.

I would remark that the numbers attached to individual names, in the regular series, have no significance as to the prominence of the individual, but are inserted to give an idea of the extent of the family, and for reference. Many names were received too late for numbering in their proper place, without breaking the general order of numbering.

Perhaps explanations of abbreviations or arrangement are unnecessary in these days when almost every family owns some Genealogical work, and I will only explain that the Roman numerals, at the left of various names in this work, indicate the generation; and the Arabic figures at the right, in parenthesis, refer to a preceding number in the regular series, where will be found the date of birth, with that of other members of the same family.

With regard to dates, and the spelling of names, they have been inserted as they were received, as far as the (in some cases) obscure chirography could be deciphered. Town and family records have been often at variance, and, for a decision betwee them, the judgment of the compiler has been the only resource.

Acknowledgments for assistance in collecting the early records of the family, are due to many of the town clerks of Massachusetts and Connecticut, and the histories of Marlboro, Newbury, Shrewsbury, Mass., Acworth, N. H., and Northfield, Vt., have afforded many items. To Hon. E. S. Keyes of Jay, Me., to C W. Keyes, Esq., of Quincy, Ill., Capt. C. W. Keyes of Farmington, Me., Gen. E. D. Keyes, U. S. A., Hon. John S. Keyes of Concord, Mass., and the late lamented Judge Wade Keyes of Montgomery, Ala. our thanks are due; also to Rev. R. G. Keyes, of Watertown, N. Y., R. W. Clarke, Esq., of Brattleboro, and many others whose names we cannot here insert, for anecdotes and records.

ASA KEYES.

BRATTLEBORO, VT., January 21, 1880.

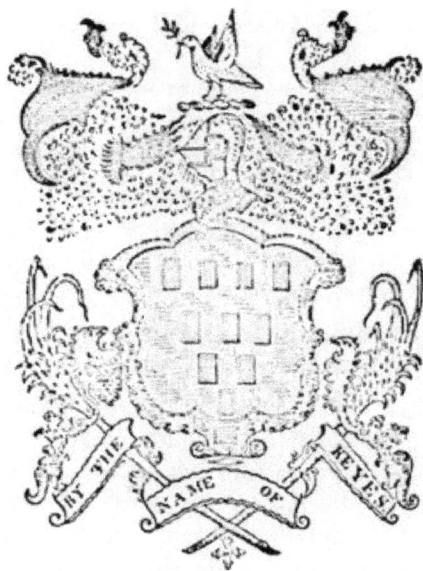

Coat of Arms.

# THE COAT OF ARMS.

From the books of heraldry we take the following descriptions of the Keyes 'Coat of Arms.'

"Keyes. (Kent.) Gu, (red), a chev, (a chevron), erm, (ermine), between three leopards' heads, ar, (silver or white). Another, or, (gold or yellow).

Keyes. The same arms. Crest, a griffin's head between two wings, holding a palm branch, ppr. (proper).

The Coat of Arms illustrated in this book belonged to Solomon of Chelmsford. It was taken from a coloured copy, which has long hung on the wall of the old homestead in Chelmsford, placed there before the recollection of any one now living. It will be noticed that it agrees in many respects with the descriptions we have copied. The shield is there represented as 'or,' the bars and other parts, 'Gu.' The ermine may be seen in our illustration, also the griffins and palm branches, supporting the shield. A descendant of John of Lancaster sends us a seal with the impression of a griffin's head between two wings, as the crest, of the arms, of that branch of the family. He has also the mailed head of a warrior, which appears in our illustration. These facts seem to make it probable that the Robert and Solomon families, are different branches of the same head.

# PART FIRST.

## ROBERT KEYES,

### AND HIS DESCENDANTS.

I. 1. ROBERT KEYES settled in Watertown, Mass., sometime before, or in, the year 1633. The earliest record we find relating to him, is that of the birth of his eldest daughter.

CHILDREN OF ROBERT AND SARAH KEYES.

2. Sarah, b. May 25, 1633.
3. Peter, probably s. of Robert.
4. Rebecca, b. Mar. 17, 1637.
5. Phebe, b. June 17, 1639.
6. Mary, b. 1641, d. 1642.
7. Elias, b. May 26, 1643.
8. Mary, b. June 16, 1645.

The birth of all these children is recorded in Watertown, with the exception of Peter, and the second Mary, who was born in Newbury, Mass., and her birth there recorded. The death of Robert, is recorded at Watertown, Newbury, Plymouth and Sudbury, Mass. The Watertown record says: "Robert removed to Sudbury, Mass., June 16, 1645, where he died 1647." Another record, makes his death occur July 16, 1647. His history seems to be, that he was in Watertown, in 1633 if not earlier, removed to Newbury between 1643 and 1645, and to Sudbury during the latter year, and died in 1647. His widow was married to John Gage, in 1658, or according to the Plymouth record, Nov. 1664.

II. KEYES, SARAH (probably dau. of Robert), married Samuel Buzzell, 1656, at Salisbury, Mass.

II. KEYES, PETER (3), whose wife was Elizabeth, is mentioned in Plymouth and Sudbury records, as having a dau.,
9. Esther, b. Feb. 1668.

1

II. KEYES, ELIAS (7), of Sudbury, s. of Robert, m. Sarah, dau. of John Blanford, or Blanchard, Sept. 11, 1665.

### CHILDREN, B. IN SUDBURY.

10. Elias, b. Nov. 15, 1666.
11. John, sup. s. of Elias, b. probably 1668.
*p. 20* —12. James, b. Sept. 13, 1670.
13. Sarah, b. Apr. 9, 1673.
*p. 23* ——14. Thomas, b. Feb. 8, 1674.

III. KEYES, ELIAS (10), s. of Elias. We learn from "Ward's History of Shrewsbury," that Elias was in Marlboro, Mass., where he had a family, between 1696 and 1702. We find no record of his marriage there or elsewhere, or of the birth of children.

III. KEYES, JOHN (11), sup. s. of Elias of Sudbury, lived for a time in Lancaster, Mass. He first appeared in Shrewsbury as a town officer, in 1727, and was living in the North Parish, at Spring Garden, on house lot, No. 42, in 1729. This lot was granted to "John Keyes, Sen." Dec. 30, 1718. Ward, in his history of Shrewsbury says, "Dea. John Keyes, whose wife was Sarah, was one of the founders of this church, a strong pillar therein, and its first deacon." He was chosen 1723. He was one of the Selectmen, and Assessor, and the first Town Clerk. His name does not appear as a town officer after 1743, at which time he must have been at least 79 years of age. He is supposed to have d. about 1748, or '9.

### CHILDREN.

15. Ebenezer, b. about the year 1700.
16. Phebe, who joined the church in Shrewsbury, 1728, and d. Sept. 16, 1748.
*p. 12* —17. John, b. 1712.
18. Huldah, b. 1713, d. Dec. 19, 1726.
19. Elkanah, b. 1718, m. Elizabeth Warner, Jan. 11, 1759.
    Elkanah, d. Jan. 19, 1806, at Harvard, Mass., aged 88.
    Elizabeth, d. Mar. 30, 1816, at Harvard, aged 97.

IV. KEYES, EBENEZER (15) m. Tamar, dau. of Dea. Samuel Wheelock, July 31, 1726, and lived in the North Parish of Shrewsbury, now Boylston. He d. probably, about 1780.

CHILDREN.

20. Huldah, b. April 19, 1727, m. Elijah Rice, about 1748.

21. Elisha, b. Feb. 15, 1729.

22. Tamar, } b. Jan. 5, 1731, m. Jon Knight, of Worcester, Oct. 20, 1756.

23. Tryphena, } b. Jan. 5, 1731, m. Jacob Hinds, 1756.

24. Ebenezer, b. Nov. 4, 1733.

25. Hepsibah, b. June 2, 1736, m. Bezaleel Gleason of Worcester, Dec. 6, 1758.

26. Hannah, b. April 17, 1742, m. Ebenezer Drury, Oct. 29, 1761.

V. KEYES, ELISHA (21) m. Catherine Baker, dau. sup. of Thomas Baker, July 19, 1757, lived in the S. W. part of Shrewsbury, and d. there, Feb. 18, 1811. Catherine, his wife, d. Nov 9, 1797.

CHILDREN.

27. Eber, b. Aug. 29 1758.

28. Azubah, b. May 13, 1760, m. Henry Baldwin, Jr., 1786.

29. Ashley, b. May 3, 1762, d. 1763.

30. Elizabeth, b. Oct. 31, 1763, m. Calvin Newton, 1787.

31. Ashley, b. Nov. 29, 1765.

32. Lewis, b. July 31, 1768.

33. Mary, b. June 16, 1773, d. Oct. 26, 1784.

34. Nahum, b. Dec. 15, 1776.

VI. KEYES, ASHLEY (31) son of Elisha, m. Oct. 20, 1788, Anna Willard, who was b. in Grafton, Mass., Aug. 11, 1769, d. July 8, 1803, at Newfane, Vt.

CHILDREN.

35. Mary b. July 18, 1789, at Shrewsbury, m. Sept., 1813, Timothy Kidder, a descendent of James Kidder, who was born 1626, at East Grinstead, Sussex Co., England, came to New England before 1650, located at Cambridge, Mass., married, and removed to Billerica, Mass., where he died. Mary d. Sept. 1814, at Wardsboro, Vt.

36. Betsey, b. Feb. 12, 1791, at Newfane, Vt., d. Sept. 24, 1794.

37. Willard, b. Oct. 28, 1792, at Newfane, Vt.

38. Royal b. April 23, 1795, at Newfane, Vt.

39. Philinda, b. Jan. 22, 1797, at Newfane, Vt., d. May 23, 1823, at Middlebury, Vt.

40. Eber, b. Jan. 15, 1799, at Newfane, Vt.

41. Luke, b. Nov. 3, 1800, at Newfane, Vt., d. May 20, 1851, at Quincy, Ill.

42. Anna, b. May 26, 1803, at Newfane, Vt., m. Henry Baker, d. May 22, 1824, at Jamestown, N. Y.

Ashley, m. 2nd, Tirzah Baker, Feb., 1805, who was b. at Brattleboro, Vt., June 17, 1777, and d. June 19, 1838, at Bristol, Ohio.

43. Ashley, Jr., b. Feb. 18, 1806, at Newfane, d. Nov. 27, 1835, at Bristol, Ohio.

44. Emily, b. Sept. 27, 1807, at Newfane, m. Samuel Strickland, now of Iowa.

45. Nahum, b. Nov. 2, 1809, d. Marquette, Mich.

46. Clarissa, b. June 14, 1812, m. —— Jones, d. Jan. 31, 1837, at Bristol, Ohio.

47. Benjamin Lewis, b. March 28, 1814,

Ashley Keyes, d. Jan. 27, 1853, at Greenville, Penn.

VII. KEYES, WILLARD (37) eldest s. of Ashley, removed to the West, in 1817, and was one of the original settlers of the now city of Quincy, Ill., in 1824. He m. 1st., Dec. 22, 1825, Laura Harkness, b. in Bradford Co., Penn., April 13, 1809, d. May 8, 1832.

#### CHILDREN.

48. Mary Ann, b. Sept. 27, 1826, m. Edward F. Humphrey, Sept. 19, 1850, d. April 20, 1853.

49. John Harkness, b. April 2, 1829, d. March 20, 1834.

50. Philinda, b. Feb. 14, 1832, d. Sept. 4, 1832.

Willard, m. 2nd, March 5, 1834, Cornelia Burgess, b. in Guilford, Conn., 1803, d. Nov. 22, 1834. m. 3d, March 29, 1836, Mary C. Folsom, b. Nov. 9, 1800, at Exeter, N. H., d. Nov. 2, 1864.

51. Martha, b. March 3, 1837, d. Oct 5, 1838.

52. Lucy Emily, b. April 20, 1838, m. Oct. 19, 1870, George V. Rutherford, who d. Aug. 1876. No Children.

53. Cornelia, b. Sept. 19, 1839, m. June 8. 1871, Dr. Henry J. Smith.

SON.

54.　　　Harry Keyes Smith, b. Jan. 30, 1873.

55. Charles Willard, b. July 24, 1841.

56. Sarah Folsom, b. July 3, 1845.


VIII. KEYES, CHARLES WILLARD (55) graduate of Williams College, 1864, m. Oct. 25, 1866, Mary Louisa Collins. Residence Quincy, Ill.

CHILDREN.

57. Mary, b. Nov. 22, 1867.

58. Edward Collins, b. Jan. 1, 1869.

59. Willard, b. Jan. 7, 1872, d. March 8, 1872.

60. Charles Frederick, b. Nov. 10, 1874.

61. Willard Collins, b. March 1, 1876.

62. Allen Collins, b. May 6, 1878.


VIII. KEYES, SARAH FOLSOM (56) m. Nov. 15, 1866, Edward W. Hope.

CHILDREN.

63. Willard Keyes, b. August 13, 1867.

64. Marian, b. March 20, 1872, d. Dec. 27, 1872.

65. Charles Keyes,　} b. Nov. 11, 1873.
66. Edward William,} b. Nov. 11, 1873.

Charles K. Hope d. July 17. 1874.

Son (not named) b. March 1, 1875.

Willard Keyes d. Feb. 7 1872, at Quincy, Ill.


## WILLARD KEYES.

It is fitting that a small space be given to commemorate the worth of one who through a long life bore living testimony to the value of a well balanced mind, united with inflexible integrity of purpose in all the affairs of life. The life of Willard Keyes was in more senses than one a successful life—not perhaps as the altogether worldly man estimates success—but in all that goes to make up a record for enterprise, honorable dealing, and true philanthrophy, leaving behind a memory cherished and remembered by all who knew him—in this his life was a grand success.

The only record we have of his earlier years, is from a diary, from which we should like to quote largely, did the plan and scope of this work allow. This diary, kept from 1817 to 1820, shows that the moral excellence which he afterward attained, and the influence for good which he exercised, were the result of high aims and resolves in early life. He says:

" I was born among the rugged mountains of Vermont, whose robust inhabitants are mostly cultivators of the soil they possess, in independence and peace, and where luxury and dissipation, those deadly foes to religion and liberty are hardly known. My father removed from Shrewsbury, Mass., to Newfane, Vt., about the year 1788, and entered on a small farm, entirely new, and with a soil as rough and heavily timbered, as perhaps any of the Vermont mountains produce."

After alluding to the large family which his father brought up in habits of industry, he says: "The country being new, I had but a slender chance of getting instruction at school. However, I was early taught that learning was better than riches, that without education I should be liable to repeated embarrassments and must expect to rank with the dregs of society. These early precepts and a natural taste thereto, excited me to learning, and reading soon became my ruling passion, and every leisure moment was employed in poring over some musty author. Days, weeks and years glided by with little variation, and reading continued to be my chief delight."

In his twentieth year Mr. Keyes served a three months campaign as a volunteer in the war of 1812, and the succeeding five years were varied by farm work in summer and teaching school in winter. But this monotonous life was illy calculated to satisfy the requirements of a disposition naturally so enterprising and ambitious. So on the 2nd day of June, 1817, we find him setting forth on foot, with a scantily filled purse, to seek his fortune in the far West, at that time little more than a desolate wilderness.

At the end of a month he had reached Oswego, on the shores of Lake Ontario, performing nearly the entire journey on foot. Crossing the lake to Toronto (then called York), he fell in with a party of gentlemen from New York City, on their way to examine a large tract of land on the Mississippi, at Prairie du Chien, and was persuaded to join the party.

From this point the narrative portrays with fascinating vividness the adventures of the party, as in their boat propelled by oar and sail, they coasted along the shores of the great lakes, camping out in the wilderness each night.

Their course was from Toronto north by land to Lake Simcoe, thence with their own boat through the river that connects the latter with lake Huron, thence along the shore of that lake, and through the straits of Mackinac into Lake Michigan.

From the head of Green Bay, they went by the Fox river to the portage, where it became necessary to transport their boat overland, a distance of little over a mile, to the Wisconsin river and down the Wisconsin to its junction with the Mississippi at Prairie du Chien. The route was about 2000 miles.

Mr. Keyes passed a year and a half at Prairie du Chien, engaged in such pursuits as opportunity offered. The winter of 1818-19, was spent in the prairies of Black River, amid hardships and privations which we of later times can perhaps have no conception. The early spring finds him afloat on the broad waters of the Mississippi, sole proprietor of a large raft of pine timber, and with one assistant he sets forth for St. Louis, where in due time he arrives in safety and disposes of his raft for a good price. The ensuing fall and winter were passed in explorations, with a view to finding a place, which by the aid of a strong arm and a willing heart, could be made to serve for a home.

This spot, however, was not found until some three years later, when with Mr. John Wood (since Governor of the State of Ill.), he built his cabin where now stands the beautiful city of Quincy, Ill.

In a sermon preached by Rev. Mr. Emory, in 1861, upon the occasion of the death of Judge Snow, also an early resident of Quincy, he says (in allusion to Willard Keyes, Esq.) "In 1821, sometime during the month of September, forty years ago, lacking nine months, an adventurous traveller, journeying from the South, was overtaken by the night, as he reached what is now the city of Quincy. He built a camp-fire on the banks of the river, turned out his horse to graze, and clambered up the steep bluff to enjoy the prospect. It was a pleasing prospect. The country was well timbered, well watered, choice streams, noble forests, grand old trees of a century's growth, rich lands, a magnificent river, the father of waters, vast facilities for a settlement, a livelihood and a trade, were opened up before the bright vision of our traveller, and as he laid himself down to sleep that night, doubtless his dreams of the years to come, made him quite ready to resolve—as is recorded of him—that if 'God would give him a foothold here, he would make it his dwelling place in all the future, nor would he forget God, and fail to speak of his goodness.' That resolve built the first log cabin in Quincy, in 1823, a year or two afterward, under the bluff, on what is now called Front Street, and was the happy home of the three first settlers, Keyes, Rose and Wood. That resolve did more and better. It prepared the way for a church organization in Quincy, which was effected in Dec. of 1830."

Here he lived and labored for almost fifty years, and here he died honored and respected, as one of the founders and fathers of a large and prosperous city. With what anxious solicitude he watched the gradual growth and development of this infant settlement, from a desolate wilderness to a populous city there are few left to testify.

His life was marked by a rare spirit of enterprise and progress, coupled with an unyielding integrity that won for him respect and friends from all classes with whom he come in contact. He possessed a quiet and inoffensive disposition, with a want of self assertion which prompted him to shun rather than to seek for public life or station, for which otherwise he would have been well fitted.

He loved a generous act for its own sake, and for the sake of the inward consciousness it brought of a duty fulfilled. He was always ready to extend a helping hand to suffering and needy humanity, and this quality led him to feel and express a large measure of sympathy for the negro in slavery, and he was an active and outspoken abolitionist, at a time when to be such was unpopular with a large portion of the community.

For many years, and up to the time of his death he was deacon in the church (Cong), which he was instrumental in founding.

Feeling keenly his own lack of educational advantages, it was his earnest wish to give his own children a liberal education, and to exert his influence for the establishment of educational institutions, at home and abroad. To this end he gave liberally to the endowment of a Professorship in the Chicago Theological Seminary. But at the solicitation of the managers of that institution, he consented to a diversion of the fund, and it was applied instead to the construction of the original Seminary building bearing the name of Keyes Hall.

VII. KEYES, ROYAL (38), 2d s. of Ashley, m. Feb. 8, 1818, Amanda Kidder, b. at Wardsboro, Vt., March 7, 1794, and d. Jan. 2, 1875. Royal Keyes, d. July 1, 1852.

CHILDREN.

67. Mary Kidder, b. Nov. 18, 1818, m. Rev. Milo N. Miles, Sept. 24, 1839. Res. Des Moines, Iowa.

CHILDREN.

68. Ada, b. Nov. 19, 1840, m. Sept. 12, 1865, Maj. Geo. J. North, b. Dec. 18, 1836, d. Feb. 2, 1870. Mrs. North is State Librarian of Iowa. Two chil. Howard M., and Georgia.

69. Isabel, b. Aug. 1st. 1842, m. May 15, 1866, Charles H. Ward, b. Nov. 9, 1843. Chil. Geo. Guy, dec.; Percy, dec.; and Winnifred.

70. Clarence Royal, b. Dec. 13, 1845. Res. Culla, Pawnee Co. Nebraska.

71. Albert Hale, b. June 3, 1847. m. May 5, 1875, Della Whiting, b. June 1, 1852. Res. Des. Moines.

72. Carroll, b. Feb. 4, 1859. Res. Des Moines.

Also two chil. who d. in infancy.

73. Melissa Malvina, b. Jan. 1, 1820, m. Aug. 8, 1839, Hon. Lysander Farrar, a Lawyer of Rochester, N. Y., who dec. Dec. 25, 1876. CHILDREN.

74. Ellen, b. July 6, 1841, m. May 2, 1866, Col. Samuel

2

C. Puree. Their dau. Ellen F., was b. Jan. 30, 1867, d. Mar. 14, 1867. Mrs. Farrar had also, Elizabeth, b. Nov. 20, 1842; Harriet, b. Mar. 12, 1845; Raleigh, b. Dec. 3, 1856, now in the University of Rochester, and Mary, b. Oct. 26, 1865.

75. Alcey Eddy, b. March 12, 1822, m. Charles Kennedy, Sept. 28, 1843. Res. Washington, D. C.

76. Philinda Anna, b. May 10, 1824, m. George G. Blanchard, June 17, 1847, d. April 15, 1848, at Jamestown, N. Y.

77. Sarah Antoinette, b. Nov. 11, 1827, m. John B. Forbes, Nov. 10, 1852. Res. Fredonia, N. Y.

78. Lydia Amanda, b. March 6, 1831, m. John B. Forbes, March 22, 1849, at Fredonia, N. Y., d. July 16, 1850.

VII. KEYES, EBER (40), 3d s. of Ashley, m. Aug. 30, 1827, Lydia Kidder, b. at Wardsboro, Vt., March 27, 1806, d. at Jamestown, N. Y., Oct. 7, 1828. Eber m. 2d, Aug. 23, 1831, Clarinda J. Gray, b. Sept. 20, 1809, d. Oct. 24, 1845. Res. Elgin, Ill.　　　　　　　CHILDREN.

79. Emerson Willard, b. June 30, 1828.

80. Addison, b. Nov. 23, 1832, d. Aug. 16, 1834.

81. Lydia Kidder, b. April 4, 1834, m. John H. Becker, 1864. Res. Elgin, Illinois.

82. Ellen Gray, b. Feb. 14, 1839, m. Alfred Wallen, 1868. Res. Redwood Falls, Minnesota.

83. Addison Ashley, b. Oct. 3, 1842.

VIII. KEYES, EMERSON W. (79), s. of Eber, studied law, was admitted to the bar in 1862, and has edited several law books. His "Savings Banks Reports," 1868, is regarded as standard authority throughout the United States, and has largely influenced Legislation in many of the States, it being the foundation of the present New York law upon that subject. His second and last volume of "History of Savings Banks in the U. S." is now going through the press. He was Dep. Sup. of Public Instruction in N. Y., from 1857 to 1865. Has also been Dep. Superintendent of the Banking Dep. afterwards chief Examiner of Savings Banks, under the law. Res. 48 E. 14th Street, N. Y.

Emerson Keyes, m. 1st Sarah M. King, April 5, 1849.

CHILDREN.

84. Ella L., b. January 10, 1850.

    Emerson m. 2nd, Mary A. McGowen, Jan. 1861.

85. Willard Emerson, b. April 17, 1862.

    Emerson m. 3d, Rowena R. Saxe, June, 1863.

86. Arthur Saxe, b. Aug. 3, 1864.

87. Conrad Saxe, b. Sept. 11, 1874.

88. Homer Eaton, b. Dec. 21, 1875.


VIII. KEYES, ADDISON A. (83), 3d s. of Eber, was in the army most of the time during the war of the rebellion, attaining to the rank of Captain. Graduated from the Albany Law School, in 1865, and has been connected with the educational department of New York, having been President of the Board of Education for the city of Albany, and chief clerk in the Department of Public Instruction. Now editor of the Albany Morning Express. Res. Albany, N. Y.

He m. in Chicago, Ill., July 27, 1865, Mary Agnes Bradley.

CHILDREN.

89. Edward Ashley, b. April 27, 1866.

90. Mary Ella, b. April 9, 1868.

91. Juliette Gray, b. Nov. 24, 1870.

92. Annie Rowena, b. Dec. 31, 1872.


VII. KEYES, BENJAMIN L. (47), youngest s. of Ashley was twice married.

CHILDREN.

93. Augusta, m. Henry Gibson. Res. Omaha.

94. Eugenia, m. Andrew McAusland, Res. Neb.


VI. KEYES, LEWIS (32), s. of Elisha, m. Sarah, dau. of Joseph Stone, Oct. 30, 1793, d. March 25, 1798. His widow, Sarah d. June 16, 1799.

CHILDREN.

95. Emerson, b. Oct. 5, 1794, d. Dec. 2, 1816.

96. Lewis, b. March 6, 1796, d. young.

Here ends the record of descendants of Ebenezer, s. of Dea. John.

IV. KEYES, JOHN, JR. (17), s. of Dea. John, and the only one who appears to be so of record, m. Abigail, dau. of Dea. John Livermore, Nov. 26, 1741.

### CHILDREN.

97. Simon, b. Oct. 17, 1742, m. Lucy Wheeler.

98. Abigail, b. Dec. 25, 1743, m. Will A. Hawkins of Northboro, Mass. 1776.

99. Phebe, b. March 19, 1745, m. Stephen Buss, Wilton, N.H.

100. Elizabeth, b. April 6, 1746, m. Joshua Blanchard, Feb. 1770, Wilton.

101. Submit, b. Sept. 2, 1747, m. Israel Howe, Princeton, Mass.

102. Lydia, b. May 7, 1749, m. Uriah Smith, Wilton, 1771.

103. Sarah, b. June 20, 1751, m. 1st Timothy Hall, 2nd —— Jewett.

104. John, b. Aug. 7, 1753.

105. Thomas, b. July 8, 1755.

106. Silas, b. Aug. 7, 1757.

107. Rhoda, b. Mar. 31, 1759, m. William Beals, Wilton, N.H.

108. Ephraim, b. March 14, 1761.

John is said to have d. at Boylston, Mass., age unknown.

V. KEYES, SIMON (97), eldest s. of John and Abigail, m. —— Hosmer, perhaps 2nd wife, settled in Wilton, N. H. d. 1800.

### CHILDREN.

109. VI. Simon, who had 10 children, 4 s. and 6 dau.

### SONS OF SIMON.

110. Amos.

111. Samas.

112. Bigar.

113. Solomon, who was b. 1797, at Shirley, Mass.

114. And had Leonard, James and John. Res. Worcester, Mass.

115. VI. Jeduthan.

### CHILDREN.

116. Ezra Willard, b. at New Chester, March 8, 1807.

117. Albert, b. May 14, 1809.

118. Jeduthan, b. Jan. 29, 1811.

119. David, b. Nov. 21, 1812.

Susanna, wife of Jeduthan, d. at Orford, N. H., April 26, 1814, aged 29.

V. KEYES, JOHN (104), 2d s. of John and Abigail, m. Lucy Hale, of Boxford, Mass., Sept. 4, 1777, and moved to Wilton, N. H., where the two eldest s. were b. They moved to Princeton, Mass., 1781. John Keyes d. Aug. 23, 1839, at Princeton, Mass.

### CHILDREN.

120. John, b. Aug. 28, 1778.

121. Jotham, b. Aug. 12, 1780, m. 1st, Sally Moore, m. 2nd, Susan Hartwell, no children, d. May 26, 1866.

122. Lucy, b. April 16, 1783, d. Jan. 31, 1850, unmarried.

123. Betsey, b. Aug. 3, 1785, m. Charles Gregory of Princeton. 11 children, only 2 dau. now living. Betsey d. June 5. 1868.

124. Ruth, b. Aug. 27, 1787.

125. Susannah, b. Nov. 14, 1789.

126. Amos, b. April 30, 1792.

127. Phebe, b. Jan. 4, 1795, d. Oct. 10, 1870, unmarried.

128. Moses, b. Oct. 2, 1797.

VI. KEYS, JOHN (120), s. of John and Lucy, graduated from Dartmouth, 1803, studied Divinity with Rev. Dr. Richards, of Morristown, N. J., was ordained at Perth Amboy. N. J., Aug. 4, 1807, preached at Sand Lake, N. Y., Wolcott, Conn., at Talmadge, and in the Western Reserve, Ohio, then removed to Dover, Ohio, disabled by ill health. He m. Mary Carmichael of Morristown, April 25, 1804, d. at Dover, Jan. 21, 1867. His wife d. 1850. Like many of the name in early days, he wrote his name "Keys," omitting the second e, which some of his children afterward adopted.

### CHILDREN.

129. Mary Ogden, b. Feb. 7, 1805, at Morristown, N. J.

130. John Alexander, b. Sept. 7, 1806, at Perth Amboy, N. J.

131. William Mulford, b. May 4, 1808, at Morristown, N. J. Has 2 children, both married. Res. Roca, Neb.

132. Richard Montgomery, b. Jan. 18, 1810, at Sand Lake, N. Y. Res. Fresno, Cal. The town of Keyesville, Tulare, Co., Cal., named for him on account of his discovery of the first gold mine there.

133. David Carmichael, ⎫ b. July 10, 1812, at Albany, N. Y., m. in Ohio, 3 children. d. in Cal., March 27, 1865.

134. Huldah Bryon, ⎬ b. Jul. 10, 1812, at Albany, N.Y., d. Oct. 14, 1813.

135. Catharine Sophia, b. May 31, 1814, at Albany, N. Y.

136. Lucy Hale, b. May 6, 1816, at Wolcott, Conn.

137. Charles Francis, b. April 26, 1819, at Wolcott, Conn., d. July 2, 1845. in Miss.

138. Augusta Albertina, b. July 3, 1822, at Wolcott, Conn., d. June 30, 1825, in Talmadge, Ohio.

139. Luther Hart, b. Sept. 9, 1826, at Talmadge, Ohio.


VII. KEYS, MARY O. (129), m. William Kingsbury.

CHILDREN.

140. William Vanhorn, b. 1825, m. Lucy Keyes. Res. Cal.

141. Mary, b. 1827, d. in infancy.

142. Louise Dutcher, b. Dec. 16, 1829, m. Jan. 2, 1851, Alexander Reed, in Maumee City.

CHILDREN.

143.          William Henry, b. Jan. 8, 1852.

144.          George Frederic, b. Jan. 2, 1855.

145.          Edward Montgomery, b. June 25, 1857.

146.          Mary, b. Sept. 10, 1862.

147.          Bessie Louise, b. March 12, 1869.

148. Alonzo, b. 1832, m. 1867, Clarissa Church.

149.          s. Alonzo.  Res. Alleghany City.

150. Ogden, s. of Mary O., died in childhood.

151. Frank,  "          "          "          "


VII. KEYES, JOHN A. (130), lived in Peoria, Ill., and was Deacon of his church. Removed to Cal., elected to the office of County Judge, and has been Post Master in Visalia, 17 years. Res. Visalia, Cal. He m. Mary W. Taylor, in 1850.

CHILDREN.

152. Rina, d. at eight months of age.
153. Georgiana, b. about 1862.

VII. KEYES, CATHARINE S. (135), m. May 30, 1833, Marius Moore. Res. Dover, Ohio.

CHILDREN.

154. Van Ness, b. July 12, 1837.
155. Augusta Jane, b. Jan. 21, 1838.

VI. KEYES, LUCY HALE (136), m. Feb. 15, 1838, Rev Caleb Abbott. Res. Cleveland, Ohio.

CHILDREN.

156. Mary Jane, b. Nov. 19, 1838, deceased.
157. John Knox, b. June 22, 1840, was in the late war.
158. John Francis, b. Oct. 31, 1842, was in the late war.
159. Merlin Howard, b. Jan. 5, 1845, deceased.
160. Alfred Augustine, b. Oct. 12, 1847.
161. Marion Clarice, b. July 13, 1850.
162. Charlotte Elizabeth, b. Sept. 23, 1852, Deceased.

VII. KEYES, LUTHER HART (139), is a graduate of Charity Hospital Medical College (now a department of the University of Wooster, Ohio), Cleveland, Ohio. Was in the war of the Rebellion in the year 1865, on detached service at General Hospital, Fort Gaines, Alabama, the Hospital, Mobile, and at Sedgwick General Hospital, New Orleans. He m. May 30, 1852, at Cedar Rapids, Iowa, Mary Frances, dau. of John and Emeline Nelson. Dr. Keyes resides in Junction City, Kansas.

CHILDREN.

163. John Norwood, b. April 7, 1853, Cedar Rapids, Iowa, Lawyer, and Police Judge at Junction City.
164. Earnest Mulford, M. D., b. at Cedar Rapids, Iowa, May

14, 1855, graduate of "College of Physicians and Surgeons," Keokuk, Iowa, m. Jennie Carter, Earlville, Iowa. Residence Earlville.

165. Charles Carmichael, b. Aug. 12, 1857, at Cedar Rapids. Druggist. Res. Junction City, Kansas.

166. Luther Montgomery, b. July 25, 1859, at Cedar Rapids. Farmer. Res. Westmoreland, Kansas.

Mary Frances, wife of Dr. Luther Keyes, d. at Springville, Iowa, April 21, 1860, aged 28. He m. 2d, July 4, 1861, Cyrene Maria, dau. of Rev. Joy and Rhoann Bishop, of Readsboro, Vt.

167. Merton Joy, b. June 3, 1862, in Linn Co., Iowa.

168. Flora Ettie, b. July 10, 1864, Buchanan Co., Iowa.

169. Mary Rhoana, b. Feb. 4, 1867, Greely, Iowa.


VI. KEYES, RUTH (124), m. Nathan Merriam of Westminster, Mass., Nov. 1811. He was the eighth generation from William Merriam, of Hadlow, Kent Co., England.

### CHILDREN.

170. Abner Holden, b. May 11, 1812.

171. Elizabeth Howard, b. July 17, 1815, d. Aug. 20, 1837.

172. Abigail, b. July 17, 1817.

173. Nathan, b. June 2, 1819, d. Aug. 25, 1837.

174. Joseph H., b. Aug. 28, 1821, m. Maria Allen. Two children, both with the mother, deceased.

175. Phebe Keyes, b. Nov. 10, 1823, d. May 18, 1836.


VII. MERRIAM, ABNER H. (170,) s. of Nathan and Ruth (Keyes) Merriam, m. Emily Wood of Leominster, April 14, 1842. Res. Templeton, Mass.

### CHILDREN.

176. Charles Holden, b. Aug. 16, 1845, m. April 18, 1875, L. C. McKenley of Jackson, Me., s. Clarence Eugene, b. July 11, 1876.

177. Emily Maria, b. Aug. 29, 1847, m. June 25, 1873, Lewis W. Bryant of Templeton. Two children, Olive, b. Apr. 27, 1875, d. Apr. 27, 1875; Wm. Lewis, b. Aug. 18, 1876.

178. Olive Elizabeth, b. April 17, 1849, m. June 25, 1873, Moses Leland, Gardner, Mass., s. Walter Wood, b. Feb. 25, 1875.

179. Susan Adeline, b. Aug. 10, 1850, d. Aug. 10, 1852.

180. Mary Abby, b. Oct. 1, 1857, d. May, 7, 1860.


VI. KEYES, SUSANNA (125), m. 1st, Peter Kendall; m. 2d, Moore; 3d, Benjamin Rice of Northboro, Mass. She d. Feb. 19, 1863, leaving    TWO SONS,

181. Amos Edwin Kendall, m. Mary Mason, of Princeton, Mass. No children. Res. New York City.

182. John Hervey Moore, b. Sept. 2, 1826; m. Oct. 20, 1847, Phebe Ann Hapgood. Res. Marlboro, Mass.

### CHILDREN.

183.        Edwin W., b. Oct. 21, 1850.
184.        Fred A., b. July 11, 1854.
185.        Emma A., b. Nov. 30, 1858.


VI. KEYES, AMOS (126), m., June 17, 1817, Sophia Robbins, of Sterling, Mass. Res. Princeton, Mass.

### CHILDREN.

186. Peter Kendall, b. Mar. 11, 1819.   Res. New York City.
187. Ezra Sawyer, b. Sept. 20, 1820.   Deceased.
188. Amos Hervey, b. Mar. 22, 1824.   Res. Princeton, Mass.
189. Charles Nelson, b. Apr. 29, 1829.   Res. Princeton, Mass.


VI. KEYES, MOSES (128), m. Mary Baxter, of Boston.

### CHILDREN.

190. William F.   Deceased.
191. Moses W., m. Eliza J. Burdy.
192. Charles H.   Res. New York City.   Unmarried.
193. Melville B., d. at St. Charles, Mo.
194. Theodore L., m. Charlotte D. Downing, dau. Effie L.
195. Mary, m. Augustus Wilder.
196. Edwin K., m. Sarah S. Keyes, s. Murray.

V. KEYES, THOMAS (105), 3d s. of John and Abigail, m. 1st, the widow of —— Davis, (maiden name, Ruth Atherton.) He d. Nov. 2, 1845, at the age of 90, in the full possession of all his faculties, and in the christian faith. His life was an active one, he was much engaged in town business, possessed of some literary talent, and distinguished himself among his acquaintance as a rhymer. He served three years in the Revolutionary War.

### CHILDREN.

197. Ruth, b. 1782, in Princeton, Mass.; probably d. young.
198. Molly, b. 1784.
199. Thomas, Jr., b. 1786, in Northboro, Mass.
        Ruth d. Jan. 13, 1788.
        Thomas m. 2d, Eunice Knight, of Bolton.
200. Ruth, b. 1790, m. had several children.
201. Ira, b. Apr. 20, 1792, d. Jan. 18, 1843, unmarried; a teacher, and of considerable note in that capacity.
202. David, b. Apr. 19, 1794, m. Linda, dau. of Daniel and Mary Bruce. They had three children, two d. in infancy, one now living.
        Addison, b. May 3, 1827, m. Mary J. Smith.
203. Ziba, b. Dec. 9, 1796.

VI. KEYES, ZIBA (203), m. 1828, Lois, dau. of Daniel and Mary Bruce, d. Nov. 27, 1850. Mechanic, with considerable inventive genius and mechanical talent. He leaves to his decendants the remembrance of his keen moral perceptions and the example of his upright and Godly life.

### CHILDREN.

204. Mary J., b. Sept. 23, 1828, Berlin, Mass.
205. Francis, b. Oct. 23, 1830, d. Dec. 20, 1830.
206. Charles G., b. Oct. 19, 1831.
207. Henry F., b. May 25, 1833.
208. John F., b. Feb. 5, 1835.
209. Ellen L., b. Nov. 9, 1839, m. Nov. 24, 1869, William G. Sawyer. Res. Berlin, Mass.

VII. KEYES, CHARLES G. (206), m. Nov. 6, 1860, Juliet
A. Whipple.　　　　　　CHILDREN.
  210. Charles D., b. June 7, 1864.
  211. Carrie Edith, b. June 5, 1868, d. Dec. 24, 1872.
  212. Mary Juliet, b. May 14, 1872, d. Jan. 4, 1873.
       C. G. Keyes is a lawyer, office 28 State St., Boston.

VII. KEYES, HENRY F. (207), m. Sept. 22, 1859, Mary
J. Winch, dau. Maud Alice, d. in infancy.

VII. KEYES, JOHN F. (208), m. 1st, June 6, 1860, Han-
nah A. Newton; 2d, Oct. 22, 1873, Louisa J. Wilder.
  Freddie, s. of John F. and Hannah A. Keyes, d. in infancy.
Henry F. and John F. Keyes are Carriage manufacturers,
Clinton, Mass.

V. KEYES, SILAS (106), 4th s. of John and Abigail, m.
Sarah Lovejoy, of Methuen, d. Aug. 18, 1840. Sarah d. 1830.
　　　　　　CHILDREN.
  213. Sarah, b. in Wilton, N. H., May 1, 1782. d. unm.
  214. Jemima, b. in Wilton, Feb. 16, 1784, m. 1820, Nat.
Howard, Wilton, N. H.
  215. Silas, b. 1785, m. Rebecca Pratt, Temple, N. H.
  216. Phebe, b. 1787, m. Moses Tyler, Boston, Mass.
  217. Ephraim, b. 1789.
  218. Jonathan, b. Mar. 6, 1791, m. Miriam Tyler of Wilton.
Sons Geo. H., res. Wilton, and Silas, b. Feb. 1831, res. Boston.
  219. Joanna, b. Nov. 7, 1793, m. Hubbard Currier, Bow, N. H.
  220. Persis, b. 1795, m. Azor Maynard, Northboro, Mass.
  221. Abigail, b. 1797, m. William Rand Stacy.
  222. Warren, b. June 23, 1799, m. Lucy W. Cummings, Nov.
6, 1823, d. Sept. 14, 1876, in Temple, N. H. No chil.

V. KEYES, EPHRAIM (108), 5th s. of John and Abigail,
m. at Boylston, Feb. 16, 1790, Sally Gerry, b. Feb. 28, 1767.
Ephraim d. Feb. 17, 1837. For this family see appendix.
　　　　　　CHILDREN.
  223. Ephraim, b. Oct. 8, 1791. Res. with a dau. Mrs. Geo.
Botterie, in Sterling, Mass. Another dau. res. in Hartford, Mass.

224. Sally, b. Nov. 7, 1793, m. John Murdock of Westminster, May 15, 1821.

225. Abby, b. Sept. 23, 1795, m. 1816, Jon. Whitcomb of Stow.

226. Silas, b. Oct. 1, 1797, m. Julia Brooks. m. 2d Martha Keyes.

227. Betsey, b. Sep. 20, 1799. m. 1823, Asa Sawyer, of Fitchburg, Mass.

228. Lydia, b. Dec. 2, 1801, m. Earl C. Gordon, Salem, N. H., s. George.

229. Persis, b. Jan. 26, 1804, m. 1842, Rev. R. W. Fuller, Westmoreland, N. H.

KEYES, SARAH, called niece of Dea. John (11), possibly his dau., was added to the church in Shrewsbury, from that in Lancaster, in 1724. She m. Peter Butler and had 7 children.
Here ends the record of Dea. John Keyes' descendants.

III. KEYES, JAMES (12), 3d s. of Elias, of Sudbury, m. Hannah——of Marlboro, Mass. He was one of the proprietors of the Indian Plantation, in Marlboro, 1693. His name is on the Bolton records as third in a list of twenty-two town clerks. He d. in Bolton, Mass., Sept. 25, 1746. His wife d. Mar. 19, 1742.

CHILDREN.

230. Elias, b. 1694.
231. James, b. 1696.
232. Mathias, } b. 1698.
233. Jonathan, } b. 1698.
234. Elizabeth, b. 1701.
235. Hannah, b. 1704.

IV. KEYES, ELIAS (230), eldest s. of James, and g. s. of Elias of Sudbury, m. Keziah Brigham, at Marlboro, Dec. 13, 1718, and was one of the 16 founders of the church in Shrewsbury, Mass. About 1742 or 3, he removed to New Marlboro, Mass., and was dismissed to the church in that place, from the one in Shrewsbury. Elias, (probably 230), d. Feb. 27, 1756.

CHILDREN.

236. Elias, b. July 22, 1719.
237. Mary, b. Apr. 13, 1721, d. 1724.
238. David, b. Sept. 20, 1722.

239. Robert, b. Apr. 18, 1725.  see appendix.

240. Mary, b. Dec. 12, 1726.

241. Charles, b. Apr. 29, 1728.

242. Keziah, b. Feb. 13, 1730.

243. Paul, b. Sept. 16, 1731.  In Sheffield, Mass., is a record of birth of Reuhamah, b. Apr. 18, 1761, and Elias b. Jan 31, 1763, children of Paul and Mary Keyes.

244. Zenas, b. Mar. 9, 1733, d. 1740.

245. Martha, b. June 27, 1736.

246. Thaddeus, b. June 17, 1738.  A Thaddeus Keyes went to East Bloomfield, N Y., as surveyor, about the time of its first settlement, 1789.  No descendants there now.

247. Deliverance, b. 1740.

V. KEYES, ELIAS, Jr. (236), m. Apr. 15, 1741, Sarah Twill, of Grafton, Mass., soon after which, with his father Elias, he removed from Shrewsbury to a new town at Housatonic, called No. 2, now New Marlboro, Berkshire Co., Mass.

CHILDREN.

248. Zenas, b. May 20, 1742, in Shrewsbury.

249. Deliverance, b. May 25, 1744, in New Marlboro.

VI. KEYES, ZENAS (248), m. Massa———.  This marriage recorded in New Marlboro, Mass.

CHILDREN.

250. Elias, b. Nov. 10, 1766.

251. Moses b. Aug. 30, 1768.

252. David, b. Aug. 16, 1770.

253. Diadama, b. Jan. 1774, dec.

254. Zenas, b. Oct. 1776.

255. Rhoda, b. 1778, dec.

256. Hiram, b. 1780.

257. Massa, b. 1783, dec. 1791.

VII. KEYES, ELIAS (250), m. Phebe Gates, and had one s.

258. Henry, b. Nov. 16, 1793, in New Marlboro.

In 1814, Elias Keyes removed, with his family, to Conneaut, then Salem, Ohio, where he, with his son Henry, located as land-holders and capitalists.  Elias d. in Conneaut, in his 55th year; his wife, Phebe, in her 69th year.

VIII. KEYES, HENRY (258), was an extensive land-owner, and leader in all business enterprises in Conneaut. He was instrumental in starting one of the first newspapers in the State, the material being brought from Buffalo on an ox sled. At an early day he gave his attention to navigation and built the steamer N. America, and other smaller craft. He was Gen. of Militia and known as Gen. Keyes. He m. 1st Jan. 19, 1819, Mary, dau. of Asa Cole, of N. Marlboro. who d. Dec. 1824. He m. 2nd, 1829, Vesta, dau. of Asa Bates, of Commington, Mass. Gen. Keyes d. in Conneaut, July 21, 1873. Mrs. Keyes is still living in Conneaut, Ohio.

### CHILDREN.

259. Henry Plummer, b. Feb. 14, 1820, graduated at Yale, New Haven, 1843, studied law, m. Nov. 1859, Sarah Marin Huntington, who d. Mar. 1877. 3 dau. Res. Cedar Rapids, In.

260. Alvin Cole, b. Oct. 25, 1821, m. Minnie Kopp; 7 chil. living, 1 dec. Wholesale grocer at Cedar Rapids.

261. Mary Cole, b. Nov. 4, 1823, m. Edward Grant, of Conneaut, who was lost on Lake Erie, Mar. 23, 1850.

262. Marcus Bates, b. Mar. 30, 1830, m. 1st, Louisa Gordon, of Beloit, Wis.; no chil. m. 2d, Frank Brock of Conneaut. s. Henry A., foreman on the Journal of Commerce, St. Louis, Mo. Also a dau. Marcus d. in Beloit, Nov. 7, 1859.

263. Martin Bates, b. Nov. 4, 1831, m. Eliza Loyd of Chicago, dec.; 2 children; dau. d. in infancy. P. M. in Conneaut.

264. Charles William, b. Dec. 23, 1832, d. Oct. 8, 1852.

265. Elias Asa, b. May 9, 1834, m. Charlotte Elizabeth Fenton, who d. Oct. 19, 1877; has one s. Res. Conneaut.

266. Phebe Ann, b. Jan. 25, 1836, m. Dr. E. D. Merriam, has two children living, two dec. Res. Conneaut.

267. Russell Melzo, b. Dec. 22, 1837, graduated at Beloit College, Beloit, Wis., 1861, studied theology at Union Theological Seminary, New York City, graduating 1865. Began to preach in Conneaut, 1865, where he remained to 1878, when he removed to Chardon, O. Rev. R. M. Keyes (Cong.), m. Mrs. Catherine Lyon Smith; 2 dau.; the youngest d. in infancy.

268. Milo Osborn, b. Apr. 9, 1840; unm. Res. Conneaut, O.

IV. KEYES, JAMES (231), 2d s. of James, was living on house lot, No. 19, in Shrewsbury, in 1730. His 1st wife's name unknown.

### CHILDREN.

269. Jonas, d. 1735.

James m. 2d, Jan. 4, 1739, Abigail Rugg, of Sudbury, Mass.

270. Jonas, b. 1739.
271. Meliscent, b. 1741, m. 1762, Levi Goodenow, of Marlboro, Mass.
272. Submit, bap. Apr. 24, 1743.

IV. KEYES, MATHIAS (232), 3d s. of James, m. Sarah —

### SON.

273. Joseph, b. Nov. 5, 1726, who m. Elizabeth ———.

### CHILDREN.

274.     Dorothea, b. May 9, 1750.
275.     Leles, b. Dec. 7, 1751.
276.     Joseph Annis, b. May 16, 1754.
277.     Christopher, b. Sept. 4, 1757.
278.     Charles, b. July 17, 1761.
279.     Hannah, b. Sept. 1, 1764.

This account of the family of Mathias, taken from Bolton records.

Here ends the record of the family of James Keyes, 3d s. of Elias of Sudbury.

III. KEYES, THOMAS (14), youngest s. of Elias, of Sudbury, and g. s. of Robert, m. in 1698, Elizabeth, dau. of John Howe (spelled How in the old records), and g. d. of John and Mary Howe, 1st white settlers of the town of Marlboro, Mass. She was sister of Mrs. Peter Josslyn, of Lancaster, Mass., and in 1692, when a young girl, while visiting her sister, was taken captive by the Indians and carried to Canada. She remained there four years, when she was redeemed by government, returned home and m. Thomas, afterward, Dea. Thomas Keyes, to whom she was engaged before her captivity. It was sixteen years earlier that the town was attacked by 1,500 Indians and destroyed, and numbers carried into captivity. But Lancaster was, for many years, a frontier town, and it was probably during some raid of lesser historical moment that her capture occurred. Dea. Thomas Keyes and wife settled on a new farm in the East part of Marlboro, where they resided during their lives, and which is still in possession of the descendants of Dinah, who m. John Weeks.

### CHILDREN.

280. David, b. 1699, was killed 1720, when nearly 21.

281. Jonathan, b. Nov. 19, 1702.

282. Cypron, b. 1706.

283. Dinah, b. Mar. 4, 1710, m. John Weeks, 1731.

284. Thomas, b. 1713, d. young.

> Dea. Thomas, d. Aug. 25, 1742.
> His wife d. Aug. 18, 1764.

IV. KEYES, JONATHAN (281), 2d s. of Dea. Thomas, m. 1727, Patience Morse, of Marlboro, Mass., and settled in Shrewsbury. Was Dea. in the North Parish.

### CHILDREN.

285. Jonathan, b. Jan. 21, 1728.

286. Miriam, b. Oct. 7, 1729, d. young.

287. Dinah, b. Aug. 22, 1731.

288. Timothy, bap. Nov. 4, 1733.

289. Miriam, b. Dec. 14, 1735, m. Artemus Maynard, of Princeton, Mass., May 27, 1762.

290. Thomas, b. Dec. 24, 1739, m. Mary Temple, of Westminster, 1765, d. 1812.

291. Benjamin, b. Jan. 29, 1740, m. Lucy Merriam, d. about 65 years of age.

292. Asa, bap. July 4, 1742, d. 1745.

293. Catherine,⎫ b. Aug. 15, 1744, d. infant.
294. Dinah,  ⎭ b. Aug. 15, 1744, d. 1752.

295. Catherine, b. Oct. 9, 1747, sup. m. Jonathan Warren Smith, 1774, and lived to be nearly 100.

Dea. Jonathan d. suddenly at Shrewsbury of apoplexy, June 25, 1778.

V. KEYES, JONATHAN, Jr. (285), s. of Dea. Jonathan, m. Jan. 23, 1752, Sarah Taylor, and lived in the North Parish of Shrewsbury.

#### CHILDREN.

296. Solomon, b. June 25, 1753.
297. Dinah, b. Jan. 23, 1755, d. 1756.
298. Sarah, b. Dec. 21. 1756.
299. Perhaps Thomas.
300. Ebenezer, b. Oct. 24, 1760.
301. Salma, b. Sept. 6, 1762.
302. Francis, b. Oct. 13, 1765.

## JONATHAN KEYES, JR.

It is said that somewhere about the year 1774, Jonathan Keyes, Jr., in company with one Richardson, taking with him his son Ebenezer, then about fourteen, went into the woods at Bethel or Rumford, Me. In the Autumn following, he went back to Massachusetts, leaving his son in the care of the Indians, but returning to him in the Spring. The next Autumn, Ebenezer, finding the same treatment to be repeated, ran away, going by a spotted line to Massachusetts, where he enlisted in the Revolutionary Army, and served three years. It is thought by some that Jonathan returned to Shrewsbury after this escapade of his son, and did not again appear in the Maine woods for two or three years. Be that as it may, "It was in December, 1776, that Jonathan, then said to be of Shrewsbury, Mass., purchased four rights in the township of New Pennacook, now Rumford, Me. This township was situated on both sides of the Androscoggin River, in the present county of Oxford, seventy miles from Portland. It had just been granted to Timothy Walker and others, of Concord, N. H. On the 10th of March, 1777. Mr. Keyes, with his wife and youngest son Francis, set out from Shrewsbury, for New Gloucester, Me., then a border town. The distance was 50 miles to New Pennacook, from New Gloucester,

where he left his wife, and with his son, then about twelve years
of age, made the journey through the wilderness, arriving at
New Pennacook, in August. He commenced a clearing in the
place which he afterward occupied, and which he transmitted to
his son Francis. His wife joined him in the Autumn of 1779,
making the journey on foot, and was the first white woman in
the settlement. Mr. Keyes frequently went to New Gloucester
while his wife was there, leaving his son in care of the Indians,
under whose instructions he learned to shoot, and soon became
familiar with the use of the bow and arrow. Other families
began to move in, and in 1781 there were four or five families
in the township. In the month of August, 1781, a party of St.
Francis Indians from Canada, made a raid into Sudbury, now
Bethel, Canada a township joining New Pennacook on the
West, and in which were ten families. The Indians killed some
and carried others captive into Canada. The settlers of New
Pennacook, alarmed for their own safety, fled through the wilderness to New Gloucester. Mr. Keyes did not return to his
farm until the Spring of 1783, when he found his cabin as he
left it. The settlers were now unmolested, and the township
rapidly filled up. Mr. Keyes settled on a beautiful interval
farm, which he cultivated to the time of his death. He was a
man of great physical powers, and a fine specimen of a pioneer
settler of Maine. He d. Nov. 9, 1786, aged 58. His wife Sarah
d. Nov. 14, 1799, aged 75.

VI. KEYES, EBENEZER (300), then a resident of Shrewsbury, bought a farm, Dec. 10, 1784, in that part of Gardiner,
Mass., which was formerly Templeton, and June 12, 1787, m.
Jemima Jackson, b. March 11, 1765. June 7, 1805, he bought
Lot 14, Range 7, in Jay, Me., and moved his family to it, Jan.
1806, and spent there the remainder of his life. He was an ec-
centric old gentleman, and believed in all events both of fact
or fortune changing once in seven years. He died at Jay,
Me., May 31, 1838, aged 77 years, 7 months and 7 days.

His name was K-e-y-e-s, but because they called him Keys,
he dropped the first e, when he moved to Jay.

## CHILDREN.

303. Solomon, b. March 30, 1788, d. Sept. 25, 1793.
304. Ebenezer, Jr., b. March 9, 1790, d. August 24, 1794.
305. Elisha, b. Feb. 18, 1792.
306. Jemima, b. April 19, 1794, d. March 29, 1803.
307. Ebenezer, b. April 25, 1796.
308. Solomon, b. June 2, 1798.
309. Naomi, b. Oct. 12, 1800, d. Nov. 26, 1819.
310. Lucy J., b. Oct. 25, 1802, d. March 26, 1820.
311. Jemima, b. April 22, 1805.
312. Lorenzo, b. June 10, 1807.

VII. KYES, ELISHA (305), s. of Ebenezer, Sen. m. Dec. 3, 1818, Katherine, dau. Dea. Oliver Fuller, of Jay. Elisha was a successful merchant, farmer, and post master at North Jay for twenty years, and one of the leading men of Franklin County.

### CHILDREN.

313. Abel J., b. Dec. 11, 1819.
314. Columbus, b. July 29, 1821, d. Oct. 10, 1847.
315. Lucy J., b. March 24, 1823, m. 1st in 1852, George W. Dickerson of Boston, 2d 1871, Charles Robins. Residence New York City.
316. Elisha, Jr., b. Feb. 7, 1825.
317. Gustavus, b. Jan. 9, 1827.
318. Catharine F. b. Feb. 15, 1829, m. April 18, 1852, Sulviro Merrit, lives on the Col. David Merrit homestead farm, on Jay Hill.    CHILDREN.
319.            Elia S., b. Nov. 1853, d. March 22, 1854.
320.            Victor S., b. Nov. 19, 1862, at Boston.
321. Oliver, G., b. Sept. 27, 1831.
322. Salma, b. July 22, 1833, d. San Francisco, Cal., Nov. 4, 1875, was a merchant at Jay Bridge.
323. Infant dau., b. Mar. 9, 1837, d. at two months of age.
324. Edward, b. May 6, 1838, m. Aug. 8, 1866, Lucy Keyes, d. Dec. 24, 1866.
325. Ebenezer S., b. Jan. 22, 1842.

VIII. KYES, ABEL (313), s. of Elisha and Katherine, m.
March 4, 1857, Mercy Rose of Turner; farmer in Jay.

### CHILDREN.

326. Infant dau., b. Jan. 22, 1858, d. Jan. 24, 1858.
327. Ellen F., b. Oct. 24, 1859.
328. Horace A., b. Mar. 4, 1863.

VIII. KYES, ELISHA, Jr. (316), m. 1835, Rachel Har-
ring.

### CHILDREN.

329. Columbus, b. at East Somerville, Mass.
330. Emma L.
331. Chester.
332. Martha, deceased.
333. Calvin, deceased.
334. Nellie, deceased.
335. Mary G., b. Apr. 15, 1869, deceased.
336. Edward.

VIII. KYES, GUSTAVUS (317), m. Nov. 21, 1852, L.
Anna D. Merritt of Jay.   ONE SON.
337. George E., b. Mar. 21, 1854.   Merchant and Station
Agent at North Jay.

VIII. KYES, OLIVER G., (321), m. June 1, 1856, Harriet
Niles of Jay.   Flourishing farmer of Jay.
338. Alice M., b. March 29, 1859.
339. Leslie G., b. Apr. 19, 1863.
340. Cora H., b. June 19, 1868.
341. Earnest V., b. Nov. 19, 1870, d. Dec. 29, 1876.

VIII. KYES, EBENEZER S. (325), was educated at Bowdoin College, served as private, orderly sergeant and captain
in 28th, 31st and 32nd Maine Volunteers and was breveted
Major, U. S. Vols. for gallant and merritorious conduct at the
capture of Petersburg, Va., Apr. 2, 1865, was in thirteen battles, and wounded at Coal Harbor, June 3, 1864.   Read law

with Judge Luce of Auburn, admitted to the Androscoggin Bar, member of the Senate of Me., 1876 and 1877, Chairman of Judiciary Committee, 1877, President of the Senate, *pro tem*. half the session, Supervisor of Schools and resides on the homestead built by his father. m. Caroline M., dau. of Maj. Elisha Coolidge of Jay, Mar. 12, 1864.

### CHILDREN.

342. Edward, b. Feb. 3, 1868, d. Nov. 27, 1870.
343. Paul M , b. Oct. 25, 1869, d. Sept. 5, 1870.
344. Preston, b. Jan. 24, 1875.
345. Howard F., b. March 29, 1876.


VII. KEYES, EBENEZER; Jr. (307), s. of Ebenezer, Sen. m. June 18, 1821, Lucy Axtell of Jay. Farmer. He d. Mar. 31, 1842. His wife d. Jan. 6, 1836.

### CHILDREN.

346. Warren, b. April 24, 1822, m. June 2, 1844, Mary W. Fenderson, of Wilton. He d. Nov. 29, 1865.

### CHILDREN.

347.          Lucy M., b. March 25, 1845, m. Oct. 1863, John
              P. Covell, 2d Edward Morse of Jay, Jan. 8,
              1868, d. Sept. 17, 1873.

### CHILDREN.

348.          Mary P. Covell, b. Jan. 17, 1866.
349.          Lizzie E. Morse, b. Nov. 5, 1869.
350.          Edward W. Morse b. Feb. 7, 1871.
351.     Mary Frances, b. Oct. 9, 1846, d. Aug. 31, 1847.
352.          Frances, b. June 16, 1848, m. Calvin Chambers,
              May 1868. Res. Redwing, Minn.

### CHILDREN.

              Infant.
              Harry, b. Oct. 14, 1875.
              Daughter b. Jan. 14, 1878.
353.     Lizzie F., b. Nov. 1850, d. Aug. 1866.
354.     Olive F., b. Dec. 21, 1852, m. April 1874, F. A.
              Hanscomb, child  Winnifred P., b. Dec. 9,

1877.   Res. Madeira, Minn.

355.        John F., b. Feb. 1855.   Teacher, Minn.

356. Naomi, b. Jan. 23, 1824, m. June 2, 1844, Robert L. Smith of Wilton.   Res. Worcester, Mass.   Boot and Shoe manufacturer.   d. Aug. 6, 1854.

### CHILDREN.

357.        Frank, b. April 28, 1845, d. March 28, 1869.
358.        Ellen, b. June 3, 1847, m. George H. Soule, June 3, 1868.

359. Lucy Ann, b. July 11, 1831, m. Nov. 29, 1849, A. K. P. Childs, M. D. of Jay, d. July 19, 1856.   Res. now at Worcester, Mass.

### CHILDREN.

360.        Lucy Ella, b. Oct. 1850, d. July 17, 1861.
361.        Naomi S., b. Sept. 6, 1855.

VII. KYES, SOLOMON (308), s. of Ebenezer, Sen., m. June 17, 1821, Rhoda N. Eldridge of Readfield, Me.   Farmer in Jay, d. at Wilton, Jan. 27, 1871.

### CHILDREN.

362. Jonathan O., b. July 3, 1822.

363. Aurilla S., b. Jan. 11, 1824, d. Aug. 11, 1826.

364. Ebenezer, b. Feb. 25, 1826, d. Apr. 9, 1840.

365. Solomon N., b. Dec. 27, 1827.

366. Rhoda N., b. July 17, 1830, m. May 17, 1848, Dr. John Powers, dentist, of Wilton.

### CHILDREN.

367.        Rosamond A., b. Feb. 15, 1856, m. Feb. 12, 1878, Charles S. Robinson.
368.        Moors, b. Feb. 2, 1858.

369. Delia A. b. Aug. 19, 1832, d. May 6, 1841.

370. Francis, b. Sept. 10, 1834.

371. Horatio A. B., b. Jan. 19, 1837.

372. Rutillus W., b. Nov. 26, 1838.

373. Albert F., b. June 26, 1841.   Lieut. in 8th Me. Vols., wounded twice; d. of wounds at Fortress Monroe, Va., Nov. 16, 1864.

374. Jemima W., b. Aug. 12, 1843, d. Jan. 15, 1858.

VIII. KYES, JONATHAN O. (362), m. Jan. 14, 1847, Annarilla R. C. Rowell of Jay, who d. Mar. 4, 1860.

### DAUGHTER.

375. Delia A., b. Sept. 21, 1852, m. Nov. 25, 1871, Alvarus N. Goodrich of Industry. Farmer. Delia, d. May 6, 1841.

Jonathan m. 2nd, Julia E. Haskell of East Livermore, Me. Is one of the Maine State Board of Agriculture and has been County Commissioner.

VIII. KYES, SOLOMON N. (365), m. May 12, 1852, Mary R. Adams of Hopkinton, Mass. Was in the Mass. 3d Vols. in the late war. Lived on a farm in Jay; d. at Hopkinton, Nov. 18, 1870.

### CHILDREN.

376. Anna R., b. March 10, 1853, at Hopkinton, m. Horace Wood, of Hopkinton, Jan. 1, 1874. Children, Ervin B. Wood and Leon H. Wood.

377. Arthur N., b. Mar. 24, 1862, in Hopkinton, Mass.

VIII. KYES, FRANCIS (370), m. Dec. 28, 1857, Minnie Brown of Earlville, Ill., where he now resides.

### CHILDREN.

378. Rutillus W., b. about 1856.
379. Solomon A., b. about 1867.
380. Helen, b. about 1870.
381. Son, b. about 1872.

VIII. KYES, HORATIO A. B. (371), m. Jan. 22, 1860, Miranda Kimball of Patten, Me. Res. Industry. Farmer. Was in 8th Reg. Me. Vols.

### CHILDREN.

382. Albert F., b. about 1866.
383. Gayton H., b. about 1868.
384. Alberta, b. about 1870.
385. Winona, b. about 1874.

VIII. KYES, RUTILLUS W. (372), m. Oct. 5, 1864, Helen
M. Lake, and lives on the homestead of his father. Was in
Co. K, 28th Me. Vols.

### CHILDREN.

386. Minnie H., b. July 31, 1865.
387. Arthur K., b. June 25, 1869.
388. Earnest N., b. Jan. 24, 1872.

VII. KEYES, JEMIMA (311), dau. of Ebenezer, Sen., m.
Nov. 29, 1821, Silas Jones, Esq., of Jay. She d. at Jay, Mar.
18. 1830.

### CHILDREN.

389. Andrew J., b. Jan. 14, 1823, d. March 21, 1839.
390. Naomi K.,  ) b. March 30, 1825, m. Jan. 9, 1854, George
  M. Robinson, of L— Falls.
391. Jemima K., ) b. March 30, 1825, m. 1st Jonathan E.
Bradford of Turner; 2nd, Amos Proctor of Bolton, Mass., and
d. 1863.
392. Emory C., b. March 14, 1828, d. Dec. 15, 1828.

VII. KEYES, LORENZO (312), m. Dec. 7, 1830, Lucy
Powers of Jay, now lives on the old Ebenezer Kyes farm in
Jay.

### CHILDREN.

393. Emily, b. Feb. 2, 1832, m. Nov. 9, 1853, Henry V. Rowell of Jay. Res. Bath, Maine.

### CHILDREN.

394.        Mary L., b. Feb. 11, 1854, d. April 30, 1861.
395.        Clara M., b. Aug. 27, 1857.
396.        Emma J., b. Sept. 29, 1859.
397.        Mary E., b. Nov. 29, 1862.
398.        George H., b. April 23, 1865.
399.        Lucy H., b. Aug. 25, 1867.
400.        Florence E., b. March 26, 1873.
401.        Rosie F., b. Aug. 27, 1875.
402. Lorenzo M., b. Feb. 28, 1834, d. at Bowdoin College,
in his Sophomore year, Aug. 9, 1857.

403. Adeline, b. June 12, 1836, m. Nov. 9, 1853; Artemus L. Richardson of Jay, gardener at Westbrook. Adeline d. June 3, 1860.

CHILDREN.

404.　　　George A. Richardson, b. Sept. 15, 1854, d. Oct. 21, 1855.

405.　　　Charles E. Richardson, b. about 1858.

406.　　　Flora A., b. about 1860.

407. Julia R., b. March 9, 1839, d Dec. 9, 1865.

408. Lucy, b. April 24, 1841, m. Aug. 8, 1866, Edward Kyes of Jay, d. June 3, 1871.

409. Mary F., b. July 9, 1843, m. 1st Feb. 19, 1865, Lewis A. Packard of Winthrop; 2nd George R. Smith, July 3, 1873, son, Roy B. Smith, b. March 1875.

410. George, b. May 10, 1846, m. M. F. Sullivan, of Mass.

411. Martha P., b. Jan. 3, 1851, m. Jan. 19, 1875, Henry R. Dascomb of Wilton, Me., merchant.

412. Naomi,　} b. Nov. 3, 1852.
413. Henry P.,} b. Nov. 3, 1852.　Res. Riverside, Cal.

414. Ella, b. Nov. 29, 1855, d. May 8, 1864.

415. Jessie E., b. May 21, 1858, d. May 5, 1864.


VI. KEYES, SALMA (301), left home when a boy, and for many years there was no news of him. At length a letter came, post-marked "Keyes Mills, Va." Letters directed to that place were never answered, and nothing more is known of him.


VI. KEYES, FRANCIS (302), youngest s. of Jonathan Keyes, Jr., was about twelve years of age when his parents moved to Maine. His means of obtaining even the rudiments of an education were very limited, but he made the best use of what he had. He was chosen Clerk of the plantation of New Pennacook, at the time of its organization, and of the town of Rumford, at its incorporation, and filled the office with ability and fidelity for many years. He was a surveyor of land and draughtsman, a Justice of the Peace, and a useful citizen of the new town. He married Dolly, daughter of Josiah and Molly (Crocker) Bean of Sudbury, now Bethel, Canada. The father

5

of Dolly was descended from Lewis Bean or Bane, who came from the Isle of Jersey, and was an early settler of York, Me.

### CHILDREN OF FRANCIS AND DOLLY.

416. Sally, b. June 9, 1792.

417. Polly, b. Nov. 14, 1794.

418. Jonathan, b. April 24, 1797, killed by bursting of a musket at a military muster in Rumford.

419. Josiah, b. Dec. 24, 1799.

420. Lydia, b. Aug. 23, 1802.

421. Winthrop S., b. Dec. 5, 1804, d. Nov. 22, 1825.

422. Dolly B., b. Nov. 10, 1806.

423. Francis, b. Oct. 13, 1810, d. young.

424. Hannah, b. July 19, 1813.

VII. KEYES, SALLY (416), m. Nov. 13, 1813, Peter C. Virgin of Rumford, Me., youngest son of Ebenezer and Dorcas (Lovejoy) Virgin, of Concord, N. H. He was born in Concord, July 23, 1783. His grand-father, Ebenezer Virgin, came from England about the year 1722, was one of the first proprietors of Pennacook, now Concord, N. H., and one of the very first settlers. He married Mary Chandler of Andover, Mass. Peter Chandler Virgin came quite early to Maine, and opened a law office at Rumford corner, where he resided more than sixty years. He served two terms in the Mass. Gen. Court, before the separation, was a member of the Convention that formed the constitution of Maine, and of the first and second Maine Legislatures. He was County Attorney for Oxford County and Postmaster at Rumford many years, besides holding other offices of honor and trust. He was a safe Counsellor, a good advocate, a gentleman of the Old School. For a long time he was the Nestor of the Oxford County Bar, and when he passed to the better land, and his erect and venerable form was missed from the Court room, a vacancy was made which was not easily to be filled.

### CHILDREN OF PETER C. AND SALLY (KEYES) VIRGIN.

425. Maria Caroline Lovisa, b. April 13, 1814, became the second wife of Otis C. Bolster.

## CHILDREN.

426.     William H., b. April 17, 1844.

427.     Dolly M., b. Mar. 14, 1846, d. May 25, 1867.

428.     Noris D., b. May 22, 1850.

429.     Sarah V., b. April 30, 1853.

430.     Marietta, b. Nov. 17, 1859.

431. Patrick Henry, b. Aug. 29, 1816, m. Lavina, daughter of Luther Bean. Farmer in Rumford.

## CHILDREN.

432.     Charles C., b. Sept. 26, 1847, d. Sept. 13, 1873.

433.     William Wirt, b. April 6, 1854.

434. Joseph W., b. Sept 5, 1820, d. Aug. 7, 1822.

435. William Wirt, b. Sept. 18, 1823.

436. Theodore F., b. Feb. 5, 1831.

437. Dorcas Courtney, b. June 24, 1833, m. James Dingley, Jr. of Auburn, and died leaving one child.

## JUDGE VIRGIN.

VIII. WILLIAM WIRT VIRGIN (435), s. of Peter C. and Sally (Keyes) Virgin, fitted for college at Bridgton and Bethel, Me. academies, graduated at Bowdoin College, class of 1844, read law with his father and established himself in practice at Norway, Me. in 1848. He was county attorney for Oxford in 1859, and served one term. He was a member of the State Senate in 1865, re-elected in 1866, and chosen President of that body. In 1866, he was appointed Reporter of Decisions of the Supreme Judicial Court, and re-appointed in 1871. In 1872, he resigned this position, to accept the office of Associate Justice of the Supreme Judicial Court, which position he now holds (1878). At the breaking out of the war of the Rebellion, he was one of the Major Generals of the Maine Militia, and early in the summer of 1861, was put upon duty, in the State recruiting service. In the fall of 1862, he resigned this position to accept of the Colonelcy of the 23d Me. Vols., which was mustered into service in Sept., and assigned to duty on the defences of Washington. It was stationed at Edward's Ferry and at other places on the Potomac. He was mustered out with his regiment in June, 1863. He is the author of two volumes of Digests of the Maine Judicial Reports, which are models of their kind. As a lawyer he was successful, and is an able and popular Judge. He was married Sept. 18, 1851, to Sarah H., daughter of Horatio G., and Parmelia (Stowell) Cole, of Norway, and has one SON.

438. Harry R., b. Aug. 25, 1854, a member of the Junior Class, in Tufts College.

VII. KEYES, POLLY (417), 2d dau. of Francis and Dolly Keyes, m. Jessie Putnam, and lived and died at East Rumford.

### CHILDREN.

439. Prentiss Mellen, b. Nov. 21, 1824, m. Esther C., adopted dau. of Joel Howe of Hanover, where he was a merchant, but now lives on the old Putnam homestead.

### CHILDREN.

440.        Sarah Marcella, b. Oct., 1851.          .
441.        Adah, b. Oct., 1854, d. Feb., 1857.
442.        Solon A., b. Aug. 10, 1860.
443. Sarah Ann, b. Oct. 3, 1827, m. Robert Taylor. No children. Res. California.
444. Edwin Alonzo, b. Nov. 21, 1829, m. Sarah Ross. 2 children. Res. Cal.
445. Solon Thurston, m. Caroline Evans. 1 child, d. at 6 years of age.

VII. KEYES, JOSIAH (419), m. Rachel, dau. of Capt. Samuel Barker, formerly of Newery, afterwards of Rumford.

### CHILDREN.

446. Frances Ophelia, b. Sept. 30, 1836, m. March 11, 1856, Stephen Abbott Russell of Bethel. Jeweller and watchmaker at Augusta.          CHILDREN.

447.        Alice A., b. Nov. 22, 1858.
448.        Sylvanus H. b. Dec. 8, 1861.
449. Cincinnatus, b. July 13, 1839. He was in the 10th Me. Reg., and was killed at Cedar Mountain, Va.

450. William Tell, b. Aug. 23, 1843, m. 1st, Thirza A. Little. Res. Colebrook, N. H.    CHILDREN.

451.        Llewellen T., b. Feb. 2, 1871.
452.        Nettie R., b. Aug. 30, 1873.

His wife Thirza d. April 12, 1875.    He m. 2nd, Oct. 30, 1875, Sarah A. Keyes.

453. George D., b. Sept. 15, 1848, m. Carrie Lowder of Rockland.


VII. KEYES, LYDIA (420), m. Francis Cushman, Esq., a trader and active business man at Rumford Pt.

### CHILDREN.

454. Georgiana Francis, b. May 15, 1835, m. James Buckland, St. Louis, Mo.

455. Francis Ebenezer, b. May 11, 1837, d. unmarried.


VII. KEYES, DOLLY B. (422), m. Otis C., son of Isaac and Hannah (Cushman) Bolster of Paris, Me., to whom she was pub. Sept. 9, 1827.    She d. Aug. 15, 1840.

### CHILDREN.

456. Horatio A., b. Sept. 8, 1828, d. Nov. 1, 1836.

457. Henrietta L., b. Jan. 29, 1835, d. Nov. 17, 1843.

458. Mellen E., b. Sept. 19, 1837, m. 1st, Ann Sophia, dau. of Dea. Thomas Roberts of Rumford, had dau., Eva I., b. Aug. 2, 1862, and Hattie W., b. Dec. 4, 1865; m. 2nd, Mary S., dau. of Geo. Smith of Hanover, and has Freelon E., b. Mar. 30, 1873. Mellen E., is a member of the firm of Locke, Twitchell & Co., wholesale Dry Goods merchants, Portland, Me.

459. Freelon K., b. August 8, 1840, d. Oct. 20, 1855.


VII. KEYES, HANNAH (424), was published to Loammi B. Peabody, Sept. 9, 1832, and m. soon after. She d. young leaving one child,

460. Franklin Dexter, b. Oct. 14, 1833, who m. Lucy Bryant of Woodstock, and they have 2 children.

V. KEYES, TIMOTHY (288), 2nd s. of Dea. Jonathan Keyes, m. May 1, 1755, Prudence Wilder of Shrewsbury, d. 1810.

### CHILDREN.

461. Jonas, b. May 10, 1756, d. Dec. 7, 1757.
462. Betty, b. Mar. 21, 1759.
463. Patience, b. 1761.
464. Jonas, b. 1764.
465. Lemuel, b. 1768, lived in Chicopee.
466. Cate, b. 1770.
Timothy was said to be of Rutland, Mass.

VI. KEYES, JONAS (464), s. of Timothy, m. 1st, 1789, Delana Parker.

### CHILDREN.

467. Oren, b. 1789. Farmer. Res. Springfield, Mass.
468. Sally, b. 1791, deceased.
469. Willis, b. 1793. Farmer. Res. Ludlow.
470. Electa, b. 1795. Res. Springfield. Deceased.
471. Francis, b. 1797. Farmer. Lived and died at Longmeadow, Mass.
472. Mary, b. 1801. Lived at the West.
473. Harriett, b. 1803. Lived at the West.
474. Levi, b. 1806. Farmer. Colon, Mich.
475. Ely, b. 1808.
and d. there.
476. Justin, b. 1810, d. about 1875, in Chicago. Railroad Man.
Jonas m. 2nd, Sally Ingalls. Carpenter. Res. in Wilbraham, Mass, d. 1836.

VII. KEYES, OREN · (467), eldest s. of Jonas, m. Anna Frost.

### CHILDREN.

477. Oren D., b. 1812, m. Jane C. Crane.

### CHILDREN.

478.  William D., b. 1837, m. M. S. Belknap.
479.    s., J. Dwight, b. 1869. Res. Springfield.
480.  Elias S., b. 1839, m. Ellen Mosely.
481.    s., Eugene, b. 1870. Res. Wilbraham, Mass.
482.  John F., b. 1844, d. 1866.
483. Elias F., b. 1813, 2nd s. of Oren, m. Elizabeth Pettis.

### CHILDREN.

484.  Mary, b. 1342.
485.  Elbert M., b. 1852. Farmer. s., Wilbur, b. 1876.
486.  Morris O., b. 1854.
487.  Homer J., b. 1856.

VII. KEYES, WILLIS (469), 2nd s. of Jonas, m. Chloe Frost.   CHILDREN.

488. Samuel F., b. 1820, m. Thankful Taylor. Farmer. Resided in Ludlow, Mass.

### CHILDREN.

489.  Henry W., b. 1845. Railroad Manager. son, Henry S., b. 1875.
490.  Wyan H., b. 1858. Res. Indian Orchard.
491. Angelica, b. 1823.
492. Eliza, b. 1828.
493. William L., b. 1833, m. Amanda Pease. Res. Indian Orchard, Mass.

### CHILDREN.

494.  James H., b. 1858.
495.  Harley L., b. 1860.

VII. KEYES, FRANCIS (471), 3d s. of Jonas, m. 1822, Irene Prince, who d. 183-.

### CHILDREN.

496. Sophia P., b. 1823.
497. Irene, b. 1825.
498. Eliza, b. 1828.
499. Francis b. 1831, m. Lucia B. Alden, 1854. Res. Palmer, Mass.

## CHILDREN.

500.        Amy L., b. 1857.

501.        Herbert F., b. 1861.

502.        Agnes L., b. 1867, deceased.

503.        Edith J., b. 1870.

504.        Marguerite E., b. 1876.

505. Henry, b. 1838, m. 1857, Lucy A. Plympton of Wardsboro, Vt. Merchant in Springfield, Mass.

## CHILDREN.

506.        Fred H., b. 1858.

507.        Lucy B., b. 1867.

VII. KEYES, LEVI (474), 4th s. of Jonas, lived for a time
in Mt. Morris, Livingston Co., N. Y. He moved to Michigan
in 1836, and lived in Leonidas. P. O. address, Colon, Mich.
He d. March 10, 1871.

## CHILDREN.

Justin E., b. Nov. 6, 1828. Farmer. David, b. Jan. 9, 1831,
Clarissa, b. April 17, 1834, d. Feb., 1843, Rawdon, b. in Mich.,
Jan. 4, 1839.

The wife of Levi d. Dec. 29, 1850. He m. Mar. 6, 1851,
Mrs. Scholfield. Their children were Parmelia, b. Mar. 31,
1852, Clara, b. Jan. 20, 1855, Edward, Levi, b. April 30, 1862.

VII. KEYES, ELY (475), 5th s. of Jonas, moved to Colon,
Mich., in 1837, d. Feb. 5, 1843.

## CHILDREN.

George, b. June 8, 1830, in Springfield, Mass., Horace, b. Jan.
31, 1833, in Springfield. Both farmers in Colon. Albert, b.
Aug., 1835, Haney M., b. 1837.

VI. KEYES, LEMUEL (465), 2d s. of Timothy.

## CHILDREN.

508. Betsey.

509. Sophia.

510. Cotton.   s. Alanson.   Lives in New York State.

511. Emily.

512. Lucy.
513. Marther, b. 1799.
514. Anson, b. 1808.
515. Lemuel, b. 1809.
516. Dassy.
517. Delocia.

VII. KEYES, MARTHER (513), m. Oriel Chapin, South Hadley Falls, Mass.

### CHILDREN.

518. Marther, b. 1833.
519. Ann M., b. 1836.
520. Caroline H., b. 1839.

VII. KEYES, ANSON (514), m. Ann M. Atwood.

### CHILDREN.

521. George A., b. 1831, m. Eliza I. Lawrence. Res. Chicopee Falls, Mass.
522. John A., b. 1833.
523. Edwin S., b. 1835, dec.
524. Helen M., b. 1840.
525. Edwin L., b. 1844.

VII. KEYES, LEMUEL (515), m. 1st, Eliza Covley. Res. Chicopee Fails, Mass.

### CHILDREN.

526. Eliza, b. June 9, 1833.
527. Julia A., b. Dec. 2, 1834, dec.
528. Isabella, b. April 8, 1836.
529. Julia A., b. July 5, 1841.
530. Isabella, b. Oct. 31, 1847.
531. William L., b. Dec. 24, 1849, dec.
532. Frank P., b. Oct. 31, 1852, Chicopee Falls, Mass. unm.
        Lemuel m. 2nd, Caroline M. T. Carleton.
533. Ella J., b. Nov. 11, 1859.
534. Winfield S., b. Nov. 15, 1861, dec.
535. Fred L., b. July, 25, 1864, dec.
536. Jennie C., b. May 12, 1868.

V. KEYES, THOMAS (290), 3d s. of Dea. Jonathan, m.
April 25, 1765, Mary, dau. of Isaac Temple of Shrewsbury, b.
Mar. 9, 1741.

### CHILDREN.

537. Lucy, b. Aug. 18, 1765, d. Apr. 4, 1776.
538. Thomas, b. Jan. 20, 1767, at Westminister, Mass.
539. Asa, b. Sept. 21, 1768.
540. Francis, b. April 15, 1771.
541. Luther, b. Sept. 21, 1772, d. Nov. 5, 1773.
542. Lucy, b. July 27, 1778.
543. Luther, b. May 8, 1781.

  Thomas Keyes d. Dec. 21, 1812.
  His wife Mary, d. Jan. 21, 1800.

VI. KEYES, THOMAS (538), eldest s. of Thomas and
Mary, m. May 26, 1791, Lydia, dau. of Micah Harthan of
Boylston. She was born Feb. 18, 1765. His parents removed
to the North West part of Shrewsbury, now Boylston, about six
weeks after his birth. The farm upon which he resided almost
the entire period of his life, was taken up and occupied by Benjamin Bigelow, in 1735, who sold it to Ephraim Temple in 1750.
It came into the possession of Thomas Keyes (290), in 1767.
Upon his death in 1812, it descended to his son Thomas.

  Thomas d. June 25, 1856.

### CHILDREN.

544. Benjamin Franklin, b. April 15, 1793.
545. Polly, b. Jan. 13, 1795, d. Sept. 18, 1800.
546. Betsey, b. Nov. 17, 1796, d. May 11, 1839, unmarried.
547. Sally, b. Mar. 2, 1799, d. Sept. 18, 1800.
548. Thomas, b. April 20, 1802, was a young man of more
than ordinary promise. He m. April 13, 1827, Eveline, dau.
of Dea. Artemus Murdock, who d. suddenly, Sept. 24, 1828, in
the 25th year of her age. Thomas Keyes survived his wife
about three years, and d. Oct. 30, 1831.
549. Jonathan, b. Nov. 17, 1808, d. Aug. 12, 1813,

VII. KEYES, BENJAMIN F. (544), m. Dec. 10, 1822,
Lois, eldest dau. of Thaddeus Nichols of Holden, when they

took possession of the house built and formerly occupied by his grandfather, Thomas Keyes, which has been their dwelling ever since. She was b. July 17, 1797.

### CHILDREN.

Infant, b. Oct. 9, 1823.

550. Jonathan Mason, b. Aug. 13, 1825.

Infant, b. Jan. 9, 1827.

551. Eveline Murdock, b. July 1, 1828, d. Oct. 25, 1829.

552. Thomas Nichols, b. March 18, 1830.

553. William Wirt, b. Jan. 29, 1832, m. Oct., 1861, Hannah Tabor Peck of Warren, R. I., no children. Res. Township No. 17, Barton Co., Kansas.

554. Lydia Eveline, b. July 15, 1835, m. Mar. 26, 1873, Dea. John H. Brooks of Worcester, Mass. 1 child, Albert Raymond, b. Jan. 23, 1878.

555. John Quincy, b. Oct. 13, 1837, d. Feb. 20, 1838.

VIII. KEYES, JONATHAN M. (550), m. Mar. 20, 1849, Esther Damon of Kirby, Vt.

### CHILDREN.

556. George Harvy, b. Sept. 28, 1850.

557. Benjamin Franklin, b. Nov. 24, 1857.

VIII. KEYES, THOMAS N. (552), m. Dec. 4, 1856, Thankful, eldest dau. of Jerry and Lucy (Keyes) Smith of Marathon N. Y. Res. West Boylston.

### CHILDREN.

558. Florence Gertrude, b. Oct. 27, 1858.

559. Thomas Smith, b. Feb. 14, 1863, d. Mar. 12, 1863.

560. George Franklin, b. Oct. 26, 1868.

561. Mary Evalyn, b. July 27, 1870, d. April 12, 1871.

562. Eva Maria, b. May 28, 1874.

VI. KEYES, ASA (539), 2d s. of Thomas and Mary, m. May 31, 1798, Sarah Thurston of Westborough, when they settled on a farm in Sterling, where they resided during their lives.

## CHILDREN.

563. Asa, b. Feb. 4, 1800, d. Aug. 31, 1803.

564. Sarah, b. July 15, 1801, d. Dec. 12, 1830.

565. Mary, b. April 25, 1803, m. Simeon Partridge of Boylston, d. April 18, 1836.

566. Asa, b. Sept. 17, 1805.

567. Lucy, b. Jan. 25, 1807.

Sarah, wife of Asa, d. Feb. 26, 1807.

He m. 2d, Tamer Eager, May 31, 1808.


VII. KEYES, ASA (566), m. April 10, 1833, Lucy W. Hubbard, of West Boylston, Mass., who d. Sept. 6, 1846.  He m. 2d, Mrs. Martha J. Morse of Westboro, May 18, 1847.

Mrs. Keyes d. Feb. 25, 1867.

### CHILDREN.

568. Charles B., b. Jan. 24, 1834, d. May 23, 1863, at Brashear City, La., Co. K., 53d Reg. Mass. Vols.

569. Mary, b. Jan. 21, 1837, d. Dec. 21, 1844.

570. Martha J., b. Oct. 9, 1838.

571. Susan M., b. Mar. 23, 1842, d. Mar. 11, 1843.

572. Mary F., b. Oct. 24, 1845, m. Everett Kendell.  Res. Worcester, Mass.

573. George H., b. Aug. 30, 1848.   Res. Sterling, Mass.


VII. KEYES, LUCY (567), m., Oct. 30, 1827, Welcome Johnson of Nahant, Mass.  Mrs. Johnson d. Feb. 14, 1878.

### CHILDREN.

574. Asa, K., b. Oct. 26, 1828, d. Oct. 1, 1829.

575. Sarah E., b. Aug. 31, 1830, m. Bradley B. Hawks, Buffalo, N. Y.   5 children.

576. Caleb T., b. Aug. 2, 1832, d. Jan. 22, 1833.

577. Caleb H., b. April 26, 1834, m. Sept. 25, 1864, Julia Connors.  Res. San Francisco, Cal.

578. Martin K., b. Aug. 16, 1836, d. Nov. 15, 1840.

579. Charles T., b. Oct. 16, 1838, m. July 2, 1863, Elizabeth Edson.  Clergyman, Palmer, Mass.   2 children.

580. Herbert E., b. Nov. 22, 1840, m. Feb. 7, 1864, Cynthia Ann Taylor.

581. Edwin W., b. July 28, 1843, m. July 15, 1868, M. T. Crandall of Nahant.

582. Harriett L., b. April 26, 1845, d. Aug. 28, 1848.

583. Frederic K., b. Feb., 1848, d. Sept. 21, 1851.


VI. KEYES, FRANCIS (540), 3d s. of Thomas and Mary, m. May 2, 1805, Thankful Fairbank of Sterling, Mass. They removed to Marathon, N. Y., where Mrs. Keyes died.

Francis m. 2d, Lydia Surdam of Salisbury, Conn.

### CHILDREN.

584. Persis, b. April 9, 1806, m. Ira Surdam of Hector, Penn.

585. Thankful, b. May 22, 1809, m. Jonathan Nichols, Sterling, Mass.

586. Lucy, b. Nov. 21, 1811, m. Jerry Smith, Marathon, N. Y.

Francis d. 1851, at Hector, Penn.

His wife d. 1853, aged 82 years.


VI. KEYES, LUCY (542), youngest dau. of Thomas and Mary, m. Jan. 15, 1805, Lewis Glazier of Gardiner, Mass.

She lived in Gardiner, and d. there Jan. 21, 1873, in her 95th year.

### CHILDREN.

587. Betsey Coolidge, b. Nov. 17, 1805, m. Harvey M. Bancroft of Ashburnham, Mass.

### CHILDREN.

588.  James H., b. April 1, 1829, m. Rebecca Laws.

589.  Sarah b. Sept. 1, 1831, m. Samuel Piper. 5 children.

590. Thomas Edwin, b. Mar. 5, 1807, m. Lucy Brown.

### CHILDREN.

591.  Thomas K., b. May 10, 1832, d. Aug. 15, 1832.

592.  William W., b. June 7, 1834., m. Anna P——, dau., Ella B——.

593.  Mary Ann, b. April 19, 1836, d. July 2, 1847.

594.  Francis B., b. May 3, 1843, d. Oct. 30, 1865.

595.        Lucy E., b. July 3, 1846, m. Charles H. Greene.
            They have 4 children.
596.        Charles E., b. June 6, 1849, m. Lucy M. Scollay.
597. Mary Ann, b. May 1, 1812, d. Jan. 8, 1813.
598. Lewis L.,  } b. Dec. 2, 1813, d. Dec. 23, 1813.
599. Smyrna S., } b. Dec. 2, 1813, d. Dec. 23, 1813.
600. Lucy Ann, b. Oct. 18, 1816, d. Feb. 15, 1838, unm.
601. Mary K., b. June 3, 1818, d. Jan. 14, 1876, unm.

VI. KEYES, LUTHER (543), youngest s. of Thomas and
Mary, m. May 8, 1803, Lydia Parker of Concord. Settled in
Hubbardston, removed to Cincinnatus, N. Y. His wife d. Mar.
3, 1816, and he m. 2d, Mary Benedict.

  He d. in Cincinnatus, now Marathon, N. Y., Aug., 1828.

     CHILDREN.

602. Breighton, d. after arriving at mature age.
603. Sumner.
604. Grosvenor.
  There were two other children who d. in infancy.

VII. KEYES, SUMNER (603), m. Catherine Lathrop.
Res. Berksier, Tioga Co., N. Y. Farmer.

     CHILDREN.

605. Sarah.
606. William.
607. Benjamin.

VII. KEYES, GROSVENOR (604), m. Feb., 1844, Rhoda
Parker. Res. Marathon, N. Y.

     CHILDREN.

608. Fernando C., b. Dec. 10, 1844. He was in the Union
Army during the war of the Rebellion, taken prisoner Oct. 19,
1864, at Cedar Creek, Va., died a captive in Salsbury, N. C.,
Feb. 12, 1864, aged 20 years.

  609. Lesley L., b. April 24, 1847, m. ———— 1 son, 6 years
of age. Res. Otis, Richfield Junc., Oneida Co., N. Y. Telegraph operator.

V. KEYES, BENJAMIN (291), fourth s. of Dea. Jonathan, m. 1737, Lucy Merriam of Oxford, Mass.

#### CHILDREN.

610. Benjamin, b. 1768.
611. Joel, b. 1770, d. unmarried.
612. Amasa, b. 1773.

VI. KEYES, BENJAMIN (610), m. Annice Bigelow. Resided in West Boylston.

#### CHILDREN.

613. Artemus, deceased.
614. Hezekiah, deceased.
615. Annice, deceased.

VI. KEYES, AMASA (612), m. Dorothea Goodnow.

#### CHILDREN.

616. Levi, b. Nov. 17, 1798.
617. Harrietta.
618. Amasa, b. Nov. 3, 1802, d. in San Francisco, Feb. 14, 1855.
619. Dorothea G., m. —— Godden, d. Aug. 25, 1874.

VII. KEESE, LEVI, M. D. (616), graduated from the University of Ohio, passed many years of his life at the South, and is now located at Lowell, Mass. He m. Susan Lee Micou, b. at Richmond, Va. In reference to the spelling of his name, Dr. Keese says: "When quite young it occured to me that Keese was an improvement upon Keyes, so I made the change."

#### CHILDREN.

620. Susan Lee, b. April 1, 1844.
621. William A., b. Dec. 23, 1846.
622. Julia Eliza, b. July 29, 1849.
623. Mary Jean, b. Jan. 31, 1852.
624. Alice Roy, b. Aug. 27, 1859.

VIII. KEESE, WILLIAM A. (621), graduated from Amherst, 1869, took his 2d degree, A. M., 1871, and graduated

from Newton Theo. Sem. 1873.    He m. Feb. 15, 1876, Lizzie
E., dau. of Rev. H. D. Hodge of East Charlotte, Vt.   Rev.
Mr. Keese (Baptist), preached for a time in Maine and is now
settled in Salem, Mass.

VIII. KEESE, JULIA E. (622), m. Jan. 29, 1875, A. F.
Drinkwater, Esq., of Ellsworth, Me.

IV. KEYES, CYPRIAN (282), 3d s. of Dea. Thomas Keyes,
m. in Sudbury, Mass., Dec. 15, 1729, Hepisbah Howe.   She was
added to the Church in Shrewsbury from that in Sudbury, in
1736, and d. 1792, aged 86.    Dea. Cyprian Keyes, was Selectman, Town Clerk and Assessor in Shrewsbury, and was Deacon
in the Cong. Church there and in the North Parish.   He was
elected Deacon, April 27, 1735.   He d. June 18, 1802, at
Boylston.

### CHILDREN.

625. Hepsibah, b. Nov, 9, 1730, m. Jotham Bush, 1750.
626. Betty, b. 1732, sup. m. Oliver Dakin of Sudbury, 1749.
627, Zenas, b. 1733.
628. Cyprian, b. 1735.
629. Levinah, b. Feb. 2, 1737, d. 1756.
630. Persis, b. 1739, m. Ezra Beaman, 1758.
631. David, b. 1741, d. 1745.

V. KEYES, CYPRIAN, Jr. (628), m. in Shrewsbury, May
27, 1756, Martha, dau. of John Bush.   Cyprian d. in Pittsfield,
Mass., about 1805.

### CHILDREN.

632. David, b. July 13, 1757, d. Nov. 23, 1775.
633. Cyprian, b. Jan. 31, 1759, d. in the Revolutionary war.
634. Israel, b. July 20, 1760.
635. Patty, b. Feb. 4, 1762, or Mary, according to another
record.
636. Peabody, b. Nov. 1, 1763.
637. Levinah, b. Mar. 25, 1765.
638. Persis, b. April 5, 1767.

639. Betty, b. Jan. 1, 1768, m. Daniel Cheever, d. in Prince-
.on, Mass., aged about 75.

640. Lucy, b. May 13, 1770, m. Alpheus Stratton, d. in Rutland, about 1830.

641. Jotham, b. June 23, 1772, at Princeton, Mass.

642. Ezra, b. 1774, at Princeton, Mass. d. young.

643. David.

644. There was also a dau., Hypey (Hepsibah), d. at 9 years.

Cyprian is supposed to have had 14 children.

Levinah Keyes, dau. of Cyprian, Jr., m. Joseph
Baker, d. at Guilford, N. Y.

Patty and Persis, dau. of Cyprian, Jr., m. and d. in
Milford, N. Y.

VI. KEYES, ISRAEL (634), 3d son of Cyprien, m. Mar.
7, 1782, Dolly, dau. of Lieut. and Olive (Keyes) Temple. Israel was in the Revolutionary War, and survived, while his two
elder brothers died of small-pox. He was one of an artillery
company, commanded by Capt. David Henshaw, at Castle William, now Fort Independence, after the evacuation of Boston, by
British troops. He lived in Princeton and died there, Sept. 18,
1841.

### CHILDREN.

645. Dennis, b. Sept. 20, 1784, d. Sept. 21, 1847.

646. Ezra B., b. Aug. 8, 1786.

647. Jonas, b. Oct. 28, 1788, had one child, Mrs. Dolly T.
Lent, now living in Chelsea, Mass. Jonas d. in Eastport, Me.,
Oct. 29, 1831.

648. Abigail, b. May 21, 1791, m. Feb. 28, 1813, Seth Whit-
temore of Paxton, Mass., d. in Eaton, N. Y., May 20, 1823.

649. Jotham, b. Dec. 3, 1793, d. Feb. 23, 1871. He m. probably, Roby Robbins, and had six children. None of them
married, and the only one now living, is Geo. W. Keyes of
Princeton, Mass.

650. Dolly T., b. Oct. 26, 1798, m. 1st, Abram Hager, Mar.
19, 1821; she m. 2d, in 1838, Charles Brown, dec. Has had
6 children, 3 s. and 2 dau. The 3d s., A. M. Hagar, has been

conductor on the Hannibal and St. Joseph R. R. most of the time for twenty years. Res. Cato, Crawford Co., Kansas.

651. Cornelia B., b. Dec. 17, 1803, m. Oct. 26, 1826, Col. Ezekiel Brown of Eaton, N. Y., who d. in Kansas, about 1873. They have had 3 sons, and 6 dau. of whom 4 have died. The sons are Henry B. Brown, merchant, Israel K. and Charles, farmers. Res. Cato, Kansas.

VII. KEYES, DENNIS (645), eldest s. of Israel, had 6 children, of whom four are now living. Dennis d. Sept. 21, 1847.

CHILDREN.

652. John L.
653. David D.
654. Israel N.
655. Lydia.

These children of Dennis reside in Worcester, Mass., and the sons have a large trade in lumber. The dau. is m., name of her husband not at hand.

VII. KEYES, EZRA B. (646), 3d s. of Israel, married and lived in Princeton, Mass. He died there Aug. 9, 1877. He had seven children, four d. in infancy. There are three now living.

CHILDREN.

656. George W., b. Dec. 28, 1822. Res. Pecatonica, Ill., no children.

657. Louise H., b. Sept. 18, 1827, m. June 28, 1849, Charles Pierce. They have one son, Frank Eugene, who is married, and has a daughter.

658. Persis B., b. Oct. 18, 1831, m. A. W. Hubbard. Res. Princeton, Mass.

CHILDREN.

George Wheeler, b. Dec. 14, 1853, who is m. and has dau., Della May; Abbie Louise, b. May 8, 1856; Martha Caroline, b. April 2, 1861; Ida Sarah, b. April 4, 1862; Charles Upham, b. Jan 23, 1864; William Bailey, b. Feb. 9, 1866, Edgar E., b. Oct. 2, 1868; Elmer A., b. Mar. 4, 1871; Emma A., b. Feb. 2, 1873; Edward J., b. April 14, 1875.

VI. KEYES, PEABODY (636), 4th s. of Cyprien, Jr., m. Persis Brooks of Princeton. His children were born before his removal to Penn. The exact date of removal is uncertain but is supposed by his grandson to have been about 1802. He settled at Jackson, Tioga Co., probably near Daggett's Mills, as that was their Post Office and letters addressed to that place still reach the family.

The country was new, and they were among the first settlers. Persis, wife of Peabody, died after his removal to Penn., and he married again, but it does not appear that there were children. Peabody died some years after his removal to Penn. He was found dead in the road, and from his position, it is supposed that he slipped and fell on the ice

#### CHILDREN.

659. William.

660. Mary, m. John Mapes and lived in Erie, Penn.

661. Roxana, m. and lived in western New York.

662. Asenath, m. Samuel Kress of Dundee, New York. dec.

VII. KYES, WILLIAM (659), m. in 1809, in Tioga Co., Penn., Selome Daggett, probably dau. of the proprietor of Daggett's Mills, and had two children.

663. Seth Q., b. July 3d, 1810.

664. William B., b. Mar. 16, 1812.

William (659), d. June 1813, when his youngest son was one year old, and when he was three, his widow married again, and shortly moved to Vermont, taking her children with her.

At the age of 15, Seth, eldest s. of William went to sea. He m. in Ireland, had two children, and died in Liverpool, Eng., at 42 years of age.

#### CHILDREN.

665. Seth.

666. Mary.

VIII. KYES, WILLIAM B. (664), returned from Vermont to Penn. in 1831, when he was 19 years of age, and made

for himself a home near the old home of his father and grandfather.  He settled in Tioga and became a man of position and
substance.

He m. Aug. 14, 1841, Sarah M. Wells.  Res. Tioga Village.

CHILDREN.

667.  Austin O., b. July 9, 1842, d. July 17, 1855.
668.  Sarah M., b. May 18, 1844, m. G. W. Hazelett.  */. . 3)2
669.  Sevellon C., b. Aug. 14, 1848, m. Gertrude Blatchley.
670.  Bell, b. Feb. 22, 1847, m. William Hazelett.
671.  Annette, b. June 16, 1851, m. H. W. Lawnsberry.
672.  Ada M., b. Dec. 6, 1855.

W. B. Kyes, Esq., took charge of Seth the orphan
son of his brother, who after a time went abroad in search of
his mother and sister.

VI.  KEYES, JOTHAM (641), 5th s. of Cyprian, Jr., m.
Aug. 5, 1794, Mary Harriet Everett, b Oct. 11, 1772, probably
at Rutland, Mass., and settled in Holden, Mass., the marriage
recorded at Rutland.    He removed to Ohio in the summer of
1817, and lived in Windsor, Morgan Co., on the Muskingam.
P. O., Stockport, Ohio.

Jotham d. May 5, 1854, at Marion, Linn Co., Iowa.
His wife d. April 12, 1853, at Marion.

.CHILDREN.

673.  Tylar, b. Jan. 13, 1795.
674.  Harriet, b. Nov. 9, 1796, d. at two years.

The record of birth, of Tylar and Harriet, found at
Rutland, Mass.

675.  Phinnehas Clapp, b. Jan. 13, 1799.
676.  Amory, b. May 17, 1801, merchant in Marion, Iowa.
677.  Mary H., b. May 11, 1803, m. Richmond Cheadle, removed to Oregon in 1849, where she died May, 1862.
678.  Cynthia E., b. Oct. 30, 1805, m. 1st, Asa White.

CHILDREN.

John W., M. D., m. 1st, Martha White, m. 2d, Mary
Edablate;  Addison, m. Mary Evans;  Melissa died
young;  David, m. Lucy Ellis, res. Western Iowa;

Mary, m. Charles Cooper; Cyprian and Charles, both died in the war of the rebellion; Newell, m. Sarah F. Buntin. These all, with one exception, reside in Marion.

Cynthia m. 2d, David White.

679. Horace, b. May 17, 1809, in Waldo Co., Me.

680. David B., b. Dec. 30, 1811, in Waldo Co., Me., lives near Sedalia, Mo.

681. Jotham, b. Mar. 6, 1814, in Waldo, Co., Me. d. Jan. 1868.

VII. KEYES, TYLAR (673), eldest s. of Jotham, m. 1st, Sally Sidelinher. They lived for a time in Richmond, Ind., and moved from that place to Center Point, Iowa.

CHILDREN.

682. Phinehas.

683. Jotham, m. Harriet Smith. No children.

684. Charles.

685. George, accidentally killed when a young man.

686. Mary, m. Mr. Trump. Lived near Cincinnatti. Both dec.

687. Cynthia, m. Mr. Gates.

Tylar m. 2d, Mrs. Mary Nicely.

He m. 3d, Mrs. Roxanna Andrews. He d. Jan. 1, 1878, at Center Point.

VII. KEYES, PHINNEHAS C. (675), m. April 15, 1822, Mary Aiden Gould. Lived in Marshall, Ohio, d. Oct. 30, 1864, in Albion, Iowa.

CHILDREN.

688. George Everett, b. Mar. 2, 1823, m. Nov. 28, 1850, Joanna Evans. Resides near Jewell Center, Jewell Co., Kansas. They have 6 children.

689. Harriet Newell, b. Jan. 1, 1825, graduated at Oberlin, and m. Oct. 4, 1853, Rev. Harvey Jones, (Cong.) Res. Wabaunsee, Kansas.

690. Martha Bush, b. July 18, 1826, unmarried.

691. Edwin, b. July 21, 1828, graduated at Marietta Coll., Ohio, m. April 13, 1854, Sybil D. Sargent. He d. July, 1864, at Lynchburg, Va., from wounds received in his country's service. Was Capt. of a company in 116th Reg. Ohio Vols. Left one son. His widow resides at Hockingport, Ohio.

692. Juliette, ) b. Nov. 28, 1830, m. May 14, 1855, Rev. J.
                . H. Barker, (Bap.). Res. McConnelsville, O.
693. Mariette, ) b. Nov. 28, 1830, d. Mar. 26, 1837.

694. Hiram, b. Dec. 5, 1832, m. May 16, 1858, Lucinda C. Hovey. 6 children living. Res. Pavillion, Wabaunsee Co., Kansas.

695. Chandler, b. July 9, 1834, d. Feb. 6, 1835.

696. Emily, b. May 2, 1836, m. Jan. 7, 1858, Rev. Henry C. Cheadle (Pres.). Res. Blue Earth City, Minn.

697. Mary Gould, b. Sept. 19, 1839, m. Aug. 20, 1872, Levi M. Benedict. Res. Wabaunsee, Kan.


VII. KEYES, AMORY (676), m. Lovisa Cheadle.

CHILDREN.

698. Caroline, m. Thomas Downing.

699. Eliza, m. Robert Homer.

700. Mary Ann, m. Preston Daniels.

701. Josephine, m. Lemuel Parkhurst.

702. Helen, m. James D. Griffin.

703. Arthur, m. Stella Chapin.

704. Everette. Lost his life by an accident at 22 years.

705. Laura, d. in infancy.

706. Sarah, d. in infancy.

These children of Amory all reside in Marion, Iowa.


VII. KEYES, HORACE (679), Post Master at Pleasant Ridge, northern Kansas. m. Nov. 24, 1831, Sarah Reader, in Morgan Co., Ohio.

CHILDREN.

707. Ebenezer, b. Jan. 6, 1833, d. at the age of 6 weeks.

708. Mary Arabella, b. Dec. 23, 1833, m. Sept. 11, 1855, William M. Willis. Res. Oregon.

709. Rosina, b. Jan. 11, 1836, d. at 22 years.

710. Melissa W., b. Dec. 13, 1837, m. Dec. 27, 1860, Geo. W. Mitchell. Res. Leavenworth Co., Kan.

711. Sarah Eleanor, b. Aug. 24, 1839, d. at 14.

712. Lucy Adelia, b. Feb. 14, 1841, m. April 28, 1861, Valentine Devinny. Res. Denver, Col.

713. Cynthia Lovisa, b. Jan 18, 1843, m. Dec. 28, 1865, William McCartney, now living in South Park, Col.

714. Helen Frances, b. July 8, 1846, d. at 14 months.

715. Elizabeth Ermina, b. Sept. 25, 1848, d. at one year.

716. Margaret Eveline, b. June 2, 1851, d. at 2 years.

717. Hepcy Howe, b. Sept. 20, 1853, m. Jan. 2, 1876, Edwin Pike. Res. South Park, Col.

Sarah, wife of Horace Keyes, d. July 13, 1864, aged 52.

Horace m. 2d, Jan. 11, 1866. Sallie Hail.

718. Edna Lillian, b. Jan. 6, 1867.

719. Parmela Emma, b. Aug. 24, 1870.


VII. KEYES, DAVID B. (680), m. Salome Cheadle.

CHILDREN.

720. Almond.

721. Newell.

722. Martha, m. Henry Hanford. Res. Blairstown, Iowa.

723. Laura.

724. Sarah.}
725. Mary, } d. young. Res. Windsor, Mo.

726. Judson, unmarried. Res. Windsor, Mo.

727. David E., unmarried. Res. Windsor, Mo.


VII. KEYES, JOTHAM, Jr. (681), youngest s. of Jotham, m. Jane Gabaudon in Ohio, went with other members of his father's family to Cedar Rapids, Iowa, thence to Coffee Co., Kan., was made Judge, and was an active Union man during the Rebellion. After the war he moved to Wilson Co., Kan., where with his son-in-law, he engaged in mercantile pursuits. Some months after, three of the desperate men with which

Kansas was at that time infested rode to the door of his place of business and called his name. When he responded to their call in person, they shot him dead as he stood in the door.

He had two daughters, the eldest,

728. Pamela Ward, m. a Mr. Sylvester, and lives at or near Coyville, Kan.

729. Mary, the youngest daughter, m. Mr. F——, and lives at Neodosha, Wilson Co., Kan.

The widow of Jotham, Mrs. J. A. Keyes, now resides at Neodosha.

VI. KEYES, DAVID (643), youngest s. Cyprian, Jr., m. Ruby Adams of Milford, N. Y., and had several children, whose names we do not succeed in obtaining. Perhaps news of them may be obtained from Frank J. Keyes, printer, now of Binghampton, N. Y., where David Died, at an advanced age.

Here ends the record of the family of Dea. Thomas Keyes, son of Elias of Sudbury, and grandson of Robert of Watertown.

# PART SECOND.

## SOLOMON KEYES

### AND HIS DESCENDANTS.

# SOLOMON KEYES

## AND HIS DESCENDANTS.

I. 1. SOLOMON KEYES. A tradition prevailed among the earlier descendants of Solomon, and is now current among the older members of the "Keyes" family, that two brothers from England, settled in this country and were the ancestors of all of the name in America. Various names have been ascribed to the brothers, and different ports have been mentioned as their place of landing, but I find no record relating to either of them, earlier than that of the marriage of

"Solomon Keies and Frances Grant at Newbury, Mass., Oct. 2, 1653."

The birth of the five elder children is recorded at Newbury.

In 1664 and 1665, Solomon and Joseph Keyes took up land in Chelmsford, Mass., and in that town is recorded the birth of the other children of Solomon and Frances.

There appears to be no record of the marriage of Joseph, supposed to be the the brother of Solomon, or of the birth of children. He might have had children born in England, or before he came to this country.

Solomon was town clerk and tything man in Chelmsford, and seems to have been a man of influence in those early days.

"The old Keyes homestead, par excellence, a roomy, two story white house, now more than two hundred years old, stands in the town of Westford, which was set off from Chelmsford, and incorporated in 1729, and most of the families of the name in that vicinity, are now said to be of Westford. The village according to an old writer, is handsomely situated on a swell of fine land, commanding a beautiful prospect of great extent, and contains an academy of ancient date and respectable standing."

There are beautiful views of the Monadnock mountain from certain points in the town, and a fair amount of summer visitors, gives variety to the society, while the academy gives to it a tone of unusual intelligence.

In an old town book of Chelmsford, we find the following:

"Sar g nt Solomon Keys,
dyed, Mch 28, 1702."

His wife Frances, died, 1708.

The name is spelled Keyes in the Newbury records, with one exception, where the second *e* is omitted, probably by mistake. At Chelmsford, the records make it Keies, generally, during the life of Solomon, although during the few years preceding, as in the record of his death, we find it sometimes Keys.

### CHILDREN OF SOLOMON AND FRANCES.

2. Hannah, b. Sept. 4, 1654.
3. Sarah, b. Aug. 24, 1656.
4. Mary, b. Sept. 26, 1658.
5. Jane, b. Oct. 5, 1660, m. May 17, 1680, Sam'l Cleaveland.
6. Judith, b. Sept. 16, 1662.
7. Solomon, b. June 24, 1665, said to have been born in Billerica, Mass. There is no record of his birth in that place.
8. Joseph, b. May 24, 1667.
9. Ruth, b. April, 1669.
10. Moses, b. Mar. 21, 1671.
11. John, b. Aug. 14, 1674.

II. KEYES, SOLOMOM (7), eldest s. of Solomon and Frances, m. Mary ———

### CHILDREN.

12. Elias, b. Oct. 17, 1692.
13. Hannah, b. Jan. 28, 1698.
14. Henry, b. Jan. 23, 1699.
15. Solomon, b. May 11, 1701.
16. Eunice, b. Dec. 17, 1704.
17. Ruth, b. June 8, 1707.
18. Zebediah, b. Jan. 11, 1710.  s. of Solomon and Priscilla, 2d wife.

III. KEYES, ELIAS (12), s. of Solomon and Mary, and grandson of Solomon and Frances, m. Mary ———

### CHILDREN.

19. Ephraim, b. July 5, 1715.
20. Stephen, b. July 15, 1717.
21. Sampson, b. Nov. 21, 1719.
22. Mary, b. Jan. 19, 1721.
23. Zechariah, b. Jan. 5, 1723.
24. Solomon, b. July 15, 1728.

Elias d. Feb. 22, 1767.
Mary, his wife, d. Nov. 27, 1753, aged 58.

Elias was born in Chelmsford, and was perhaps married elsewhere, as, although we find no record of his marriage in Chelmsford, we find that of the birth of the two elder children. The record of these two children of Elias and Mary is also found in Ashford, Conn., together with that of their other children. An Elias Keyes was one of the original proprietors of Londonderry, New Hampshire, which was settled in 1719, by a colony of Presbyterians from the vicinity of the city of Londonderry, in the north of Ireland, to which place their ancestors had emigrated about a century before from Scotland. They came to New England in the summer of 1718, and applied to the government of Mass., for the grant of a township, and were allowed to select a place for their location. Having selected Londonderry, sixteen families accompanied by their pastor, took possession of the place and in 1720 purchased the Indian title. If the Elias mentioned as having been there from 1720 to 1735, emigrated with the party from Ireland, who are his descendants? If not one of the emigrants, it is possible that Elias, the son of Solomon, prospected in the wilds of New Hampshire, previous to his removal to Ashford, Conn. It is also possible that Elias, son of Elias of Sudbury, of whose settlement, wife or children we know nothing, might have taken up land in Londonderry, and lived there those fifteen years. He would have been more than fifty years old at that time. It is curious, that although Ward mentions that Elias had a family in Marlboro', between the years 1696 and 1702, he does not give names or dates.

IV. KEYES, LIEUT. EPHRAIM (19), eldest son of Elias and Mary, m. 1st, Sarah Wadkins, at Ashford, Conn. He m. 2d, widow Glazier of Rockingham, N. H. He removed from Ashford to Acworth, N. H., in 1769, one year later than his son William, and died at Acworth, Sept. 6, 1802. His wife Sarah, died June 15, 1790, in the 71st year of her age. The birth of the two brothers Ephraim and Stephen, recorded both in Chelmsford and Ashford as the children of Elias and Mary, leaves no doubt as to the identity of Ephraim. Add to this that the names of Elias and his family disappear from the Chlemsford records after the birth of Stephen in 1717, while the record is continued in Ashford.

### CHILDREN OF EPHRAIM AND SARAH.

25. William, b. Oct., 1740, at Ashford, Conn.

26. John, who gave part of the common to the town of Acworth, but probably never lived there. We have no clue to him, unless he was the founder of the Keeseville family whose first ancestor is supposed to have been named John, and who must have been born about the time of the son of Ephraim.

27. Sally. The wife of Perley Keyes, grandson of Ephraim, remembered a daughter of Ephraim of this name who married Nathan Wales. Perhaps the Nathan Wales, Jr., who married (as Justice of the Peace) John, afterward Gen. John Keyes and Mary Wales, at Ashford, Conn., in 1767. If so, she must have been one of the older children of Ephraim.

28. Edward, b. 1746, d. at Acworth, July 24, 1823.

29. Jonas, b. 1748, d. at Acworth, July 8, 1820.

30. Joseph, d. of measles contracted in the Revolutionary War.

31. Heiress. In a list of the children of Ephraim, in possession of one of his descendants, the name of Heiress is found last on the list, but it does not appear that she was the youngest. Perhaps she was born about 1752. That such a person really existed there is no doubt, as she married Henry Coffeen and they moved from Acworth to Schuyler, N. Y., where he acted as County Judge. In 1799 he bought land in Watertown, N. Y., and moved there in the year 1800, being, if not the first

settler, among the first. His mother belonged to a prominent family of N. H., the Hale family, and they had a son, named Hale.

32. Hannah, b. Jan. 20, 1754.

33. Henry, b. probably about 1756 or 7. Of weak mind owing to an accident in childhood, and lived with his brother Amos. The Acworth Register gives the date of his death as May 25, 1792, in his 34th year, which would make the date of his birth 1758.

This must be a mistake, as the next son, Frederic, was born that year.

34. Frederic, b. 1758, m. Sarah Grout, and had one son,

35.     Frederick, bap. June 23, 1785, who d. young.

Frederic was in the Revolutionary War. He d. April 30, 1785, and his widow m. 2d, Eusebius Silsby. Their son Joseph, m. Mary, dau. of Amos and Polly (Grout) Keyes.

36. Amos, b. 1761, d. in Acworth, Aug. 30, 1820.

V. KEYES, CAPT. WILLIAM (25), supposed to be the eldest son of Ephraim, m. in 1767, Hannah. dau. of Stephen and Margaret (Stowell) Scarborough. She was born Sept. 18, 1744.

William Keyes was the first settler of Acworth, N. H., moving to that place in 1768, his wife Hannah and one child Huldah, with his ox team, a common mode of conveyance among the early settlers. A log house would be in place for their first dwelling. Upon this subject the chronicles are silent, but it is recorded that in 1797, Capt. William moved into his new house, where probably his grandson, Perley G., son of Perley and Lucinda (White) Keyes, was born in 1798. He was in the Revolutionary War, and died April 21, 1813.

Hannah, the wife of Capt. William, was of tall stature, a feature which many of her descendents have inherited. She d. Feb. 26, 1808, aged 63.

CHILDREN.

37. Huldah, b. Feb. 6, 1768, at Ashford, Conn.

38. Philharma, b. April 11, 1769. She was the first child born in Acworth, and d. in Ashford, Mar., 1772.

39. Frederic, b. Feb. 21, 1771.
40. Stephen, b. April 21, 1772.
41. Perley, b. Feb. 24, 1774.
42. Miriam, b. Jan. 23, 1776.
43. William, b. Sept. 18, 1777.
44. Sally, b. July 16, 1779.
45. Ephraim, b. May 17, 1781.
46. Andrew, b. June 11, 1783, d. at Holland Purchase, N. Y., June 27, 1803.
47. John, b. Sept. 11, 1785, d. Dec 1, 1840.


VI. KEYES, HULDAH (37), eldest child of Capt. William, m. July 1, 1788, Andrew, son of Daniel and Elizabeth (Adams) Grout. He was b. 1764.

### CHILDREN.

Philharma, b. 1789, m. Thomas Slade; Andrew; Frederic, m. —— Brown; Huldah, m. Joseph Ball; Hannah; Azubah; Daniel; Elizabeth A., m. Joseph Dickey; John, m. Hannah Allen; Sally, m. Joseph Dickey; William R., m. Nancy Hayward; Patty W., d. young; Linda, m. Albert Pearson.


VI. KEYES, FREDERIC (39), 3d child of Capt. William, m. Rachel Jacobs, who was b. May 4, 1776, and settled in Northumberland, N. Y. It is said that he was a model man, agreeable in his manners and of fine talents. He was in the Revolutionary War. He was at one time engaged in the lumber business in Argyle, Washington Co., N. Y., and afterward became a farmer. He lived a long time near Ballston, Saratoga Co., and d. near Syracuse of consumption, Sept. 17, 1834. His wife Rachel d. Jan. 29, 1840.

### CHILDREN.

48. William W. b. Nov. 13, 1797.
49. Samuel J. b. July 26, 1799.
50. Elizabeth, b. July 12, 1801.
51. Charles, b. May 30, 1804.
52. Hannah, b. May 21, 1806.
53. Archibald, b. July 26, 1808.

54. Stephen P., b. Nov. 13, 1811.
55. Sarah A., b. Mar. 5, 1814.
56. Perley G., b. July 13, 1816.

VII. KEYES, WILLIAM W. (48), eldest son of Frederic Keyes of Northumberland, m. Laura Rice. He was a carpenter and lived in Northumberland, until about 1868, when he removed to Rockford, Ill., and lived with his son Charles. He died and was buried in Rockford, Mar. 15, 1874.

Laura, his wife d. 1842.

He m. 2d, Jemima Rice, July 2, 1846, who d. May 14, 1864.

### CHILDREN.

57. Charles Edwin, b. Sept. 12, 1830.
58. Marsdin, b. Feb. 15, 1832.
59. Abigail J., b. Mar. 17, 1834, m. James Milier. Res. Wis. No children.
60. Laura Emmeline, b. May 26, 1840. d. young.

VIII. KEYES, CHARLES EDWIN (57), has been a railroad man all his life. After considerable experience on Vermont railroads, he went west, Aug., 1852, and occupied positions on the Chicago, Pittsburg and Fort Wayne R. R. For the last fifteen years, has been Road Master, on the Chicago and North Western R. R. He m. Aug. 26, 1852, Elizabeth Burkby. Res. Rockford, Ill.

### CHILDREN.

61. Ellen Augusta, b. July 26, 1853, d. June 5, 1859.
62. Frederic Angustus, b. Oct. 25, 1855. R. R. man.
63. Alford Burkby, b. April 3, 1857, d. May 25, 1859.
64. Ellen Elizabeth, b. Sept. 25, 1859.
65. Jessie R., b. July 18, 1866.
66. Charles Herbert, b. Oct. 6, 1870.

VIII. KEYES, MARSDIN (58), m. July 2, 1856, in Nova Scotia, Margaret Purves, b. Mar. 15, 1832.

9

## CHILDREN.

67. Harlow William, b. July 9, 1857.
68. Laura Anna, b. June 27, 1860.
69. George P., b. Dec. 23, 1863, d. Jan. 25, 1864.

Marsdin moved to Mt. Vernon, Iowa, where his wife Margaret d. Dec. 30, 1863. He m. 2d, Mar. 15, 1866, Martha Worthington, b. Aug. 22, 1845.

## CHILDREN.

70. Carrie Ellen, b. May 24, 1867.
71. Hattie Julia, b. Sept. 9, 1868.
72. Chas. Ruben, b. May 5, 1871.
73. Margaret Bertie, b. April 3, 1873.
74. Geneva May, b. Feb. 10, 1876.

VII. KEYES, SAMUEL J. (49), 2d child of Frederic, m. Oct. 13, 1835, Joanna Gahan. After living 40 years in his native town, in the Spring of 1841, he removed to Monroe Co., N. Y. In 1845 he went west, was three years in Chicago, thence to Dane Co., Wis., in 1848, and in 1854, to his present residence, Strongs Prairie, Wis.

## CHILDREN.

75. Mary Elizabeth, b. July 26, 1836, unmarried. Res. Kan.
76. Charles, b. Nov. 6, 1838, m. Gertrude Hinkley. No children. He was a lumberman, accidentally killed on Yellow River, April 24, 1867.
77. Sarah, b. Nov. 29, 1840, d. young from her dress taking fire, from a fire place.
78. John B., b. Nov. 2, 1842, was Capt. in the Union Army, in 16th Wis. Reg. was Ass't Comm. of Musters, was mustered out as Capt., Jan. 17, 1866, unm. Res. Strongs.Prairie.

VII. KEYES, ELIZABETH (50), 3d child of Frederic, m. Rev. William Fowler (Meth.) of Palmyra, N. Y. His voice failing, he removed to Rockford, Ill., about 1841, being one of the early settlers, became a farmer, and occupied a prominent position in the Church there.

## CHILDREN.

Edward Fowler, who started for Cal., and d. near Ft. Laramie; Mary, who m. J. B. Skinner, but d. in a few years, leaving a dau., Mary; Jane, who d. young; Sarah, who m. Shelden Smith, architect, of Detroit, Mich., about 1861; Adam C., who m. and was Lieut. in the 8th Ill., Cavalry. Res. Genoa, Wis.; Frederic, m. in Kansas, was in Union Army; John Emory, m. Mary Chirk, 4 children; Rachel Nellie, m. Mortimer Smith of Detroit, Mich., d. soon, one son Frederic.

Mrs. Fowler d. at Rockford, Dec. 13, 1858.
Her husband resides in Los Gatos, Cal.

VII. KEYES, CHARLES (51), 4th child of Frederic, m. Oct. 14, 1841, Mary Viele. He was a farmer, went west about 1847, and settled in Rockford, Ill., where he d. Aug. 19, 1854.

### CHILDREN.

79. Charles Frederic, b. Aug. 10, 1842, m. Sept., 1871, Mary A. Hale of Geneva Lake, Wis. He was accidentally killed in Aurora, Ill., Aug. 13, 1876. One child, Kate Louisa, b. Dec. 6, 1863.

80. Lydia Ann, b. April 28, 1844, d. May 1845.

81. Francis, b. Oct. 10, 1848, unmarried. Res. Rockford, Ill.

82. Sarah Ann, b. Nov. 10, 1852, unmarried. Teacher in Rockford.

VII. KEYES, HANNAH (52), 5th child of Frederick, m. Dr. Ely Osborn who had a large practice at Saratoga Springs where he lived. They had a dau. who m. and resides in Saratoga.

Hannah d. Mar. 17, 1866.

VII. KEYES, ARCHIBALD (53), 6th child of Frederic, m. June 18, 1834, Elizabeth Clarke, who was b. Oct. 15, 1807. He went west in 1845, and still (1878) resides in Rockford, Ill. Farmer.

### CHILDREN.

83. Elizabeth Ann, b. Mar. 20, 1839, d. Sept. 15, 1841.

84. Miles Gardiner, b. Nov. 18, 1842. Farmer, unmarried,

living with his parents, in Rockford, on the homestead.

85. John Clark, b. July 5, 1844, m. Mar. 25, 1868, Mary Esther Hemenway. They have a dau., Carrie Marilla, b. May 12, 1872. John Keyes is a farmer, living on part of the homestead.

VII. KEYES, REV. STEPHEN P. (54), 7th child of Frederic, passed three years in the Lima Seminary, N. Y. Entered the ministry of the M. E. Church in 1834, and received his first appointment to Milo and Starkey circuit, in Yates Co., N. Y. Removed to Ill., in 1837, and was regularly transferred from the Genesee Conf. to the Ill., and received his appointment to Ottawa, La Salle Co., Ill. In 1839 he received an appointment as chaplain in the Union Army, in which capacity he served for three years, when he returned to his regular work in the Rock River Conf. After being stationed for two years in Chicago, he was elected to the General Conference, which held its session in Boston, in 1852, and again in 1856, was presiding elder from 1854 to 1856, when his health failed, and he received a superannuation relation, and now resides in Aurora, Ill. He m. Sept. 22, 1746, at Dixon, Ill., Amelia Bassett.

CHILDREN.

86. Emma Therese.
87. Mary Amelia.
88. Herbert Duane, d. in infancy.

VII. KEYES, SARAH ANN (55), 8th child of Frederic, m. 1st, Mr. Hoag. He d. leaving a dau., Sarah Jane, who m. Wm. W. Dutton of Chelsea. They have one dau., Thirza. Sarah Ann m. 2d, Thomas Marshall. They lived at Victory Mills, Saratoga Co., where she d. Aug. 11, 1870.

VII. KEYES, PERLEY G. (56), 9th child of Frederic, m. Kate Ostrander, went west, settled in Dane Co., Wis., from which place he removed to Strongs Prairie, Wis., May, 1854, where he d. April 14, 1874.

#### CHILDREN.

89. Stephen, who m. Lucia Vancuren.

#### CHILDREN.

90. Ellsworth, Ave and Eve, twins, and Bessie. Res. Strongs Prarie, Wis.

91. Mary Ellen, m. William Cannon, one son.

92. Sarah Ann, m. Riley Hammond, dec.

93. George Henry, m. Name of wife not at hand.

94. Amelia, m. Resides in Minn.

VI. KEYES, STEPHEN (40), 4th child of Capt. William, m. Dec., 1792, Hannah Gregg. Lived in Augusta, Oneida Co., N. Y., in 1800, d. about 1820.

#### CHILDREN.

95. Ephraim.

96. Andrew.

97. Hiram.

98. William.

They were living in Cataraugus Co., N. Y., in 1856.

VI. KEYES, PERLEY (41), 5th child of Capt. William, m. Nov. 20, 1796, Lucinda White, b. Feb. 28, 1776, supposed to be a descendant of Peregrine White, the first child born in New England after the landing of the Pilgrims. Peregrine White d. 1704, aged 83, and was buried on Webster's farm at Marshfield. Lucinda White went to Walpole, N. H., Oct. 4, 1795, and to Acworth, May 7, 1796, was m. Nov. 20, the same year. She had a retentive memory, and kept a diary, from which have been gathered many facts relating to the earlier members of the Acworth families.

Perley Keyes, soon after the Rev. War, went to Saratoga Co., N. Y., and engaged in lumbering on the Hudson River. In 1799, he took up 500 acres of land in what is now Rutland, Jeff Co., N. Y., and moved there in 1800. He removed to Watertown, five miles from Rutland, in 1809, and became a prominent man in Jeff Co., holding successively the offices of Magistrate, Judge of the County Court, Sheriff and Coll. of Customs at Sackett's Harbor.    Was twice State Senator, and once a member of the Council of Appointment.    He wielded a strong political influence in Jeff Co., and when in the Legislature, made his presence felt.    He was the personal, as well as the political friend of such men as Silas Wright, Jr., Will L. Marcy, Martin Van Buren, &c.    In a letter from the above mentioned gentlemen and others, to Van Buren in 1830, recommending him for the office of Gov. of the territory of Wis., they speak of him as a plain, unlearned man, with a sound, strong mind, and in the practical exercise of an unusual amount of common sense.    A correspondent of the Utica *Observer* writes: "No man ever lived in Jeff Co., who, for a quarter of a century, exercised so great a political influence as Perley Keyes."    He was nicknamed the "King" by his political opponents.    Among the best known anecdotes of Judge Keyes, is that of the "Whittlesey case," familiar to the readers of the Acworth history, where also may be found the way in which, as a boy, he turned the tables upon Capt. Duncan, his military commander.    The following has never been in print, and will illustrate his facility at repartee.

Micah Sterling, one of the ablest lawyers of Jefferson county, N. Y., where Keyes resided, in a heated political discussion, had been knocked down by Sam Brown, the brother of Gen. Jacob Brown.    Shortly after this occurrence, a couple of hogs belonging to Judge Keyes, had broken out into the highway, and been shut up in the Pound.    As the Pound Master knew very well that it was an accident, Keyes was indignant, and going to the Pound, without further ceremony lifted his hogs, which weighed some two hundred pounds apiece, out of the enclosure, and proceeded to drive them home.    Quite a number witnessed the performance, and among them Micah Sterling.    As Judge Keyes passed by, driving his pigs before him, Sterling thought it a good opportunity to banter him, and cried out, "Keyes, I understand that you can handle a hog better than any man in Jefferson county."    Keyes's quick retort was, "Oh, no, Sterling, not as well as Sam. Brown."

Perley Keyes, d. May 13, 1834.
Lucinda, his wife, d. Feb. 23, 1855.

CHILDREN.

99. Solon, b. Aug. 22, 1797, d. Aug. 29, 1797.

100. Perley Gardiner, b. Sept. 6, 1798, at Acworth, N. H.

101. Cynthia C., b. Oct. 31, 1802, m. Jan. 27, 1820, William Wood. Cynthia d. May 11, 1821. Wm. Wood m. 2d, Anna, sister of Gen. Joe Hooker. Mr. Wood d. and his wife now resides in Watertown.

102. Marietta W., b. Jan. 26, 1810, m. Dec. 31, 1834, Gilman Wood. She d. May 30, 1836.

VII. KEYES, PERLEY G. (100), m. 1st, Mar. 7, 1824, Laura Becker, b. April 13, 1805. She d. June 8, 1828. Perley G., or Gardiner, as he was generally called, m. 2d, Sept. 22, 1829, Lydia Pearce,

He was a year and a half old, when his parents moved into the Black River country in the western part of New York, was candid, upright and conscientious, formed an extensive acquaintance throughout the region where he resided, and had many warm friends At an early period in the anti-slavery movement, he became an active, outspoken, anti-slavery man. He was a lawyer but did not practice his profession the latter part of his life.

He d. Nov. 25, 1856.

CHILDREN.

103. Richard G., b. Jan. 6, 1826, at Watertown, N. Y. Rev. R. G. Keyes, graduated at Hamilton College, 1848, and at Auburn Theological Seminary, 1857, was ordained by the Oneida Cong. Association at Paris Hill, Sept. 29, 1852. He is a clergyman, and resides at Watertown, N. Y., in the house built by his grandfather, Perley Keyes, in 1831. Unmarried.

104. Laura B., b. May 25, 1828, d. Aug. 7, 1829.

VI. KEYES, MIRIAM (42), 6th child of Capt. William, m. 1793, John Mitchell, b. July 28, 1771.

Mrs. Mitchell, d. July 29, 1817.

John Mitchell, d. Dec. 6, 1838.

CHILDREN.

Nancy, b. Mar. 20, 1794, m. Benj. Alexander, June 26, 1810;

Perley, b. Oct. 13, 1795, m. Phebe Lewis, residence, Terre Haut, Ind., d. July 20, 1878: Sally b. Aug. 29, 1797, m. Merrill Coburn, Feb. 3, 1817, res. Carthage, N. Y. Her dau. m. Chas. Follinsbe, now one of the wealthy men of Chicago; Asenath, b. April 6, 1799, m. —— Blanchard; William, b. Nov. 11, 1800, m. Polly Briggs; John, b. Sept. 25, 1802, d. June, 1834; Andrew, b. Aug. 15, 1804, m. Laura Smith; Almon, b. Sept. 27, 1806, d. young; Stephen, b. Aug. 15, 1808, d. young; Ephraim, b. Mar. 30, 1810, d. young; Franklin, b. Feb. 8, 1812; Frederic, b. May 17, 1814, d. 1844; Miriam, b. June 21, 1816, m. Woster Donner. She d. 1844.

VI. KEYES, WILLIAM (43), 7th child of Capt. William, m. Hannah Prior, was in the war of 1812, d. Dec. 1812, at Ogdensburg, N. Y., of Camp Epidemic, or Spotted Fever. He resided in Rutland, N. Y., and was buried there.

His widow m. Amos Stebbins. Their dau. Cornelia b. Nov. 8, 1815, m. Dr. Isaac Munson.

#### CHILDREN.

105. Solon, b. 1805, m. Sybil H. Goodrich. He d. Dec. 24, 1857.

#### DAUGHTER.

106.      Mary L., b. Feb. 8, 1828, m. Sept. 30, 1847, Rufus Scott, who d. Aug., 1861.

#### SON.

107.      Frank Keyes Scott, b. July 18, 1859.

108. Calista, b. Mar. 7, 1812, m. July 10, 1832, Stephen White. Res. Watertown, N. Y.

#### DAUGHTER.

109.      Mary B., b. June 10, 1835, m. Oct. 21, 1855, John C. Streeter, who is now (1878) Mayor of Watertown, N. Y. Mrs. Streeter d. Dec. 2, 1869, leaving a son, born about 1858.

VI. KEYES, SALLY (44), 8th child of William, m. Aug. 1809, James Burnam, who was b. April 10, 1799.

Mrs. Burnam d. Mar. 3, 1814.

Mr. Burnam d. Jan. 30, 1852.

### CHILDREN.

110. Ambrose, b. Aug. 7, 1811, m. April 29, 1841, Rhoda Bradley Reynolds, at Joliet, Will Co., Ill., d. Oct. 21, 1870.

#### CHILDREN OF AMBROSE.

Alston, b. Feb. 17, 1843, d. May 21, 1844; Arthur, b. May 27, 1845; Lisle, b. Sept. 10, 1847; Frank, b. Aug. 18, 1850; Miles, b. Sept. 23, 1857. Arthur, Lisle and Frank are now living in Chicago, Cook Co., Ill. Miles is in San Francisco.

111. Harman, b. July 11, 1812, m. April 18, 1838.

#### CHILDREN OF HARMAN.

Roscoe, b. Sept. 4, 1839, d. April 20, 1860; James E., b. Feb. 4, 1842, d. June 21, 1863; Anna J., b. June 21, 1846, d. April 12, 1857; Sarai M., b. Aug. 10, 1852, m. Mr. Leddy of Chicago. Harman resides at Watertown, N. Y.

112. Sally, b. Feb. 24, 1814, d. Oct. 8, 1836.

VI. KEYES, EPHRAIM (45), 9th child of Capt. William, m. in 1800, Esther Rogers. He settled in Middlesex, Washington Co., Vt., in 1804, emigrated to Ohio in 1814, where he d. in 1822.

#### CHILDREN.

113 Loren, b. May 3, 1801.

114. Daniel, b. Mar. 11, 1803.

115. Andrew, b. Mar. 4, 1805.

116. Harriet, b. Sept. 16, 1809, d. Sept. 11, 1822.

117. Elias, b. Sept. 8, 1812.

118. William, b. April 22, 1815, d. in Arkansas. Had one child.

119. John M., b. Nov. 3, 1818, d. 1864, in Louisiana, in the southern army.

120. Emily, b. Jan. 12, 1822, d. 1825.

VII. KEYES, LOREN (113), m. Lydia Morse. He d. 1861, in Madison Co., Ohio.

#### CHILDREN.

121. Lydia E., b. Oct. 12, 1823, m. Elisha Calender. Eight children living in Ohio and Ind.

122. Esther Ann, b. Sept. 21, 1825, m. John W. Smith. Ten children. Res. Union Co., Ohio.

123. Renewa E., b. Oct. 29, 1827, m. Amos Culver. Had one child, dec.

124. Harriet A., b. Jan. 5, 1830, m. Henry Newman. Three children.

125. Perley M., b. Nov. 13, 1832, m. Roselphe Bigelow.

### CHILDREN.

126. Loren B., b. July 8, 1866.
127. Orval B., b. Nov. 27, 1868.
128. Lydia B., b. May 22, 1871.

These children of Perley reside in Madison Co., Ohio.

129. Loren A., b. Dec. 29, 1834, unmarried.

130. Elizabeth A., b. Sept. 20, 1837, m. Jacob Yozel, four children.

131. William H., b. Aug. 1, 1840, m. Almira McAdams. These three children of Loren res. in Union Co., O.

132. Adela Gannett, b. Sept. 6, 1843, m. Porter McDowelle. Res. Plain City, Madison Co., Ohio.

133. Josephine B., b. Aug. 12, 1848, m. G. Morse, four children.

VII. KEYES, DANIEL (114), m. Elizabeth Carr about 1825, had several children. The only son now living,

134. George, married and has a large family. Lives in the east part of Marion Co., Ohio.

135. Mary, m. John Jolly, lives in Richmond, Union Co., O.

136. Another dau. m. John Granger, had large family in Ind., and d. there. Daniel d. 1878, in Marion Co., O.

VII. KEYES, ANDREW (115), m. in 1829, Rebecca Sabine. Res. Marysville, Union Co., O.

### CHILDREN.

137. Cynthia, b. June 30, 1833, m. Justin P. Woodworth, Sept. 12, 1853. Two children, Julia and Justin.

138. Abi, b. Sept. 1, 1835, unmarried.

139. Beverly W., b. Aug. 6, 1837, m. Abbie Baxter.  Three children.  Res. Marysville.

140. Daphney, b. July 6, 1841, m. Dwight Webb.  Two children living.  Res. Marysville.

VII. KEYES, ELIAS (117), m. in 1837, Mary Neal.  Res. Mechanicsburgh, Champain Co., Ohio.

### CHILDREN.

141. Emily, m. Joseph —— and has children.

142. Ann, unmarried.

143. Josephine. m. Alexander Reed.  Two children.

144. Lylla Belle, unmarried.

145. Edwin R., unmarried.

146. Warren, unmarried.

VI. KEYES, JOHN (47), youngest child of William, m. 1st, Anna Keyton.

### CHILDREN.

147. Frank, b. July 28, 1806, d. Mar. 26, 1814, of Spotted Fever.

148. Fielding, b. Sept. 29, 1807.

149. Lauriston, b. Mar. 22, 1809.

150. Philharma, b. Feb. 3, 1811, m. Mr. Lothrop.  One child, John, d. young.  Res. West Roxbury, Mass.

151. Nancy F., } b. Dec. 23, 1813.
152. Fanny F., } b. Dec. 23, 1813, d. Feb., 1814, of Spotted Fever.

 Anna, wife of John, d. Mar. 20, 1814, of Spotted Fever.

 John m. 2d, Lucia Hubbard.

153. Frank H., b. Nov. 23, 1820.  Living at Webster, Mass., in 1868.

154. Caroline F., b. Jan. 10, 1823, m. Mr. Heyward.  Res. Concord, N. H.

 John, m. 3d, Lucy Thornton.

 He d. in Acworth, Mar. 1, 1845.

## VII. KEYES, FIELDING (148), m. Martha Mitchell.

### CHILDREN.

155. Matthew P., m. Ellen Patterson.   Res. Sharon, Vt.

### CHILDREN.

156.          Fielding.
157.          George F., d. young.
          Fielding, m. 2d, Maria L. Whittaker.

### DAUGHTER.

158. Martha Mitchell.


## VII. KEYES, LAURISTON (149), m. 1st, Susannah Burgess, who d. Jan. 17, 1849, aged 42.   He m. 2d, Martha E. Hibbard.   Res. Claremont, N. H.

### CHILDREN.

159. William H., b. Aug. 31, 1854.
160. John C., b. Oct. 3, 1857.
161. Martha Ella, b. April 15, 1860.


## VII. KEYES, NANCY F. (151), m. Enos P. Hoag.   Res. Lincoln, Vt.

### CHILDREN.

162. Alonzo, d. July 4, 1858.
163. Amelia, m. A. J. Cushman, d. July 9, 1870.   She left two children, a son, b. Nov. 18, 1865, a dau., who d. Feb. 31, 1876


## V. KEYES, EDWARD (28), son of Lieut. Ephraim, m. Patty Sawyer, d. at Acworth, July 24, 1823.

### CHILDREN.

164. Perley, b. April 7, 1789.   Resided in Jeff Co., N. Y., dec.
165. Zealy, b. Mar. 25, 1791, m. Mar. 18, 1812, Shuah Mason.
166. Judith, b. May 12, 1793, m. 1st, Feb. 18, 1813, Rex Keyes.   Judith m. 2d, Mr. Barker, Crown Point, N. Y.
167. Avis, b. Jan. 30, 1796, m. Nov. 3, 1814, John Ober of Crown Point, d. Mar. 4, 1874.   Her husband d. July 19, 1875.

### CHILDREN.

Israel, Abner, Martha, John, Milo, deceased. Eight are living, Almira, Edward, Sarah, Dapheria, Abner, Luthera, Stebbens, Hiram. Edward Ober is now living at Crown Point, N. Y.

168. Luthera, m. Amos Burge. Res. Herman, St. Lawrence Co., N. Y.

169. Almira, m. —— Burge, dec.

170. Edward, b. June 20, 1803, m. Mar. 18, 1823, Elmira Abbott. Res. Unity, N. H.

### SON.

171.   Ephraim A., b. Dec. 27, 1841. He was in the Union Army in the war of the Rebellion, and d. there. He left a son,

172.   Edward Ephraim, b. May 14, 1863.

V. KEYES, HANNAH (32), dau. of Lieut. Ephraim, m. July 11, 1771, Mehumen Stebbins. He was b. Nov. 3, 1752, and d. Feb. 11, 1839 He went to Acworth, from Ashford, Conn. They were the first couple married in Acworth, and the whole village assembled to witness the ceremony.

### CHILDREN.

Elizabeth, b. Sept. 16, 1772, d. June 17, 1787; Amos, b. July 20, 1775, d. Aug. 3, 1849; Ruth, b. May 16, 1777, d. May 11, 1778; Ruth, b. Oct. 13, 1779, d. Oct. 5, 1848; Hannah, b. Mar. 15, 1783, d. Dec. 25, 1837; Mehumen, b. June 29, 1785; Frederic, b. Dec. 1, 1787, d. 1853.

V. KEYES, JONAS (29), 4th son of Lieut. Ephraim, m. 1st, Esther —— and the birth of one son, Amasa, is recorded at Ashford, Conn. He went to Acworth before 1775, with his 2d wife.

He d. at Acworth, July 8, 1820.

### CHILDREN.

173. Amasa, b. Mar. 11, 1771, at Ashford, Conn.

174. Mazelda, b. 1773.

175. Sally, bap. at Acworth, Mar. 5, 1775, m. Nathan Ol-
cutt. Two children, Olive and Esther. Res. Unity.
        Jonas m. 2d, Mehitable Wadkins.

176. Phile, b. Feb. 9, 1779, m. John Abbott.

177. Anne, b. Dec. 21, 1782, m. Dec. 25, 1806, Rufus Blanchard. He lived in Vershire, Vt., and d. 1840.

178. Esther, b. Sept. 29, 1785, m. John Huntoon. Settled in
Unity, N. H. Two children.

179. Rex, b. May 29, 1789, m. Feb. 18, 1813, his cousin Judith Keyes. He d. of Spotted Fever, April 15, 1814. An Infant d. Dec. 23, 1813.

180. Morses, d. young.

181. Morses, b. May 22, 1792.

182. Ada, b. June 3, 1795, m. Asa Howe.

183. Lima, b. Jan. 4, 1798, m. Aug. 7, 1817, William Board-
man. Res. Vershire, Vt.

184. Elizabeth, b. July 15, 1800, m. Sept. 22, 1818, Ambrose
Alexander.

185. Vine, b. Oct. 3, 1805.


VI. KEYES, AMASA (173), m. Catherine Blood of Acworth, and d. in Acworth, Mar. 23, 1815.

### CHILDREN.

186. Asa, bap. April 22, 1792, d. in Acworth of consumption, May 27, 1820.

187. Mazelda, bap. Mar. 16, 1794, probably d. Mar. 12, 1801.

188. Orenza, bap. Aug. 14, 1796, d. April 7, 1804.

189. Harland, bap. Mar. 4, 1799, taxed in Acworth, 1820-
21-22.

190. Sally, bap. June 20, 1802.

191. Larned, bap. May 27, 1804.

192. Lucinda, bap. June 15, 1806.

193. Corinna, bap. Jan. 18, 1809.


VI. KEYES, MAZELDA (174), m. Sarah Foster, Nov. 12,
1795.
        Mazelda d. at Acworth, Oct. 1, 1843.
        Sarah, his wife, d. July 22, 1854.

CHILDREN.

194. Anson, b. Sept. 20, 1796, d. April 20, 1815.

195. Theda, b. Feb. 21, 1799, m. Otis Field of Lempster, N. H

196. Mazelda, b. April 26, 1801, d. unmarried.

197. Linda, b. Aug. 1, 1803, d. Mar. 23, 1815.

198. Lima, b. Sept. 23, 1806, m. Nov. 24, 1825, N. B. Hall.
Two children.

199. Amasa, b. June 26, 1811, d. Feb. 9, 1815.

200. Adna, b. July 28, 1813.

201. Ephraim, b. Sept. 17, 1816.

202. Orison, b. April 2, 1819.

203. Zana, youngest child of Mazelda, m. Ebenezer Grout.
Res. Acworth.


VII. KEYES, ADNA (200), m. Betsey Hilliard.    Res. So.
Acworth.

CHILDREN.

204. Adson D., b. Oct. 22, 1842.   Graduated at Kimball Union Academy, Meriden, N. H., in 1868, at Dartmouth College in
1872, m. Aug. 17, 1872, Mary E. Weston, also a graduate of
K. U. A., class 1869, of Ascutneyville, Vt.   He went west the
same year, studied law with Gordon E. Cole, ex-Attorney of
State, was admitted to the Bar, Nov. term of 1873.   Since that
time, has been in practice at Faribault, Minn.

205. Sarah Jennie, b. Oct. 31, 1853, m. May 31, 1877, Rufus
Merriam, Commercial Agent of Minneapolis, Minn.   Dau. Ina
J., b. Jan. 8, 1878.


VII. KEYES, EPHRAIM (201), m. Ruth Clement.   Res.
West Brome, Can. E., d. in the Autumn of 1860.

CHILDREN.

206. Janette, d. young.

207. Janette, m. Richard Robinson.   Res. West Brome, Can.

208. Sarah Jane, m. —— Clement.   Res. Nopana, Can.

209. Mary, d. unmarried.

210. Edna,  }
211. Emma, } twins, unmarried.

VII. KEYES, ORISON (202), m. Dec. 2, 1841, Lucina A. McClure, b. Jan. 11, 1825. He d. Oct. 9, 1877. His widow lives with her son Frank, at Lempster, N. H.

### CHILDREN.

212. Anson L., b. Feb. 6, 1843, fitted for college at Kimball Union Academy, graduated from Dartmouth, 1872, graduated from the Albany Law School, 1873. Has been Principal of the High Schools at Franklin, N. H., and at Biddeford, Me. Now, in the summer of 1878, enters upon the practice of Law at Faribault, Minn. He m. June 30, 1873, Hattie O. Lufkin of Great Falls, N. H. Dau., Lulu May, b. May 25, 1876.

213. Zenas, b. Sept. 28, 1845, d. Aug. 6, 1858.

214. Nettie E., b. Feb. 12, 1848, m., Jan. 2, 1878, William, son, of Chapin K. and Pamelia (Graham) Brooks of Acworth. He was b. Oct. 4, 1840. He is a merchant and holds the offices of P. M., and Town Clerk.

215. Martin L., b. Feb. 19, 1850, m. Oct. 4, 1876, Isadora V. Stowell of Unity, N. H.

216. Frank E., b. Sept. 22, 1852, unmarried.

These two brothers, carriage manufacturers at Lempster, N. H.

217. Charles W., b. July 1, 1856, d. Jan. 14, 1859.

218. Nellie L., b. July 18, 1859.

219. Angie M., b. May 17, 1862, d. Nov. 22, 1874.

220. Susan Belle, b. Aug. 4, 1866.

VI. KEYES, MORSES (181), m. Aseuath Dickey. He d. at Acworth, Nov. 21, 1847.

### CHILDREN.

221. Hannah, m. Dexter R. Way, two children. Res. Springfield, Vt.

222. Frances Jane, m. Orin D. Wood. Res. Bethel, Vt.

223. Mehitable W., m. Olivet S. Carey. Res. Washington, N. H.

224. Mercey Aseuath, m. 1st, Albert E. Spaulding, daughter, Ellen M.

She m. 2d, Charles Carey. Res. Charleston, N. H.

225. Orpha, b. about 1826, d. at Nashua, Nov. 14, 1843.

226. Graham, b. Sept. 21, 1828, m. Feb. 13, 1850, Calista M. Rogers of Lempster, N. H.

### CHILDREN.

227.　　　Edgar M., b. Oct. 24, 1850, at Acworth, m. May, 25, 1873, Ada Taylor, Marlow, N. H.

228.　　　Etta A., b. June 13, 1852, m. Mar. 25, 1870, Lucius D. Tinker of Marlow. Daughter,

229.　　　　　　Neta, b. Sept. 20, 1872.

230.　　　Nellie E., b. June 10, 1865, at Marlow.


VI. KEYES, VINE (185), youngest son of Jonas, m. Mary Taylor. He enlisted in the 1st N. H. Cavalry, 1864, and d. July 29, 1864, in Andersonville Prison. Moved from Acworth to Unity, N. H., in 1832. His widow res. at East Alstead.

### CHILDREN.

231. Roseltha L., b. Feb. 23, 1836.

232. Angeline Calista, b. Dec. 19, 1838, at Lyttleton, N. H., m. April 29, 1858, George Gilmore. Res., probably, Charleston, N. H.

233. George W., b. Dec. 7, 1840. Enlisted in the 1st N. H. Cavalry in 1862, and served to the end of the war.

234. Annette S., b. Jan 27, 1843, d. April 17, 1856.

235. Hiram A., b. Feb. 21, 1845. Enlisted in the same company, and at the same time with his father and died at Andersonvill, date not known.

236. Amasa W., b. Sept. 9, 1847.

237. James A., b. Mar. 4, 1853.


V. KEYES, AMOS (36), youngest s. of Lieut. Ephraim, m. April 27, 1788, Polly, dau. of Daniel and Elizabeth (Adams) Grout. The farm of his father Ephraim, came into the possession of Amos. He kept a Hotel and was a prominent man. Res. Claremont, N. H.

Amos Keyes d. Aug. 30, 1820.

Mrs. Keyes d. Jan. 8, 1807, in the 39th year of her age.

### CHILDREN.

238. Harry, b. July 12, 1792, d. Mar. 7, 1832, unmarried.

239. Amos, b. Aug. 15, 1794, m. Jane McClure, April 5, 1826. He d. 1868, in Claremont, N. H.

### CHILDREN.

240.  Daniel M.  Res. Boston, Mass.

241.  George A.

242.  Samuel D.  Res. Boston. Mass.

243. Ralph, b. Feb. 9, 1797.

244. Betsey, b. Mar. 30, 1799, m. Mar. 31, 1823, William Warner.  She now lives in Acworth, N. H.

245. Mary, b. Aug. 4, 1802, m. Joseph G. Silsby, Esq.  Both d. in Acworth.

246. Docia, m. July 19, 1827, Isaac Houston.  Both removed to Utah.

Miss Christian McClintock was published to Amos Keyes (youngest s. of Lieut. Ephraim) at Charlestown, N. H., Mar. 24, 1811.  After the death of Amos, Miss Christian m. Daniel Farnsworth of Washington, N. H.


VI. KEYES, RALPH (243), m. Feb. 6, 1820, Hannah Wilson of Acworth, b. 1797.  Res. Goshen, N. H.  Mrs. Keyes d. 1846.

### CHILDREN.

247. Amos, b. 1820, in Acworth, m. in 1853, Martha Ginn. Res. Somerville, Mass.  Address, 20 Clinton, and 26 Blackstone Sts., Boston, Mass.  Wholesale Comm. Produce dealer.

### CHILDREN.

248.  Charles A. Keyes, b. 1854, in Charleston, Mass.

249.  Carrie, b. 1855, in Somerville, Mass., d. young.

250.  S. Emma, b. 1857, in Somerville, Mass.

251.  Fred L., b. 1859, in Somerville, Mass.

252.  Jennie M., b. 1864, in Somerville, Mass.

253. Hiram, d. unmarried.

254. Lauretta, b. May 14, 1823, in Acworth, m. Charles Train of Washington, N. H.  He d. and she m. 2d, Noah Jackson.  Res. Hillsboro Bridge, N. H.  No children.

255. Dean W., b. Aug. 24, 1828, at Acworth, m. Nov. 1, 1860, Sarah A. Snaith, who was b. in Boston, Jan. 1, 1838.

Address, 16, So. Market St., Boston, Mass.

DAUGHTER.

256. Nellie Dean, b. Aug. 22, 1861, d. Oct. 28, 1861.

257. Marietta.

258. Orson H., b. Sept. 19, 1829, at Acworth, m. Mrs. Emma Evens, née Perley. One boy about 12. Res. San Francisco.

259. Maria, m. —— Burnham of Hillsboro Bridge, N. H.

260. Julietta E., b. Dec. 4, 1837, m. May 25, 1854, Fred S. Little, then of Antrim, N. H. They resided at Newport, N. H. Mrs. Little d. Sept. 29, 1869.

CHILDREN.

261. Nellie L., b. Nov. 2, 1855.

262. Willie W., b. Nov. 9, 1859, d. Mar. 14, 1866.

263. Freddie O., b. Sept. 30. 1867.

264. Arthur T., b. July 9, 1839, at Washington, N. H., m. in San Francisco, a widow lady, maiden name Perley. Res. San Francisco.

265. Louisa N., b. in Washington, N. H., m. John McQuestion, of Manchester, N. H. Two dau. 15 and 18.


IV. KEYES, STEPHEN (20), 2d s. of Elias and Mary, b. in Chelmsford, Mass., m. Abigail Peabody, children recorded at Pomfret, Conn.

CHILDREN.

266. Amasa, b. Nov. 3, 1744.

267. Peggy, b. Feb. 18, 1747, d. of Paralysis, unm.

268. Luce, perhaps Percey, b. April 16, 1749.

269. Abigail, b. Aug. 16, 1751, m. Seth Grosvenor of Pomfret, moved to Windsor, Berkshire Co., Mass., had a large family, and d. there.

270. Stephen, b. Dec. 6, 1753.

271. Peabody, b. April 14, 1756, went south, d. without issue.

272. Lucy, b. Nov. 15, 1758, m. Sampson Keyes, Jr.

273. Jerusha (name doubtful), perhaps comes in here. She m. a Mr. Durkee. They moved to Vt., where they lived and

died. It was probably the Durkee who settled in Stockbridge, Vt., with Elias, afterward Judge Elias Keyes.

274. Elnathan, b. July 9, 1762.

275. Mary, b. Aug. 27, 1764, d. Aug. 6, 1766.

276. Mary, b. Feb. 13, 1767, m. Capt. Robert Centre of Hartford, Conn., removed to Hudson, N. Y., thence to New York City, where she died.

V. KEYES, COL. AMASA (266), eldest son of Stephen, m. Nov. 26, 1772, Mrs. Penelope Williams, sister-in-law of Hon. Elisha Williams of Hudson, N. Y. Res. West Hartford, Conn.

CHILDREN.

277. Eleazur, b. April 17, 1774, d. Sept. 7, 1775.

278. Eliezer, b. Sept. 12, 1776, m. Permelia, dau. of Col. Ethan Allen. She was b. before they came to Vt., it is supposed, perhaps in Sheffield, Mass., or in Sunderland, Vt , where the family of Ethan Allen lived from 1777 to 1789, when they removed to Burlington. Eliezer was a lawyer, lived in Burlington, and d. probably at St. Albans, Vt. No children.

279. Eliza, m. Major Henry Stanton, d. in New York, about 1836.

280. Henry, d. in Hartford, unmarried.

281. Mary,        These two sisters m. successively, E. T. En-
282. Abby,        glesby, a prominent man and President of a Bank in Burlington, Vt., and d. leaving no children.

283. Jerushy, m. Lewis Williams, d. soon. No children.

284. Julia, removed to Ohio, with her brother, d. unmarried.

285. Charlotte. This name on Church records at West Hartford.

286. Stephen Peabody, m. and d. in Ohio. No children.

287. Chester d. at sea, or in one of the West India Islands, where he was supercargo on one of his uncle Centre's trading vessels.

V. KEYES, PERCEY (268), m. Nov. 28, 1775, Rev. Nehemiah Williams of Brimfield, Mass. She was left a widow in 1796, with eight children. She d. at the house of Col. Amasa Keyes, Sept. 28, 1827.

## CHILDREN.

Peggy, b. Sept. 10, 1776, d. Nov. 22, 1818. Eben, b. Nov. 24, 1777, d. June 26, 1856. Stephen K., b. Feb. 25, 1779, d. Aug. 4, 1798. Nehemiah, b. June 7, 1781, d. May 18, 1862. Samuel, b. Jan. 22, 1782, d. Aug. 8, 1838, dau. not named. Lewis, b. Sept. 16, 1784, d. Aug. 19, 1852. Percey, b. May 31, 1786, d. April 7, 1856. Charles, b. Aug. 16, 1788, d. May 15, 1876. William, b. May 16, 1790, d. Aug. 20, 1874. Sarah Porter, b. July 22, 1792, d. June 1, 1846.

The name of Luce (Lucy) is found on the record of Stephen's children at Pomfret, as b. April 16, 1749. This date is given in Mrs. Williams's family Bible, as the date of her own birth. Name probably changed. C. L. Williams, grandson of Percey, is now living in Rockford, Ill.

V. KEYES, COL. STEPHEN (270), 2d s. of Stephen, emigrated to Vt., about the year 1791. He is said to have studied, but did not practice, law, in Vermont, but "became one of the earliest merchants of Burlington, at a time not remote from its settlement, when there were not more than seven framed houses in the village," and except on Water St. and its neighborhood, the forest was almost unbroken.

The following anecdote of him, in giving an account of the visit to this country of Prince Edward, afterward Duke of Kent, in 1793, is taken from Miss Hemenway's Vt. Gazetteer.

"Among the earlier settlers of Burlington was Col. Stephen Keyes, a gentleman of the old school, who wore a cocked hat, kept a hotel on Water street, and was collector for the district of Vt. He proposed to pay his respects to the Prince, and with several young gentlemen of the village, made a call in the evening. Col. Keyes introduced himself to the Prince, and then stated that he had brought with him some young gentlemen of the law and merchants, who wished to pay their respects to him. Among those young gentlemen were Elnathan Keyes, Joshua Stanton, Levi Henri and Zacheus Peaslie. They were severally presented, and the Prince respectfully bowed to each. This was apparently the commencement of a pleasant evenings entertainment. It opened auspiciously if not flatteringly to the Col. and his party, but what must have been their dismay, when the Prince and his aids very informally and abruptly retired to their own apartments without deigning an apology or an explanation. The Col. would not brook this, and in unmeasured terms and unchosen phrases vented his indignation and among the mildest of his expressions, said the prince was no gentleman.

An anecdote of the Col. should here be told, which will illustrate the effect which this rebuff was likely to produce. Two or three British officers with their dogs stopped at the Hotel kept by the Colonel. It was a humble house, but its best and largest north room, kept in the nicest order, with its clean sanded floor, was not an uninviting place for British gentlemen to dine in, and particularly on such a dinner as the Col. never failed to set forth. The officers went in to dinner, with their dogs, which they soon begun to feed on the floor. The Col. looked upon it as an indignity and bringing in a brace of loaded pistols, laid them formally on the table, and denouncing the conduct of the officers, swore he would protect the respectability of his house, and was ready to do it."

Col. Stephen Keyes m. Elizabeth, dau. of the late Col. Elisha Sheldon of the Rev. War, and sister of Maj. Sheldon. Col. Stephen d. at St. Albans, Vt., about 1804.

### CHILDREN.

288. Samuel Willard, dec.
289. Stephen Sheldon, dec.
290. William, d. unmarried.
291. Sarah Bellows, b. June 7, 1782.
292. Elizabeth.

VI. KEYES, SAMUEL W. (288), m. Sarah B., eldest dau. of Major Sheldon. They had one dau., Lucy Sheldon, who m. George H. Mallory, s. of R. C. Mallory, M. C. Res. New York City.

VI. KEYES, STEPHEN S. (289), m. Miss Barlow, dau. of

the late Col. Barlow of Fairfield, Vt. They had five children, four are living, all married, and one,

293. William, a lawyer, res. in Highgate, Vt.

VI. KEYES, SARAH B. (291), m. 1st, Mar. 6, 1802, Maj. Nathaniel B. Platt of Plattsburg, N. Y.

### CHILDREN.

Elizabeth Sheldon, b. July 22, 1803, d. Oct., 1874. Stephen Keyes, b. April 22, 1805, d. Sept. 15, 1819. Mary VanWych, b. Feb. 6, 1808, d. June 10, 1869. Theodore S., b. Dec. 19, 1811, res. in Brandon, Vt. William Totten, b. Oct. 6, 1817, d. Feb. 18, 1818. Samuel Keyes, b. May 11, 1820.

Sarah, m. 2d, Orange Ferriss of St. Albans, Vt.
She d. Aug. 7, 1845.

VI. KEYES, ELIZABETH (292), m. Mr. Parsons; their dau. m. Heman S. Royce, lawyer, St. Albans, Vt.

V. KEYES, ELNATHAN (274), 4th s. of Stephen and Abigail, m. Sarah, youngest dau. of the late Col. Sheldon of Sheldon, Vt.

Judge Elnathan Keyes lived in Sheldon, Vt., and d. there of apoplexy.

### CHILDREN.

294. Peabody, m. late in life, the widow of a s. of Col. Amasa Keyes. No children. He d. about 1856.

295. Robert, d. unmarried, about 1853.

296. Chester.

297. Stephen, supposed to be still living, but has not been heard from of late.

298. Maria.

299. Sarah.

300. Hetty, d. at about 20, unmarried.

301. Elizabeth.

302. Hetty M.

VI. KEYES, CHESTER (296), was a prominent physician of Fairfield, Vt. He m. a Miss Northrop of Fairfield, and d. there on fast day, April, 1850.

### CHILDREN.

303. Ell Nathan, m. his cousin Elizabeth Little of Cleaveland, Ohio, and d. about 1870, leaving a son,

Frank, b. about 1863.

304. Delia, m. Elisha Mix of Henryville, P. Q., and moved to Ohio.

VI. KEYES, MARIA (298), m. Mr. Cook, and d. early, leaving two children, Sarah and Chester Cook. Sarah m. 1st, Dr. Dorothy of Albany, who d., and she m. 2d, Dr. James Little of Cleaveland, O., where she d. about 1862, leaving one dau., Elizabeth, who m. her cousin, Ell Nathan Keyes, s. of Dr. Chester Keyes.

VI. KEYES, ELIZABETH (301), m. Dr. Lyman Little of Cleaveland, and d. about 1866, leaving a dau., Sarah, who m. John, s. of Gov. Todd of Ohio. She has five dau. who res. in Cleaveland.

VI. KEYES, HETTY M. (302), b. after the death of her sister Hetty, m. Dr. Hiram H. Little of Cleaveland, Ohio, d. July 7, 1875, leaving no children, their only dau. having d. at the age of 10.

This family, with not more than one exception, were noted for their large stature, personal beauty, and stylish deportment.

IV. KEYES, SAMPSON (21), 3d s. of Elias and Mary.

### CHILDREN.

We give the names of the children of Sampson without regard to the order of their ages.

305. Anna.

306. John, b. 1744, at Ashford, Conn.

307. Zachary, d. young.

308. James, b. 1752.

309. Sampson.

310. Olive, m. a Weeks.

311. Mary, never married.

312. Abigail, m. a Hall.

313. Avis m. a Bullard.

V. KEYES, ANNA (305), dau. of Sampson, Sr., m., in 1759, at Ashford, Conn., Col. Thomas Knowlton, a native of Ashford. Gen. Washington, in a general order after his death, termed him "the gallant and brave Col. Knowlton, who would have been an honor to any country." Col. Knowlton was at the battle of Bunker Hill, and was killed at Harlem Heights in 1776. He had a young son with him in the battle, probably the eldest, Fred.

Anna, wife of Col. Knowlton, d. May 22, 1808.

CHILDREN.

Fred, b. 1760. Sally, b. 1763. Thomas, b. 1765. Polly, b. 1767. Abygail, b. 1768. Sampson, b. 1770. Anna, b. 1773. Lucinda, b. 1776.

V. KEYES, JOHN (306), son of Sampson, Sr. "Ashford, Sept. 28, A. D., 1767. These may certify that Mr. John Keyes of said Ashford, son of Mr. Sampson Keyes of said town, was this day joined in marriage with Miss Mary Wales, dau. to Capt. Elisha Wales of said Ashford, by Mr. Nathan Wales, Jr., Justice of the Peace."—*Ashford Record.*

Gen. John Keyes, a commissioned officer for the State of Conn., was the companion in boyhood and mature years of Gen. Israel Putnam and Col. Thomas Knowlton, and, with the latter, who married his sister, Anna, he was always on the most intimate terms of friendship. He was also under Col. Knowlton when that officer fell, at Harlem Heights, in 1776. He was a most devoted patriot, and contributed his energies and property freely to his country's cause. It is said that he kept eight of his negroes in the service, throughout the Revolutionary War. He was not without his peculiarities. He frequently took his negro servant Cæsar, behind him on his horse in going to Battle. A lady of Schenectady, a descendant of Gen. John, says: "I have heard much of his servant Cæsar, he was with his master through the war, and in the battle of Bunker Hill, in the midst of the fight, a brave soldier.

Soon after the war, he emigrated to Vermont, where he probably remained but a short time, and subsequently having obtained a township, under the Act of Congress, according grants

12

to the officers and soldiers of the Revolution, removed to Canajoharie, N. Y., then a wilderness. He resided at intervals with his son Zackariah, at Amsterdam, N. Y., then an important point, seven miles west of Schenectady.

A slave holder, and living at a time when social distinctions were pronounced and acknowledged, the habits of the camp did not detract from the influences which made him a pronounced and punctilious gentleman of the old school. Besides being thoroughly public spirited, he was very generous, also genial, methodical, prompt and honest, and very tenacious in adhering to friendships.

The following is taken from the Charlestown *Courier*, a newspaper of the period, published in Montgomery Co., about thirty miles west of Schenectady:

"*Died*, in the town of Canajoharie, Montgomery Co., N. Y., on 13th inst. (13th April, 1824), Gen. John Keyes, aged 80 years. As a Revolutionary officer, he exhibited a peculiar degree of devotion to his country's cause—regardless alike of fatigue and danger. He has lived many years to share the fruits of that Revolution, in the obtaining of which he acted an honorable part. He retained to the day of his death, a degree of vigor, both of body and mind, which the ravages of eighty years leave to but few. The day previous to his death, he rode nearly three miles to transact some business with tenants on land, of which he had the agency. After his return he retired at his usual hour, and in apparent health. At about three o'clock next morning, he was discovered lifeless, having expired apparently without a struggle. As a friend he was ardent; as a neighbor, benevolent; and in his death the community sustains a very sensible loss.

Mary, his wife, and the mother of his children, d. in Montgomery Co., N. Y., Sept. 11, 1806, and he m. 2d, Oct. 18, 1807, at Farmington, Conn., Mercy Scott, a lady much younger than himself, spoken of by the grandchildren as an accomplished and elegant woman. She m. 2d, Capt. Palmer of Stillwater, N. Y., who served under Gen. Gates at Saratoga. They lived at Stillwater, on an elevation adjoining and overlooking the battle

. field. She died at Geneva, N. Y., at the age of 92, about the year 1860.

314. Clarissa, b. April 30, 1768, at Ashford, Conn.

315. Elnathan, b. 1770.

316. Laura, m. Mr. Thrall, d. at an advanced age at Grand Rapids, Mich.

317. Zackariah, b. 1778.

318. Almira Catherine, b. 1785. .

VI. KEYES, CLARISSA (314), eldest child of Gen. John Keyes, m. Rev. Winslow Paige, and d. May 14, 1846, in Gilboa, Schoharie Co., N. Y. Her husband d. Mar., 1838.

319. Col. John Keyes Paige, b. at Hardwick, Mass., Aug. 2, 1788, was clerk of the Supreme Court at Albany many years, and d. Dec. 10, 1857, in Schenectady, N. Y. Son,

320.         John Keyes Paige, b. at Albany, Dec. 14, 1843, m. Nov. 20, 1873, Janet McClellan, dau. of Hon. Richard Franchot, dec. Res. Schenectady. They have two children.

321.         John K. Paige, Jr., b. Feb. 11, 1876.

322.         Richard Franchot Paige, b. Jan. 22, 1878.

323. Hannah Winslow, b. Aug. 13, 1791, at Stephentown, N. Y., m. Archibald Croswell, d. in Gilboa, N. Y., April 3, 1852.

324. Maria C., b. at Schaghticoke, N. Y., Mar 24, 1794, m. David Cady, and d. at Schenectady, Aug. 11, 1874.

325. Aldigo C., b. July 31, 1798, at Schaghticoke, N. Y., was Judge of the New York Court of Appeals. He d. Mar. 31, 1868, at Schenectady, where his family now reside.

326. Diana C., b. Feb. 25, 1800, m. Allen H. Jackson, d. May 19, 1863, at Schenectady.

327. Antoinette, b. Aug. 11, 1805, at Schaghticoke, m. Judge Platt Potter. She has one dau., Mary. Res. Schenectady.

VI. KEYES, ELNATHAN (315), 2d child of Gen. John Keyes, graduated from Dartmouth in 1790, read law, and was long prominent in his profession in Burlington, Vt., represent-ing it in the State Legislature in 1796, 1797, 1799, 1800, 1801.

He is represented by a late writer, as "a prominent lawyer of the early times, a man of powerful mind and ability, an honored and distinguished citizen of the town, county and state."

He m. a dau. of Gen. John Fellows of Sheffield, Mass., had four children, and removed about 1820, to the vicinity of Rochester, N. Y., where he d. in 1853.

### CHILDREN OF ELNATHAN.

328. John. A daughter of John was adopted by Judge Edmonds of New York.

329. Stephen. Lived at Grand Rapids, Mich., some years ago.

330. Henry. Resided at Grand Rapids, dec.

331. Charlotte, m. a man by the name of Wilson, and both d. at Auburn, N. Y., many years since.

VI. KEYES, ZACKARIAH (317), 4th child of Gen. John Keyes, m. 1st, Oct. 5, 1800, at Burlington, Vt., Lydia, dau. of Judge Stanton of Burlington. She d. Dec. 18, 1822, at Sharon, N. Y. He m. 2d, Sept. 4, 1823, at Sharon, Nancy Whittaker, who d. at Cherry Valley, N. Y., July 4, 1837.

Zackariah Keyes d. at Cherry Valley, Nov. 4, 1834.

### CHILDREN.

332. Stephen Pearl, b. Nov. 2, 1801, drowned at Lake St. Peters, below Montreal, June 22, 1827, unmarried.

333. Norman Landon, b. July 4, 1804.

334. Mary Wales, b. Oct. 6, 1806.

335. Eliza C., b. Feb. 22, 1810, at Sharon, N. Y.

336. Henry Stanton, b. Jan. 22, 1812, d. Aug. 25, 1850, at Amsterdam, N. Y., unm.

The only child of the 2d marriage was,

337. John W., b. at Cherry Valley, N. Y., Aug. 26, 1825.

VII. KEYES, NORMAN L. (333), m. May 15, 1830, Sarah E. Whittaker at Sharon, N. Y. No children. He d. July 26, 1848, at Cherry Valley, N. Y. Sarah, his wife, d. April 28, 1861, at Cherry Valley.

VII. KEYES, MARY W. (334), m., Dec. 17, 1823, John N. A. Waldron, at Sharon, N. Y. She d. Sept. 6, 1852, at Binghamton, N. Y.

### CHILDREN.

Cornelius, Stephen, Charles, residing at Binghamton, Henry and George at Dalles, Oregon, Zachariah and another brother at Chicago, Ill.

VII. KEYES, ELIZA C. (335), m., May 28, 1829, at Sharon, N. Y., George Warnick, who d. Dec. 7, 1865. Mrs. Warnick res. at Amsterdam, N. Y.

### CHILDREN.

George Warnick, Jr., b. Oct. 25, 1831, m. at Mohawk, N. Y., Aug. 12, 1857, F. Carolyn Prince. Children, A. C. Paige, b. 1860, Grace b. 1863. Res. Burlington, Iowa. Stephen Keyes, b. Mar, 15, 1834, d. Oct. 19, 1839. Arthur, b. Aug. 1, 1836, m., Oct. 25, 1870, Harriet McDowell. Children, Mary A. Warnick, b. 1871, and Lee, b. 1876. Res. La Grande, Union Co., Oregon. John Keyes, b. Feb. 19, 1840, m., Oct. 17, 1872, at Poughkeepsie, N. Y., Ada B. Tooker, son, Harry Tooker, b. Jan. 5, 1874. Res. Amsterdam, N. Y. Mary Antoinette, b. Feb. 24, 1843, m. Dec. 12, 1866, at Amsterdam, J. W. Waite. Children, Nelson W., b. Nov. 5, 1867, George Warnick, b. Sept. 12, 1869, and Mary F., b. July 20, 1876. Res. Sandy Hill, N. Y. Middleton, b. Oct 15, 1845, m. Oct. 13, 1869, at Amsterdam, Marian Kellogg. Children, Lauren K., b. Sept. 19, 1870, George, b. Mar. 16, 1873, d. 1873, Spencer Kellogg, b. Sept. 14, 1874, Catherine, b. Sept. 23, 1876.

VII. KEYES, JOHN W. (337), m. Sept. 16, 1847, at Amsterdam, N. Y., Abi B. Wager, who d. Oct. 12, 1859. J. W. Keyes res. at Amsterdam.

### CHILDREN.

338. Edward S., b. June 15, 1848, dec.
339. Sarah E. Young, b. Sept. 20, 185-.
340. Charlotte E., b. Sept. 11, 1856.

VI. KEYES, ALMIRA C. (318), youngest child of Gen. John Keyes, was born probably in Conn., and emigrated with her father to Canajoharie, N. Y. In 1795 she was a member of the first fashionable boarding school that was established west of Albany, held in a log house at Cooperstown, N. Y. Fennimore Cooper, the novelest, then a four years old, attended, and was described by Mrs. Peck as a fretful child, fond of following the girls. A French master taught music, dancing and drawing. At this early age she showed great self-reliance and fondness for adventure. One day a sleigh, loaded with produce, passed the school, on its way to Troy. Taking a school-mate with her, she jumped on, in a frolic, and the two children continued, what, in the then sparsely settled condition of the country and the hardness of the roads, was considered a very adventurous journey, to its end. The advent of such youthful visitors in midwinter, from such a distance and by open conveyance excited the astonishment and admiration of the hospitable Trojans, to whom Gen. K. was well known. Social parties in honor of the little truants became the order of the day. These terminated only in the arrival of Gen. K., in quest of the little runaways. In 1808, she m. John Peck (see Peck Gen., page 301), who became a prominent merchant, and from 1832 to 1855, was an active co-worker in nearly all the leading enterprises of the day.

Her father disliked the match. His consent however, was not waited for, yet it is presumed that he became reconciled, for as a token of his good wishes, his daughter received three silver table, and six silver tea spoons. Mrs. Peck had great force of character, decided opinions, was quite frank and thoroughly honest in their utterance. Of course she made many enemies and many sturdy friends. She was a devoted mother, and a reliable and exceedingly tenacious friend.

Almira (Keyes) and John Peck had ten children, of whom four died in childhood. The surviving six were,

341. John Henry, eldest son of Almira, b. Dec. 24, 1810, in Burlington, Vt., was educated a merchant, but the last year of his minority, owing to weak health, was spent in travelling in

the South, the West Indies, and southern Europe. He was for a time, a member of the firm of J. & J. H. Peck, was prominent and active in several railroad enterprises in Vt., and in 1855 removed to New York City, and was there engaged in prominent railroad and other enterprises, until failing health compelled his return to his native place in 1874. He d. of heart disease at Burlington, Aug. 18, 1877, was buried at Lake View Cemetery. Col. Peck was a man of fine culture, of courtly and dignified demeanor, and of true delicacy of feeling. In 1833, he m. Mary, dau. of the late Luther Loomis, Esq. She d. in 1834. Their son, Charles Loomis Peck, b. 1834, d. and was buried in Lone Mountain Cemetery, San Francisco. He m. 2d, in 1837, Lucia, dau. of the late Harry Bradley, Esq. She now res. in Burlington, Vt.

342. J. Cassius Pomeroy, 2d son of Almira, b. in Burlington, Dec. 17, 1812, studied at Castleton, and at U. V. M., which he left an undergraduate in 1829. He was in the mercantile business at Ausable Forks and at Burlington, also in New York city. He was Gen. of Militia in Vt., and was generally known as Gen. Peck. In 1833, he m. Lucia, dau. of the late Col. Marmaduke Wait, of the war of 1812. He d. suddenly of apoplexy, at the residence of Mrs Joseph Wait, his sister-in-law, in Jersey City, N. J., Aug. 5, 1872. His widow d. of rheumatism of the heart, in Hyde Park, T. U., June 19, 1878, and was buried in Lake View Cemetery.

343. Theodore Augustus, 4th s. of Almira, b. in Burlington, Aug. 8, 1817, was druggist and apothecary and had one of the most tasteful establishments in the Union. Was in business in Burlington from 1840 to 1862, when he removed to Watertown, N. Y. In 1842, he m. Delia, 4th dau. of Rev. Hiram Safford, pastor of the First Baptist Church in Burlington, who, assisted by Rev. Geo. Ingersoll, performed the marriage ceremony. He d. suddenly, of apoplexy of the heart, May 18, 1872, and his remains lie in Lake View Cemetery. Their surviving children, b. in Burlington, are,

344. Theodore Safford, b. Mar. 22, 1843, who served creditably in the war of the Rebellion, having entered the military service as a private and returned a captain. Afterward

he was appointed chief of staff to the Governor, with the rank of Colonel. He was also made Col. of the 1st Reg. of Infantry, N. G. Vt., is now Col. Commanding, 1st and only Reg. Vt. Vols. and State Guard. Res. Burlington.

345. Edward Sprague, A. B., M. D., b. Oct. 24, 1844, graduated from U. V. M., in 1864, was assistant Professor in surgery in its Medical Coll. in 1872, was afterward abroad three years, pursuing special studies with a view of practicing as an Oculist and Aurist, and is now established in New York city.

346. Charlotte Almira, b. Nov. 25, 1846, m., Sept. 11, 1873, William Van Schoonoven Woodward, Esq., s. of the late Hon. J. Douglass Woodward, a lawyer and now ass't U. S. District Attorney. Res. Plattsburgh, N. Y.

347. George Huntington, 5th s. of Almira, b. Mar. 4, 1819, in Burlington, graduated from U. V. M., in 1837, receiving the degree of A. B. and his second degree in 1838. His health failing, he made a cod fishing voyage in 1838, to Labrador, and spent the winter of 1839-40, in the West India Islands. He was admitted to the Bar, in 1841, but giving up the practice on account of ill health, he shipped before the mast, and following the sea for a time, finally landed in San Francisco in Dec., 1849. He was at Big Bar, a noted mining camp on American River, and opened a law office at Dutch Flat, in Placer Co. He taught the first school in Sacremento, was teacher and Dept. Supt. of the San Francisco Industrial School, and Principal of the Spring Valley Grammar School. He finally purchased a farm in El Monte, Los Angeles Co., in which county he has been School Superintendant two years. Res. El Monte. He m. 1st, in 1851, Mrs. Sarah Thornton, from whom he was legally separated in 1862.

CHILDREN.

John Henry Fenton, b. in Yolo Co., Jan. 25, 1853, now Purser on S. S. Great Republic. Geo. H. Peck, Jr., b. Oct. 15, 1856.

G. H. Peck m. 2d, April 30, 1864, Mary Wanostrocht, dau. of Nath. Chater, Esq. of London, Eng. They have two children, Kate W., b. Jan. 28, 1866, and Mary Chater, b. Nov. 1, 1867.

348. William Ware, 6th s. of Almira, b. in Burlington, Vt., Jan. 21, 1821, graduated from U. V. M., 1840. Read law in Burlington with the late Hon. Jacob Marsh, and with Judge Story at Harvard, was second in a large class graduating in 1842, receiving the B. L. degree. He was admitted to the Bar, and began practice at Burlington in 1843. He had as partners, Geo. R. Platt, and afterward Hon. J. McM. Shafter, now (1878) of San Francisco. He removed to New York City, where he remained nineteen years, having as partner, part of the time, the late gifted and brilliant John VanBuren. In 1878, he was appointed U. S. District, and assistant Sup. Judge of Wyoming Ter. In 1846, he m. Hannah, dau. of Benj. Mumford Esq. of Schenectady, N. Y. Children, John, b. 1847, Catherine, Benj. Mumford, civil engineer, Clara, Joseph, Harriet.

349. Edward Williams, 7th son of Almira, was b. Jan. 20, 1823. He was in the mercantile business at Burlington, until 1878, when after a successful career he retired from active business, having been for over forty years closely attentive to business in the place where his father began in 1806. He m. about 1845, Harriet, eldest dau. of Hon. Joseph Clark of Milton, Vt. No children.

Mr. and Mrs. Peck are now living on College St., Burlington, Vt.

V. KEYES, JAMES, SEN. (308), s. of Sampson, Sen., b. at Ashford, Conn., m. Miriam Badcock, and in 1780, moved to Andover, Vt., four years after the settlement of the town. Here his eldest s. James, was b., the first male child b. in the place, and here they were subject to all the hardships of pioneer life. A descendant relates that Miriam rode six miles on horseback, to an adjoining town for fire, one day, when the male members of the family were absent hunting. Miriam also plumed herself on being the smartest and handsomest woman in town, when she was the only one there. Tired of life in the backwoods, and the severity of Vermont winters, James, after a year or two, returned to Mass., probably remaining in Mason, N. H., two years. "James Keyes was taxed in Mason in 1781 and 1782."

He afterward settled in Northboro, Mass., where is the record of birth of his seven younger children, and where he lived and died. He represented the town in the State Legislature nine years, and d. Dec. 18, 1824.

Miriam, his wife, d. Oct. 31, 1823, aged 67.

### CHILDREN.

350. James. b. 1780.
351. Erastus.
352. Amos, b. Sept. 30, 1785.
353. Prentice, b. Mar. 25, 1787.
354. Annah, b. April, 29, 1789.
355. Abigail, b. Sept. 15, 1791.
356. Clarissa, b. July 22, 1794
357. Roswell, b. Mar. 23, 1796.
358. Sampson, b. Dec. 10, 1800.

VI. KEYES, JAMES (350), eldest s. of James and Miriam, m. Nov. 1, 1803, in Andover, Vt., Jane Babcock. He was a farmer, in which pursuit he actively engaged, until eight years previous to his death, when he gave up active business, and passed the remainder of his life with his dau., Miriam. James Keyes was a man of clear intellect, sound judgement, sterling integrity, and rare independence and energy of character, possessed of a large share of sharp, mirth-provoking wit, and distinguished for his brilliant story telling propensities. He and all his sons were eminently successful in teaching school, a profession which many other of his descendants have successfully followed. He retained remarkable physical and intellectual vigor, until his death, reading without spectacles, and relating amusing anecdotes, until within a few hours of that event. He united with the Protestant Episcopal Church, at a somewhat advanced age. He d. Sept. 2, 1865, aged 85, and was buried in Clarendon, Vt., where lie also, the remains of his wife and three children.

### CHILDREN.

359. Abigail, b. Aug. 12, 1804.
360. Lucy, b. July 14, 1805, m. in 1829, Burley Davis of

Fairhaven, Vt. She had ten children, of whom, one s., Horace, d. in the army, during the late war.

361. Rebecca, b. Sept., 1806, m. in 1831, Isaac Davis. Res. Token Creek, Dane Co., Wis. Four children.

362. Prentice, b. 1807, last heard from in 1840, at N. O.

363. Jonas, b. 1809, d. 1813.

364. Henry, b. Nov. 1, 1811, m. 1836, Priscilla Percival. Six children. Res. Lockport, N. Y. One son,

365.       James, a few years since, res. at Marathon, Lapeer Co., Mich.

366. Franklin, b. Nov. 2, 1813.

367. Williams, b. 1815, d. 1832.

368. Miriam, b. Mar. 9, 1818.

369. Albert, b. Sept. 10, 1820.

VII. KEYES, ABIGAIL (359), m. Dec., 1823, Asa B. Foster of Weston, now of Pittsford, Vt.

### CHILDREN.

370. Mary, b. Dec. 9, 1824, d. Feb. 28, 1842.

371. Asa G., b. Dec. 29, 1826.

372. James H., b. April 11, 1829.

373. Annette N., b. April 30, 1835, d. April 11, 1868.

374. Agnes, b. July 8, 1839.

Asa G. Foster, 2d child of Abigail, was Capt. of the 16th Vt., in the war of the Rebellion, and was a brave soldier. His s. Clarence M., was educated at Dartmouth, has since practiced law in N. Y. City, and San Francisco.

VII. KEYES, FRANKLIN (366), a man of great intelligence and energy of charater, for many years engaged in mercantile pursuits, in which he was eminently successful, and amassed large wealth. He m. 1st, in 1836, Alona A. Lawrence, of Weston, Vt., and had two children. He m. 2d, in 1842, Eliza A. Lawrence of Weston. Three children. Res. Wabash, Ind.

### CHILDREN.

375. Frank. Resided in California many years, at St. Mary's where he owned extensive vineyards, and elsewhere, has also travelled extensively in China, and elsewhere. Sup. unm.

376. A dau., educated at College Hill, O., m. Ovid W. Connor, a prosperous merchant of Wabash, and has four sons.

377. Another dau. m. Horatio Connor, brother of Ovid. Res. Wabash, Ind.

378. Bessie, b. about 1866.

VII. KEYES, MIRIAM (368), m. Oct. 30, 1838, John Downs, who d. in 1861.

#### CHILDREN.

379. Caroline Williams, b. Nov. 26, 1839, m. Aug. 15, 1867, Vincent C. Meyerhoffer, now publisher of the Rutland Inquirer. Mrs. Downs res. with her dau. in Rutland.

380. Eliza Ann, b. Sept. 20, 1841, d. Sept. 10, 1865.

381. Miriam Keyes, b. May 30, 1843, d. Aug. 13, 1865.

VII. KEYES, ALBERT (369), m. in 1839, Roxana Strong. Albert d. and his widow res. in Center Rutland.

#### CHILDREN.

382. Daughter, m. Mr. Graham, and since his decease resides with her two children, James and a dau. 13 years of age in Rutland.

383. Another dau. m. Truman Lawson and d. of consumption in Rutland, Aug. 21, 1878.

384. James, the only s., enlisted when he was sixteen, and served two years in the war of the Rebellion. He was much extolled for his bravery, returned home ill and soon after d.

VI. KEYES, ERASTUS (351), 2d s. of James and Miriam, m. Polly —— and lived at or near Clarendon, Vt. He had a good education and taught school. He d. of a prevailing malignant fever (perhaps Spotted Fever) about 1814–15.

#### CHILDREN.

385. Cyrus, b. 1803.

386. James.

387. Artemus, was twice m. and d. at Sudbury, Vt., many years ago.

388. Erastus.

389. Samuel, was living in Bronson, Mich., in 1875.

390. Polly.


VII. KEYES, CYRUS (385), went to N. Y. State, when about twelve, with some of the Farwell family. When eighteen years of age returned to Vt., and commenced the study of law, which he was obliged to relinquish, on account of ill health, and in two years returned to N. Y. He m. about 1824, Lucy Alton, and settled in Centerville, Alleghany Co., where his widow now resides. After removing to N. Y., Mr. Keyes dropped the first e in his name, making it Kyes.

Cyrus Kyes, d. April 12, 1853.

### CHILDREN.

391. Samuel, d. in infancy.

392. Marcus, d. in infancy.

393. Marium II., b. 1835, d. at the age of 27.

394. William E., b. Feb. 27, 1841.

395. Andrew J., b. 1851, d. 1876, in Stanton, Mich., unm.

396. Benton Duilleris, b. 1853, m., and has son,

397.        Arthur, b. 1877.

Benton D. res. in Rushford, N. Y.


VIII. KYES, WILLIAM E. (394), m. —— merchant. Res. Rushford, N. Y.

### CHILDREN.

398. Eliza Marium, b. 1863.

399. Lena Jane, b. 1872.

400. Stacy C., b. 1877, dec.


VI. KEYES, AMOS (352), 3d s. of James and Miriam, m., May 2, 1811, Eunice Spafford of Berlin, Mass. Has had eight children, only three now living. Amos d. in Rindge, about 185-.

### CHILDREN.

401. Sarah, m. —— Stephens, res. in Caladonia, Wis.

402. A dau. living in Bolton, has eight children.

403. George W., b. 1814, in Rindge, N. H., m. 1st, Mary Flagg, and had four dau., b. in New Ipswich, N. H.  He m. 2d, Sept. 16, 1870, Lucy A. Avery, and d. in New Ipswich, May 6, 1876.

404. Charles E., res. Lyndeboro, N. H.

405. Eliphalet, was living in Hudson, Mass., a few years since.

VI. KEYES, CAPT. PRENTICE (353), 4th s. of James and Miriam, m., May 1, 1814, Anna Brigham of Berlin, Mass. He lived on the old James Keyes place in Northboro, Mass., and d. there Nov. 26, 1842.

Anna, his wife, d. Oct. 19, 1848, aged 55.

### CHILDREN.

406. James Brigham, b. Jan. 26, 1815.

407. Stephen Prentice, b. Oct. 17, 1819.  Supposed m. in Conn.

408. Adaliza Miriam, b. Dec. 1, 1824, m. Nov. 1, 1849, Chas. O. Longley of Westboro, Mass.

409. Angeline Augusta, b. June 27, 1827, m. April 12, 1849, George L. Boynton of Westboro, Mass.

VII. KEYES, JAMES B. (406), m. Nov. 15, 1837, Elizabeth Kelly.

### CHILDREN.

410. Harriet Maria, b. Aug. 2, 1838, m. Joseph Neff of Shrewsbury.

411. Henry Prentiss, b. Sept. 27, 1841, d. at Shrewsbury, May 25, 1860.

James B. d. Nov. 21, 1844.  Elizabeth, his wife, was burned to death by her clothes taking fire, Dec. 6, 1858, age 47.

VI. KEYES, ROSWELL (357), 5th s. of James and Miriam, m. Jan. 4, 1821, Lois Howe of Berlin, Mass., went west in 1856. His wife d. while there, and he returned and m. again in Rindge, N. H., where he d. about 1876.

CHILDREN.

412. William P., b. in 1821, in Berlin, Mass.

413. Curtis, b. Sept. 27, 1827, in Hague, N. Y.

414. Ellen Loisa, b. Sept. 26, 1831, m. Dec. 27, 1847, Josiah Moore of Berlin, and d. in the summer of 1856.

Another dau. b. probably Mar. 9, 1836, d. in infancy.

VII. KEYES, WILLIAM P. (412), went west and settled in Braidwood, Will Co., Ill. Had a number of dau., and one s., who with one dau., is now living.

CHILDREN.

415. Josephine Aldora, m. Oscar A. Sykes. Res. Chebanse, Ill.

416. Nye P., b. Feb., 1869.

VII. KEYES, CURTIS (413), m. 1st, Nov. 27, 1848, Julia M. Harris, b. in Lancaster, Mass., Jan. 19, 1829, and d. Jan. 19, 1855. Curtis m. 2d, Oct. 11, 1856, Mary E. Ball, b. in West Boylston, Mass., Aug. 14, 1835, and d. Feb. 5, 1873. Res. Wilmington, Will Co., Ill.

CHILDREN.

417. Jennie A., b. May 20, 1859, in Wilmington, Ill.

418. Ella L., b. Jan. 24, 1865, in Wilmington, Ill.

419. Francis, b. Oct. 24, 1868, in Wilmington, Ill.

420. Edward, b. Jan. 16, 1870, in Wilmington, Ill.

VI. KEYES, SAMPSON (358), 6th s. of James and Miriam, m. Betsey —— He d. July 9, 1850. His widow d. 187-.

CHILDREN.

421. Elizabeth, m. Geo. B. Chase, 1842, and d. July 9, 1850. No children.

422. Charles Augustus, b. April 10, 1829.

423. Washington Fayette, b. Mar. 2, 1831, d. May 5, 1839.

VII. KEYES, CHARLES A. (422).   Res. Worcester, Mass.
Florist.

### CHILDREN.

424. Stella E., d. at 5 years.
425. George C.
426. Fred E.
427. Dora M.
428. Mabel F.
429. Stella A.


V. KEYES, SAMPSON, JR. (309), probably the youngest
of the sons of Sampson Keyes, Sen., m. Nov. 13, 1787, at Ashford, Conn., his cousin Lucy, dau. of Stephen Keyes (20).

### CHILDREN.

430. Harriet, b. June 18, 1789, d. at about 18.
431. Stephen, b. Oct. 19, 1790.
432. Peggy, m. a Mr. Pitts of Ashford, Conn.
433. Sarah, m. a Burnham, and in 1876, was living in Hartford, Conn., a widow.  She had two dau. and four sons, the
youngest of whom, Col. Burnham, is now Post Master of Hartford.
434. Penelope, m. Ira Peck of Hartford, and d. leaving three
sons and two dau., and a large fortune.

Sampson, Jr. m. 2d, Eunice Burnham Snow, and had
two sons,
435. John, d. in Iowa, about 1874.
436. Henry, went to Alabama.

Sampson, Jr. m. 3d, Perses Holt Babcock.


IV. KEYES, ZECHARIAH (23), s. of Elias and Mary.
The only trace we can find of him, is the record, at Pomfret,
Conn., of the birth of a dau., Rhoda, to Zechariah and Mehita-
ble Keyes, June 3, 1754.


IV. KEYES, SOLOMON (24), youngest s. of Elias and
Mary, m. Sarah Sumner, who was b. Feb. 11, 1729.

CHILDREN.

437. Solomon, b. Mar. 28, 1755.
438. Elias, b. April 14, 1757.
439. Edward, b. June 4, 1759.
440. Elizabeth, b. Jan. 26, 1761.
441. Percy, b. Jan. 20, 1763.
442. David, b. April 20, 1765.
443. Justus, b. Sept. 10, 1767.
444. Sarah, b. Oct. 14, 1769.
445. Mary, b. June 20, 1773.

V. KEYES, SOLOMON (437), eldest s. of Solomon and Sarah, m. Esther and lived in Ashford, Conn.

CHILDREN.

446. Elizabeth, m. William P. Sessions, lived in Union, Tolland Co., Conn., and d. there, leaving no children.

447. Cyril, m. Margaret, lived and died in Ashford, Conn. He had three dau. Only one, Olive Louisa, b. Nov. 21, 1823, lived to womanhood, and has since d.

448. Edward Sumner, b. 1784.

449. Percy, b. Aug. 8, 1786, d. in Henrietta, N. Y., unm.

450. Huldah, b. Dec. 14, 1789, m. Mr. Corbin, d. in McComb Co., Mich., leaving two children.

451. Solomon, } b. July 22, 1793.
452. Isaiah, } b. July 22, 1793.

453. Jeremiah, b. April 2, 1796.

454. David, b. Sept. 7, 1798. Still living (1878) in Woodstock, Conn., has one son,

455.        Amasa, b. Nov. 22, 1824.

VI. KEYES, EDWARD S. (448), s. of Solomon and Esther, lived in Ashford, Conn., until 1845, when he moved to Dudley, Worcester Co., Mass., where he d. Oct., 1854. He m. 1st, Hannah Sessions.

CHILDREN.

456. Edward S., Jr., b. Sept. 30, 1815, now living in Henrietta, N. Y.

14

457. Jerome, b. in Ashford, Conn., Nov. 15, 1817, m., in 1856, in Henrietta, N. Y. His wife d. 1861, and he m. again, 1863. He moved to Rochester, N. Y., about 1874. Has one child living,

458.       George J., b. about 1871.

459. Esther, b. Nov. 29, 1819, dec.

460. Mary Ann, b. Aug. 15, 1821.

461. Elizabeth, b. Jan. 21, 1824.

462. Hannah Maria, b. May 27, 1826.

Hannah, wife of Edward S. (448), d. in 1828, and Edward m. 2d, Nancy Haskell.

463. James H., b. Oct. 22, 1830. Res. Wheatland, Yuba Co., Col.

464. Nancy Lucretia, dec.

465. Andrew S. Res. Dudley, Worcester Co., Mass.

466. John Milton, dec.


VI. KEYES, SOLOMON (451), s. of Solomon and Esther, m. about 1821, Sophia Stearns of Vermont, and with his brothers, Isaiah and Jeremiah, removed to Monroe Co., N. Y., about 1822, and settled near Rochester, the two first in the town of Henrietta. Neither of them are now living.

### CHILDREN.

All b. at West Henrietta, N. Y.

467. Esther, b. Jan. 25, 1822, m. William Bullard, and d. June, 1853, leaving no children.

468. Lorenzo, b. Mar. 23, 1824, d. May 10, 1833.

469. Edwin Ruthven, b. May 7, 1826.

470. Warren Sumner, b. May 10, 1829.

471. Elizabeth, b. Sept. 5, 1832, d. April 21, 1833.

472. Homer Eldridge, b. Feb. 5, 1834.

473. Jeremiah Judson, b. Aug. 5, 1836.

474. Sophia Jane, b. June 8, 1838, m. Charles F. Moon, d., Feb., 1875, leaving no children.


VII. KEYES, EDWIN R. (469), is a graduate of the Wesleyan University at Middletown, Conn., of the class of 1848, having prepared for college at Lima, Livingston Co., N. Y., Genesee, Wesleyan Sem. After his graduation, he taught the Academy at Henrietta, during the winter of 1848-9, taught the Academy at Livingston, eight months, when he was compelled to leave on account of his anti-slavery views, and his support of the Wilmot Proviso. Then taught in Madison, Ind. In Oct., 1850, was admitted on trial as a preacher in the Genesee Conf. of the M. E. Church. Preached at Williamsville, Niagara Falls and at Alexander, N. Y. Was then transferred to the N. Y. Conference and stationed at Vestry St., New York City, to fill an unexpired term. Afterward, he preached at Tarrytown, Newburg, N. Y., in Westchester Co., at Sing Sing and Yonkers. Was chaplain of the N. Y. Heavy Artillery from May to Sept., 1863, when, on account of ill health, he resigned. He was then stationed at Oswego, Tioga Co., N. Y., at Poughkeepsie, N. Y., in Cannon St. Church, and in the Chestnut St. M. E. Church in Portland, Me., being transferred thither at the request of that church. About this time, Mr. Keyes dissolved his connection with the M. E. Church, in consequence of having embraced the doctrines of Swedenborg, and preached for a time for the New Church in Portland, Me., then as a New Church Missionary, mostly in the Hudson River towns. From Oct., 1871, he preached two years in the New Church Society on Broad St., Philadelphia, Penn. His health failing, he removed to Yonkers, Nov., 1873, where he has since resided. Mr. Keyes was admitted to the Bar, May 12, 1862 (having graduated at the Law School of the University of New York City), and opened a law office in Yonkers, April, 1874. He has a large law practice, and holds various offices, connected with educational and other departments. He m., Aug. 4, 1849, at Livingston, Nelson Co., Va., Sarah Ann, eldest dau. of Benj. and Rhoda Ann Bradshaw, b. at Fabers Mills, Nelson Co., Va., June 14, 1827. They were m. by Rev. John Howard.

### CHILDREN.

475. Edwin Ruthven, b. Jan. 23, 1853, at Alexander, Genesee Co., N. Y. Custom House broker, office 69 Wall St., New York City. Unmarried.

476. Malcolm Sidney, b. July 2, 1859, at Sing Sing, West-chester Co., N. Y.

477. Charlotte Lilian, b. April 20, 1861, at Sing Sing.

478. Frank, b. Nov. 15, 1864, at Owego, Tioga Co., N. Y.

VII. KEYES, WARRREN S. (470), m. Oct. 16, 1851, at Rush, Monroe, Co., N. Y., Mary Jane Sears, who was b. Mar. 15, 1829, at Butler, Wayne Co., N. Y. Res. West Henrietta, N. Y. Carpenter.

#### DAUGHTER.

479. Mary Adelaide, b. May 30, 1856.

VII. KEYES, HOMER E. (472), m. at Rochester, N. Y., Oct. 31, 1855, Harriet S. Snow. Res. West Henrietta, N. Y. Farmer.

#### CHILDREN.

480. Esther, b. Feb. 10, 1859.

481. Carrie Julia, b. Nov. 28, 1861.

482. Homer E., b. April 14, 1866, d. July 4, 1875.

VII. KEYES, JEREMIAH J. (473), studied at the University of Rochester, N. Y., not graduating, but receiving in 1870, the honorary degree of A. M. He was ordained to the ministry (Bap.), Jan 29, 1859, at Penfield, N. Y. Served during the war, as Chaplain of the 58th reg. of N. G. of N. Y. Preached at Foxburgh, Penn., and other places, and is now doing newspaper work at Olean, N. Y. Rev. Mr. Keyes m. Emma Henry Bradshaw, who was b in Livingston, Nelson Co., Va., Jan. 9, 1835. Res. Olean, N. Y.

#### CHILDREN.

483. Irving Judson, b. Dec. 6, 1859.

484. Kittie Bell, b. Jan. 7, 1862.

485. Mary Louisa, b. Jan. 7, 1767.

VI. KEYES, ISAIAH (452), s. of Solomon and Esther, m. Jerusha Wood, had two sons, both dec., and one dau., now living. He removed to Monroe Co., N. Y., in 1822, where he d. His wife res. in West Henrietta.

VI. KEYES, JEREMIAH (453), s. of Solomon and Esther, m. Martha Cornwall, moved to N. Y., with his brothers, and settled in the town of Mendon, Monroe Co. Dec. His wife still lives in Rochester.

#### CHILDREN.

486. Prudentia, b. Nov. 13, 1830, m. Res. Rochester.
487. Sarah, b. Aug. 1, 1833.
488. Albert, b. Dec. 13, 1841. Res. Rochester.

V. KEYES, ELIAS (438), 2d s. of Solomon and Sarah, emigrated to Vt., and with John Durkee, Asa Whitcomb and Joshua Bartlet, commenced the settlement of Stockbridge, in Windsor Co., in 1783. He was a lawyer, Judge of the County Court, Member of Congress for that district, and "held most of the offices in the gift of the town, for many years." He was a tall, large featured man, somewhat careless in his dress, and of great simplicity of character.

Judge Elias Keyes, d. July 9, 1844.

Olive, his wife, d. March 18, 1843, aged 83, and both were buried in Stockbridge.

"The Judge possessed a strongly marked character, and lived in times when one's individualism was but little shaped and restricted by the conventialisms of polished society. A lover of abstract justice, a hater of shams, he was nevertheless almost grotesque in his peculiarities, as the following anecdote related of him will show.

While holding his Court in Windsor County, a worthless fellow was tried and convicted before him for stealing a lot of boots and shoes from Gen. F., a leading man and merchant of the county. When his Honor come to pass sentence upon the prisoner, after treating the poor fellow to a severe lesson upon the nature and gravity of his offence in a general way, he broke out in this wise.

'Prisoner, you not only must steal these boots and shoes, not from some worthless fellow like yourself, but must needs add to the turpitude of the offence by stealing them from Gen. F., one of the most respectable and respected men of the county, and for this perverseness, I shall add one year more to the term of your imprisonment.' "

The following anecdote is probably familiar to many.

Judge Keyes of Vermont had about him a large number of workmen. Among them was a young man named Amasa. One day he ordered Amasa, or as the Judge always called him, Sampson, to cut down a crooked unsightly tree, on the brink of his mill pond.

The Judge stood by, watching the progress of the work. "Sampson" was, like most young Vermonters, at home with the ax, and soon reached the heart of the tree; two or three strokes more would suffice. Seeing the Judge was in a position to be hit by the limbs of the tree when it fell, he said:

" You had better move, Judge, or you will be hit."

"Cut the tree right down, Sampson," was the response.

Two more strokes, and then, seeing that unless the Judge moved, he would be hit sure, Sampson renewed his suggestion.

" Cut the tree right down, Sampson, just as the old man tells you," said the Judge.

One more stroke, and the last; down came the tree, and down came the old Judge also, into the water. Sampson quickly jumped into the water, and dragged him on shore, his face all scratched and bleeding, and nearly strangled by his sudden bath. Blowing the water from his mouth, like a spouting whale, and wiping his face, he said:

"That's right, Sampson, that's right; always do just as the old man tells you."


V. KEYES, EDWARD (439), 3d s. of Solomon and Sarah, m., at Ashford. Conn., Mary Work, who was b. Jan., 1759. He was familiarly called Esq. Ned, lived in Eastford, a village set off from Ashford, and was a business man, well known and esteemed. He d. May 1, 1827.

### CHILDREN.

489. Roxanna, b. Dec. 11, 1778.
490. Justus, b. Nov. 9, 1780.
491. Elias, b. Mar. 9, 1783, d. June 23, 1801.

492. Elizabeth, b. Feb. 23, 1785; d. May 13, 1803.
493. Danforth, b. April 24, 1787.
494. Mary, b. Nov. 9, 1788.
495. Esther, b. Jan. 23, 1791.
496. Edward, b. Jan. 20, 1793.
497. Sarah, b. Oct. 20, 1795.
498. Anna, b. Mar. 8, 1798.
    Mary, wife of Edward, d. Mar. 9, 1798.
    Edward Keyes m. 2d, Feb. 15, 1801, Sarah Whitmore.
499. Giddings Whitmore, b. Aug. 31, 1802.
500. Joseph Flagg, b. Nov. 23, 1803.
501. David, b. Jan. 31, 1808.

VI. KEYES, ROXANNA (489), m. a Mr. Brooks, and lived in Vt. She had a son, Deloma, who studied medicine with his uncle, Dr. Justus Keyes of Brimfield, Mass., moved to Ohio, about the year 1818, m. and had a s. born about 1821. This son had a military education, and after about twenty years service, was a Gen. of Volunteers (Gen. W. H. T. Brooks), in the late war, and d. at Huntsville, Ala., July 19, 1870.

VI. KEYES, JUSTUS (490), was a physician and surgeon of great ability and eminence of Brimfield, Mass., and prominent in town affairs. He m. in 1806, Betsey Corey, b. in Sturbridge, Mass., in 1781. The original progenitor of the Corey family was a man of wealth and importance in England, of the rank of gentleman, who left his native country, on account of religious persecution, and brought with him to the colony, a large amount of family silver, etc., and enjoyed distinction in colonial times. One of his descendants was John Corey, who settled in Sturbridge, in 1750. He had many children of whom Jacob, the father of Betsey, was the youngest son, b. in 1755. He m. in 1779, Matilda Walker, b. 1761. Jacob Corey had ten children. Betsey, the wife of Dr. Justus, was the eldest child, and of his other children, two sons survive, George V. Corey, now living in the old homestead built one hundred years ago, at Sturbridge, and Frances E., residing in Chicago. Dr. Justus

Keyes d. in Brimfield, Mass., Sept. 21, 1835. Mrs. Keyes, wife of Dr. Keyes, and the mother of his children, d. Mar. 3, 1826. Mrs. Polly Keyes (2d wife), widow of Dr. Keyes, d. in 1874.

### CHILDREN OF DR. JUSTUS KEYES.

502. Mary Ann, b. Mar., 1808, in Brimfield. She m. in 1826, Russel T. Wheelock, had two s., and one dau., and d. at Amherst, Mass., in 1843.

503. Erasmus Darwin, b. May 29, 1810, in Brimfield.

504. Edward L., b. Aug 3, 1812. He was first named Elias and changed his name to Edward L.

VII. KEYES, ERASMUS D. (503), s. of Dr. Justus and Betsey, m. 1st, Nov. 8, 1837, Caroline Maria Clarke, who was b. in New York City, Mar. 21, 1816, and d. in the city of Brooklyn, Nov. 26, 1853.

The father of Mrs. Keyes, James B. Clarke, was a graduate of Yale, and a lawyer, a man of property and culture. Her grandfather Clarke was a native of Scotland, educated, and a vestryman of Trinity Church, New York, in Revolutionary days.

Erasmus D. was fifteen years old when he left Brimfield, and went to Maine to live with his uncle (by marriage) Morse, with a view to becoming a soldier, in opposition to the wishes of his father, who preferred for his son, a mercantile career. He applied through the Hon. Peleg Sprague, Kenn Co., Me., M. C., for a Cadet's warrant, and failing one year, renewed the application in the winter of 1827-8. Mr. Sprague being unable to obtain the warrant, wrote him, advising to give up the search. Our young aspirant however, immediately wrote a full account of himself to Barbour, Sec. of War, asking for an appointment as Cadet, which he received by return mail. He was eighteen years old when he entered the West Point Military Academy, and graduated, June, 1832, tenth in a class which entered (July 1, 1828), one hundred and thirty in number. On graduating, he immediatly volunteered for the Black Hawk war, and took service with a detatchment of recruits, as far as Buffalo, and thence to Detroit, where on the morning of their arrival, the Asiatic Cholera broke out, on the steamer, "Robert Paine." The infected were left in a hospital near the city, and the others sped on by water, to Fort Dearborn on the present site of Chicago. Shortly after leaving Detroit, the pestilence appeared on their steamboat, and the cases increased so rapidly that all disembarked at the village of St. Clair, and the following morning, only two men reported for duty. It is said that at that early stage of his military life, amid the universal panic, the young soldier exhibited the coolness and composure which were his companions in his subsequent career, reading from some book of poetry he had with him, and committing various passages to memory.

The command to which he was attached, being destroyed by cholera, he was ordered back to West Point, and was attacked by the disease on the way, and laid up for a time at Rochester. His next attempt at war, according to his own account, was in Charleston Harbor, in Nov., 1832, at which time, Gen. Scott was in command on shore. Having attracted the notice of Gen. Scott, he was ordered to join the staff of that Gen. in 1833, and only left it in the Autumn of 1838, to accept promotion, to be Captain and Ass't Adjutant General. He was ordered to join Gen. Gaines at St. Louis, but did not remain long, and accepted Gen. Scott's invitation to return to his staff, remaining with him on the Canadian frontier, in the winter of 1837–8, and in the winters of 1838, 39 and 40. It was in 1838, that he accompanied Gen. Scott to remove the Cherokee Indians, and en route for the South, via Charlestown for the Cherokee country, took his young wife (to whom he had been married, Nov. 8, 1837), to Washington, and was invited with her, to dine with President Van Buren, about whom were grouped Mr. Clay, Mr. Preston of South Carolina, Gen. Scott, Mr. John Sergeant of Philadelphia, and his two beautiful daughters, and other distinguished persons. After the removal of the Cherokee Indians, he went to St. Louis to join Gen. Gaines. Thence rejoining Gen. Scott, was at Augusta, Me., when that Gen., with Gov. Fairfield, negotiated through the mediation of Sir John Collville, the settlement of the N. E. boundary dispute.

In Nov., 1841, his service as aid de camp to Gen. Scott ended, he having been promoted to be Captain of Artillery, and ordered to Florida, thence to New Orleans, where he remained five months, most of the time in command of the Barracks, below the city. From New Orleans he was ordered to Charleston, S. C., where he remained until May, 1844. Among those on duty at Fort Moultrie, were W. T. Sherman, Geo. H. Thomas, Braxton Bragg, Thomas W. Sherman, and John F. Reynolds, all of the 3d Artillery, and all of whom rose to be Major Generals in the civil war. He left Charleston in May, 1844, to be a member of the West Point board of visitors which was composed solely of Army Officers, and Gen. Scott was President. It was during this year that he was appointed Chief Instructor of Artillery and Cavalry at West Point, and was only relieved Christmas eve, 1848. During this time he supervised the instruction, in those two branches, of McClellan, Stonewall Jackson, Burnside, Hancock, Sturgis, Stoneman and many others who shone in the late war.

In 1848, he was ordered to California, which he reached via the Isthmus, was assigned to the Post of San Francisco, which post he held off and on for nine years. Part of this time was passed in quelling the Indian troubles on the Pacific Coast, in the Puget Sound district, W. T., in the campaign of 1858, second in command to Col. Geo. Wright against the Yackima, Pelouse and Coeur d' Alene Indians, said to be the most effective campaign known, and those Indians never rose afterwards. He was five times engaged in battle with the savages, while in service on the N. W. Pacific coast, either as principal or second in command. Travelling over so large an area of country and amid such dangers, many anecdotes of war and service might be told, did it come within the scope of this work.

Having been promoted to the rank of Major of Artillery in 1858, he was ordered from Fort Van Couver to the East, but, delayed in San Francisco, he did not arrive in New York, en route for Fort Monroe, until Dec., 1859. His old friend Gen. Scott, being in New York, he called on him and was offered the post of military secretary on his staff, in case Col. Robert E.

Lee, to whom the post had been offered, should refuse. As the rank of military secretary was only that of Lieut. Col., Gen. Scott expected Lee to refuse, which he did, and Keyes was appointed. To his room afterward came Robert Lee, with whom he was intimate many years before the war, to ask if Gen. Scott was in, and to tell him he had been approached with an offer of the command of the northern army, which the next day, he refused.

In the Spring of 1861, he was ordered, in concert with M. C. Meigs of the Engineers, now Quartermaster General of the Army, to draw up a plan for the reinforcement of Fort Pickens, Pensacola Harbor. Their plan was approved by the President and Secretary Seward, who took an active interest in it, and they were ordered to carry it into immediate effect, and that stronghold was made secure in a short time, and with such secrecy, that Bragg, who commanded the confederates at Pensacola, learned too late, that the Fort was too strong for him to capture.

It was after the Fort Pickens affair, on his return to Washington, that occurred the estrangement between him and his old friend, Gen. Scott, due perhaps to the fact, that Scott, with Cameron, Sec. of war, had had the question of reinforcing Fort Pickens, under discussion and that the intervention of Mr. Seward in the project was not altogether relished by them.

Gen. Scott, however, sent him an order on the application of the Gov. of N. Y., to assist in the organization of the N. Y. troops for active service. He was complimented by Gov. Morgan, and returned to Washington to receive his commission, as Col. of one of the new regiments of Infantry, the 11th.

Gen. Keyes served during the late rebellion of the Southern States "on the staff of Gov. Morgan of N. Y., assisting in dispatching the state quota of Volunteers to the field from April 21, to June 25, 1861; in recruiting his regiment at Boston, June 25 to July 3, 1861; in the defences of Washington, D. C., July, 1861; in the Manassas campaign of July, 1861, being engaged in the battle of Bull Run, July 21, 1861; in the defenses of Washington, D. C., July 22, 1861 to Mar. 10, 1862; in the Virginia Peninsular campaign, commanding the 4th corps (Army of the Potomac), from March to September, 1862, being engaged in the action at Lee's Mills, April 5, 1862; at the siege of Yorktown, April 5 to May 4, 1862 (Maj. Gen. of Volunteers, May 5, 1862); at the skirmish at Bottoms Bridge, May 22, 1862; action near Savage Station, May 24, 1862; battle of Fair Oaks, May 31, 1862; battle of Charles City Cross Roads, June 29, 1862; battle of Malvern Hill, July 1, 1862, and skirmish at Harrison's Landing, July 2, 1862; in command of the 4th Army Corps on the Virginia Peninsular, Aug. 25, 1862 to July, 1863, being engaged in the organization of a raid to the White House, Va., Jan. 7, 1863; in command of an expedition to West Point, Va., May 7, 1863; and in an expedition under Maj. Gen. Dix, toward Richmond, June—July, 1863, being engaged in several skirmishes; and on the Board for Retiring Disabled Officers, July 15, 1863 to May 6, 1864." Resigned May 6, 1864.

Gen. Keyes was brevetted a Brigadier General in the Regular Army, for "gallant and meritorious conduct" in the battle of Fair Oaks. He commanded the 4th Army Corps, and was engaged alone, more than half the time in the battle of the 31st, in which the principal fighting was done the first day, by the 4th Corps. Col. C. C. Suydam, ex-chief of staff to Gen. Keyes, speaks of him as "ever vigilant, ever on the alert, foreseeing and foretelling events as with a second sight, and devoting to the service, that acute intelligence and perception of military affairs, which his thorough training in the old army, had made a part of his very nature."

In the 12th Vol. of the "Rebellion Record," is the report of Gen. McClellan, in which he publishes at length, the letter of Gen. Keyes to Senator Ira Harris of New York, and praises his conduct in saving the trains of the army, and an immense amount of property, when, after the battle of Malvern Hill, he commanded the Rear Guard. See also, Gen. Keyes's report of the battle of Bull Run, Vol. 2, page 15 of "Rebellion Record." Read also in same Vol., page 9, the report of Gen. David Tyler, and mark his high approval of General Keyes. See also, book published by Gen. George M. Cullum, containing a synopsis of the history of all the graduates of the Military Academy, part of which we have quoted. During his time of service in San Francisco, Gen. Keyes became somewhat identified with the place, and after retiring from the army, bought lands and planted a vineyard of forty thousand vines, built one of the largest wine cellars in California, and was elected chief officer of the Vinecultural Society, for the county of Napa. He also took part in the organization of a Saving and Loan Society, and was made Vice President and Director.

In March, 1872, he went to Europe, where he travelled extensively, and where he remained more than five years.

CHILDREN OF ERASMUS D. AND CAROLINE M. (CLARKE) KEYES.

505. Winfield Scott, b. Nov. 17, 1839.

506. Eleanor Fisher, b. Nov., 1841, in Elizabeth, N. J., m. 1862, Bradbury C. Chetwood, a lawyer of N. Y., and has three children, George J., Edward L. and Charles C.

507. Edward Lawrence, b. Aug. 28, 1843.

508. Caroline Maria, b. June 4, 1848, at West Point, N. Y., m., Mar. 4, 1871, Capt. Samuel R. Franklin, U. S. N.

509. Florence Adele, b. Oct. 12, 1853, in Brooklyn, N. Y., m. Dec. 6, 1876, Lieut. Sam. H. Gibson, U. S. N.

Gen. Keyes m. 2d, Nov. 22, 1862, Mary Loughborough, who was b. Aug. 30, 1831, widow of the late Geo. W. P. Bissell, at one time partner in the mercantile house of Alsop & Co., N. Y. The father of Mary, was a prominent lawyer, and her grandfather, Nathan Loughborough, a large land holder, and a gentleman of the old school.

CHILDREN OF ERASMUS AND MARY.

510. Alexander Darwin, b. Jan. 6, 1864, in Baltimore, Md., now (1878) in college at Aix en Provence, France.

511. Bessie Maria Corey, b. Feb. 18, 1868, in San Francisco, d. June 15, 1873, at Brussells, Belgium.

512. Henry Erasmus, b. Sept. 19, 1870, in San Francisco.

513. Agnes Geraldine, b. Nov. 18, 1871, in San Francisco.

514. Francis Walker Corey, b. Sept. 22, 1873, in Brussels, Belgium.

VIII. KEYES, WINFIELD S. (505), eldest s. of Gen. Keyes, b. at the house of his maternal grandfather, in Brooklyn, N. Y., during the life of his mother, resided with his parents at Fort Moultrie, West Point, on the Hudson, and other military posts. Later, he attended the Columbia College Grammar School, at New York, and Burlington College, N. J., under the late Bishop Doane. He studied at Taunton, Mass., and entered Yale in 1856, graduating with honors in 1860. In the Autumn of 1860, he sailed for Europe, in order to pursue the higher branches of science, entered the Royal School of Mines at Freiburg, Saxony, and remained until the beginning of 1863, studying Chemistry, Mineralogy, Geology, Mining, Engineering and Metallurgy. In ten out of eleven elective branches he received the highest mark. The principal mines and reduction works on the Continent, were critically examined by him, and on his return to America, he proceeded at once to California, intent upon the practical exercise of his profession. He visited first, the principal mining districts of California, and studied the mines, mills and processes of Washoe, Nev. For more than two years, he was Superintendant of a large silver mill in Sonora, Mexico. In 1866, he returned to San Francisco, and was chosen Superintendant of the Silver Smelting and Refining Works at Argenta, Montana. While there, he acted as deputy of the U. S. Mineral Commission, and wrote the chapter on the mineral resources of that section, which appears in the report of the Hon. J. Ross Browne. Having left Montana in the Spring of 1869, he was appointed to the charge of the smelting works in White Pine Co., Nev., and in Jan., 1871, was appointed General Manager and Superintendant of the mines and furnaces of the Eureka Consolidated Mining Company at Eureka, Nev., and this enterprise he made a grand technical and financial success. He remained Chief Manager of mines for himself, and various corporations, until the Summer of 1876, when he served on his appointment by the Centennial Commission, as a member of the Board of Judges, for Mining, Metallurgy, &c., at the International Exhibition at Philadelphia. In the Spring of 1878, he was appointed by the President of the U. S., Honorary Commissioner to the Paris Exposition to represent the

State of Nevada.   Pressure of other duties however, prevented
his attendance.   At the same time he was offered, and refused,
the position of Mining Engineer in Chief, by the Viceroy of
Northern China, to explore that country, for its precious and
useful ores and minerals.   He has acted as scientific mining ex-
pert in all the prominent lawsuits in California and Nevada,
during the last few years and with great success.   Various scientific papers have been contributed by him to the reports of
the Mineral Commissioners, and to the Engineering and Mining
Journal of New York.   He wrote also, the article on the mineral resources of California in Langley's Directory.

Winfield S. Keyes was m. April 25, 1878, at the Cathedral,
San Francisco, by Father Alemany, Archbishop of California,
to Flora Azalea, b. at Bernicia, Cal., Oct. 11, 1857, 2d dau. of
the Hon. S. Clinton Hastings, Ex-Supreme Judge of the States
of Iowa and California, and Ex-Attorney General of the latter
State.   Judge Hastings is one of the millionaires of the Pacific
Coast, and has recently endowed munificently the Hastings Law
College, an adjunct to the University of California.

VIII. KEYES, EDWARD LAWRENCE (507), 2d s. of
Gen. Keyes, b. at Fort Moultrie, Sullivan's Island, Charleston
Harbor, S. C., graduated from Yale College in 1863, graduated
M. D. in 1866, in New York, studied in Paris (France), about
two years, is now practicing medicine in New York, as a partner of Dr. Wm. H. Van Buren.   Address, 210 Madison Avenue,
New York.   Dr. Keyes is Professor of Dermatology in Bellevue Hospital Medical College, New York, since 1871.   Adjunct
Professor of Surgery in the same institution since 1875.   Con-
sulting Dermatologist to Bellevue Bureau of out door Relief,
since 1872.

Visiting Surgeon to Bellevue Hospital, since 1876; visiting
Surgeon to the Charity Hospital from 1871 to 1876; also, Con-
sulting Surgeon to the same Hospital since 1876.   For notice of
Dr. Keyes, see Biographies of eminent living American Sur-
geons and Physicians, which has lately, or soon will appear in
Philadelphia.

Dr. Keyes is the author of various Medical works, from 1870 to 1877.

He m., April 26, 1870, Sarah Maria **Loughborough** of Georgetown, who was b. Oct. 15, 1847, and is the sister of his father's 2d wife.

#### CHILDREN.

515. Edward Loughborough, b. May 15, 1873.
516. Hamilton Augustine, b. Dec. 24, 1876, d. Sept. 12, 1877.
517. Eleanor, b. June 18, 1878.

VII. KEYES, EDWARD L. (504), 2d s. of Dr. Justus and Betsey, m., May 30, 1843, Lucy, b. Mar. 25, 1818, in Medford, Mass., dau. of Col. Alex. S. Brooks, U. S. A., and granddaughter of Gov. John Brooks of Medford, Mass.

Col. Alex. Scamnel Brooks, father of Mrs. Keyes, was b. in Medford, Oct. 19, 1781, and m. Sarah Turner of Pembroke, Mass. He joined the army in 1808, and continued there, until his death, which occurred Dec. 17, 1836. At the close of the Florida War, he was (then Col. of the 4th Artillery) killed by the bursting of the boiler of the steamer, Dolphin. His body was washed ashore at St. Johns, Florida, and taken to Medford, where it was buried with military honors. He left two children, Lucy, m. to E. L. Keyes, and John, a midshipman, who d. 1843. Edward L. Keyes "had only the education which may be acquired at a common school with one or two terms at an Academy. His keen taste for literature, and his youthful ambition led him to employ his leisure time in the acquisition of knowledge, and he distinguished himself in the Lyceums and was regarded as a brilliant youth. He went to Boston as a clerk in a wholesale store, and availed himself of the facilities for acquiring knowledge, so abundantly afforded by that city. While there, he wrote articles for the daily papers, the excitement and success of which, made merchandizing distasteful. He took a leading part in the formation of the free soil party of which he was an ardent and untiring advocate. In 1844, he bought the printing establishment of the Dedham Gazette."

Henry O. Hildreth, the successor of E. L. Keyes, as editor of that paper, writes of him thus, at the time of his death.

"Hon. Edward L. Keyes, a resident of this town (Dedham), for several years, during most of which he was editor of this paper, died from softening of the brain, in the hospital at Taunton, June 6, 1859, at the age of 47. He represented Dedham for two years in the House of Representatives and in 1851 and 1852 represented the County of Norfolk, in the State Senate. In 1848, he was a member of the Executive Council, and in 1853, represented the town of Abington in the Constitutional Convention. He was also one of the Commissioners for the erection of the State Alms Houses. For several years, Edward L. Keyes was one of the foremost young men of the State, exercising a degree of influence seldom attained even by men of riper years and larger experience. He weilded a vigorous and earnest pen and as a speaker, was possessed of remarkable power, which, combined with graceful manners, commanding presence and a clear, musical and deep toned voice, made him one of the most brilliant and effective political speakers in the country. He was a perfect master of invective, and no person who had listened to him, could ever forget the blistering, withering power with which he invested human speech, or the burning words with which he pleaded the cause of suffering humanity, and called down the execration of men, and the vengeance of Heaven upon the oppressor.

He dared to speak bold, brave words for human rights, at a time when interest, position and reputation were endangered thereby, for which, his name will long be held in grateful remembrance.

The funeral services took place at the Indiana Place Chapel, and were attended by many friends and former associates of the deceased, among whom were Henry Wilson, John A. Andrew, Wendell Phillips, Edmund Quincey and others. The remains were interred in the tomb of Gov. John Brooks in Medford, Mass."

### CHILDREN.

518. Caroline Florence, b. Mar. 23, 1844, in Boston, m., Nov. 25, 1870, to Edmund Tileston Mudge of Baltimore, Md., who was b. in Baltimore, Sept. 15, 1844.

519. Alex. Brooks, } b. July 28, 1846, in Dedham, Mass.
520. George Stuart, }

521. Edward L., b. Sept. 26, 1848, in Dedham.     Appointed
to 5th Cavalry, in 1872, and left in 1877.  Unm.

VIII. KEYES, ALEXANDER S. B. (519), enlisted as
Sergeant-major of the 59th Mass., Oct., 1863; 2d Lieut., Jan.,
1864; transferred to 2d Lieut., 1st Mass. Art., July 5, 1864;
mustered out, Oct. 20, 1865.   Appointed to the Regular Army,
as 2d Lieut., 12th infantry, Feb. 23. 1866; transferred to 30th
Infantry, Sept. 21, 1866; 1st Lieut.. Feb. 9, 1867; unassigned.
Mar. 23, 1869; transferred to 10th Cavalry, April 2, 1870.
Now Capt. in the 10th Cavalry, stationed at Fort Concho, Tex-
as.   He m. Mar. 30, 1870, Virginia G. Maxwell, who was b.
Dec. 12, 1850, at Taos, N. M.

### CHILDREN.

522. Berenice Mary, b. Nov. 21, 1870, at Fort Sill, I. T.
523. Alex. Hugh, b. Mar. 4, 1872, at Fort Sumner, N. M., d.
Aug. 27, 1872.
524. Maxwell, b. July 15, 1873, at Fort Sill, I. T.
525. Lucy Beatrice, b. Sept. 11, 1874, at Fort Sumner, N. M.
526. Alex. S. S., Jr., b. Nov. 23, 1877, at Fort Sumner, N. M.

VIII. KEYES, GEO. STUART (520), enlisted as Sergeant-
major, Oct., 1863; was promoted to 2d Lieut., Jan., 1864; was
in Battery A, 2d Mass. Artillery, in 1864; mustered out, April,
1865.  He m. Sept. 27, 1869, Emma C. Reed, who was b. in
Boston, June 7, 1848.  Res. Baltimore, Md.

### SON.

527. George Stuart, b. in Quincy, Mass., June 17, 1872.

VI. KEYES, DANFORTH (493), 5th child of Edward and
Mary, m. Sept. 22, 1811, Olive Chapman, and lived in Ashford, Windham Co., Conn.

### CHILDREN.

528. Julius, b. Jan. 7, 1813, at Ashford, Conn.
529. Caroline, b. Oct. 20, 1814.

530. Danforth, b. May 27, 1816.
531. John, b. June 20, 1818.
532. Mary W., b. Dec. 19, 1819.
533. Edward Francis, b. Jan. 29, 1822.
534. Esther C., b. Sept. 23, 1824.
535. Edwin R., b. April 4, 1826.
536. Lucy Ann, b. Dec. 28, 1829.
537. Joseph, b. July 18, 1832.

VII. KEYES, JULIUS (528), eldest child of Danforth, m. Oct. 5, 1837, Abby Ursula Brown of North Windham, Conn., and moved to Michigan in 1839. He was Township Clerk and School Inspector in Olivet Mich., also Secretary and Treasurer of Olivet College. He d. in Lansing, Mich., Oct. 26, 1869. His wife, Abby, d. in Lansing, April 27, 1876.

CHILDREN.

538. George W., b. Aug. 27, 1838.
539. Jane Isabella. b. Jan. 7, 1840, m. Charles Hurd, about 1864 and d. Mar. 28, 1865.
540. Sophia Antoinette, b. Oct. 22, 1842, graduated at Olivet College, d. July 8, 1871, unm.
541. David Edwin, b. Jan. 30, 1850, m. Mary Armes, Feb., 1878. Res. Lansing, Mich.

VIII. KEYES, GEORGE W. (538), graduate of Oberlin College in 1864, was in the army, during the late war, four months, as sergeant, was appointed Postmaster of Olivet, June, 1867, and in the same month was elected Secretary and Treasurer of Olivet College, which offices he still holds. Is also Justice of the Peace, &c. He m. Nov. 10, 1864, Annabelle Amy Howe.

CHILDREN.

542. Karl Drury, b. Jan. 12, 1867.
543. Gertrude, b. Sept. 23, 1870.

VII. KEYES, CAROLINE (529), 2d child of Danforth, m. Mar. 23, 1836, Fielder S. Snow, b. in Ashford, Conn., May 17,

1814. They removed to Clinton, Mich., soon after their marriage, and res. there until her death, April 17, 1878.    Her husband d. at Clinton, May 22, 1878.

### CHILDREN.

544. Mary Ellen, d. at eight months of age.

545. Mary Kathleen, d. at nine years of age by drowning.

546. Arthur Herbert, b. Sept. 20, 1841.

547. Alice Augusta, b. Jan. 11, 1845, m., Aug. 7, 1867, A. B. Cotton.    Merchant.    Res. Tecumseh, Mich.

VIII. ARTHUR H. SNOW (546), s. of Caroline (Keyes) Snow, graduated at Mich. University, Ann Arbor, Mich., in 1865.   He is a lawyer, County Attorney of Winona Co., Minn., also, member of the Board of Education of the city of Winona.    He m., Aug. 28, 1867, at Homer, Mich., Martha A. Westcott.    Res. Winona, Minn.

### CHILDREN.

George Herbert, b. Mar. 13, 1869, at San Francisco.   Harold Fielder, b. June 17, 1872, at Winona.    Clinton and Clyde, twins, b. June 19, 1875, at Winona, where Clyde d., July 30, 1876.

VII. KEYES, DANFORTH (530), 3d child of Danforth, res. at Clinton, Lenawa Co., Mich., where he has been Notary Public, twenty-five years, also, Postmaster, eight years, Supervisor in Tecumseh, 1863-4-5, also, First Supervisor of Clinton (a town divided from Tecumseh, in 1868), in 1869-70, Town Representative, 1875-6, and has held other offices.    He m., Dec. 24, 1841, at Salem, Washtenaw Co., Mich., Mary Ann, dau. of Dea. Isaac Hamilton.    She was b. July 12, 1819, in Pelham, Mass.

### CHILDREN.

548. Charles Danforth, b. July 25, 1844.    Res. Grand Rapids, Mich.

549. Arthur Hamilton, b. June 2, 1847, m., Oct. 31, 1871, Celia Augusta Miller, at Dummerston, Vt., who was b. in that

town, Sept. 10, 1852. Res. Grand Rapids, Mich. They have one child,

550.   Lillian Mary, b. Mar. 9, 1873.

551. Mary Olive, b. Jan. 10, 1855.

552. John Edward, b. May 2, 1859.

VII. KEYES, JOHN (531), 4th child of Danforth, m. Nov. 1, 1846, Angeline E. Pease of Wilson, Niagara Co., N. Y., who was b. Sept. 25, 1829. John Keyes was a lawyer, and d. at Winona, Wis., Dec. 2, 1876, where his widow and family still reside.

#### CHILDREN.

553. Mary Angeline, b. Dec. 13, 1847.

554. Anna Genevieve, b. Dec. 12, 1848, m. Sept. 22, 1875, Dr. D. F. Brooks. Two children. Harry, b. Sept. 4, 1876; Infant, b. Mar. 31, 1878. Res. Minneiska, Minn.

555. Carrie Eliza, b. May 21, 1854.

556. Lillie, b. July 30, 1856, d. Aug. 20, 1857.

557. Edward Danforth, b. Jan. 9, 1859.

558. Lizzie Adams, b. Sept. 1, 1860.

559. Emma Olive, b. Sept. 27, 1863.

560. Belle Waldo, b. Jan. 22, 1865, d. May 9, 1876.

561. John Pease, b. Mar. 19, 1868.

562. George Andrews, b. Aug. 31, 1871.

VII. KEYES, EDWARD F. (533), 6th child of Danforth, m. Mary Dennis, and had three children. He d. of consumption, and was buried in Ashford, Conn. His widow res. at Abington, Conn.

#### CHILDREN.

563. Frank, d. of consumption at about twenty-two years of age.

564. Darwin, d. at about sixteen years of age.

   Infant.

VII. KEYES, EDWIN R. (535), 8th child of Danforth, m., Nov. 26, 1851, in Killingly, Conn., Louisa J. Sumner, b. in

Ashford, Nov. 30, 1829. He was a graduate of the Conn. State Normal School, by profession a teacher, and a successful one. In 1862, enlisted in 26th Reg., Co. G, Conn. Vols., was 3d serg't. Was wounded at Port Hudson, May 27, 1863, d. in the hospital at Baton Rouge, June 12, 1863, his remains interred at Ashford. His widow now resides at Pomfret, Conn.

### CHILDREN.

565. Ruthven Sumner, b. June 28, 1854, in Eastford, Conn. Clerk in a store in Providence, R. I. Unm.

566. Amy A., b. Dec. 3, 1855, in Ashford, Conn. Graduate of Mt. Holyoke Sem., class of 1877, m. Sept. 30, 1878, Rev. Charles E. Gordon (Cong.), East Hardwick, Vt.

567. Ellen L., b. Sept. 30, 1857, in Brooklyn.

568. Rosie M., b. Oct. 1, 1861, in Pomfret, Conn., d. Dec. 16, 1865.

569. Minnie F., b. Mar. 14, 1863, in Pomfret.


VII. KEYES, JOSEPH (537), 10th child of Danforth, m. and res. with his wife and dau. at Lansing, Mich


VI. KEYES, EDWARD, JR. (496), 8th child of Edward, m. Mary Hughs, and lived in Ottawa, La Salle Co., Ill. He d. at Galena, Ill., July 3, 1835.

### CHILDREN.

570. Elias H., b. Nov. 5, 1823.

571. Sarah M., dec.

572. Roxy E., dec.

573. Esther, dec.


VII. KEYES, ELIAS H. (570), m., Feb. 7, 1845, Ann D. Hanson, is a farmer and res. in Clyde, Jasper Co., Iowa. Was in the Union Army, during the late war.

### CHILDREN.

574. Mary B., b. Feb. 12, 1848, at Vinton, Ia., m. H. Skinner, had two children, d. at Clyde, Ia., June 6, 1875.

575. Emily Hannah, b. Aug. 9, 1850, at Vinton, m., Sept., 1871, A. E. Jeffries. Res. Vail, Crawford Co., Ia.

576. Edward Dustin. b. Feb. 16, 1852, at Marseilles, Ill., d. Dec. 6, 1871, at Clyde, Ia.

577. Antonia C. A., b. Feb. 14, 1854, d. at Clyde, July 15, 1856.

578. Andrew Flagg, b. Oct. 13, 1855, at Clyde, d. Feb. 7, 1856, at Clyde.

579. Sarah Esther, b. July 30, 1859.

580. Theo. Ellsworth, b. Oct. 5, 1861, at Clyde, d. Sept. 18, 1863.

581. Alfred Elias, b. Feb. 18, 1864.

582. Carrie May, b. May 19, 1870.

VI. KEYES, GIDDINGS WHITMORE (499), s. of Edward Keyes and Sarah Whitmore, m., Feb. 25, 1829, Emily Gaylord, who was b. Sept. 14, 1806. He removed to Beaver Dam, Wis., in 1860, and d. there, Sept. 8, 1875. Emily, his wife, d. at Beaver Dam, Wis., Oct. 5, 1873.

### CHILDREN.

583. Dwight Whitmore, b. Mar. 29, 1830.

584. Hamlin Wales, b. Feb. 14, 1833.

585. Herbert William, b. Nov. 2, 1834.

586. Sarah Parmelia, b. Jan. 8, 1836.

587. Helen Eliza, b. Nov. 30, 1837.

588. Charles Henry, b. July 23, 1839, d. Aug. 5, 1843, at Willimantic, Conn.

589. Egbert Le Roi, b. Feb. 28, 1841.

590. Edwin Eaton, b. Oct. 8, 1844, d. Mar. 13, 1864.

591. Frank Gerald, b. Feb. 17, 1852, d. Nov. 4, 1852.

VII. KEYES, DWIGHT W. (583), m., Jan. 8, 1852, at Willimantic, Conn., Jane Strong Huntington, b. Jan. 22, 1831. Res. Milwaukee, Wis. Connected with the Chicago, Milwaukee and St. Paul R. R.

### CHILDREN.

592. Louise Emily, b. Nov. 18, 1853.

593. Charles Dwight, b. June 9, 1855.

594. Henry Walter, b. April 2, 1858, d. Jan. 1, 1873.

VII. KEYES, HAMLIN WALES (584), m. Nov. 28, 1855, at Boston, Mass., Emma Pierce, who d. in Boston, April 7, 1859.

Col. Keyes m. 2d, July 6, 1863, in Boston, Josie Braston. No children.

He entered the army, in the late war, as Maj. of the 5th Mass. Reg., was immediately appointed Captain of the 14th U. S. Infantry, Reg. U. S. Army. Was mortally wounded on the eighth day of the Wilderness fight, at Spottsylvania, May 12, 1864, and d. at Douglass Hospital, Washington, June 16, 1864.

VII. KEYES, HERBERT WILLIAM (585), m., July 16, 1866, at Winona, Minn., Sarah Jane Isham.    Res. Milwaukee.

### CHILDREN.

595. Louise Isham, b. April 19, 1868.
596. Lizzie Emily, b. Feb. 10, 1870.

VII. KEYES, SARAH PARMELIA (586), m., July 23, 1855, at Willimantic, Conn., Charles P. Huntington.    She d. at Milwaukee, Aug. 1, 1863.

### CHILDREN.

597. William Herbert, b. Mar. 15, 1858.
598. Jennie Keyes, b. July 4, 1860.

VII. KEYES, HELEN ELIZA (587), m., Sept. 29, 1857, at Portage City, Col. Elias Ahira Calkins.    Res. Milwaukee, Wis.

### CHILDREN.

599. Hattie Lillian, b. Aug. 31, 1858.
600. Keyes, b. Mar. 5, 1865.

VII. KEYES, EGBERT LE ROI (589), m., July 5, 1864, Mary Jane Smith, from whom he was afterward divorced.

### CHILDREN.

601. Kate Kearney, b. June 28, 1865.
602. Helen Adelle, b. July 31, 1867.

VI. KEYES, JOSEPH FLAGG (500), s. of Edward Keyes and Sarah Whitmore, m., Mar. 25, 1830, Clarissa Bugbee, b. Aug. 23, 1807. He d. Nov. 23, 1848.

### CHILDREN.

603. Andrew Flagg, b. May 13, 1832.

604. Sarah M., b. Sept. 11, 1833.

605. David L., b. Mar. 31, 1838, m., Oct. 5, 1859, Sarah A. Sherman.

VI. KEYES, DAVID (501), s. of Edward Keyes and Sarah Whitmore, m., Nov. 21, 1831, Betsey Bill. No children.

A David Keyes (supposed to refer to the s. of Edward and Sarah), d. Oct. 24, 1835.

V. KEYES, DAVID (442), fourth son of Solomon and Sarah, m., Jan. 30, 1793, in Ashford, Conn., Sally Sumner, and they had one daughter,

606. Delotia, b. Aug. 9, 1793, who m. a Mr. Lewis, and had four children, of whom Sarah and David Keyes Lewis, are still living. David m. 2d, Mary Caswell, who outlived him and m. again. He was a well known business man, known as "Sheriff Keyes," and d. about 1839 or 40.

III. KEYES, HENRY (14), 2d s. of Solomon and Mary, and g. s. of Solomon and Frances of Chelmsford, m. Ruth —— Henry was probably b. in Chelmsford, but was in Shrewsbury before 1728, as his wife was added to the church there that year. He was living on house lot No. 45, in 1729, and d. before 1757, "soon after his return from camp." Isaac Temple and Cyprian Keyes were his executors.

### CHILDREN.

607. Ruth, b. July 24, 1728.

608. Reuben, b Feb. 19, 1730.

609. Priscilla, b. Aug. 25, 1731, m. Dan. Hastings, Jr., 1753.

610. Mary, b. Feb. 12, 1734.

611. Elizabeth, b. May 27, 1736, sup. m. Bezaleel Maynard, 1754.

17

612. Olive, b. May 17, 1738, m. Lieut. Jonas Temple, 1756.

613. Simeon, b. 1740.

614. Son, name not distinct on the original record, probably Henry, b. Nov. 16, 1743.

615. Eunice, b. April 19, 1745, sup. m. Abel Holt, Oct. 21, 1765.

IV. KEYES, SIMEON (613), s. of Henry, m. Lucy, dau. of Isaac Temple, Dec. 5, 1765, lived in the North Parish of Shrewsbury, and d. Jan. 21, 1782. His wife Lucy, d. Oct. 9, 1779, aged 35.

### CHILDREN.

616. Reuben, b. Sept. 15, 1766.

617. Henry, b. Aug. 22, 1768.

618. Ruth, b. July 12, 1770.

619. Elizabeth, b. Mar. 21, 1773.

620. Tabitha, b. Mar. 15, 1775.

621. Isaac, b. May 13, 1777.

622. Simeon, b. Aug. 26, 1779.

Simeon Keyes, perhaps the father of these children, was published to Abigail Ward of Sutton, Nov., 1780.

III. KEYES, CAPT. SOLOMON (15), third of the name, and fourth child of Solomon and Mary, was noted for his personal bravery. He was in Capt. Lovewell's company on its famous excursion to Pequawket, now Fryeburg, Me., and was one of the very few survivors of the fight. The story was thus given, more than forty years ago, in the North American Rev. "It was on the 18th of April, 1725, that Capt. John Lovewell of Dunstable, Mass., with thirty-four men, fought a famous Indian chief, named Paugus, at the head of about eighty savages, near the shores of a pond in Pequawket, Me. Lovewell's men were determined to conquer or die. They fought till Lovewell and Paugus were killed, and all Lovewell's men but nine (or as some say, two) were either killed or dangerously wounded. The savages having lost, as was supposed, sixty of their number, and being convinced of the fierce and determined resolution of their foes, at length retreated and left them masters of the ground."

"Solomon Keys received three bullet wounds, and was apparently dying. To save his dead body from being mangled by the savages, he rolled himself down the beach to a canoe, which chanced to be there. Almost senseless, he succeeded in creeping into it. A gentle breeze blew the canoe across the pond, diagonally, and landed it but a short distance from the stockade fort, into which he contrived to creep."—*Abbott's History of Me.*

"Loveweil's pond," a beautiful sheet of water, lies a short distance from the village of Fryeburg, and is often visited with interest, as being the scene of a bloody combat, and of the overthrow of a powerful Indian tribe.

Capt. Solomon Keyes, in some accounts of this fight, has been accorded to Billerica, as was also the birth of his father, the son of Solomon and Frances. But no record of the birth of either father or son has been found in that place, and both are recorded in Chelmsford, where the second Solomon lived, and where Capt. Solomon probably passed his early life. Later he removed to Western (now Warren), Mass., then a part of Brookfield, and lived in a house built on an eminence near the village. This house may have been built by the second Solomon, father of Capt. Solomon of the Pequawket affair, who probably moved from the vicinity of Chelmsford, as we find no record there of his death. Capt. Solomon lived thirty years after the fight at Pequawket, and was killed at Lake George, Sept. 8, 1755, in the French and Indian War.

He m. Sarah —— and had eight

CHILDREN.

623. Solomon, b. May 19, 1727.

624. David, b. Sept. 1, 1729.

625. Sarah, b. Nov. 30, 1731, m., Feb. 3, 1759, Jonathan Belding of Northfield, Mass. She d. Jan. 17, 1762.

626. Asa, b. Jan. 18, 1734.

627. Rebecca, b. Feb. 16, 1736, m., Feb. 24, 1759, Francis Faulkner of Acton, Mass., d. April 10, 1812.

628. Mary, b. May 18, 1738, d. Dec. 10, 1756.

629. Danforth, b. July 6, 1740.

630. Martha, b. Nov. 20, 1742, d. Jan. 14, 1821.

IV. KEYES, SOLOMON (623), eldest s. of Capt. Solomon, was wounded in the same battle in which his father was killed, at Lake George, was taken to Fort Edward, and d. Oct. 1, 1755.

IV. KEYES, DAVID (624), 2d s. of Capt. Solomon, m., July 30, 1757, Submit Belding of Northfield, Mass.    They moved to Albany, and had three

### CHILDREN.

631. Jonathan, b. Nov. 6, 1758, d. Aug. 13, 1760.
632. Hepsibah, b. April 3, 1760.
633. Sarah, b. Oct. 8, 1861.

David Keyes d. in Albany, Oct. 8, 1861, the day of the birth of his youngest child, and Col. Danforth Keyes, their uncle, brought the daughters on horseback to Warren, the son having died the previous year.   Subsequently Mrs. Keyes m. John Eastman of Amherst, Mass., became the mother of Rev. John Eastman, who was settled in Hawley, now of Amherst, Rev. David Eastman, who d. in New Salem, and Keyes Eastman, who lived on the old homestead in Amherst, and d. there a few years since.

IV. KEYES, ASA (626), 4th child of Capt. Solomon, m., Oct. 28, 1753, Phebe Smith, both of Western (now Warren), Mass.   He is supposed to have lived and died in Arlington, Vt.   He d. Jan. 28, 1771.

### CHILDREN.

634. Daniel, b. July 25, 1754.
635. Solomon, b. Feb. 22. 1756, in Arlington, Vt.
636. Mary, b. Nov. 8, 1757, m. a "Stone."
637. Anna, m. Thomas Lincoln.
638. Phebe.

There were three other dau.   One dau. of Asa, m. an "Allen," and lived in Fairhaven, Vt., another, m. a "Field" of Warren.

V. KEYES, DANIEL (634), eldest s. of Asa, moved to Ohio, and had two children.

639. Asa.
640. Mary.

Perhaps others. The son returned and commenced the study of law in Rutland. Place of residence unknown.

V. KEYES, SOLOMON (635), 2d s. of Asa, lived with his uncle Danforth in Western, Mass. He went to Reading, Vt., about 1783, built a log cabin, and cleared a farm on land belonging to his uncle, obtaining in 1785, a grant of 125 acres. The same year, he m. Thankful Lincoln of Western, Mass., taking his bride to Reading on an ox sled. *23 March* He was in the Revolutionary War, was eleven years Town Clerk, two years Town Representative. Besides being Selectman and Lister, he was long Justice of the Peace, and "old Esq. Keyes" was always referred to with respect, as well on account of the judgement and impartiality of his decisions, as of his personal popularity.

CHILDREN.

All b. in Reading, Vt:

641. Asa, b. Jan. 9, 1786.

642. Nancy, b. June 7, 1787, m. Asahel Goddard, and is still living in Reading.

643. Sophia, b. May 27, 1789, d. Aug. 17, 1876.

644. Royal, b. 1790.

645. Harriet, b. April 11, 1792, m. David Wetherbee, d. Sept. 12, 1831.

646. Thama, b. Feb. 10, 1794, d. June 6, 1804.

647. Solomon, Jr., b. Feb. 4, 1796.

648. Sally, b. July 11, 1798, d. June 12, 1804.

649. Washington, b. Sept. 2, 1802.

650. Laura, b. Dec. 18, 1803, m. James Whitten. Res. So Woodstock, Vt.

VI. KEYES, ASA (641), eldest child of Solomon and Thankful, m., Jan. 6, 1806, Sally Gilson. Res. in Reading, Vt., and d. July 22, 1856.

CHILDREN.

651. Pardon, b. Dec. 6, 1808, in Reading.

652. Thama, m. Danforth Brown.

653. Adaline, m. John Wait, Windsor.

654. Lucinda, m. —— Bisbee Severance, Durham, Conn.

655. Sarah.

656. Mary Ann, m. —— Watrass of Windsor.

657. Phidelia, m. —— Ramsdell.

VII. KEYES, PARDON (651), m. Jan. 22, 1835, Christina Newton of Reading, had one dau., and one

### SON.

658. Augustus Solomon, b. in Reading, Aug. 16, 1842, who m. in 1865, Clara Etta Burnham.

### CHILDREN.

659.      Mac Augustus, b. Nov. 1, 1865.

660.      L. Leon, b. Oct. 3, 1867.

661.      Anna Frances, b. Sept. 3, 1870.

662.      Ruth Hammond, b. May 13, 1875.

VI. KEYES, ROYAL (644), 4th child of Solomon and Thankful, m. Eleanor Annis. Children with one exception, b. in Reading, Vt.

### CHILDREN.

663. Sarah M., b. 1813, m. Stephen Folsom, now dec. She res. in Chelsea, Vt.

664. Ozander A., b. 1815, d. Mar. 8, 1871. He res. at Plattsburg, N. Y. Only one child living, Mrs. Laura Udel, Boon, Ia.

665. Sarepta, b. May 31, 1818, m. Benjamin F. Tibbetts, Jan. 1, 1843. Res. Milford, Mass.

### CHILDREN.

666.      Lizzie L., b. Jan. 21, 1844.

667.      Charles, b. Sept. 7, 1845.

668.      Arthur H., b. Sept. 9, 1847, graduated at Bangor, 1872. Rev. Mr. Keyes is now a Cong. minister.

669.      Georgia M., b. Sept. 30, 1850.

670.      Fred, b. Aug. 1, 1855.

671. Lucinda B., b. 1821, m. Dudley Cabot. Res. Chelsea, Vt.

672. Susan C., b. 1823, m. Adam Dickey. Res. Chelsea.

673. Solomon M., b. 1827, in Northfield, Vt.

VII. KEYES, SOLOMON M. (673), m. Olive Hanson. Res. Chelsea, Vt.

### CHILDREN.

674. Carlos K., b. 1856, in Chelsea.
675. John A., b. 1859, in Chelsea.

VI. KEYES, SOLOMON, JR. (647), 7th child of Solomon and Thankful lived in Reading, Vt., where he was a farmer and took and active part in all the business affairs of the town. Was Deputy Sheriff and Constable, Town Representative three years, and held for many years most of the town offices. Having quite a knowledge of the common law and of law practice, he inspired his fellow townsmen with a large share of confidence in his judgement, so that he was often employed as arbiter, to settle differences between neighbors and to settle estates, &c. He was free hearted, hospitable and social. He m. in 1825, Sophronia, dau. of Peter Darby of Reading, and d. Sept. 19, 1872.

### CHILDREN.

676. Charles Melvin, b. Feb. 16, 1829, m., in 1856, Mary L., dau. of Hon. Benoni Buck of Reading, Vt., and settled in Springfield, Vt., as a merchant. They had a dau. who d. in 1876, aged 20 years.

677. Melvina Elizabeth, b. Feb. 17, 1831, m. her cousin Solomon Keyes Goddard. One dau., Mina. Mrs. Goddard, now a widow, res. in Lexington, Mass.

678. William Wallace, b. July 20, 1832, was at the west some years, returned, bought and settled on the "old farm" owned by his father. Was Sergeant in Co. H, 16th Vt. Vols., during the war, was a member of the last Constitutional Convention, and has been Town Clerk several years. He m., in 1863, Mary S. Mahoney, has one

### SON.

679. Wade, b. Jan. 1, 1865.

680. Marion Sophia, b. Oct. 7, 1833. Unmarried. Res. Lexington, Mass.

681. Amanda Sophronia, b. Feb. 6, 1835, m., 1868, Merritt E. Goddard of Reading, d. Dec. 3, 1870.

682. Gould Darby, b. Feb. 9, 1837, was in Co. D, 4th Reg. Vt. Vols. in the late war, learned the tinman's trade, and m., in 1858, Eliza Royce.

#### CHILDREN.

| | |
|---|---|
| 683. | Fred C., b. Nov. 26, 1858. |
| 684. | Gertrude E., b. Jan. 17, 1861. |
| 685. | Minnie Bell, b. Sept. 7, 1867. |
| 686. | Alice May, b. Nov. 1, 1870. |
| 687. | Mary Sophronia, b. Mar. 17, 1875. |

VI. KEYES, WASHINGTON (649), 9th child of Solomon and Thankful, was a farmer, Town Representative, Selectman, Lister and Overseer of the Poor. He m., in 1831, Eliza Robinson, who d. in 1861. Washington Keyes d. May 8, 1876.

#### DAUGHTER.

688. Laura Melvina, who m. William M. Williams, and res. in New York City.

IV. KEYES, DANFORH (629), 7th child of Capt. Solomon, was b. at the old homestead built by his father in Western (now Warren), Mass., in 1740. He was the first child b. in the house, and was carried to Brookfield (to which that part of Western formerly belonged) to be christened in the old meetinghouse on the hill, which was burned by the Indians the next year.

Although only sixteen years old at the time, he was in the same battle in which his father was killed at Lake George, but came out unharmed. After the affair at Lake George, he still continued in the French war service, and was in the disastrous assault of Gen. Abercrombie upon the French lines at Ticonderoga, 1758. Also, he was with Gen. Amherst in the army raised for the conquest of Canada, took part in the final capture of Ticonderoga and Crown Point, 1759, and was with Amherst engaged in the capture of Isle aux Noix, St. Johns and Montreal. With part of his regiment he came across the State of Vermont from St. Albans in the winter, and most of the men were barefooted before arriving at Charleston, No. 4.

• "The town of Hardwick, Cal. Co., Vt., was granted to Danforth Keyes and his associates, Nov. 7, 1780, and chartered Aug. 19, 1781."

At the outbreak of the American Revolution, he was among the first to take the field, and was in the battle of Lexington and Bunker Hill, at Providence with Gen. Sullivan and subsequently served throughout the war, being at home but twice during that time.

' He was a personal friend of Washington, who visited him after the war, and his descendants still preserve many letters with the signature of the great chief appended."

"The same house is now standing in Warren, Mass., where Col. Danforth Keyes, grandfather of Danforth Keyes, now living in Warren, was notified more than one hundred years ago of the battle of Lexington, and that war had actually begun, and was ordered to start with his regiment at once for the scene of action. The regiment was collected on the common at Brookfield, and in twenty-four hours was ready to march. The same old well is now in use on the premises from which Gen. Washington and some of his army drank on their march from Boston to New York, and the old Oak tree in whose shade the soldiers rested, still stands erect and waves its branches in defiance of the ravages of time."

Col. Danforth Keyes m., Dec. 6, 1764, Sarah Cutler of Warren, who was b. April 2, 1745. He lived in Warren and d. there, Sept. 14, 1826.

Sarah, the wife of Col. Danforth Keyes d. Aug. 19, 1831.

### CHILDREN.

689. Anna, b. Nov. 25, 1765, in Warren, Mass.
690. Solomon, b. Feb. 13, 1768.
691. David, b. Mar. 15, 1770.
692. Sally, b. July 3, 1772.
693. Thomas, b. Nov. 3, 1774.
694. Washington, b. Nov. 8, 1777.
695. Warren, b. May 31, 1781.
696. Pardon, b. Aug. 26, 1783.

18

V. KEYES, ANNA (689), eldest child of Col. Danforth, m.,
1783, Nathaniel Read, s. of Maj. Reuben Read of Warren,
Mass., remained there until the year 1800, when they came to
Vermont, and settled in Cambridge, Lamoille Co., where Anna
d. Aug. 23, 1844.

### CHILDREN.

697. Rensselaer, b. in Warren, Mass., Sept. 10, 1784, d. at
Cambridge, Vt., Feb. 22, 1866.

698. Sally Keyes, b. at Warren, April 9, 1786, d. Sept. 15,
1839, at Cambridge.

699. Nathaniel Read, Jr., b. at Warren, June 4, 1788, d. at
Cambridge, June 30, 1873, graduated at U. V. M., in 1811.

700. Fanny, b. in Warren, Nov. 10, 1790, d. in Cambridge,
Jan. 9, 1842.

701. Keyes, b. Nov. 2, 1792, in Warren, d. at Cambridge.
Unmarried.

702. Horace, b. Jan. 26, 1795, at Warren, d. at Du Page, Du
Page Co., Ill.

703. Thomas, b. June 7, 1797, at Warren. Res. at Kanka-
kee City, Ill.

704. David, b. July 24, 1799, at Warren.

705. Adaline, b. April 15, 1803, at Cambridge, and d. there,
Sept. 24, 1873. She m. Andrew Story and had two sons, Hampton L., and George, the latter dec.

706. George W., b. at Cambridge, Feb. 22, 1806. Is m. and
has a large family. Res. Wayne, Du Page Co., Ill.

707. Tennison E., b. in Cambridge, Nov. 15, 1808, d. at Batavia, Ill., in 1868, leaving six children.


VI. JUDGE DAVID READ (704), s. of Anna, m. 1st,
Judith Maria Hazeltine.

### CHILDREN.

708. Adilia Maria, b. in Fairfield, Vt., July 4, 1825, m. Rev.
M. M. Colburn of So. Dedham, Dec. 14, 1852, d. Nov. 8, 1861.

709. Eldon Willard, b. in St. Albans, Vt., July 7, 1827, and
d. there, Aug. 19, 1835.

710. Harriet Sophia, b. in St. Albans, July 14, 1829, d. there Aug. 30, 1831.

Judge Read m. 2d, Emily Marsh of Hartford, Vt.

711. James Marsh, b. in St. Albans, Nov. 19, 1833, graduated at U. V. M. in Aug., 1853, was four and a half years in the U. S. exploring expedition in New Mexico and the Western Plains, under Capt. Pope of the U. S. Army. Was in the war of the Rebellion and commissioned First Lieut. and Adjutant, also, Captain by brevet, in the 10th Vt. Vol. Reg. in the 6th Corps, Army of the Potomac. Was successively engaged in the battles of Big Bethel, Kelly's Ford, Brandy Station, Locust Grove, Mine Run, Wilderness, Spotsylvania, Gaines' Mills, Cold Harbor, Bermuda Hundred, Winchester, Fisher's Hill, Cedar Creek, and the seige and capture of Petersburgh. In the last named battle, in the assault upon the Rebel lines, April 2, 1865, he received a wound from the effects of which he died, at the 6th Corps Hospital at City Point, Va., April 6, 1865, his remains were embalmed, sent to Burlington and interred in the family burial place in Locust street Cemetery, April 14, 1865.

712. Harriet Eldon, b. in St. Albans, July 30, 1835, m. Jan. 1, 1863, Rev. M. M. Colburn of So. Dedham. She now res., a widow, in St. Joseph, Mich., where her husband became pastor (Cong.), after leaving Dedham, and where he was buried, at the request of his Church and people.

713. Emily Arabella, b. in St. Albans, April 15, 1838, d. at Burlington, May 28, 1843.

714. William Jeffries, b. at Burlington, Oct. 10, 1840, d. there Dec. 4, 1841.

715. Ogden Benedict, b. in Colchester, Vt., Sept. 16, 1843. After two years study at U. V. M., he enlisted in the U. S. Army, was commissioned First Lieut. and Adjutant, and Maj. by brevet, in the 11th U. S. Infantry, and is now stationed at Fort Custer, in Montana Ter. He first enlisted in the 10th Reg. Vt. Vols., in Aug., 1862, leaving College for that purpose. He afterward received a Captain's commisson, and was stationed in front of the enemies' lines at Petersburgh, and with his compa-

ny was in the desperate charge upon the Rebel works at the time of the explosion of the mine which had been laid under them, receiving a severe wound and losing a majority of his company. He has remained in the U. S. Service, stationed at various Posts to the present. He m., at Fort Richardson, Tex., Jan. 1, 1872, Edith, dau. of Lieut. Sage of the U. S. Army.

716. Edward Mason, b. in Colchester, July 25, 1846, m. Elizabeth S. Platt of Plattsburgh, N. Y., April 24, 1873. He is engaged in mercantile pursuits and res. in St. Louis, Mis.

V. KEYES, SOLOMON (690), 2d child and eldest s. of Col. Danforth Keyes, while he was quite young, with his brothers, David and Thomas, emigrated to the then wilds of Vermont, and settled, the latter in Vershire, the two former in the north part of the State, on the Lamoile river, in the town of Cambridge, the res. of their sister Anna. Solomon m. Mary Newell, who d. in Leicester, Mass., July 2, 1836, aged 64.

### CHILDREN.

717. Danforth D., b. in Cambridge, Vt.
718. Louisa.
719. Sarah.
720. Thomas N., b. June 29, 1807, in Cambridge, Vt.
721. Lucy.
722. Mary.
723. Harriet.
724. William, b. Mar. 15, 1818, in Cambridge, Vt.

The daughters of Solomon all m. and had children, who are scattered over the West. The daughters and their husbands are not now living.

VI. KEYES, DANFORTH D. (717), m., May 2, 1832, in Newark, N. J., Phebe Ann Thompson of New York City.

### CHILDREN.

725. Elizabeth P., b. April 7, 1833, d. Aug. 25, 1833.
726. George B., b. Feb. 12, 1835, in New York City.

727. Alfred P., b. Feb. 22, 1838, d. Jan. 30, 1841, in New York City.

728. Edgar D., b. April 11, 1843, in New York City.

Danforth D., d. Nov. 2, 1864, in Chicago, Ill.

His wife, Phebe, d. Mar. 2, 1850, in Madison, N. J.

VII. KEYES, GEORGE B. (726), early in life went to sea, made voyages to China, Japan, Europe and South America, was in San Francisco early in 1852, and travelled thence to Colorado and Nevada. He was a merchant in Dayton, Ohio, in 1857 and 58, and married there, went to Texas in 1859, entered the Confederate Army in 1861, was A. Q. M. and Commissary of Engineers, served in Arizona, La., Texas, &c., up to May, 1865, removed to San Antonio, Texas, and raised cotton, returned to Ohio in 1866, has been connected with the Miami Powder Company, Xenia, O., since 1869. He m., May 31, 1857, in Dayton, O., Elvira J. Granger who was b. Aug. 7, 1837, in Westfield, Mass.

### CHILDREN.

729. Arthur G., b. Feb. 11, 1858, in Dayton, Ohio.

730. Robert D., b. Oct. 9, 1859, in Texana, Texas, d. Feb. 7, 1861.

731. Clara J., b. Aug. 9, 1861, in Indianola, Texas.

732. Edgar D., b. Dec. 20, 1865, in Gonzales, Texas.

733. Wallace B., b. Aug. 19, 1868, at Beam Station, near Xenia, O., d. Sept. 18, 1868.

734. George H., b. April 13, 1871, at Xenia, O.

735. Frank F., b. Dec. 1, 1873, at Xenia, O.

VII. KEYES, EDGAR D. (728), studied at various institutions in New York and New Jersey, was several years in the grocery business, and in the Spring of 1872, entered Drew Theological Seminary, graduating May, 1876. Removed to Ohio, was admitted to the Cincinnatti Conference of the M. E. Church, Sept., 1876. Preached in Winchester and Marshall Circuits. Rev. Mr. Keyes m., Sept. 19, 1877, at New Russellville, Brown

Co., O., Mary A. Fenton, who was b. Dec. 13, 1853, and in
Sept., 1878, was appointed to Sugar Tree Ridge Circuit, where
he now is.

### SON.

736. Earl F., b. Sept. 30, 1878, in Sardinia, Brown Co., O.

VI. KEYES, THOMAS N. (720), m., Jan. 2, 1837, Mary A.
Flint of Randolph, Vt.    Res. Bellows Falls, Vt

#### CHILDREN.

737. Marshall S., b. Sept. 2, 1840.   Graduate of Union College, Schenectady, N. Y., was a student at the Law School in
Cambridge, Mass., which he was compelled to leave on account
of insanity, produced by excessive study, and is now at the
Asylum in Concord, N. H.

738. Alfred G., b. Nov. 26, 1842, m. Carrie Winch, and has
one daughter,

739.          Fannie C., b. April 27, 1875.

Alfred G. res. in Florida and New York City.

740. John W., b. June 21, 1845.   Is a graduate of Harvard
University.   Now in dental practice at Bellows Falls, Vt.

VI. KEYES, WILLIAM (724), removed to Illinois in 1857,
and in April, 1859, m. Lodema F. Pickering, who was b. in
Winchester, N. H.   They now res. in Mendota, La Salle Co., Ill·

#### CHILDREN.

741. Hattie Eliza, b. Oct. 8, 1861.

742. Edward Leslie, b. Aug. 4, 1864.

743. Lena May, b. Feb. 17, 1869, d. Oct. 28, 1872.

V. KEYES, DAVID (691), 2d s. of Col. Danforth, lived
but a short time after emigrating to Vt., and d. unm., in Cambridge, Vt., Aug. 10, 1799.

V. KEYES, SALLY (692), m. William Tufts, and settled
in New Braintree, Mass.   They had four children, of whom,
only one survives,

744. Washington, the youngest son.   Res. Brookfield, Mass·

V. KEYES, THOMAS (693), 3d s. of Col. Danforth, m., in Chelsea, Vt., Margaretta McArthur, who was b. in Thornton, N. H. Thomas d. Mar. 26, 1850, probably in Vershire, Vt., to which place he came sometime before the year 1800, and where he passed the remainder of his life. Margaretta, his wife, d. Aug. 15, 1853, in Newbury, Vt.

### CHILDREN.

745. Freeman, b. Oct. 3, 1807.
746. Henry, b. Jan. 3, 1810.
747. Sally, b. July 5, 1812, d. July 13, 1812.
748. Horace T., b. Nov. 14, 1813.
749. Harriet N., b. May 4, 1816, d. Mar. 10, 1832.
750. J. D. W., b. Jan. 19, 1823, d. Feb. 2, 1848.

VI. KEYES, FREEMAN (745), at the age of sixteen, in the year 1823, left his home in Vershire, and began his business career as a clerk in the firm of Messrs Reed & Goold in Newbury, Vt. On the death of Mr. Goold, in 1829, he became partner in the firm, of which he continued a member under different names during life, most of the time in company with his brothers and son. He m., Nov. 1, 1831, Emmeline C., dau. of Dr. Calvin and Sallie (Parker) Jewett of St. Johnsbury, Vt. Three weeks after this event, they connected themselves with the church (Cong.) of Newbury, of which he continued a leading and active member for forty years, and Deacon for the last eighteen years of his life. He was a constant and generous giver to all the benevolent societies and enterprises of the day, was active in the cause of Temperance and president of the County society. The "Howard Mission" and "Burlington Home" were much in his heart and many of the poor will regret his loss. He was superintendant of the Sabbath School for almost twenty-five years. In May, 1871, Deacon Freeman Keyes left home for a journey to Kansas and other points at the West, in company with his son Edward and others and died in Chicago, June 11, 1871. Mrs. Keyes died June 20, 1878.

### CHILDREN.

751. Edward P., b. Feb. 1, 1836, m., Nov. 23, 1863, Anna E. Atkinson. No children. Res. Boston, Mass.

752. Charles F., b. Mar. 23, 1839, d. Jan. 21, 1840.

753. Harriet E., b. Sept. 14, 1841.

754. Thomas C. b. Jan. 1, 1844. Res. Newbury, Vt.

755. Ellen M., b. April 13, 1846, d. Aug. 27, 1847.

756. John F., b. May 14, 1849, d. Jan. 10, 1851.

757. Emmeline E., b. May 27, 1851, m., June 23, 1875, Mayhue P. Aiken.

VI. KEYES, HENRY (746), m., Oct. 2, 1838, Sarah P. Pierce, who d. Dec. 8, 1853. He m. 2d, May 6, 1856, Emma F. Pierce. Henry Keyes was a prominent business man of Newbury, Vt., President of the Conn. and Passumpsic River R. R., also, of the Atchinson, Topeka and Santa Fee R. R. He d. Sept. 24, 1876. His family res. in Boston, during the winter, and in Newbury, in the summer.

### CHILDREN.

758. Isabella F., b. June 21, 1859.

759. Henry W., b. Mar. 23, 1862.

760. Martha G., b. April 27, 1864.

761. George T., b. Sept. 7, 1867.

762. Charles W., b. Jan. 16, 1871.

VI. KEYES, HORACE T. (748), the only son of Thomas, who is now living, m., May 19, 1842, Sarah Powers, who d. April 9, 1852. No children. Horace m. 2d, May 18, 1863, Lucy E. Rhodes. They have one

### SON.

763. John L., b. Sept. 5, 1866.

Horace Keyes res. in Newbury, Vt.

V. KEYES, WASHINGTON (694), 4th s. of Col. Danforth, graduated from Dartmouth, Class of 1800, and d. early, in Richmond, Va.

V. KEYES, WARREN (695), 5th s. of Col. Danforth, m., May 18, 1815, Cynthia Bonney of Hadley, Mass.  He lived in Warren, Mass., and d. there, Nov. 17, 1851.  Cynthia, his wife, d. Dec. 14, 1867.

### CHILDREN.

764. Sylvester, b. June 24, 1816.

765. Sophronia, b. April 7, 1818, d. Oct. 7, 1820.

766. Caroline E., b. June 27, 1820, m., Oct. 21, 1854, John Stiles of Westfield, who d. Sept. 25, 1855, and left no children.

767. Sophronia C., b. May 16, 1822.

768. Sarah A., b. Mar. 9, 1824.

769. Franklin W., b. Mar. 7, 1826.

770. David, b. Aug. 26, 1828, d. June, 1831.

771. Susan J., b. Dec. 6, 1831.


VI. KEYES, SYLVESTER (764), m., Feb. 28, 1860, Mabel Hall of Port Allen, Iowa, and d. Mar. 27, 1867.  They had one                              SON.

772.          Warren S., b. Aug. 10, 1864.

Mrs. Keyes married again, and now lives in Port Allen.


VI. KEYES, SARAH A. (768), m., Oct. 16, 1850, Warren G. Butterworth of Warren, who was b. Aug. 28, 1822.

### CHILDREN.

Edgar W., b. April 29, 1852; Albert P., b. Sept. 12, 1854; Lillie C., b. Jan. 8, 1858; Mary A., b. Feb. 22, 1863, d. Aug. 3, 1864; Emma, b. July 29, 1870.  Res. Warren.


VI. KEYES, FRANKLIN W. (769), m., June 22, 1854, Charlotte Shepherd of Warren, who was b. April 24, 1824. Res. Warren.

### CHILDREN.

773. Frederick, b. Nov. 24, 1855.  Res. Indian Territory.

774. Jennie, b. Mar. 24, 1858.

775. Charles D., b. June 30, 1860.

V. KEYES, PARDON (696), youngest s. of Col. Danforth, m., May 21, 1812, Martha Davis of Brookfield, Mass., and lived on the old homestead built by his grandfather, Capt. Solomon Keyes of Pequawket memory. He lived in Warren, Mass., and d. there, Sept. 26, 1861. Martha, his wife, d. Mar. 6, 1877.

### CHILDREN.

Born in Warren, Mass.

776. Washington, b. July 16, 1814.
777. Danforth, b. Aug. 19, 1816.
778. Henry A., b. 1822.
779. George G., b. Jan. 17, 1830.

VI. KEYES, WASHINGTON (776), m., June 1, 1847, Julia A. P. Stacy. He is a merchant and res. formerly in Montague, Mass. Present res., East Greenwich, R. I.

### CHILDREN.

780. Marion Ida, b. April 11, 1859.

Son, not named, b. Aug. 20, 1850, d. Sept. 3, 1850.

VI. KEYES, DANFORTH (777), m., Sept. 5, 1843, Elizabeth Lincoln of Warren, and lived for a time on the old homestead. Later, he built his present residence in the village of Warren, where he is a merchant, and a prominent man. The old homestead still remains, in part, in his possession.

### CHILDREN.

781. Charles Danforth, b. May 23, 1846, d. Nov. 27, 1857.
782. Charlotte Eliza, b. Mar. 5, 1849.
783. Martha Warriner, b. May 8, 1851, d. July 20, 1853.

VII. KEYES, CHARLOTTE E. (782), m., Oct. 25, 1871, Walter L. Demond of Ware, Mass. Present res., Spencer, Mass., where he is Cashier of a Bank. They have two children, Alice Belle, b. Mar. 2, 1873, and Helen, b. Jan. 23, 1877.

VI. KEYES, HENRY A. (778), is Postmaster and Supervisor in Port Allen, Iowa, is unm. and writes thus in regard to the genealogy. "And here it ends as far as I am concerned, for I have neglected to obey the divine injunction, 'Multiply and replenish' until now in my fifty-sixth year, I feel that it is altogether too late, and in all human probability, I shall go down to my grave, unwept, unhonored and unsung. I have no wife— I never had. I have no child who bears my name."

VI. KEYES, GEORGE G. (779), m., Mar. 25, 1856, Ruth A. Streeter of Plainfield, Mass. Mr. Keyes is a merchant, Justice of the Peace, Town Clerk and Special State Treasury Agent in Delton, Sauk Co., Wis., where he has res. the last eleven years.                   SON.

784. Harry D., b. June 1, 1862, in Warren, Mass.

*60*

III. KEYES, ZEBEDIAH (18), s. of the second Solomon and Priscilla (his second wife), and g. s. of Solomon and Frances, m. Mary —— He d. in Chelmsford, Mass., Nov. 4, 1758.

CHILDREN.

785. Mary, b. 1738.
786. Daniel, b. 1741.
787. Esther, b. 1744.
788. John, b. 1749.
789. Solomon, b. 1752.

IV. KEYES, DANIEL (786), is probably the person who, with Abiel his wife, both of Chelmsford, Mass., sold land in Goffstown, Hillsborough Co., N. H., between 1771 and 1780, to Phœba Butterfield of Goffstown. Other parties who joined in the deed, resided in Wilton, N. H.

Daniel, John and Solomon Keyes, probably sons of Zebediah, were in "Captain Ford's company" in the Battle of Bunker Hill, where the eldest was sergeant and all were wounded.

Here ends the record of the descendants of Solomon Keyes, the son of Solomon of Chelmsford.

II. KEYES, JOSEPH (8), 2d s. of the first Solomon, b. in Chelmsford, Mass., May 24, 1667, m., 1690, Joanna Cleaveland. He is mentioned in Chelmsford records as one of the town "Commity" until 1720, perhaps later. His descendants seem to have remained generally in, or in the vicinity of Chelmsford and Westford. While the descendants of the second Solomon have emigrated to New Hampshire, Vermont, Conn., and later to New York and the far West, so that their names are not found on book or gravestone, the Westford town books show pretty full lists of Joseph's descendants for three or four generations. The names of Joseph and Jonathan Keyes are to be seen in numbers on ancient gravestones, in the old graveyard, while a modern tomb bears the names of Keyes and Fletcher, with which family this branch of Keyes have often intermarried.

Joseph d. June 9, 1757, aged 90 years and 3 days.

Joanna, his wife, d. Mar. 18, 1758, aged 87 years and 11 months.

### CHILDREN.

790. Lydia, b. 1693, lived in the village of Chelmsford, carried on a store and did quite a large business. She d. unm.

791. Joanna, b. 1695.

. 792. Joseph, b. 1698.

III. KEYES, JOANNA (791), is probably the Joanna Keyes who m., in 1716, Thomas Kidder, b. Oct. 30, 1690, s. of John Kidder of Chelmsford. Benjamin, the brother of Thomas, was with Lovewell in his expedition to Pequawket. Another brother, Joseph, went to sea, and after his return in 1734, kept the Green Dragon tavern in Boston.

III. KEYES, JOSEPH, JR. (792), m. Elizabeth —— and lived in Westford, Mass.

### CHILDREN.

793. Elizabeth, b. 1720.

794. Jonathan, b. 1721.

795. Sarah, b. 1723.

796. Lydia, b. 1724.

797. David.

IV. KEYES, JONATHAN (794), s. of Joseph, m. 1st, Jan. 20, 1746, Elizabeth Fletcher of Westford, m. by Rev. Mr. Huil, Pastor.

### CHILDREN.

798. Joseph, b. Nov., 1746.

799. Joanna, b. 1748, d. 1753.

800. Aaron, b. 1751, d. 1753.

801. Stephen, b. 1754, d. Aug. 3, 1758.

802. Joanna, b. 1757, m., 1781, Timothy Adams of Chelmsford, and became the mother of the late Hon. Joel Adams.

*//.* 803. Elizabeth, b. 1759, m., 1770, Capt. Zacheus Hildreth of Townsend, Mass.

804. Hannah, b. 1761, m., 1780, Uriah Pike of Dunstable, grandmother of Hon. Austin F. Pike of Franklin, N. H.

Elizabeth, wife of Jonathan, d. July 23, 1761, aged 41.

Jonathan m. 2d, 1762, Mrs. Betty (Hartwell) Read of Lyttleton (probably Mass.).

805. Jonathan, b. Mar. 30, 1763.

806. Lydia, ⎫ b. Nov. 15, 1765, m. Isaac Patten and was left
⎬ a widow.
807. Lucy, ⎭ b. Nov. 15, 1765, m. Jesse Fletcher.

808. Miriam, b. Mar. 13, 1767.

809. Patty, b. 1769, m., Dec. 5, 1785, a Fletcher, and d. Dec. 9, 1786.

810. Frances Grant, b. 1771.

811. Aaron, b. 1774, d. young.

"Elizabeth Hartwell, 2d wife of Jonathan Keyes, b. in Westford, Feb. 17, 1731, m. 1st, a Mr. Read, by whom she had six children. At his decease, she became the 2d wife of Jonathan Keyes (794), by whom she had seven children. At the decease of Jonathan she m. Pelatiah Fletcher, and at his decease, she returned to the old Keyes mansion, and passed the remainder of her days, which was from fifteen to twenty years. She had three pairs of twins. There were, it is said, about forty who called her mother, either by blood or marriage. Her two husbands were widowers. At, or about the time she died, her grand-children numbered 119, and her great-grand-children about 90. There were at one time five generations at one table

in the old Keyes mansion. She could say "arise my daughter,
go to thy daughter, for thy daughter's daughter hath a daughter."
She either died or was buried on her birth-day, at the age of
ninety-five. She was successively,

   Elizabeth Hartwell.

   Mrs. Elizabeth Read.

   Mrs. Elizabeth Keyes.

   Mrs. Elizabeth Fletcher.

She lived and died a pious and godly woman."

V. KEYES, JOSEPH (798), eldest s. of Jonathan and
Elizabeth, m. 1st, 1768, Ruth Forbush of Acton, Mass.

CHILDREN.

 812. Ruth, b. 1769.

 813. Joseph, b. 1771, d. Aug., 1775.

 814. Stephen, b. 1772, d. Aug., 1775.

 815. Rebecca, b. 1774, d. Sept., 1775.

 816. Joel, b. Oct. 22, 1776.

 817. Salla, b. 1778.

 818. Anna, b. 1780.

 819. Jonas, b. 1782.

   Ruth, wife of Joseph, d. 1785, aged 36.

   Joseph m. 2d, Sarah Boyden.

 820. John, b. Mar. 24, 1787.

 821. Joseph, b. 1789, d. Mar. 8, 1796.

 822. Polly, b. 1791.

 823. Imla, b. 1793.         •

 824. Patty, b. 1797.

   Joseph, father of these children, d. Feb. 22, 1823.

   His widow Sarah, afterwards m. a Dalrymple, and
    d. 1839.

VI. KEYES, JOEL (816), s. of Joseph and Ruth, m., Nov.
27, 1800, in Westford, Mass., Polly Boyden, who was b. in Groton, Mass., Nov. 20, 1775.

They moved from Westford to Tyngsboro, thence in 1810, to
Dunstable, Mass., where Polly, wife of Joel, died Jan. 9, 1844,
aged 68 years.

He married 2d, Feb. 18, 1845, Mrs. Mary Foster, who died July 26, 1848.  Joel Keyes d. Dec. 15, 1858, in Dunstable, Mass.

"Mr. Keyes was a man of commanding personal presence.  He was six feet in height, and well proportioned, weighing two hundred pounds or upwards for many years before his death. He had a strong, well rounded character, constituting him one of those men on whom others felt they could rely.  In his bearing, he was hearty and genial to all; but along with these qualities there was an unassuming dignity that impressed even strangers.  He possessed clear judgment, and marked intelligence, reading books of a far higher grade than those usually read in his day by men upon the farm.  He was a man of the utmost sincerity.  Said an old acquaintance: "I always liked to hear him talk, he seemed so sincere."  If he uttered words of praise it was because he felt they were deserved.  If his lips spoke censure, it was because his judgment told him that it was needed.  He would reproove a man who had done wrong, with great plainness, but with that transparent sincerity and kindness that the one reproved respected him the more.  He lived a life of spotless integrity.  To abide in justice and righteousness, was natural to him, for these elements lay at the foundation of his character.  A vein of quiet but effective humor sprung from his heart, and distilled a peculiar charm over his conversation. There was in him a depth of affection that drew his children and friends closely to him.  To his grandchildren he showed a playful love, which, according to their natures, they answered with love and reverence.  They grew up proud of their grandfather, and to them, as to his children, his memory is a constant benediction.

The farm to which he moved in Dunstable was a good one, but it was greatly improved under his cultivation, and that of his son.  Few rural homes are more attractive in their situation and surroundings than the one where he abode.  The buildings stood upon a kind of shelf upon the side of a sloping hill.  Above them, beyond the green mowing, is the woodland, crowning the summit of the hill and forming a beautiful background to the scene. Before them, a wide, grassy lawn slopes downward to the road. Around them are several large elms that have stood as friendly sentinels for many years. Under these elms the aged owner would often sit of a summer day reading his favorite newspaper, or looking out upon the peaceful fields before him. Here also in thought, he often looked out upon the eternal scenes that lay around, hid from his mortal eyes. His memory dwelt lovingly upon the many friends who had gone before him; and when the end came he went trustfully home to them, and to the unseen glory."

### CHILDREN OF JOEL AND POLLY BOYDEN.

825. Mary, b. Oct. 29, 1801 in Tyngsboro, Mass., m., July 4, 1837, Willard Dalrymple of Charlestown, Mass. She d. Mar. 28, 1878.

826. Joel, b. April 26, 1804, in Tyngsboro.

827. Sophia, b. June 4, 1806, in Tyngsbsro, d. Aug. 28, 1810.

828. Ann, b. July 3, 1808, in Tyngsboro, d. Aug. 26, 1810, in Dunstable.

829. Caroline, b. April 11, 1810. Still living in Groton, Mass.

830. Sophia, b. Aug. 30, 1812, in Dunstable, d. Jan. 20, 1869 in Groton.

831. Ann, b. June 22, 1814, in Dunstable, m., July 4, 1843, Lyman Smith. Res. Groton.

VII. KEYES, JOEL (826), m., Dec. 29, 1836, Phebe Cutter of Jaffrey, N. H., and d. Aug. 11, 1867.

### CHILDREN.

832. Darwin Perry, b. Dec. 5, 1837, in Dunstable, Mass.

833. Joseph Willard, b. Sept. 30, 1839, in Dunstable.

Joel cultivated for a time his father's farm in Dunstable. It afterward became his own, and several years before his death, he transferred it to his eldest son Darwin. Like his father, Joel was a man of strict integrity, thorough sincerity and kindness of heart. In this age of railroads it is a little remarkable that he never journeyed over fifty miles from the place where he was born.

VIII. KEYES, DARWIN P. (832), m., April 24, 1867, Lizzie Cheney of Hollis, N. H. They have one dau.,

834. Edna L., b. Oct. 15, 1869.

Mr. Keyes cultivated for some years the farm which was owned by his father and grandfather and is still the proprietor, though he has lived several years near the center of Groton, Mass. He received a good Academic education, and has proved himself an energetic farmer and a successful teacher of schools.

VIII. KEYES, JOSEPH W. (833), m. 1st, May 15, 1866, at Minneapolis, Minn., Anna M. Cooper of that city. They had one child, now living.

835. Bertha A., b. April 18, 1868, at Arlington, Mass.

Anna, wife of Joseph, d. Mar. 3, 1871, at Webster, Mass. He m. 2d, Oct. 6, 1874, Ellen Cutter of Pelham, N. H.

DAUGHTER.

836. Mary W., b. May 23, 1876, at Auburn, N. Y. Just a century from the year of her great-grand-father's birth.

"Mr. Keyes is a clergyman (Univ.). He graduated from the normal school in Westfield, Mass., July, 1859, and after teaching and preaching a little, entered the Theological Department of the St. Lawrence University at Canton, N. Y., where he graduated in 1864. Immediately after, he went to the North West, and took charge of a newly organized parish in Minneapolis, Minn. Here he remained nearly two years, then with health seriously impaired, returned to the seaboard. When he was ordained over the society, its members worshipped in a hall in the third story of an unpainted building. At leaving, they had a fine church edifice nearly completed. Coming East, he was pastor of a church in Arlington, Mass., and later in Webster, Mass. From Webster he accepted a call to Auburn, N. Y. During this settlement, by his persistent efforts, the church edifice in which he ministered, was rebuilt, making it one of the most beautiful, as it is one of the most spacious in the Denomination. At Auburn, his health became greatly imperilled,

20

in part from overwork, which led him to resign, and take up his residence in Shirly Village, Mass., where he still ministers to the Universalist church of that pleasant town."

VI. KEYES, JONAS (819), s. of Joseph and Ruth, is probably the Jonas who m. Sally Read in Chelmsford, Mass., in 1808. He lived in Tyngsboro, Mass., many years, and d. there. He had eight

### CHILDREN.

Jonas, Abial, Willard and William, twins, Sarah, Lucy, and two other daughters. It is supposed that Jonas had a son, Aaron, now dec., and still another dau. The six children of Jonas, whose names are given, are known to have died, with the exception of the first, who lived in Baltimore, Md., also probably dec. Two of Jonas' (819) dau. are living, one m. and living in Concord, Mass., the other also m. and living in Boxboro, Mass.

VI. KEYES, JOHN (820), s. of Joseph and Sarah Boyden, m., Nov. 27, 1816, Ann Stow, dau. of Timothy Shepard of Hopkinton, Mass.

### CHILDREN.
All b. in Concord, Mass.

837. Ann Alicia, b. Sept., 1817. d. April 11, 1826.
838. John Shepard, b. Sept. 19, 1821.
839. Mary, b. Mar. 24, 1827, d. Oct. 3, 1834.
840. Joseph Boyden, b. May 13, 1829, d. May 6, 1871.
841. George, b. Mar. 12, 1832.

John Keyes was b. in Westford, Middlesex Co., Mass., attended the Academy in that town, graduated at Dartmouth College, in 1809, read law with John Abbott of Westford and John Leighton Tuttle of Concord, Mass. and began its practice in Concord, in 1812. Possessed of rare ability, strong sense, keen faculties and an ardent temperament, he soon became prominent both in his profession and in politics. He rose steadily in the confidence and esteem of his fellow citizens, filled with honor many important positions in their gift and became one of the leading men of his time in the State. With a retentive memory, a fearless disposition, an earnest eloquence and a strong personality, he made a deep impression on all with whom he was brought in contact. Few men in the community had more power in a deliberative assembly or carried more conviction to hearers or more weight to the cause espoused. For thirty years he was actively engaged in useful work, widely known, truly respected, thoroughly trusted, a power in his town, county and state. His well-trained mind, stored with the principles of both legal and political science, grew rather by the experience of affairs, than by close study, for which his occupations left him little time. Independent in views, manly in tone, frank in purpose, he bore himself with dignity and resolution in every station, and left a memory to be honored and an example to be imitated by all of his name.

In person above medium height, erect, light figure, ruddy complexion, dark hair, roman nose and broad, high forehead, graceful manner and powerful voice, he attracted attention and won confidence by his demeanor. In social and domestic life he was warm hearted and impulsive, strongly attached to his home and friends, hospitable and courteous to his numerous guests. His health, never robust, served with care and prudence for all his duties without interruption till a severe attack of colic suddenly ended his life Aug. 29, 1844, in his fifty-eighth year. His life was almost uniformly prosperous and he died before old age had brought its burdens. He left a handsome estate honestly earned by his own labors, and accumulated after a prudent but liberal expenditure through life. He was Postmaster from 1813 to 1837, County Treasurer for the same term, by twenty-four successive annual elections, Member of the Constitutional Convention, 1820, Representative in 1821 and 22, Senator from 1823 to 1829, and again Representative in 1832 and 1833, and Speaker, pro tem, a portion of the Session, candidate for Congress in 1824, and defeated in a close contest by Edward Everett. He never held town office, but served on most of the important committees, frequently was Moderator at town meetings and presided at the Bi-Centennial celebration in 1835, and on other public occasions. He was Master of the Masonic

Lodge in Concord and an officer of the Grand Lodge of Mass-
sachusetts. A director from the beginning in the Concord
Bank, Savings Institution and Middlesex Insurance Co., and
President of the last at the time of his death.

> John Keyes d. Aug. 29, 1844, at Concord, Mass.
> His widow is still living, and res. in Concord.

VII. KEYES, JOHN S. (838), m., Sept. 19, 1844, Martha
Lawrence, dau. of Timothy and Abigail D. (Wood) Prescott of
Concord.

### CHILDREN.

842. John, b. Oct. 13, 1845, d. July 31, 1846.
843. Annie Shepherd, b. May 4, 1847.
844. Florence, b. Jan. 26, 1850.
845. Mary Ellen, b. July 8, 1853, d. Aug. 9, 1854.
846. Alicia Mulliken, b. June 13, 1855.
847. Prescott, b. Mar. 26, 1858.

John S. Keyes lives close by the battle ground and the old
manse, in Concord, Mass., where he began the practice of law
in 1844. He was a member of the Senate in 1849, Sheriff from
1853 to 1860, Delegate to the Chicago Convention that nomi-
nated Lincoln, and appointed by him U. S. Marshal of Mass.,
in 1861, re-appointed in 1865, resigned in 1866. Appointed
Judge of the District Court for Central Middlesex, in 1874,
which office he still holds. Judge Keyes is a prominent citizen
of Concord, having in addition to his more public appointments,
done an amount of town work, and much to ornament and im-
prove the old historic town.

VIII. KEYES, ANNIE S. (843), m., Sept. 19, 1874, Edward Waldo Emerson, s. of Ralph Waldo and Lydia (Jackson)
Emerson of Concord, Mass.

### CHILDREN.

William, b. July 11, 1875, d. July 14, 1875; Charles Lowell,
b. July 3, 1876; John, b. Jan. 6, 1878.

VIII. KEYES, FLORENCE (844), m., Sept. 22, 1875, Charles Hosmer Walcott, s. of Joel W. and Martha (Hosmer) Walcott of Concord.

### CHILDREN.

Roger, b. Sept. 9, 1876; Philip Keyes, b. Dec. 11, 1877.


VII. KEYES, JOSEPH B. (840), graduated at Harvard University in 1849, studied law and practiced in Watertown and Lowell, Mass. He m., May 17, 1855, Helen Maria, dau. of Micah and Harriot (Piper) Maynard.

Joseph B. Keyes d. May 6, 1871, and his family reside in Concord, Mass.

### CHILDREN.

848. John Maynard, b. July 1, 1862.
849. Mary Lillie, b. Aug. 28, 1868.


VII. KEYES, GEORGE (841), m., Sept. 14, 1854, Mary Elizabeth, dau. of Simon and Ann (French) Brown of Concord. Res. Concord.

### CHILDREN.

850. Bessie Van Meter, b. June 4, 1857.
851. Marion Brown, b. Oct. 13, 1860.
852. Grace Boynton, b. May 29, 1866.
853. George Shepard, } b. June 2, 1869.
854. Arthur French, }


VI. KEYES, IMLA (823), s. of Joseph and Sarah Boyden, m., Sept. 30, 1816, Hannah Fletcher of Westford. They were m. by Rev. Caleb Blake. Res. Westford, Mass.

### CHILDREN.

855. George, b. Sept. 18, 1817. Now living with his brother Joseph, at the old homestead before mentioned, situated at the head of Keyes pond in Westford.

856. Lydia, b. Feb. 14, 1819, d. at two months.

857. Joseph Warren, b. May 2, 1820, m., June 24, 1868, Rebecca H. Fletcher. No children.

858. Liberty, } b. May 22, 1822, m., June 24, 1854, Rebecca
P. Davis, and d. 1856, leaving a s. Geo. H.
859. Lydia, } b. May 22, 1822, m., 1846, Thaddeus W.
Davis of Tyngsboro. Dec.

860. Otis, b. April 9, 1824.

861. Rufus, b. Jan. 30, 1826. Unm.

862. Edward, b. Nov. 9, 1827.

863. Martha Maria, b. Nov. 2, 1829, d. Nov. 12, 1856.

864. Emmeline, b. June 29, 1831, m., Dec. 8, 1858, Francis
A. Proctor of Lunenburg, Mass.

865. James, b. 1833, d. in infancy.

866. Cornelius Freeman, b. Dec. 5, 1834, now living in Westford. Unm.

867. Sarah Elizabeth, b. July 4, 1839, d. 1866.

Imla Keyes d. Oct. 3, 1861.

Hannah, his wife, d. Dec. 5, 1856.


VII. KEYES, OTIS (860), m., June 2, 1854, Lucy Ann
Turrell of Nashua, N. H. They lived for a time in Harvard,
Mass. Present res. Westford.

### CHILDREN.

868. Rosine Turrell, b. Mar. 28, 1856.

869. Henry Otis, b. May 17, 1859.

870. Alice.

871. Edward H.


VII. KEYES, EDWARD (862), m., June 2, 1854, Lucy A.
Richardson, was in the war of the Rebellion, and d. Aug. 18,
1865, at Sumterville, S. C. He left a dau., Lucy E., b. Mar.
22, 1856.


V. KEYES, JONATHAN (805), eighth child of Jonathan
and Elizabeth m. Patty Woodward, b. Aug. 7, 1766, of Dunstable. He d. May 25, 1828.

### CHILDREN.

872. Martha, b. Aug. 16, 1787, m. Levi Heyward, of Westford, and d. Feb. 3, 1839.

873. Jonathan, Jr., b. Oct. 25, 1789.

874. Aaron, b. Apr. 14, 1791.

875. Lydia, b. Nov. 7, 1792, d. Oct. 12, 1874 in Westford. Unmarried.

876. Betsey, b. May 22, 1794, m., Oct. 28, 1830, Nahum H. Groce, Esq., of Westford, where she still lives a widow (1878).

877. Joseph, b. Mar. 7, 1796.

878. Charlotte, b. Oct. 11, 1797, m. —— Dana of Chelmsford, Mass., d. Oct. 11, 1842.

879. Nancy, b. Nov. 28, 1799.

880. Benjamin F., b. Mar. 7, 1801.

881. Sally, b. July 19, 1803, d. June 18, 1843. Unm.

882. Trueworthy, b. July 28, 1805.

883. Stephen Adams, b. Aug. 30, 1807, d. Nov. 24, 1842, in Townsend, Mass. Unm.

884. Wright Sumner, b. Mar. 5, 1809.

885. Laurinda, b. Jan. 11, 1811, d. Oct. 13, 1839.


VI. KEYES, JONATHAN, JR. (873), eldest s. of Jonathan, m. Ellen Harriman of Maine, lived on his place in Westford, Mass., and d. there May 4, 1845.

### CHILDREN.

886. Jonathan Hartwell, was in the late war, killed at Fredericksburg.

887. John Harriman, was in the late war, was wounded at Bull Run, was commissioned Lieutenant, served through the war, and d. of yellow fever at Galveston, Tex., at 23 years. Was much beloved and respected.

888. Ellen M., m. G. H. Burtt. Res. Hillsdale, Ill.

889. Nancy Elizabeth, m. Thomas Clissold. Res. Penn.


VI. KEYES, AARON (874), 2d s. of Jonathan, m. Dec. 19, 1824, Martha Warren, always res. in Townsend, Mass., where Aaron d. Nov. 28, 1842. Mrs. Keyes still lives in Townsend.

### CHILDREN.

890. Aaron W., b. Jan. 30, 1827. Res. West Townsend. Unm.

891. Charles Lowell, b. Nov. 12, 1829, n.., Nov., 1870, Sarah

D. King of Williamstown, Vt. No children. Res. Ayer, Mass. In the Express business.

892. George, b. July 23, 1832. Res. Ayer. Unm.

## VI. KEYES, JOSEPH (877), 6th child of Jonathan, m.

Sophia Strong, dau. of Rev. Mr. Blake of Westford. Joseph was a merchant in Westford, and d. there Jan. 26, 1836. Sophia, his wife, d. May 10, 1844.

### CHILDREN.

893. Joseph Hammond, b. Aug. 20, 1826, in Westford, Mass.

894. Julian Victor, of the firm Keyes & Wightman, Lowell, Mass. Has one son and two dau.

895. Sophia M., m. Charles L. Fletcher, and res. in Westford.

896. Martha S., d. Dec. 31, 1846.

897. Catherine B., d. Sept. 22, 1844.

## VII. KEYES, JOSEPH II. (893), m., June 7, 1853, Sarah A., dau. of Rev. Liba Conant, the oldest ordained (Cong.) minister in N. H. Res. Bristol, N. H.

### SON.

898. Joseph E., b. Sept. 29, 1855, in Lawrence, Mass.

## VI. KEYES, NANCY (879), 8th child of Jonathan, m.,

May 3, 1821, in Westford, B. F. Tidd of Lancaster, Mass., who d. Aug. 30, 1853. Nancy m. 2d, Nov. 17, 1856, Moses Carleton, who d. July 6, 1858. No children living. She writes: " I came to Lancaster a bride in 1821, and have always lived in the same house. I am called Aunt Tidd, by old and young, but I am proud of the name of Keyes."

## VI. KEYES, BENJAMIN F. (880), 9th child of Jonathan,

b. at the old homestead in Westford (as were probably all the children of Jonathan), m. Catherine Wight, at Dedham, Mass., her ancestors having immigrated from the Isle of Wight, and settled in Dedham, in 1637, where she was born, Aug. 28, 1798 (See Gen. of Wight family by Dr. Danforth Phipps Wight, a graduate of Harvard).

Benjamin F., d. in Dedham, April 8, 1858.

Catherine, his wife, d. in Dedham, Feb. 11, 1872.

899. Eben Wight, b. June 20, 1830.
900. Benj. Franklin, b. June 27, 1832, d. Oct. 11, 1841.

VII. KEYES, EBEN W. (899), when about nineteen, left Boston in a sailing ship for San Francisco, visited Havanna, the Sandwich Islands, Juan Fernandes, etc., returned via the Isthmus in 1853, has visited almost every state in the Union, and finally settled in Denver, Col., in which vicinity "Keyes Mountain" was named for him, and where he is well known as a contributor to the press and to the cause of Education. He m., Nov. 19, 1855, Hortense Eugenia, dau. of James and Lydia White of Belfast, Me., where she was b. Sept. 15, 1834.

901. Franklin Balch, b. Sept. 5, 1856, at South Boston, Mass., educated at the academy at Lancaster, Mass., now mining in Hortense, Lake Co., Col., a place named for his wife by E. W. Keyes.

902. James White, b. Oct. 3, 1857, at Dedham, Mass., d. Aug. 3, 1867, at Lancaster, Mass.

Hortense E., wife of Eben W., d. at Dedham, Sept. 11, 1858.

He m. 2d, Oct. 11, 1861, Mary Elizabeth, dau. of William and Lydia Carleton of Charleston, Mass. She was b. in Boston, Feb. 19, 1834.

903. Carleton, b. June 29, 1862, at Charlestown, Mass.
904. Willis, b. Jan. 10, 1864, d. Aug. 29, 1864.
905. Eben Wight, b. Aug. 27, 1865.
906. William, b. July 6, 1867.
907. Hortense Elizabeth, b. April 14, 1869.

VI. KEYES, TRUEWORTHY (882), 11th child of Jonathan, m., April 9, 1837, Sophia S. Keyes, the widow of his brother Joseph (877).

Trueworthy, d. May 23, 1871, in Westford, Mass.

908. Josephine, } b. June 6, 1838.
909. Clemantine, }

Clemantine m. Charles Sweet, well known as a teacher in the Boston schools. Res. No. 7, Rockland Court, Boston Highlands.

VI. KEYES, WRIGHT SUMNER (884), 13th child of Jonathan, m., Sept. 30, 1832, in Boston, Mass., Maria Cummings, who was b. in Westford, May 23, 1810. They were m. by Rev. Dr. Hague.

### CHILDREN.

910. Maria Augusta, b. July 11, 1833, in Boston, Mass.

911. Sarah Adelaide, b. Aug. 5, 1835, in Boston, Mass.

912. Sumner Wright, b. Mar. 2, 1841, d. Jan. 28, 1842, in Boston, Mass.

913. Sumner Wright, b. Dec. 22, 1842.

914. Stephen Adams, b. Oct. 12, 1844, in Boston, d. Aug. 10, 1863. He was in the war of the Rebellion, in Co. K, 53d Reg. Mass. Vols., was in the battle of Port Hudson, d. on the St. Marys, on his way home from New Orleans, and was buried in the Gulf Stream.

915. Hattie Anna, b. May 25, 1848, in Lancaster, Mass.

916. Charles Hartwell, b. Sept. 12, 1850, in Lancaster. Res. Boston, Mass.

VII. KEYES, SUMNER WRIGHT (913), m., Nov. 28, 1871, Emma S. Eaton, in Boston, Mass. He was in Co. I, 5th Reg. Mass. Vols. Res. Boston.

### CHILDREN.

917. George Eaton, b. June 26, 1873, in Chelsea, Mass.

918. Maria Augusta, b. July 29, 1875, in Lancaster, Mass.

The daughters of Wright Sumner Keyes (884) reside with their parents in Lancaster, Mass.

It will be noticed that Jonathan (805), although the eighth child of Jonathan (794), is not the son of Elizabeth (Fletcher) as stated on page 158. He was the son of Jonathan and Mrs. Betty Read Keyes, as will be seen by referring to the list of the elder Jonathan's children on page 149.

V. KEYES, MIRIAM or MERRIAM (808), dau. of Jonathan and Mrs. Betty Read Keyes, m. Dea. Sam. Fletcher of Westford, Mass., and d. there Mar. 1, 1869, wanting a few days of 102 years of age.

V. KEYES, FRANCES GRANT (810), dau. of Jonathan and Mrs. Betty Read Keyes, m., April 7, 1794, Joseph Fletcher, and lived in Westford.

### CHILDREN.

Joseph, Frances G., Walter, Louisa, Charles H., Polly, Nancy, Abijah, Nancy, Jonathan Varnum. Of these children, Frances G. m., in 1815, Gardiner Fletcher.

Here ends the record of the descendants of Joseph Keyes, the son of Solomon of Chelmsford.

II. KEYES, MOSES (10), 3d s. and 8th child of Solomon and Frances, was b. in Chelmsford, where he lived and died. His name is mentioned in various of the old records as having received shares at the various divisions of land, and he was town surveyor in 1705. He m. Mehitable or Mabel ____ about 1693, had six children and d. Jan. 14, 1746.

### CHILDREN.

919. Jane, b. Sept. 24, 1694.
920. Moses, b. Nov. 24, 1695.
921. Ezekiel, b. Mar. 19, 1699.
922. Elizabeth, b. Mar. 14, 1702.
923. Rachel, b. Feb. 8, 1708.
924. Zechariah, b. Feb. 18, 1713.

III. KEYES, MOSES, JR. (920), eldest s. of Moses, m., July 4, 1718, at Concord, Mass., Susanna Stratton of Concord, the ceremony performed by Justin Minot. An old town book of Chelmsford, speaks of "Land laid out to Moses Keyes, Jr., lying westerly from Hart's pond, bounded west by land of Richard Hildreth, and south west, by land that was lately John

Foster's, and on all other sides by land of Moses Keyes, Jr."
He lived in Westford, but we find no record of his death there
or that of his wife.

### CHILDREN.

925. Susanna, b. 1719.
926. Mary, b. 1720.
927. Samuel, b. 1723.
928. David, b. 1724.
929. Hannah, b. 1726.
930. Elizabeth, b. 1728.
931. Ruth, b. Dec. 9, 1729.
932. Daniel, b. Nov. 30, 1731.
933. Tabitha, b. 1738.

IV. KEYES, DAVID (928), 2d s. of Moses, Jr., is perhaps
the David who m. Mary —— and recorded at Westford.

### CHILDREN.

934. Samuel, b. July 31, 1747.
935. Mary, b. June 17, 1749, d. Aug. 17, 1758.
936. John, b. Oct. 6. 1753, d. Aug. 17, 1758.
937. David, b. April 22, 1758, d. Aug. 10, 1758.

Mary, wife of David, d. Aug. 23, 1758. A David
Keyes m. Sarah Bradley of Tyngsboro, in 1792, who may have
been the s. of Moses. He would have been sixty-eight years of
age at the time of his marriage. He removed to Tyngsboro,
and m. after the death of Sarah, the widow of Abraham Little-
hale of Tyngsboro, Mass.

### CHILDREN OF DAVID AND SARAH.

938. Patty, b. 1793.
939. Sarah, b. 1795.
940. Ebenezer, b. 1797.
941. Susanna, b. 1801.

V. KEYES, SAMUEL (934), probably s. of David, m.,
1768, Molly Davis of Acton. Recorded in Westford.

### CHILDREN.

942. Samuel, b. Oct., 1769.
943. John, b. July 4, 1774.

IV. KEYES, DANIEL (932), youngest s. of Moses, Jr., m., Sept. 17, 1754, in Westford, Mass., Abigail, b. 1738, g. dau. of Robert Proctor, who m., 1645, Jane Hildreth of Concord, Mass., where he then lived, and moved to Chelmsford in 1654, where he died in the year 1797. Daniel and Abigail were married by "Rev. Ebenezer Bridge, Pastor," and the marriage recorded in Chelmsford and Westford.

The birth of the two oldest children is recorded in both Chelmsford and Westford, and the birth of the third in Townsend, Mass., after which he settled and remained many years in the town of Washington, N. H. July 25, 1777 he sold one hundred acres of land in Westmoreland, N. H., and just one hundred years ago, April 20. 1778, bought a tract of land in Putney, Vt., thus described in the records of deeds in Putney. "Know all men by these presents, that I, Jonas More of Putney, in the county of Cumberland, in the state of New York, in consideration of the sum of 223 pounds, lawful money of said state, paid to me by Daniel Keyes," &c. This deed conveyed to Daniel, one hundred acres of land "drawn on the right of John White of Charlestown, in the state of Massachusetts Bay, lots numbered 23 and 26, each fifty acre lots, one bounded on the great river," &c., dated April 20, 1778. Daniel did not move his family to Vermont, for some years after this purchase. He is represented as a tall man of fair complexion, while Abigail was small, and the tradition of her brilliant eyes still lingers among her descendants. Daniel had great energy and determination of character, held some town offices, and being a fine penman, was often employed to draw up contracts and deeds for his neighbors and townsmen.

He d. in Putney, April 1, 1814.

Abigail, his wife, d. in Putney, in the winter of 1830, and both rest in the east cemetery.

### CHILDREN.

944. Israel, b. Feb. 1, 1756, in Westford, Mass.

945. Jacob, b. Feb. 4, 1758, in Westford, d. in infancy.

946. Jonas, b. Aug. 31, 1760, in Townsend, Mass.

947. Asa, b. 1762, probably in Washington, N. H.

949. William, b. Nov., 1766.

948. Sally, b. 1770.

950. Abel, b. Sept., 1773.

V. KEYES, ISRAEL (944), eldest s. of Daniel, m., in Washington, N. H., Abigail, b. 1758, dau. of David Lowell, then of Washington, and sister of Dr. Solomon Lowell of Westminster West. He came to Putney with his father, and built, about the year 1802, the two story dwelling, in which some of his descendants lived for four generations. It is beautifully situated, on the brow of a hill, from which sweeps away a wide extent of country, across the Connecticut, and on, to the New Hampshire hills. North of the house, is a rocky elevation, from whose summit may be seen in addition to the above, the Green Mountain Range, stretching from north to south on the west, the Monadnock on the south-east, the Ascutney on the north, and far in the north-east, the shining tops of the White Mountains. There is a lily pond on the domain which was also a skating pond for the "Keyes boys" in winter.

Israel was Deacon in the Cong. church, was an energetic, capable business man, making, even at that early day, a number of journeys, each year, to Boston in the way of business. He was also Captain of a military company, but was generally known as Deacon Keyes. He d. at the homestead, after a short illness, in the Spring of 1810. Abigail, his wife, d. Oct. 7, 1853, and both were buried in the east burying ground at Putney.

### CHILDREN.

951. Abigail, b. May 19, 1780, in Washington, N. H.

952. Daniel, b. Feb. 22, 1782, in Washington, N. H.

953. Israel, b. April 15, 1784, in Washington, N. H.

954. Joel, b. Sept. 10, 1785, in Putney, Vt.

955. Asa, b. May 30, 1787, in Putney.

956. Sally, ) b. Mar. 8, 1789, in Putney.

957. Lucy, ) b. Mar. 8, 1789, in Putney, d. in infancy.

958. James, b. July 28, 1793, in Putney.

VI. KEYES, ABIGAIL (951), eldest child of Dea. Israel, b. on the "dark day," or "New England's black Friday," m. 1st, in Putney, Simon Gilson, and had

## CHILDREN.

Israel, James, Jared, Lucy and Edwin. Lucy m. a Mr. Davis of Peru, Vt., and d. Aug., 1875, leaving many descendants. Edwin m. Elinor Bachelor, and lived first in Andover, Vt., and for some years past in Chester, Vt. They have dau., Ellen and Mary, b. from 1845 to 50. Of these dau., one m. a Mr. Church and lives in Chester, the other m. Dr. Fitch, nephew of E. W. Stoughton of N. Y., now minister to Russia. Res. Meriden, Conn.

Abigail m. 2d, in Putney, Capt. Roswell Parker, one of whose dau. m. Dr. Calvin Jewett, then of Putney, now of St. Johnsbury, Vt., and whose g. dau. m. Dea. Freeman Keyes of Newbury.

Mrs. Parker d. in Chester, in the Winter of 1866, and was buried in East Putney.

VI. KEYES, DANIEL (952), 2d child of Dea. Israel, m., in Putney, Vt., in 1808, Sally Foster, lived for a time in Putney, then removed to Gouverneur, N. Y. where he d. July 2, 1876. He was a pleasant, kind hearted, genial old man, whom to know was to love.

### CHILDREN.

959. Calvin F., b. July 25, 1809, in Putney, Vt.

960. Electa S., b. Aug. 30, 1811, in Putney, Vt.

. 961. Hale Leavitt, b. June 30, 1814, in Putney, Vt.

VII. KEYES, CALVIN F. (959), m., Aug. 16, 1832, in Gouverneur, N. Y., Rebecca R., b. Dec. 26, 1814, in Putney. Calvin d. Sept. 29, 1862, in Gouverneur. Rebecca, his wife, d. Jan. 12, 1879.

### CHILDREN.

962. George F., b. June 10, 1836, d. April 26, 1857, in Gouverneur.

963. Sarah J., b. Dec. 27, 1839, m., Nov. 21, 1861, Alden G. Gifford, now in Chicago, studying medicine. Dau., Ida Emma and Minnie Electa.

VII. KEYES, ELECTA (960), m., Sept. 22, 1835, Dr. Samuel C. Waite of Gouverneur, and d. Mar. 31, 1841. She had three dau., Mary Jane, who m. 1st, Charles Shattuck, 2d, Charles Oaks. Res. Crete, Saline Co., Neb. Also, Sarah R. and Electa R.

VII. KEYES, HALE L. (961), settled in Boston, Mass., where he m., Sept. 19, 1839, Clara A. Woodman. Has been book-keeper at the Old Boston National Bank since May, 1863. Previous to which time held the same office five years at the City Bank, Boston. Res. Newtonville, Mass.

### CHILDREN.

964. George L., b. Aug. 28, 1840, in Boston.

965. Clara Stacy, b. Aug. 27, 1844.

966. Mary E., b. Oct. 13, 1851, m., Oct. 2, 1873, Alfred Schoff, dau., Bertha, b. Oct. 15, 1874.

VIII. KEYES, GEORGE L. (964), m., Jan. 29, 1868, Fanny Woodman.

### CHILDREN.

967. Fred Hale, b. April 16, 1871.

968. Walter Prescott, b. Mar. 29, 1878.

VIII. KEYES, CLARA S. (965), m., Aug. 9, 1866, Royal Mackintosh Pulsifer, one of the proprietors of the Boston Herald. Res. Auburndale, Mass. Two children, George Royal, b. Oct. 3, 1867, Louis Warren, b. Dec. 2, 1869.

VI. KEYES, ISRAEL (953), 3d child of Dea. Israel, was noted among his townsmen for his eccentricities, also for his inventive genius, which in the hands of a more practical man, should have made his name famous. Without a liberal education, he had unusual intelligence and shrewdness, and pettifogged in later years, in Justice Courts. He m., about 1807, Hannah Grout of Westminster, and lived on the homestead in Putney.

## CHILDREN.

969. Alvan, b. 1808.

Hannah, wife of Israel, d. and he m. 2d, Feb. 22, 1814, Mrs. Betsey Elizabeth Lincoln, who was b. Betsey E. Webb, dau. of Calvin and Mary (Porter) Webb of Bellows Falls, Vt., Calvin Webb, Esq., being by the intermarriage of the Webb and Bradford families, the sixth in descent from Gov. Bradford of Plymouth Colony.

970. Rollin Webb, b. Aug. 3, 1818.

971. Calvin Webb, b. Nov. 7, 1823.

Israel Keyes d. in Putney, Nov., 1873.

Mrs. Keyes is still living in Putney at the advanced age of ninety six. By her first husband she had a dau., b. 1808, Mary Porter Lincoln, who m. Noah Edwards.

VII. KEYES, ALVAN (969), m. a Miss Russell and had two

### CHILDREN.

972. Mack R., m. Miss Morse. No children.

973. Mary, m. Mr. Eager of Fayetteville, Vt., d. 1874. No children.

VII. KEYES, ROLLIN W. (970), m., Dec. 9, 1840, Ab'by A. Chandler of Saxtons Village. He fitted for college, with a view to studying a profession, but disliking to enter the ministry in accordance with the wishes of his friends, he became a merchant in Putney, afterwards in 1850, removing to Boston. His family res. in Somerville, Mass. He studied Greek, German and Spanish, had a fine literary taste, for the cultivation of which, he made use of all the facilities which Boston so generously affords, and collected a valuable and well selected library, now in the possession of his daughter. He represented Somerville in the Mass. Legislature one year, and not long before his death became a mason, joining the John Abbott lodge in that place. The death of Col. Rollin W. Keyes occurred April 4, 1859, in Somerville, the funeral taking place under the direction of the masonic lodge of which he was a member, and his remains were taken to Putney for interment. His family removed to Chicago, Ill., after his death, where they still reside.

### CHILDREN.

974. Mary Porter Lincoln, b. Feb. 8, 1843, in Putney, Vt.

975. Charles Rollin, b. June 18, 1846, d. July 15, 1848, in Putney, Vt.

976. Arthur Rollin, b. Dec. 14, 1854, in Somerville, Mass.

977. Henry Chandler, b. Jan. 15, 1857, d. Dec. 10, 1859.

978. Calvin Douglass, b. Sept. 4, 1858, d. May 22, 1862.

VIII. KEYES, MARY P. L. (974), m. July 30, 1861, Henry H. Babcock. They lived for a time in Somerville, Mass., then removed to Chicago, Ill, where he is now engaged in teaching.

### CHILDREN.

Mabel, b. May 20, 1862, in Somerville, Mass.; Rollin Keyes, b. Aug. 30, 1863, d. Dec. 6, 1863; Mary Lovina, b. Mar. 3, 1865, d. Aug. 15, 1865; Bertha, b. Jan. 24, 1867, d. Aug. 9, 1867; Florence, b. June 29, 1869, in Chicago; Helen, b. Feb. 29, 1872; Ethel, b. Aug. 14, 1875.

VIII. KEYES, ARTHUR R. (976), m., Oct. 4, 1876, in Chicago, Kitty Dickinson Ollicer, who was b. in Chicago, Sept. 24, 1855.

### DAUGHTER.

979. Fannie, b. Apr. 1, 1878, in Chicago.

VII. KEYES, CALVIN W. (971), was in trade in Putney, then went west and located in Des Moines, Iowa, where he has been in trade, and where he m. Jan. 12, 1864, Julia B. Davis of Des Moines.

### CHILDREN.

980. Charles Rollin, b. Dec. 24, 1864, at Des Moines.

981. James Davis, b. Oct. 3, 1867, at Des Moines.

VI. KEYES, JOEL (954), 4th child of Dea. Israel, m., Dec. 15, 1812, Mary Parks, b. Nov. 27, 1790. Mary, wife of Joel, d. Sept. 4, 1818.

Joel m. 2d, Mar. 22, 1819, Susan Kittridge, b. Dec. 5, 1795. After living for a time in Putney, Joel removed to Gouverneur, N. Y., where his brother Daniel was located, and in 1851, removed to Illinois, with his s. Royal, and bought a farm in Lee Co. He also lived in Avon and Abingdon. In 1873, he removed to Fornas Co., Neb., where he d., Mar. 22, 1875. Susan, his wife, d. July 15, 1849.

CHILDREN.

982. Lucius Morgan, b. Feb. 22, 1814, in Putney, Vt.
983. Marshall Mortimer, b. Feb. 12, 1816, in Putney, Vt.
984. Roswell Kittridge, b. Aug. 19, 1820, d. Aug. 31, 1820.
985. Royal Proctor, b. Aug. 6, 1821.
986. Ellen, ) b. Nov. 23, 1830, m. Rev. Ethan O. Whitaker
          ( (Bap.), Feb. 3, 1853, d. in Ill., May 26, 1854.
987. Elton, ) b. Nov. 23, 1830, d. May 3, 1832.
988. Stephen Kittridge, b. April 20, 1836.

VII. KEYES, LUCIUS M. (982), m., May 31, 1837, Loretta Holmes in Gouverneur, N. Y. Loretta was b. June 11, 1815. They moved to Illinois soon after their marriage, and lived in Princeton and Dover. About 1848 or 9, they moved to a place on the Prairie, which in time became a farm, not far from Dover, in Berlin township. Like the first houses of all the Prairie farmers, their's was a small one story building, without partition, and the stable was built by setting forked posts in the ground and covering with poles and slough grass, and boarding the sides. There was about a quarter section in the homestead, or one hundred and sixty acres. Lucius and wife were members of the church, which they attended in Dover. The chances for education at that time, were small where Loretta had lived, and so anxious was she to learn, that while living on the Prairie, she studied at home and recited to some teacher in the vicinity. A prairie fire at one time threatened the family, and the descendants relate that after it had spent itself, they went out to view the devastations, and found that the element which had threatened their home and destroyed the grass and the Prairie flowers, had revealed to them instead, innumerable eggs of the Prairie hen, which they prepared for the table, and Prairie rattlesnakes, which were almost as great enemies as the fire. Lucius was treasurer of the "Princeton Precinct Peace Society," in 1848. In 1853, having passed through the first hard years of settling in a new country, he contemplated the building of a new and civilized dwelling and went to the town of Peru, on the Illinois river, to obtain lumber, where he was exposed to the cholera, of which he died, in Princeton, Sept. 2, 1853. Loretta probably accompanied him to Peru, and took the same disease, as she died of cholera in Berlin, Aug. 28, 1853.

### CHILDREN.

989. Joel Parks, b. Feb. 21, 1838, in Princeton, Ill. Res. Mo.

990. Susan Josephine, b. Feb. 3, 1841, m. Henry Smith and res. in Derby, Lucas Co., Iowa. They have four children. Mrs. Smith dec.

991. Isaac Holmes, b. Mar. 21, 1847.

992. Mary Gertrude, b. April 25, 1850, in Berlin township, Bureau Co., Ill. and d. there, Oct. 21, 1850.

993. Ellen Maria, b. Nov. 10, 1851, in Berlin, d. in Princeton, Sept. 16, 1853.


VIII. KEYES, ISAAC HOLMES (991), left an orphan at six years, was passed around among his relatives in the vicinity of Princeton, until he was adopted by a gentleman who gave him a good education, and at twenty-one, he went out into the world to seek his fortune. He set up farming in Iowa, but failed for want of experience, tried clerking, and after many wanderings, arrived in San Francisco. Finding nothing to do there, he took a steamer for Portland, Oregon, from thence went to Salem, where, about two miles in the country, he has made a clearing "in the timber," and with neighbors at half mile distances, is making himself a home.


VII. KEYES, MARSHALL M. (983), moved with his father's family to Lee Co., Ill., where he m., Nov. 24, 1840, Barbara McDonnell. In 1850, he emigrated to Caliornia, and is pleasantly situated on a fine farm, near Calistoga, Napa Co.

### CHILDREN.

994. Hamilton M., b. May 9, 1848, in Ill.
995. Mary A., b. May 13, 1859, in California.

VIII. KEYES, HAMILTON M. (994), m., April 21, 1870, Sarah E. Hall, and res. in Calistoga, Cal.

### CHILDREN.

996. John M., b. Mar. 6, 1873.
997. Charles Hamilton, b. Oct. 26, 1875.

VII. KEYES, ROYAL P. (985), graduated from Union College, Schenectady, studied law and emigrated to Illinois in 1851. He m. Mar. 12, 1848, Lydia T. Austin. No children. They had an adopted son George, who, after the death of Royal, married, and we know nothing further of him. Royal P. Keyes d. Jan. 29, 1874. Lydia, his wife, returned to Gouverneur after his death, and m. Mr. Leavitt.

VII. KEYES, STEPHEN K. (988), was in the Union Army in the late war. Enlisted in 1861, was mustered out Dec., 1865, and m. Mar. 17, 1867, Esther L. Edom, at Avon, Illinois. In the Autumn of 1874, he moved to Medicine Creek, Fornas Co., Neb., where he is County Commissioner, and has two hundred and forty acres of land, seventy-five under cultivation, and a railroad in prospect within two years. He says, "If any friends in Vermont have not a good home, let them come here and get a one hundred and sixty acre homestead, while they can get it cheap, for the government lands are being taken fast."

### CHILDREN.

998. Charles Percy, b. Dec. 30, 1867.
999. Albert Marshall, b. Dec. 7, 1868.
1000. Edwin Randall, b. Jan. 9, 1871.
1001. Ruby Emeline, b. July 4, 1872, d. Aug. 6, 1873.
1002. Ellen Leonora, b. July 11, 1874.

VI. KEYES, ASA (955), 5th child of Dea. Israel, fitted for college at Chesterfield Academy, graduated at Dartmouth, in 1810, and afterward taught the Academy at Chesterfield for two years. For two years he read law with Judge White in Putney,

and one year in Boston, in the office of Ebenezer Rockwood.
He was admitted to the Windham County Bar, at the December term, 1814, and began practice in Putney, as partner of
Judge White. He was Postmaster many years in Putney, Royal Arch Mason and Master of the Golden Rule Lodge there,
removing to Brattleboro in the Autumn of 1833, where he has
since remained. He represented Putney in the Vt. Legislature
in 1826 and 7, and Brattleboro in 1835, was in the State Senate
in 1855 and 1856, being both years on the judiciary committee.
He was Judge of Probate in the Westminster District, also
Register of Probate some years in that District, and after giving up the general practice of law, was Register of Probate in
the District of Marlboro, for fifteen years, resigning in the Autumn of 1878. For nearly thirty-five years he was one of the
Trustees of the Vermont Asylum, and a Trustee of the Vermont Savings Bank, from the commencement to the present.
Jan. 7, 1815, Mr. Keyes married Sarah, dau. of Asa and Sally
(Keep) Britton of Chesterfield, N. H. Of the father of Mrs.
Keyes, the following anecdote is too good to lose. He was a
tall, heavy man, weighing probably two hundred, had accumulated a large property, had held the offices of Sheriff, Justice of
the Peace, Selectman and all the other offices which give respectability and importance in a country town, insomuch that it excited the animosity of some of his ambitious but less fortunate
neighbors. Now with energy, intelligence and shrewdness, he
had a credulousness, which led him often to misplace his confidence, and at two separate times, to take as partners, young,
inexperienced and untried men, who each decamped, taking with
him much spoil. On one of these occasions, when the village
was ringing with the news of the gutted store and money box,
a party of gamins, instigated by the enemy, set the church bell
also ringing, and above the noise and confusion of the crowd,
which the sound of the bell at that unusual hour, had collected,
was heard the cry, ever louder and louder, "Great Britton
has fallen, Great Britton has fallen."

### CHILDREN.

1003. Charles Douglas, b. Oct. 31, 1815, in Putney, and d.
there June 28, 1816.

1004. Laura Britton, b. Aug. 22, 1817, in Putney.
1005. Eliza Green, b. June 13, 1819, in Putney.
1006. George Britton, b. Jan. 14, 1821.
1007. Ellen Douglas, b. Nov. 1, 1823.

VII. KEYES, LAURA B. (1004), m. in Brattleboro, Apr. 29, 1840, Judge Royal Tyler, son of the late Chief Justice Royal and Elizabeth (Palmer) Tyler. He is one of a large scholarly and literary family. On his mothers side, Mrs. Horace Mann, Mrs. Nathaniel Hawthorne and Mrs. Geo. B. Loring were his cousins, also Elizabeth Peabody and the late George P. Putnam, publisher, N. Y., and four of his brothers are and were clergymen. The late Gen. John Tyler of Boston, was also a brother. Judge Tyler fitted for college at Exeter Academy. He graduated at Cambridge, and studied at the Cambridge law school, then opened a law office in Brattleboro, where he has since remained. He was Register of Probate under Judge Whitney, and has for many years been Judge of Probate and County Clerk. Res. Brattleboro.

#### CHILDREN.

1008. Gertrude E. b. May 17, 1841, in Brattleboro, m. Dec. 29, 1863. Lieut. Comm. Allan D. Brown, U. S. N. Two children, Helen, b. in Brattleboro, Oct. 14, 1864, Ethel, b. Apr. 1, 1870, at Annapolis, Md.

Mrs. Gertrude E. Brown, d. at Annapolis, Sept. 18, 1877.

1009. Helen, b. June 28, 1846, d. Sept. 1, 1850, in Brattleboro.

1010. Edith, b. Sept. 1, 1851, in Brattleboro, m. Sept. 5, 1877. Geo. Willard, son of Rev. Geo. L. Platt, of Tivoli, N. Y. dau. Gertrude, b. Nov. 23, 1878, in Brattleboro. Res. Greenfield, Mass.

VII. KEYES GEORGE B. (1006), was admitted to the Windham County Bar, about 1845, m. Jan. 4, 1847, in Brattleboro, Julia M. Thomas, b. in Brattleboro, Feb. 21, 1826, and in the winter of 1849, sailed from Boston, in the ship Pharsalia, for a voyage around cape Horn, arriving in San Francisco late the following summer. Thence he proceeded up the Tuolumne with a prospecting party, and passed his first years of California life in Jacksonville; moved to Sonora in 1864, and after some years, to Wilmington, in Southern California. The following, is from an article in the Union (Sonora) Democrat, written after his death.

"Judge Keyes was one of the earliest settlers in Tuolumne, having arrived in the county in 1849. He mined on the Tuolumne river during the famous era, known as the "fall of '49, and the spring of '50," forsaking the sluice box and wingdam during '51 or '52, for the purpose of conducting a hotel in Jacksonville. While living in the latter place, he was elected County Assessor, and filled the office with thorough ability, and during the war was elected County Judge, serving the people faithfully, ably and conscientiously. About 1870, he left Tuolumne and made his home in the Orange groves of Los Angeles, where he found innumerable friends to smooth the pathway to the grave. As a man, Judge Keyes was respected by his acquaintances and loved by his friends; a type of the early Californian, and an outgrowth of the better elements of that early civilization on this coast, upon which our present peculiarly constituted society rests. He was quiet in his demeanor, and whole-souled in his friendships, drawing all that was noble or manly in humanity towards him, as he came in contact with it. Another Argonaut has 'gone home,' may his search for the golden fleece on the unknown shores of the El Dorado of eternity, be crowned with the success he deserves." '

George B. Keyes, d. of paralysis in Wilmington, Cal., May 22, 1877. Julia, his wife, d. there, Jan. 7, 1878. They had one

SON.

1011. Charles G., b. Jan. 31, 1848. He m. in Los Angeles, Cal., Jan. 28, 1876, Mrs. Annis Cole (maiden name Taylor), b. in 1852. They have one

SON.

1012. Asa, b. Aug. 9, 1877, in Wilmington, Cal.

VII. KEYES, ELLEN D. (1007), m., April 22, 1840, in Brattleboro, Frederic N. Palmer, M. D. He studied medicine,

practiced in Gardiner, Me., and in Newton, Mass., and removed
to Boston about 1870, where he now is.

Mrs. Ellen D. Palmer d. in W. Newton, Mass., July 24, 1861.

1013. Florence, b. May 17, 1841, d. 1843, in Belfast, Me.

1014. Sarah Keyes, b. Jan. 5, 1845.

1015. Charles Douglas, b. Aug. 15, 1847, m. in Jefferson, Tex.,
Sept. 28, 1871, Ida Purcell of New Orleans, La. Children,
Virgie Douglas, dec.; Fred; Charles Douglas, b. July 29, 1878;
C. D. Palmer, res. in Sherman, Tex.

1016. Agnes Wales, b. April 2, 1849, m., June 16, 1869,
James Valentine of Framingham, Mass. Cashier of a bank.
Children, Fred, b. April 24, 1870; Dick, b. Feb. 9, 1870.

VI. KEYES, SALLY (956), 6th child of Dea. Israel, m. 1st,
about the year 1814, Dana Miller, b. in Dummerston, Vt. He
was a lawyer, practiced in Williamstown, Vt., then in Bellows
Falls, and about 1829, moved to Mt. Vernon, Knox Co., Ohio,
where in a few years he died. After his death, Mrs. Miller m.
2d, Rev. Mr. Wordsworth, and d. many years ago.

Delia, b. 1814, m., in Mt. Vernon, Rev. Mr. Mattison about
1837, and d. about 1862, leaving four children; Sally Ann, m.
Chancy Lee, in Mt. Vernon, where he was in business, about
1836, five children, four of whom dec.; Charles, b. about 1821,
studied law at Mt. Vernon, and had been in the practice about
one year, when he went to Mexico, an officer in the Mexican
war, and d. there; Janette, m. about 1844, William T. Curtis,
res. in Mt. Vernon; James was in business in Mt. Vernon about
that time.

VI. KEYES, JAMES (958), youngest child of Dea. Israel,
was a prominent and well known business man of Putney, and
for many years identified with its progress and business propects;
a man of sound judgement, strong sense and great intelligence;
a help and adviser to the young business men of the place.
He was merchant, postmaster and manufacturer, a Royal Arch

Mason and for many years, Master of the Golden Rule Lodge in Putney. He m., in Putney, Sept. 22, 1832, Laura, dau. of Asa and Sally (Negus) Houghton. Mrs. Keyes was neice of Mrs. Gen. Mann, formerly of Brattleboro West, and cousin of the late Mrs. Mary Marcy, wife of Gen. Marcy, U. S. A. The children of James and Laura Keyes, b. some years after their marriage, were Caroline and Catharine, the latter d. in infancy.

James Keyes d. in Putney, Sept. 14, 1862, and was buried with masonic honors.

V. KEYES, JONAS (946), 3d s. of Daniel, m., Mar. 3, 1784, in Westford, Mass., Bridget Reed, who was b. July 14, 1762. They were m. by Noah Sabin. Dea. Jonas lived for a time in Athens, Vt., then removed to Putney, where he d. Sept. 20, 1840. His wife d. Dec. 20, 1839.

### CHILDREN.

1017. Raymond, b. Dec. 15, 1784.

1018. Polly, b. Aug. 23, 1786, m. Elisha Flint of Brookline, Vt., d. Feb. 1, 1861.

1019. Sally, b. May 18, 1788, m. 1st, Silas Lamb, m. 2d, Ephraim Morse.

1020. Jonas, Jr., b. Nov. 7, 1790, m. Catherine Foster in Putney and d. Mar. 17, 1831.

1021. Lucy, b. Aug. 21, 1793, m. David Reed, Boston.

1022. Abigail, b. June 11, 1801, d. Mar. 17, 1819.

1023. Nancy, b. May 13, 1803, m. L. D. Thwing.

1024. John, b. Aug. 21, 1806.

VI. KEYES, RAYMOND (1017), eldest s. of Dea. Jonas, m., Sept. 4, 1810, Mary Dickinson of Westminster, Vt., who was b. Aug. 30, 1785. Res. Putney, Vt.

Raymond d. in Putney, Dec. 24, 1852.

Mary, his wife, d. Mar. 13, 1844.

### CHILDREN.

1025. Phinehas D., b. May 16, 1812.

1026. Harvey R., b. July 24, 1813.

1027. Mary, b. June 3, 1818, m. Ahira K. Knapp, Northfield, Vt.

1028. Huldah, b. Sept. 15, 1820, m. 1st, Horace Goodrich, 2d, William G. Stearns of Westminster, Vt.

1029. Nancy, b. May 22, 1822.

1030. Electa, b. May 10, 1824.

VII. KEYES, PHINEHAS D. (1025), s. of Raymond, m., April 8, 1834, Amanda M. Burrows, b. July 22, 1814. Res. Westminster, Vt.

### CHILDREN.

1031. Melisa A., b. Jan. 23, 1835, m., Dec. 3, 1856, Dan P. Kimball. Two children, Carrie M. and Frank E.

1032. Laura A., b. Mar. 17, 1843, m., Dec. 10, 1861, Henry M. Parker. They had two children, Flora A. and Abbie M. Laura A. d. Dec. 4, 1869.

Amanda, wife of Phinehas, d. Nov. 21, 1868, and he m. 2d, Frances L. Ellsworth. He d. in Westminster, Nov. 23, 1870.

VII. KEYES, HARVEY R. (1026), m., Oct. 4, 1836, Emmeline Keyes, who d. June 12, 1853. He m. 2d, Aug. 12, 1855, Mrs. Laura U. Tilson, who d. April 1, 1847, he m. 3d, 1878, Mrs. Caroline M. Goodno. Farmer in Northfield, Vt.

### DAUGHTER OF HARVEY AND EMMELINE.

1033. Jane, b. April 9, 1841, m. Newell Byam. Res. Bethel, Vt.

VII. KEYES, NANCY (1029), m., April 16, 1843, Gilbert Denison Stedman, b. in Leyden, Mass., Jan. 16, 1818. Res. Williamsville, Vt. Children, Frederic Keyes, b. in Putney. Oct. 9, 1844, d. Aug. 17, 1847, in Putney; Charlie Keyes, b. Dec. 17, 1851; Nella Electa, b. Dec. 31, 1853; Ida Melisa, b. Dec. 9, 1855; Minnie Maria, b. in Newfane, Aug. 29, 1866.

VII. KEYES, ELECTA (1030), m., Mar. 31, 1841, Ariel Kendrick Fletcher, who d. Mar. 18, 1843. Dau., Ella S., b.

April 19, 1843. Electa m. 2d, April 16, 1845, Nelson Morse, b. in Newfane, Aug. 22, 1814. Dau., Stella Maria, b. Mar. 1, 1846 and d. Feb. 6, 1876. Res. Williamsville, Vt.

VI. KEYES, JOHN (1024), youngest s. of Dea. Jonas, m., Nov. 2, 1829, Mary Ann Morse, who was b. Nov. 12, 1810, now dec. John Keyes d. in Putney, in the Summer of 1878.

### CHILDREN.

1034. Charlotte, b. July 20, 1832, d. Oct. 12, 1841.
1035. David R., b. Sept. 12, 1835, d. Oct. 23, 1863.

V. KEYES, ASA (947), 4th s. of Daniel, moved to Troy, and m. Phebe Hatch.

### CHILDREN.

1036. William, went west when about twenty-five and dec.
1037. Payne, d. at Swanton Falls, Vt., when about thirty.
1038. Sally Ann, m., in 1820, Ira Perry and moved to western New York. Three children.
1039. Eveline, b. 1799, in Troy, N. Y., m., in Troy, Welcome Whittaker, about 1827. Four children, all dec. Mrs. Whittaker d. in Troy, in 1849.
1040. Hiram, d. at four years of age.

In 1806, Asa returned to Putney, where Phebe d. the succeeding year, and he m. 2d, in 1809, Hannah Taylor, who was b. 1778, in Stoddard, N. H. (Newport), and they had four children.

1041. Phebe H., b. 1810.
1042. Hiram Proctor, b. 1812, m., 1836, Mary Russell of Dublin, N. H. Hiram P. d. 1840, and his wife d. 1878, in Putney. Two dau., Ellen, b. 1837; Mary, b. 1840.
1043. Philemon D., b. 1814, m., 1836, Minerva Radway of Putney.
1044. Asa L., b. 1819, d. 1822.

VI. KEYES, PHEBE (1041), m., in 1829, Emery Mason of Newfane, Vt., where he was b. 1803. They had four

### CHILDREN.

Hannah E., b. 1830, m. Humphrey Atherton, 1854. Res. Brattleboro, Vt. Eveline Keyes, b. 1832, m. Alonzo F. Whitney, 1855. Res. Brattleboro, Vt. Phebe, b. 1844, m., 1868, Clinton Cooledge. Res. Detroit, Mich. Ada, b. 1849.

V. KEYES, WILLIAM (949), 5th child of Daniel, m. 1789, in Putney, Vt., Betsey Nichols. They lived for a time in Putney, then removed to Northfield, Vt., where William d. Dec. 20, 1849.

Mrs. Betsey Keyes d. Sept. 7, 1859.

### CHILDREN.

1045. Polly, b. 1791, in Putney, d. 1798.

1046. Jacob, b. 1793, in Putney, d. there, 1876, m. Catharine, widow of Jonas Keyes, in Putney, had dau., Elizabeth, who m. Ebenezer Lovell. Res. Corinth, Vt.

1047. William b. 1796, in Putney.

1048. Lucy. b. June, 1798.

1049. Sewall, b. 1800.

1050. Eliza, b. 1803, in Northfield, m., 1823, John Campbell, and d. They had ten children, of whom, one son, George, is now living in Brandon, Vt.

1051. Abel, b. 1805, d. 1807.

1052. Sally, b. 1807.

1053. Emmeline, b. 1811, m. Oct. 4, 1836, Harvey R. Keyes, s. of Raymond Keyes of Putney. Res. Northfield.

VI. KEYES, WILLIAM, JR. (1047), m , 1820, Cynthia Shipman. He d. West, 1868.

### CHILDREN.

1054. Harriet, b. 1821, m. Charles Reed. Two children.

1055. Edward, b. 1823, d. 1828.

1056. Sophia, b. 1825, m. John Baxter, and d. 1864. She had dau., Carrie, now living in Lowell, Mass.

1057. Edwin, b. 1827, d. 1842.

1058. Carrie, b. 1832, m. John Baxter, d. 1866, dau. Minnie, b. 1862.

VI. KEYES, LUCY (1048), m., Dec. 31, 1818, Henry Knapp, who d. Sept. 7, 1859. Lucy is now living in Northfield, and has children as follows. Ahira K. Knapp, b. Sept. 1, 1819; Sophia, b. Dec. 12, 1820; Henry G., b. Jan. 11, 1827, d. in rebel prison in Florence, Al., in 1864; Abel K. b. Mar. 9, 1832. Of these children of Lucy, Ahira m., Feb., 1845, Mary, dau. of Raymond Keyes of Putney. Res. Northfield. dau., Elizabeth; Sophia, m. Sam. Richmond, June 16, 1842, lived in Northfield, and had four children; Abel m., Aug. 21, 1857, Augusta B. Goodrich, and had three children.

VI. KEYES, SEWALL (1049), m., 1830, Nancy Granger.

### CHILDREN.

1059. Sarah Ann, b. 1831, m. —— Cottrill, d. about 1860.

1060. Elizabeth, b. 1833, m. Eben Dodge, about 1854. Res. St. Pauls, Minn. Ten children.

1061. Benjamin, b. 1837, dec.

1062. Jonathan.

The wife of Sewall, dec. and he m. again and had two children.

1063. Julons, m. No children.

1064. Willis.

VII. JONATHAN (1062), s. of Sewall, m., Oct. 10, 1865, Anna Hatch. Res. Owatonna, Mich.

### CHILDREN.

1065. Blanche, b. April 18, 1867.

1066. Frank E., b. April 25, 1869.

1067. Lulu E., b. June 20, 1870.

1068. Willis S., b. Oct. 7, 1873.

1069. Jenievieve, b. Sept. 13, 1876.

VI. KEYES, SALLY (1052), dau. of William, m., about 1827, Elijah Rice, who d. 1874.

### CHILDREN.

Charles, b. 1829, m. Res. Penn; Betsey, b. 1831, dec.; Olivia, b. 1833, m. Mr. Darling, res. Iowa, two children; Elizabeth, b.

1835, m. Mr. Bugbee, res. Mo.; William, b. 1837, m. Miss Chald-fuld, res. Roxbury, Vt.   Two children.

V. KEYES, SALLY (948), only dau. of Daniel, m., 1789, Jacob, b. April 7, 1762, s. of Moses Lowell of Newburyport, Mass., who was brother of David Lowell, page 110.   Jacob came from Newburyport to Putney, settled there on his farm, and d. Aug., 1819.   Sally, his wife, d. in Putney, in 1840.

### CHILDREN.

Elizabeth, b. Feb., 1790, d. Jan., 1812; Charles, b. Jan., 1792, dec.; James, b. Mar. 10, 1794, dec.; Abigail, b. 1810, d. June, 1859; Lucinda, b. Feb. 27, 1798, d. June, 1875; Sally, now living in Putney, b. June 9, 1800, m. Siebra White; Mary, b. Mar., 1802, d. Nov., 1819; Jacob, b. Mar., 1804; George, b. May 3, 1806, d. Mar., 1869; Daniel, b. Sept., 1808, d. Sept., 1829; Lucy, b. July 17, 1810; Isaac, b. Jan. 10, 1812, d. July, 1812; Nancy, b. April 9, 1814, now living in Putney.

V. KEYES, ABEL (950), youngest s. of Daniel, while pro-specting for a place in which to locate, and make a home, came to Northfield, Vt., in 1790, and decided to remain there on ac-count of its water privileges.   He m., 1793, in Putney, Mrs. Esther Nichols, sister of Capt. Benjamin Smith of that place, and in 1796, moved his family to Northfield.   He was Select-man, Lister and Justice of the Peace there, also represented the town in the Legislature two years.   The history of Northfield says, "Capt. Keyes was in many respects a most remarkable man.   Having robust health, ceaseless activity and untiring en-ergy, he could do every thing but persevere and wait.   He had a restless temperament which kept him ever on the move, and with strong religious convictions, enterprise and activity, his suc-cess in life was limited only by his habit of leaving to others, the pleasant task of reaping the reward of his labors."   In 1839, he moved to Illinois, and was Post Master in Lake Zurich in that State, one year, then moved to Lake Mills, Wis., where he d., Sept. 26, 1843, according to his grandson, Elisha W. Keyes, aged 70.   The history of Northfield makes his death occur 1848. Mrs. Esther Keyes d. in Northfield in 1831.

### CHILDREN.

1070. Joseph, b. Nov. 20, 1794, in Putney.

1071. Abigail Proctor, b. Aug. 11, 1796.

VI. KEYES, JOSEPH (1070), m. 1st, in 1815, Zeruiah Eggleston, who dec., and he m. 2d, Jan. 18, 1821, Olive Williams, b. in Chelsea, Vt., July 16, 1800.

### CHILDREN.

1072. Simon Smith, b. 1817, in Northfield, Vt.

1073. Cynthia, b. 1819.

1074. Abel, b. Mar. 25, 1822, in Northfield, Vt.

1075. Catherine W., b. Oct. 13, 1825, m. Geo. Hyer, and d. 1862, in Madison, Wis.

1076. Elisha W., b. Jan. 23, 1828, in Northfield, Vt.

1077. Oliver A., b. April 18, 1831, in Northfield.

1078. Emily, b. July 22, 1843, at Lake Mills, Wis., m. H. D. Fisher. Res. Manasha, Wis.

Capt. Joseph Keyes, d. at Manasha, Wis., Sept. 17, 1874.

Mrs. Olive Keyes d. at Menasha, Wis., Feb. 18, 1878.

We extract the following from an article which appeared in the Madison, Wis., Journal, soon after the death of Capt. Joseph Keyes.

"In the Spring of 1836, Mr. Keyes, with a powerful constitution and an indomitable energy, struck out to seek his fortune in a new country, and landed at Milwaukee in June of that year. Wisconsin was then an inviting field for men of his type. It needed intelligent, enterprising, hard working men, to develop its immense resources. Mr. Keyes being one of that class, met a cordial welcome from the few bold spirits who had preceeded him, and found an ample scope of country in which to operate. During the Autumn of 1836, he spent some time at Menomonee, north of Green Bay. At this place, he dressed the lumber for a house, which he brought to Milwaukee on a vessel in December, and erected into a dwelling in that city, which still stands as a memento of his first operations in the territory.

The family of Mr. Keyes followed him to the West in 1837, arriving in Milwaukee in June of· that year. In the fall of

1837, with his family, he removed to Lake Mills, being the first white settler of that town. He proceeded at once to the erection of a grist mill and a saw mill, that proved of vast advantage to the settlement of a new country; and very soon laid out the village of Lake Mills, being its original founder. Here, in accordance with his public spirit and liberality, he erected the first school house in the town, and employed the first teacher, being a Miss Catlin of Cottage Grove, in this county, all with his individual means. Such an act, of itself is a proud monument to his name and fame.

A short time after this, Mr. Keyes erected a saw mill at a point known as Keyesville, a short distance north of Cambridge; and not satisfied with this, with his sons Simon and Abel, he put up a superior grist and saw mill at Cambridge in this county, in 1847-8.

This was the starting point of that village. In 1850, he removed to Menasha, erected one of the first saw mills there and afterward lived for a time in this city (Madison.)

Some fifteen years ago, Mr. Keyes removed from this city to Menasha, since which time, with the exception of a brief period, he was Register of the Land Office, he has lived in quiet retirement, such as was well suited to the closing years of one whose energy had been so actively exercised in developing the resources of the State. Few men have done more zealous work in this direction; and it was a source of great enjoyment to him to have lived to witness the thinly populated territory he first entered, develop into one of the most prosperous States in the Union, with its population of 1,200,000.

We have thus followed Mr. Keyes through the years of his active life, and a mere reference to his numerous works, prove that he was no common man. Being open-handed, generous to a fault, always ready to aid with his means every good cause, he executed an immense amount of labor, and made several fortunes; but in the end, had saved but little of the results of his labors to himself. The great benefits of his work had been used for the good of others. But he had the consolation of knowing that he had done the new State of his adoption, a good service, and had been the pioneer in many valuable improvements."

VII. KEYES, SIMON S. (1072), m. Nov. 14, 1838, Marcia M. Royce, b. in Claremont, N. H., 1820.

### CHILDREN.

1079. Charles Abel, b. 1839, in Northfield, Vt. Res. Oshkosh, Wis., is m.

### SON.

1080.　　　Frank, b. 1872.

1081. Eliza, b. 1841, in Northfield, m. L. Joslin. Res. Denver, Col.

1082. Jennie, b. 1846, in Lake Mills, Wis., m. A. H. Porter. Three children.

1083. Norman D., b. 1849. Res. Iowa. Unm.

1084. Kittie, b. 1852, m. Asahel Newton. Two children. Res. Denver, Col.


VII. KEYES, ABEL (1074), m. May 1, 1844, at Lake Mills, Wis., Mary E. Cutler, b. May 26, 1827, at Darien, N. Y. He res. in Menasha, and owning land himself on which a fine mineral deposit has been lately discovered, is a dealer in "Pine, Farming and Mineral Lands." Res. Menasha, Wis.

### CHILDREN.

1085. George H., b. April 13, 1845, at Lake Mills, Wis.

1086. Edward E., b. Dec. 22, 1846, at Lake Mills.

1087. Frank A., b. Nov. 15, 1848, at Cambridge, Wis., m. Dec. 20, 1877, in Menasha, Alice Brown, b. in Clayton, Wis.

1088. Frederic P., b. Jan. 28, 1851, at Menasha.

1089. William, b. Feb. 29, 1856, at Stockbridge, d. Sept. 18, 1857, at Menasha.

1090. Carrie, b. May 18, 1861, at Menasha, d. there April 14, 1863.

Mrs. Mary E. Keyes d. in Menasha, Jan. 2, 1864. Abel Keyes m. 2d, Oct. 12, 1864, at Madison, Wis., Amelia E. Saunders, b. at Norwalk, Conn. Jan. 3, 1828, dau.

1091. Mamie A., b. May 13, 1868, at Menasha, and d. there Aug. 3, 1869.

Mrs. Amelia E. Keyes d. in Menasha, May 1, 1877.

VIII. KEYES, GEORGE H. (1085), m. Mar. 24, 1869, in Menasha, Wis., Emma M. Thatcher, b. Feb. 22, 1847, in South Royalton, Vt.

### CHILDREN.

1092. Mary A., b. Oct. 10, 1870, in Menasha.
1093. Abel, b. Sept. 22, 1874.
1094. Norman, b. Nov. 4, 1875.
1095. George H. Jr., b. May 10, 1878.

VIII. KEYES, EDWARD E. (1086), m. Oct. 12, 1871, in Cuba, N. Y., Mary E. Woodruff, b. in East Rushford, N. Y., d. Aug. 31, 1876, in Menasha.

### CHILDREN.

1096. Walter Woodruff, b. Jan. 11, 1875, in Menasha.
1097. Jessie, b. Aug. 8, 1876, d. Aug. 17, 1876.

VIII. KEYES, FRED P. (1088), m. July 6, 1871, at Cuba, N. Y., Amelia S. Woodruff, b. Sept. 25, 1850, at East Rushford, N. Y.

### CHILDREN.

1098. Florence Augusta, b. July 26, 1873, d. Mar. 24, 1875, at Menasha.
1099. Mabel Flora, b. Jan. 28, 1876, at Menasha.
1100. Clarence Edward, b. Aug. 13, 1878, at Menasha.

VII. KEYES, ELISHA W. (1076), m. May 13, 1854, Caroline Stevens, who d. July 1, 1865. He m. 2d, Dec. 4, 1866, Louise Shales.

### CHILDREN.

1101. Joseph S., b. Dec. 24, 1854, in Madison, Wis.
1102. Elisha W. Jr., b. July 6, 1858, in Madison, Wis.
1103. Katie, b. Dec. 15, 1860, in Madison, Wis.
1104. Carrie, b. June 1, 1865, d. Aug. 25, 1865, in Madison.
1105. Louis R., b. June 9, 1868, in Madison.

Col. E. W. Keyes left Northfield with his father's family in 1837, and removed with them to Wisconsin. "In early life he exhibited those traits of character which have since made him a man of marked influence in the Badger State.

At school he was first in his classes, in sports and games; following in the wake of his father and grandfather, he led the van." Entering upon the study of law while quite young, he was admitted to the Bar in Madison, at the age of twenty-three, and soon acquired an extensive and lucrative practice; present firm, Keyes and Chynoweth, Madison, Wis. In 1861 he was appointed Postmaster of Madison, which office he has held to the present time. He was Mayor of Madison in 1865 and 1866, "was States Attorney for Dane Co., two years, is now one of the Regents of the State University at Madison, and was Chairman of the State Central Committee until President Hayes' Order No. 1, forbade officers in the civil service of the government holding such an office as that of chairman of a party committee," when he resigned. Says a Wisconsin paper: "There are very few persons in Wisconsin who have not heard of Hon. E. W. Keyes, popularly known as "Boss Keyes," praised by the Republicans, and abused by the Democrats, because of his untiring energy, displayed as chairman of the "State Central Committee." He is now in the prime of life, and vigor of manhood, has great force of character; for many years has been the acknowledged head of the Republican party, and has shown himself a competent, skillful and successful leader, having many times with unfaltering step, with unerring Judgment, and with matchless generalship led the party to victory, and has well earned the title, the "Bismark of western politics." He is spoken of as an able lawyer and an entertaining, forcible and convincing speaker. He was candidate for Congress in 1878, defeated by Matt H. Carpenter.

VII. KEYES, OLIVER A. (1077), m. Dec. 29, 1853, in Menasha, Sarah M. Crampton, b. in Bergen, N. Y., June 6, 1833. Res. Menasha, Wis.     CHILDREN.

1106. Ralph C., b. Feb. 12, 1855, in Menasha, d. there Sept. 9, 1858.

1107. Arthur C., b. May 21, 1860, in Menasha.

1108. Oliver A. Jr., b. Mar. 17, 1864, in Menasha.

VI. KEYES, ABIGAIL P. (1071), only dau. of Abel and Esther, m. Nov. 28, 1813, Ariel Egerton, of Northfield, Vt. Res. Quechee, Vt., where Ariel d. Sept. 20, 1859.

Mrs. Egerton now res. with her s. in Ironton, O.

### CHILDREN.

1109. Almira Ednah, b. Sept. 2, 1814, m. Wm. D. Bragg, has four children and six grand children. Res. Lake Mills, Wis.

1110. Laura Esther, b. Nov. 3, 1816, m. Henry Goddard, has six children, two grand children. Res. Franklin, O.

1111. Olive Smith, b. 1818, m. E. M. Brayton, left dau. Olive, who m. Wm. Swayne, of the Milwaukee News. Res. Milwaukee.

1112. Cynthia Maria, b. Jan. 2, 1821, m. Rev. Ambrose Smith, settled over the Cong. church at Northfield, afterward at Boscawen, N. H., where he d. 186—. They had three children. Frank E., b. 1851; Lyndon A., b. 1853, now in the junior class, at Dartmouth, and Justin Harvey, b. in Boscawen, 1857, graduated at Dartmouth, 1877, at the head of his class, the only graduate who has ranked perfect, since Rufus Choate, and the fourth of that rank since the organization of the college.

1113. Abby Sophia, b. Apr. 14, 1823, m. Geo. C. Aiken, d. at Norwich, Vt., Aug. 29, 1877, left one child.

1114. Charles Bertie, b. Mar. 6, 1825, fitted for college at Thetford Academy, Vt., entered Dartmouth 1849, compelled by ill health to relinquish study after one year. Studied medicine, took the degree of M. D., at Berkshire College, Mass. in 1852, and removed to Ironton, O. Judge of Prob., Lawrence Co. O. in 1859, which office he held by subsequent election to 1871, when he again returned to the practice of his profession in Ironton, where he now lives. He m. Emmeline Tournay, in Ironton, four chil.

11—. John Starkweather, b. Jan. 10, 1826, removed to Wis., graduated at a medical college in Wis., d. in 1852.

1115. Joseph K., b. Oct. 20, 1828, m. Dec. 25, 1856, Sarah F. Tyler, of Claremont, N. H. He was Postmaster of Quechee, Vt., from 1853 to 1861, Justice of the Peace six years, Town Treasurer two years, and Town Agent in Norwich, Vt., from 1865 to 1875. Is a trader in Northfield, Vt. Two children, Edith and Fred.

III. KEYES, EZEKIEL (921), 3d child of Moses, Sen., lived in Chelmsford, Mass., and m. Abigail ——. He d. 1742, death recorded in Chelmsford.

### CHILDREN.

1116. Ephraim, b. Aug. 14, 1727.

1117. Abigail, b. June 8, 1731.

1118. Jonas, birth not recorded in Chelmsford. He m. Elizabeth Townsend, 1756, in Billerica, Mass.

1119. Abner, b. 1738.

There was also a dau. Sarah, b. June 1, 1724.

IV. KEYES, EPHRAIM (1116), eldest s. of Ezekiel, m. in Billerica, Mass. (marriage recorded there), July 11, 1751, Rebecca Townsend. He is said to have lived in Dunstable, then moved to Plymouth, N. H., with his brother Jonas, so early that there were no roads beyond Concord, and they had only spotted trees to guide them, while they were obliged to carry their grist on their backs fifty miles to mill. He d. in Plymouth about 1802.

### CHILDREN.

Born in Plymouth, N. H.

1120. Ezekiel, b. Aug. 24, 1752.

1121. Ephraim, b. Dec. 11, 1754.

1122. Ebenezer, b. Nov. 18, 1755.

1123. Samuel, who had two children. Charles, present res. unknown, and a daughter who m. John Dearborn.

1124. Sally, d. in Rumney.

1125. Stephen, b. Jan. 24, 1760. Probably unm.

1126. Rebecca, b. May 29, 1762.

V. KEYES, EZEKIEL (1120), eldest s. of Ephraim, m. Mariam Rowell or Rowley, lived in Orford, N. H., for a time, then returned to Plymouth, where he died about 1846. Mariam d. about 1814. He m. 2d. a widow by the name of McColester, who survived him.

### CHILDREN.

1127. Samuel, b. May 29, 1780, d. Oct. 13, 1844.

1128. Jonas, not traced.

1129. Jesse, taxed in Orford, N. H., 1806 and 1807. m. Sarah George, June 18, 1807, in Strafford, Vt.

1130. Jonathan, not traced.

1131. Laban, b. 1796.

There were four dau., Elizabeth, Deborah, Sybil and Anna.

VI. KEYES, SAMUEL (1127), m. June 27, 1805, in Orford, N. H., Betsey Finney, b. Dec. 6, 1784, d. May 1, 1868.

CHILDREN.

Born in Orford, N. H.

1132. Ebenezer S., b. July 21, 1806, m. about 1834 a Miss Plummer, of Newbury, Mass., had two s. and dec. Res. in Boxford, Mass.

CHILDREN.

1133.      William, m. Harriet Spiller, of Boxford, Res. Haverhill, Mass.

1134.      Moody, unm. Res. Georgetown.

1135. Eliezer F., b. June 9, 1808, m. Miss Plummer, and dec.

1136. Samuel T., b. Mar. 15, 1810, d. June, 1853, in Kingston, N. H., unm.

1137. Elvira, b. Aug. 29, 1812, m. Feb. 19, 1834, Pierpoint Edwards, of Landaff, N. H. Has a s. in Minn., and two dau. m., of whom one has dec. Mrs. Edwards, res. in Neenah, Wis.

11—. Mariam, b. Jan. 6, 1814, dec.

1138. Benjamin F., b. May 27, 1817, m. Lois Woodman, res. in Salisbury, N. H.

CHILDREN.

1139.      Bessie A., b. Aug. 24, 1846.

1140.      Mary D., b. Sept. 18, 1847.

1141. Laban, b. Oct. 30, 1820, unm. Res. Georgetown.

1142. Deborah, b. June 23, 1821, d. in Orford, Aug. 1838.

1143. Hartwell C., b. May 6, 1824, m. Elizabeth J. Hall.

1144. Eliza Jane, b. June 19, 1827.

VI. KYES, LABAN (1131), 5th s. of Ezekiel, left home when he was about 16, went into the U. S. army, and never returned to N. H. After leaving the army he went to the state of Penn., then to Ohio where he was married to Joan

Condion, and they removed to Monroe, Mich. They afterward removed to White Pigeon Prairie, Mich., and settled among the Indians, there being one white family within 100 miles. From White Pigeon they moved to the place where Kalamazoo, Mich. now stands, and there were no white people there. In July, 1837, they moved to Washington, Tazewell Co., Ill., where Laban Keyes d. Aug. 7, 1873. Joan, his wife, d. 1849.

### CHILDREN.

1145. David, b. Feb. 13, 1820.

1146. John.

1147. Mary Jane.

1148. James, b. Aug. 12, 1827, m. Martha S. Mais, chil. Edgar G., Cornelia L., John H.

1149. Angeline, b. Feb. 13, 1829, m. J. N. Scott, had five chil. Two sons, Charles and John S., res. in Shelbyville, Ill. Mrs. Scott d. Dec. 7th, 1871.

1150. Catharine, b. Feb. 1, 1831, m. 1st Geo. Applegate, one child. m. 2d John H. Anthony. Res. Washington, Ill.

1151. Charles Laban, b. Nov. 15, 1836, m. Mary Hampton, chil. Perry, Annah and David. m. 2d Eliza Beeham, dau. Eva.

1152. Perry A., Farmer. Res. Secor, Woodford Co., Ill.

VII. KYES, DAVID (1145), m. Jan. 1, 1846, in Tazewell Co., Hannah K. Maris, and lives in Pekin, Tazewell Co., Ill. He is a lawyer in Pekin, has been Sheriff, also a member of the Legislature in Ill., and was County Judge from Dec. 1864, to Dec. 1878.

### CHILDREN.

1153. Hannah J., b. Jan. 31, 1847, m. Mar. 8, 1866, Peter Berger. Res. Fairview, Fulton Co., Ill.

1154. Laura L., b. Dec. 9, 1851, m. June 13, 1869, Tunis Cole. Res. Garden Grove, Decatur Co., Iowa.

1155. Fletcher D., b. Dec. 9, 1854, now reading law in Pekin.

1156. Laban J., b. Aug. 18, 1857, reading law in Pekin.

1157. Julia S., b. Nov. 22, 1859.

1158. Chitty C., b. Aug. 5, 1862.

1159. Kent O., b. Mar. 10, 1864.

1160. Libby A., b. Jan. 1, 1867.

V. KEYES, EPHRAIM (1121), 2d s. of Ephraim, m. Oct. 19, 1777, Bridget Sawyer, who was b. Dec. 25, 1756. He lived in Plymouth, finally removed to Rumney and d. there, July 10, 1831.

His wife d. June 14, 1839.

### CHILDREN.

1161. Betsey, b. 1778, m. a Clifford, d. Sept. 1813.

1162. James, b. July 22, 1779, in Plymouth, N. H.

1163. Samuel, b. Dec. 18, 1784, in Plymouth.

1164. Ephraim, b. about 1786, d. 1790.

1165. Joshua, b. 1787.

1166. Sally, b. about 1790, d. July 8, 1831.

1167. Ephraim, b. 1792, d. probably in Rumney. Left an adopted s. James, in Foxboro, Mass.

1168. Isaac, b. April 26, 1796.

1169. Almira, b. 1798, m. a Willoby, d. April 8, 1837.

1170. Lewis, b. 1800.

VI. KEYES, JAMES (1162), eldest s. of Ephraim, m., Sept. 7, 1806, Mary Harvey. He was a farmer and d. in Rumney.

### CHILDREN.

1171. George, b. 1808, d. April 29, 1840, unm.

1172. Henry, b. Feb. 19, 1809, in Rumney.

1173. William, b. Feb. 15, 1812, m. Nov. 27, 1855, Editha Dickenson, of Hadley, Mass. No children. Farmer in Rumney.

1174. Ephraim, went to Decorah, Iowa, twenty years ago. No news of him.

1175. James P., b. April 19, 1820.

1176. Andrew J., now in Titusville, Penn.

1177. Mary J., m. Rufus Dickerson, of Wilmington, Vt.

1178. Martha M., res. in Lowell, Mass., unm.

VII. KEYES, HENRY (1172), m., March 8, 1832, Eliza Cleasby, of Peacham, Vt., lived in Rumney until about 1853, and taught school for a time. He was Selectman, Town Agent, Overseer, Notary Public, and Justice of the Peace. Was also

Superintending School Committee. He was afterward Farmer, Railroad Man. in Vt. until in 1870, his health failed, and he returned to Rumney, then to Concord, N. H., where he now is.

### CHILDREN.

1179. Mary Elizabeth, b. Feb. 24, 1833, m. and dec.
1180. Julian (perhaps Julia Ann), b. Oct. 5, 1834, m. and dec.
1181. Martha Adeline, b. June 6, 1837, d. unm.
1182. Henry Woodbury, b. Oct. 24, 1840, m. and dec.
1183. Emma, b. Apr. 15, 1842, m. and dec.
1184. Alice, b. July 21, 1846, now living.
1185. Ella, b. March 26, 1849, d. unm.

    Mrs. Keyes, d. March 28, 1876, aged 67.
    Henry, m. 2d, Oct. 15, 1878, Mrs. Mary —— of Post Mills, Vermont.

VII. KEYES, JAMES P. (1175), m., March 4, 1845, Elmira Haskell, of Wilmington, Vt. Farmer, res. Rumney, N. H.

### CHILDREN.

1186. George F., b. June 2, 1848, d. Nov. 21, 1848.
1187. Alvah E., b. Jan. 8, 1850, m. Res. Rumford.
1188. Henry J., b. June 18, 1852. Res. Auburndale, Mass.
1189. Nellie S., b. Oct. 6, 1855, m. Joseph C. Gillett.
1190. George E., b. July 24, 1859.
1191. Willie L., b. Oct. 23, 1863.

VI. KEYES, SAMUEL (1163), 2d s. of Ephraim, m. about 1812, Abigail Benjamin of Ashburnham, Mass. He lived for a time in Weston, Mass., but res. in Ashburnham after 1823, where he d. May 16, 1868. His wife d. there in 1869, aged seventy-nine years and eight months.

### CHILDREN.

1192. Almira, b. March, 1813, in Plymouth, N. H., m. James Cooper, Jamaica Plains, dec.
1193. John T. G., b. Nov. 13, 1815, d. about 1827.
1194. Samuel H., b. Aug. 13, 1817, d. March 22, 1843.
1195. Daniel B., b. Oct. 20, 1819, m. and had two children, both dec. He res. in Boston, d. Sept, 1859.

1196. Elizabeth J., b. Aug. 27, 1822, in Rumney, N. H.

1197. Sarah H., b. October 19, 1824, in Ashburnham, Mass., m. Lewis Ward, d. June 1854.

1198. Charles S., b. Feb. 23, 1828, unm.

1199. Caroline W., ) b. July 13, 1832, m. A. S. Sawtell of Rindge, N. H., d. Oct. 4, 1878.

1200. Catharine W., ) b. July 13, 1832, m. O. P. Butler of Rindge, N. H.

VI. KEYES, JOSHUA (1165), 4th s. of Ephraim, m. Feb. 18, 1812, Sarah Beers of So. Reading, Mass., was expressman in Old Cambridge, and d. by an accident, Aug. 18, 1831. Sarah his wife, d. about 1837.

### CHILDREN.

1201. William, dec.

1202. Nelson, m. in Valparaiso, So. America. dec.

1203. Joseph, dec.

1204. William, dec.

1205. Stillman, dec.

1206. Gilman M., b. Sept. 19, 1822.

1207. Mary E., b. Dec. 9, 1829, in Cambridge, m. J. H. Stark-weather. Res. Cambridge, Mass.

VII. KEYES, GILMAN M. (1206), m. 1845. His wife d. May 15, 1872.

### CHILDREN.

1208. Mary Jane, b. July 31, 1847, in Boston, Mass., m. Mr. Horne, a farmer, and res. in Great Falls, Me.

1209. Ella M., b. Aug. 8, 1849, in Portland, Me.

1210. Ida E., b. Feb. 27, 1851, m. Mr. Barber, res. Berwick, Me.

1211. Willie E., b. Dec. 31, 1853, in Springvale, Me.

1212. George M., b. July 27, 1858, in Springvale.

These two sons, candy manufacturers, res. one in North Conway, N. H., the other in Brunswick, Me.

VI. KEYES, ISAAC (1168), m. 1st, 1817, Abigail Stimson, m. 2d, May 5, 1864, Lucy W. Fuller.

### CHILDREN.

1213. Mary, b. Mar. 1, 1818, m. Jan. 13, 1839, John C. Appleton, who has dec.  Mrs. Appleton res. in Newton.

1214. Frances F., b. Sept. 3, 1819, dec.

1215. Abigail T., b. Oct. 1, 1825, m. a Cunningham.  Res. Newton, Upper Falls, Mass.


VI. KEYES, LEWIS (1170), m. Jan. 1, 1822, Henrietta Ramsey.

### CHILDREN.

1216. Sarah G., b. Aug. 4, 1822, m. Samuel O. Greenough, July 31, 1848.  Res. Boston.

1217. Joseph C., b. Jan. 24, 1826, m. Sarah A. George, Nov. 27, 1851.

1218. Louisa A., b. Nov. 7, 1831, m. Knight S. Osgood, Nov. 8, 1855.  Three chil.  Res. Boston Highlands.

1219. Hannah V., b. Feb. 9, 1836.  Res. Boston.

1220. Carrie M., b. Oct. 9, 1840, m. William H. Lake, Feb. 9, 1864, d. Dec. 31, 1866.

1221. Emmeline M., m. June 3, 1856, Chase W. Colley.

1222. Carpenter, has two sons, Francis A., b. 1852, and Fred C., b. 1854.

Lewis had three other dau. of whom, Mary E. only, survives.


V. KEYES, EBENEZER (1122), 3d s. of Ephraim, m. Esther Hildreth, and d. in Plymouth, N. H., about 1828 or '30.

### CHILDREN.

1223. Ebenezer Jr., b. Apr. 15, 1785.

1224. Stephen, no children, probably not married.

1225. Benjamin, b. 1791.  See appendix.

1226. Abel, d. in Paton, P. Q.   s. Marquis and Ezra.

1227. Townsend, said to have m. a Bickford.  s. Arthur.

1228. Sewell, Res. Concord, N. H.  Sons Ira and Franklin.

The daughters of Ebenezer were Esther, Rebecca, Mary, Olive, Hannah and Charlotte, twins.

**VI. KEYES, EBENEZER Jr.** (1223), m. Apr. 23, 1806, Betsey Kelley, b. July 12, 1782, lived in Rumney and Plymouth, last in Haverhill, N. H., where he died.

### CHILDREN.

1229. Ruth Hildreth, b. Mar. 16, 1807, m. Apr. 22, 1835, Joseph Hartwell, dec. Res. Bradford, Vt. No chil.

1230. Calvin Winslow, b. Jan. 1, 1809, m. Maryam Bradish, and d. in Bradford, Vt., Apr. 22, 1870. Of his two chil. the son d. at 24, the dau. with her mother, res. in Haverhill, N. H.

1231. Arad, b. Mar. 30, 1811, d. Oct. 17, 1811.

1232. Lydia Kelley, b. Sept. 9, 1812, in Haverhill, m. John Noyes. Res. Barnston, P. Q. Five chil.

1233. Luther Harvey, b. Aug. 26, 1814.

1234. Casper, b. Sept. 25, 1816, d. Jan. 30, 1817.

1235. Rufus Conant, b. June 15, 1818, m. at Haverhill, May 8, 1845, Mary St. Clair. Son and two dau. Res. Kansas.

1236. Esther, b. Jan. 18, 1824, in Haverhill, m. May 9, 1844, John H. Large, and d. Jan 23, 1852.

**VII. KEYES, LUTHER H.** (1233), m. Apr. 15, 1837, in Haverhill, N. H., Susan S. Strong. He d. Oct. 5, 1877.

### CHILDREN.

1237. George F., b. Jan. 19, 1838.
1238. Emma S., b. Aug. 3, 1839.

**VIII. KEYES, GEORGE F.** (1237), m. Aug. 3, 1856, Abbie Hardey. Farmer and res. in Haverhill, N. H.

### CHILDREN.

1239. Willie H., b. June 7, 1857, d. Sept. 12, 1858.
1240. Belle, b. Oct. 11, 1859.
1241. Clara, b. Jan. 15, 1862.
1242. Luther Frauklin, b. June 7, 1864.

**IV. KEYES, JONAS** (1118), 2d s. of Ezekiel, lived in Rumney, probably d. there. Sup. had two s. John and Ezekiel.

IV. KEYES, ABNER (1119), youngest s. of Ezekiel, m. Dec. 20, 1763, Mary Shedd, of Billerica, Mass. Birth of his 11 chil. b. between 1764 and 1785, to be found in Hollis, N. H. Abner later removed to Rumney, N. H., with two brothers, Ephraim and probably Jonas. He belonged to Capt. Fletcher's company in an expedition to Canada, 1758, an account of which is given in a journal kept by Joseph Holt, of Wilton, N. H. Abner was in the Rev. war, afterward drew a pension. He d. in Hancock, at the house of his s. Abner, about 1819 or '20. He had nine dau. and two

### SONS.

1243. William, lived in Antrim.

1244. Abner, b. 1781, in Hollis, N. H.

One of the daughters of Abner (1119), m. a Cooledge, and has a son, Cornelius Cooledge, now State Senator. Res. Hillsboro, N. H.

V. KEYES, ABNER (1244), m. Susannah Barton, and lived in Hancock, N. H. He d. Feb. 12, 1837.

### CHILDREN.

1245. Jonathan French, b. Aug. 23, 1811.

1246. Veranus, b. Sept. 22, 1813.

1247. Ruth, m. Col. Hiram Monroe, Hillsboro, N. H. She had four chil. and d. Mar. 1848. Son.

1248.　　Orvan P., of Moro, Mad. Co. Ill. only child living.

1249. Horace Wells, b. Feb. 18, 1816.

1250. Corydon D., b. 1827, d. in the late war.

1251.　　Orvan, only s. of Corydon D., d. in the war.

1252. Albert Barton, b. Jan 26, 1828.

Abner, Alfred, Ephraim and Hazen, s. of Abner, d. young.

VI. KEYES, VERANUS (1246), lived in Nashua and Ashland, N. H., removing to Newton, Lower Falls, Mass., 1878.

### CHILDREN.

1253. Frank, b. Aug. 31, 1832. He was in the late war.

1254. Flora M., b. Sept. 21, 1846. Another dau. Susan Elizabeth, b. about August, 1835, has been twice m.   Flora, m. and lives at North Adams, Mass.

**VI. KEYES, JONATHAN F. (1248).**   Is a banker.   Res. in Ashland, N. H.

### CHILDREN.

1255. Orlando W., was Captain in the late war, and lost his life.

1256. Henry F., enlisted in the late war, and lost his right arm.

1257.             Henry S. Keyes, is grandson of Jonathan F. There were also eight daughters.

**VI. KEYES, HORACE W. (1250),** res. in Milford, N. H., m. 1st Sophia King Page.   The last two children are by a second marriage.

### CHILDREN.

1258. Alfred Page, b. Nov. 22, 1845; also, Ellen R., b. Feb. 18, 1848; Edward Payson, d. young; Abbie Sophia, b. July, 1853, and d. at ten years; Emma Frances, b. Oct. 30, 1861; Anne S., b. Dec. 13, 1869; Henry M., b. April, 1870.

**VII. KEYES, ALFRED P. (1258),** m., Nov. 22, 1866, Harriet Newell Wheeler of Amherst, N. H.   Res. Nashua, N. H.

### CHILDREN.

1259. George Albert, b. Mar. 10, 1868.
1260. Clara Belle, b. Feb. 26, 1870.
1261. Dana Wheeler, b. June 20, 1877.

**VI. KEYES, ALBERT BARTON (1254),** m., Aug. 2, 1851, Hannah M., dau. of Simon L. Gordon of Ashland, Grafton Co., N. H.   A. B. Keyes has a livery stable in Washington, D. C.

### CHILDREN.

1262. Mary E., b. Sept. 12, 1864.
1263. William H., b. Sept. 20, 1866, d. Aug. 21, 1876.

**III. KEYES, ZECHARIAH (924),** youngest s. of Moses, m. Dinah —— Death recorded in Chelmsford, Dec. 21, 1759.

## CHILDREN.

1264. Abigail, b. 1736.
1265. Sybyl, b. 1737.
1266. Olive, b. 1739.
1267. Lydia, b. 1741.
1268. Abel, b. 1743.
1269. Zebulon, b. 1745, probably d. young.
1270. Issacher, b. 1747.
1271. Uriah, b. 1749.
1272. Thankful, b. 1752.
1273. Rhoda, b. 1754.
1274. Joanna, b. 1756.
1275. Anna, b. 1757, d. 1768.

IV. KEYES, ABEL (1268), m. Olive Durant, in 1768. The Abel who m. Olive Durant, was probably the s. of Zechariah. He is said to have lived in Townsend, Mass.

## CHILDREN.

1276. Sarah, b. 1769.
1277. Abel, b. 1770.
1278. Aaron, b. 1773.
1279. Zebulon, b. 1775.
1280. Hasme, b. 1776.
1281. Levi, b. 1777.

IV. KEYES, ISSACHER (1270), m., 1769, Elizabeth Richardson, and lived in Chelmsford, Mass., d. April 19, 1820.

## CHILDREN.

1282. Solomon, b. May 13, 1771.
1283. Priscilla, b. Dec. 29, 1773.
1284. James, b. Feb. 13, 1775.
1285. Sampson, b. Nov. 22, 1777.
1286. Betsey, b. Jan. 15, 1780, in Westford.
1287. Jonas, b. July 24, 1787, in Westford.
1288. Joash, b. May 29, 1792.

V. KEYES, CAPT. SOLOMON (1282), eldest s. of Issacher, m., 1794, Hulda Tenney of Littleton, Mass. He was a Farmer and Blacksmith, and Capt. of a Military company, d. in Littleton, May 10, 1850.

CHILDREN.

1289. Jeptha, b. June 30, 1795, d. at three months.

1290. Hulda, b. May 11, 1797.

1291. Sally, b. Jan. 25, 1799.

1292. Solomon, b. Nov. 6, 1800.

1293. Laura, b. July 24, 1802, m. Dea. James Brown of Littleton. No children. d. about 1840.

1294. Nancy, b. June 28, 1809, d. unm. about 1855.

1295. Walter, b. Jan. 4, 1812, d. at three months.

1296. Walter, b. Dec. 9, 1813. Farmer, unm.

VI. KEYES, HULDA (1290), m., March 4, 1815, America Hamblin of Waterford, Me. Farmer and Carpenter.

CHILDREN.

Albert H., b. Nov. 20, 1816.; Nancy H., b. Aug. 1, 1818; Maria H., b. August 13, 1820.; Almira, b. Sept. 26, 1822; Elizabeth G., b. Oct. 10, 1824, d. July 4, 1856.; Walter H., b. April 25, 1827.; Edwin, b. May 17, 1829.; Laura, b. Feb.12, 1832.; Sarah J., b. June 9, 1834.

VI. KEYES, SALLY (1291), m. Davis Parlin of Acton, Mass. Farmer and Carpenter, who d. about 1850, from injuries received from an engine on the Boston and Fitchburg railroad. s. Henry K. Parlin, b. June 5, 1834, m. Mary Parlin of Acton, Mass. Farmer and mechanic.

VI. KEYES, SOLOMON (1292), m. Almira Foster of Littleton, Mass., in 1826. Settled in Littleton, lived there until 1855, then moved to Ayer Junction, where he still lives. Blacksmith and Farmer.

CHILDREN.

1297. Sarah, b. Jan. 15, 1827, d. at seventeen days.

1298. George W., b. Feb. 3, 1828, d. 1860.

1299. John A., b. March 13, 1830.

1300. Joel E., b. June 7, 1831, d. 1870.

1301. Almira Jane, b. Dec. 3, 1840, m. William M. Turner of Ayer, Mass., s. William M., b. Feb. 12, 1861.

V. KEYES, PRISCILLA (1283), eldest daughter of Issacher m. James Baldwin of Woburn, Mass., who was b. Dec. 26, 1772. He settled in Westford, Mass., then removed to Dunstable, now a part of Nashua, was Dea. in a Baptist church and d. there Nov. 25, 1827. Priscilla, his wife d. August 4, 1849. He was a Master Mechanic, making Factorys, Water Wheels, Saw Mills, &c.

### CHILDREN.

1302. Stephen K., b. Nov. 4, 1799, m. Mary Leach of Goffstown, N. H., Feb. 29, 1827. Res. Merideth, N. H. Children, Charles Augustus, Nathan Howe, John Wesley, Samuel Josephus.

1303. Josiah, b. July 25, 1801, d. April 9, 1872, unm.

1304. Josephus, b. Oct. 15, 1803, m. Feb. 12, 1828, Nancy Blanchard of Milford, N. H., who d. Dec. 31, 1859. Mr. Baldwin m. 2d, Oct. 23, 1863, Mrs. Lucy C. Grant of Cranston, R. I. He settled in Nashua (then called Dunstable), and was the first Mayor after its incorporation into a city; was also Deacon in the first Baptist church in that city. He d. March 4, 1872, aged sixty eight. "Honorable Josephus Baldwin d. at his residence on Main street at 9 o'clock Monday, of dropsy, at the age of sixty eight years. Mr. Baldwin was born in Nashua, N. H., and has been identified with the manufacturing interests of this city, from his youth up. He was the largest manufacturer of Bobbins, Spools and Shuttles, in New England, had an extensive acquaintance and business connection, and was probably the most widely known citizen of Nashua. He was the first Mayor of the city, to which office he was twice elected. He was also Chief Engineer of the Fire Department for many years, and one of the first men of his time in every improvement and industry, that added materially to the growth and prosperity of the city. Mr. Baldwin was a member of the Baptist church, and will be missed by the society and community at large."—*Nashua Telegraph.*

### CHILDREN OF JOSEPHUS BALDWIN.

1305. Edwin, b. Nov. 16, 1828, d. Dec. 18, 1830.

1306. Ann Maria, b. Oct. 24, 1831, in Nashua, m. Dr. F. B. Ayer of Meredith, N. H., Feb. 8, 1854, s. Frank J. B.

1307.        George Wells, b. June 1, 1837, d. young.

1308.        Clara A., b. July 20, 1845, m. Roger W. Porter of Nashua, Sept. 13, 1864. Children, Clara Grace, and Pauline.

1309.        Katie, b. March 12, 1866.

1310.        Sarah, b. Sept. 8, 1871.

1311. Eliza, b. Sept. 13, 1805, m. Sept. 27, 1832, Henry Kimbal of Goffstown, N. H. Mrs. Kimbal d. Oct. 7, 1845. Her husband d. July 6, 1841. Children, Charles Otis, b. Aug. 29, 1833, dec.; Nancy Baldwin, b. June 23, 1835, dec.; Lusilla F., b. Feb. 28, 1837; Henry L., b. Sept. 2, 1839, m. One child.

1312. Caroline, } b. Sept. 7, 1807, lives in Hudson, N. H., unm.
1313. Edwin, } b. Sept. 7, 1807, m. Orpha More of Nashua, N. H., m. 2d, Mary A. Ballard, m. 3d, Mary B. Lovell of Westboro. Four children.                 .

1314. Nancy, b. Nov. 27, 1809, m. Joseph Merrill of Sedgewick, Me., Apr. 19, 1835. Dea. Joseph Merrill was a worthy and esteemed citizen, afterward of Hudson, N. H., d. 1871. His widow now resides in Hudson.

1315. James, b. May 13, 1812, m. Oct. 12, 1834, Harriet Robins of New Ipswich, N. H., he m. 2d, Mary Butrick of Concord, Mass., m. 3d, Julia Hunton of Nashua, N. H. Seven children.

1316. Priscilla, b. Oct. 6, 1814, m. Feb. 12, 1842, Luther A. Chase of Hillsboro, N. H., both dec. Two children.

1317. John, b. April 9, 1817, m. Betsey Crooker of Amherst, N. H., March 12, 1860. No chil. Betsey d. May 20, 1877.

1318. Cyrus H., b. June 22, 1820, m. Laura Ann French of Milford, N. H., June 13, 1842. One child. Mrs. Baldwin dec. May 25, 1861. C. H. Baldwin was the inventor of the seamless bag and sold his right to the Stark company.

V. KEYES, JAMES (1284), second s. of Issacher, m. 1799, Abigail Carlton, b. April 24, 1779. Marriage recorded at Westford, Mass. James d. Sept. 20, 1864.

#### CHILDREN.

1319. Abigail, b. Oct. 11, 1800, m. Samuel Wheeler, who d. Dec. 12, 1876. Abigail d. 1873. s. James K. Wheeler. Res. Bolton, Mass.

1320. James, b. Jan. 5, 1802, d. April 4, 1802.

1321. Roxa, b. Jan. 22, 1803, d. April 26, 1803.
1322. Stephen, b. Jan. 25, 1804, d. May 26, 1805.
1323. Ivory, b. May 15, 1805.
1324. James, b. April 5, 1809.
1325. Roxy, b. Sept. 24, 1811.
1326. Walter, b. May 18, 1813.
1327. Franklin, b. June 14, 1819.


VI. KEYES, IVORY (1323), m. Lucy Robbins, and d. April 6, 1867. Mrs. Keyes Res. in West Acton, Mass.

CHILDREN.

1328. Martha A., b. Feb. 17, 1834, d. March 18, 1858.
1329. George F., b. Jan. 27, 1838.
1330. Marcus M., b. Jan. 23, 1840. Res. Boston, Mass.
1331. Ellen M., b. Aug. 27, 1844. Res. West Acton, Mass.


VII. KEYES, GEORGE F. (1329), m. Belle W. Res. Boston, Mass.

CHILDREN.

1332. George S. W., b. June 20, 1870.
1333. Mattie Belle, b. Nov. 1873.


VI. KEYES, JAMES, JR. (1324), m. Nov. 11, 1834, Lydia Robbins of Acton. James Keyes, d. in Acton, May 16, 1867, and his widow now res. there with her son, George R.

CHILDREN.

1334. John Carleton, b. Feb. 25, 1837, in Lexington, Mass.
1335. George R., b. June 26, 1850, in Lowell, Mass.


VII. KEYES, JOHN C. (1334), m. April 26, 1862, Maria A. Flagg. CHILDREN.

1336. Lula Flora, b. Jan. 4, 1864.
1337. Rena N., b. Jan. 28, 1870.


VI. KEYES, WALTER (1326), m. Nov. 7, 1839, Rebecca M. Noyes of Acton, Mass., settled in Groton, Mass. Mrs. Keyes

d. July 4, 1852, and Walter m. 2d, Sept 12, 1857, S. A. Dickson of Groton, moved to Rochester, N. Y., 1858, thence to Germania, Wis., where he now res. Stove and furniture dealer. Has no children.

VI. KEYES, FRANKLIN (1327), was ordained March 31, 1872, in the Methodist Episcopal church. He m. Sept. 11, 1842, Eliza Warren Reed, b. July 10, 1822. Res. Woburn, Mass. Dau. 1338. Ellen Eliza, b. April 5, 1852, d. Sept. 15, 1852.

V. KEYES, SAMPSON (1285), 3d s. of Issacher, passed his early life in Westford in the shops and mills of his father, receiving a good common school education. He m., 1802, Betsey F. Little and settled in Wilton, N. H. In the Autumn of 1807 he removed to Wilton, Me., then called Tyngtown, took up a wild lot of land, and was now both blacksmith and farmer. Betsey, wife of Sampson, d. Aug. 26, 1810, leaving her husband poor, with three young children, amid the hardships and privations of a new country. In Feb. 1811, Mr. Keyes m. 2d, Mehitable Butterfield of Wilton, Me., dau. of a Revolutionary patriot. He filled many places of trust and responsibility in his church, town and county, all of which he discharged with efficiency and honor. During the years that intervened between his leaving Mass., and the birth of his youngest child, Mr. Keyes had cleared and improved a large farm, built a fine set of buildings, secured, for that locality and those times, a good patronage, and had placed himself in easy circumstances. He d. at his residence in Wilton, Me., April 24, 1861, and was followed by his widow, Jan. 6, 1867. All the family dead, lie buried in the beautiful country cemetery near East Wilton, and all save two, in the expensive family lot.

### CHILDREN.

1339. Zoa, b. Aug. 6, 1803, m. Joseph Hatch, and settled in Wilton, Me. She had four s. and a dau. Her oldest s. is a clergyman, M. E., the other three were in the war of the Rebellion. One, a Lieut., another severely wounded at Antietam, another languished for months in Andersonville prison.  **Mrs. Hatch** d. May 28, 1856.

1340. Betsey, b. Aug. 23, 1805, m. Abial Cheney.  Res. Wilton, Me.  She had a s. and two dau.  The s. was a soldier in the late war, wounded at Port Hudson.  Mrs. Cheney d. July 10, 1840.

1341. Sampson, b. May 3, 1807, d. Jan. 18, 1808.

1342. Alvah, b. Nov. 7, 1808.

1343. Daniel, b. Feb. 23, 1812, d. in infancy.

1344. Arvilla, b. Feb. 13, 1813, m. Bela Townsend and res. at East Dixfield, Me.  Five chil.  Her three s. were soldiers in the late war, the eldest a Lieut., the first and second, severely wounded, and the third, furloughed under a general order, for forty-five days, as being the best soldier in his brigade.  Mrs. Townsend now res. in Newfield, Me.

1345. Calvin, b. Aug. 3, 1814.

1346. Mary, b. Sept. 24, 1816, d. of consumption, Aug. 10, 1838.

1347. Fanny, b. Feb. 25, 1818.  Died in infancy.

1348. Ruth S., b. May 2, 1819.  Died in infancy.

1349. Stephen, b. May 7, 1820.  Died in infancy.

1350. S. Warren, b. Aug. 30, 1822.

1351. Edee B., b. Dec. 5, 1824, m. Elbridge G. Brewster, of Amboy, Ill.  Four children.  Present res. Cordova, Ill.

1352. Lovina, B., b. Feb. 9, 1827, m. Cotton Elliott, Jr., settled in Rumford, Me.  Three sons.

1353. Charles W., b. Feb. 1, 1831.

VI. KEYES, ALVAH (1342), m., April 24, 1837, Lucy A. Bennett of Swanzey, N. H., and settled in that place.  Now res. in Claremont, N. H.  He is a Blacksmith and Machinist.

### CHILDREN.

1354. John A., is a sailor, was connected with our Naval Service during the war.

1355. Jeannie M., m. S. E. Fuller, M. D.  Dr. Fuller has a large practice in Brooklyn, N. Y.  One child.

1356. Charles W., is a printer and journalist.  Res. Farmington, Me.

1357. Frank P., youngest child, is now studying law.

## VI. KEYES, CALVIN (1345), m. Lucy A. Moon, settled in Wilton, Me., founded the scythe and agricultural tool works, at East Wilton, an important and prosperous business enterprise, which he successfully managed until his sudden death, Dec. 19, 1864.

### CHILDREN.

1358. Marcus C., was a soldier in the late war, wounded at Peterborough, Va., m. Carinda Dunham. Res. Lawrence, Mass.

### CHILDREN. •

1359.     Wallace L.
1360.     Charles D.  Died in infancy.
1361.     Richard A.

1362. Laura E., m. W. W. Cushman, settled in Lowell, Mass. Her husband was a soldier in the late war.

## VI. KEYES, S. WARREN (1350), m. Clarissa Butterfield, settled in Grafton, Me., about 1858, removing to Chesterville, Me.

### CHILDREN.

1363. B. Roscoe, Architect and Builder.
1364. Mary O., teacher, m. F. Niles, settled in Chesterville, Me.
1365. Florence J., b. about 1864.

## VI. KEYES, CHARLES W. (1353), m. Juliette C. Lord, daughter of a Methodist Episcopal Clergyman, settled at East Wilton, Me.  Scythe maker by trade; enlisted into the volunteer service as private in 1862, rose to first Lieutenant, and was discharged from the service July 7, 1865.  He was wounded three times, one wound resulting in the amputation of his left foot, was brevetted for gallant and meritorious conduct at each of the battles of Fort Butler, Louisiana, and Spottsylvania Court House, Va.  Nov. 1866, he was appointed second Lieutenant in the U. S. Army.  In 1868, was promoted to be Captain, and after serving in various parts of the South and West, until 1873, was placed on the retired list of the regular Army, Dec. 31, of that year.  July 25, 1868, Mrs. Keyes d. leaving no children.  Feb. 6, 1875, Capt. Keyes became editor and proprietor of the Far-

mington Chronicle, located in the beautiful country town of Farmington, Me.   Connected with the Chronicle is one of the best
book and miscellaneous job printing establishments in the state,
also owned and managed by Capt. Keyes.   January 10, 1878,
he married Miss Hattie E. Park, A. M., preceptress of the Me.
Wesleyan Seminary and Female College, and settled in Farmington, Me.


V.   KEYES, BETSEY (1286), daughter of Issacher, m. 1806,
Thomas Flint, a carpenter, b. Jan. 17, 1784, in Francestown, N.
H.   Lived in Westford until 1817, then moved to Wilton, Me.,
where they remained twenty years.   They finally settled in Grafton, Mass., and passed there the remainder of their days.

### CHILDREN.

1366.  Thomas G., b. March 29, 1807, in Westford, Mass., m.
Anna Spaulding of Chelmsford, lived in various places, now
Res. in Ashburnham, Mass.   Anna, wife of Thomas d. Oct. 24,
1862.   They had four children.   Diantha, b. May 1, 1836, in
Chelmsford, m. J. Rodney Bunker of New London, N. H., No
children.   Edward Austin, b. June 17, 1838, in Littleton, N. H.,
m. Nellie S. Ford, b. in N. Y., Feb. 22, 1849.   Was in Co. H.,
36 Mass. Infantry, served from Aug. 27, 1862, to the close of the
war.   Now ornamental japanner on sewing machines in Cleveland,
Ohio.   Children, Edward G., Leonard A., and Nellie Gertrude.
Leonard Alden, b. 1840, accidentally burned to death, July 5,
1852.   Flora Ann, b. May 1, 1844, in Slaterville, R. I., m. John
Coutuer of Fayettville, Me.   One child.   Thomas Flint, m. 2d,
Mrs. Clarissa Wilson, Dec. 28, 1866.

1367.  Betsey, b. May 27, 1812, in Westford, Mass., m. John
Daisy of Wilton, Me., 1833.; daughter Eliza Ann, b. 1835, living
in Fitchburg, Mass.   Betsey d. 1837.

1368.  Julia Ann, b. April 15, 1814, in Westford, m. Henry
Wesson of Grafton, Mass., March, 1838.   Two children.   Henry
Alison, Charles Edward, both married.

1369.  Harriet, b. Oct. 31, 1815, in Westford, m 1st, William
S. Walker of Wilton, Me., m. 2d, Andrew Bissell of Grafton,
Mass., daughter Lucinda, m. Mr. Forbush of Me., Oct. 22, 1856.

She was dau. of the 1st marriage, and had three chil.

1370. Edward S., b. Sept. 2, 1817, in Westford, m. Betsey C. Glazier of Ashburnham, Mass., June 5, 1845. Res. Everet, Mass. 3 chil. Mary Elizabeth, dec., Julia E. dec., and Helen E.

1371. Sarah, b. May 7, 1819, in Wilton, Me., m. July 22, 1860, Harvey Putnam of Grafton, Mass. No children.

1372. Mary F., b. Dec. 11, 1822, in Wilton, Me., m. Lowell Sanborn of Fayette, Me. Two children, Eldora and Edward. Mrs. Mary d. 1874. Eldora m. a Lovejoy of Wayne, Me.

V. KEYES, STEPHEN 4th son of Issacher, omitted in the list of his children, is in place here, having been b. June 10, 1784, d. May 8, 1798.

V. KEYES, JONAS (1287), 5th s. of Issacher, m. 1808, Sarah P. Read of Stoddard. She was b. June 3, 1790. Jonas was a Farmer, Blacksmith and Miller. He settled in Westford, Mass., moved to Pelham, N. H., 1829, and there res. until his death which occured June 18, 1863.

Sarah, his wife d. April 19, 1874.

CHILDREN.

1373. Emrilla, b. March 20, 1809, m. January 17, 1841, Franklin Putnam of Cavendish, Vt., as his second wife. He d. Feb. 4, 1848, no children.

1374. Sarah, b. June 16, 1810.

1375. Beulah, b. May 12, 1812, m. June 18, 1867, Charles Stiles of Pelham, N. H. Hatter and Deacon of the Congregational church. No children.

1376. Marcus, b. Jan. 22, 1814.

1377. Jonas, b. Aug. 25, 1815.

1378. Stephen, b. Jan. 1, 1821.

1379. Nancy E., b. April 23, 1828, m. Aug, 1857, Robert S. Stewart, Hudson, N. H. Two children.

1380. Maria M., b. May 24, 1830, d. March 30, 1838.

VI. KEYES, SARAH (1374), m., Dec. 1, 1831, Dea. Thomas T. Farwell, b. Sept. 11, 1809, of Chelmsford, Mass., and settled in New London, N. H.

### CHILDREN.

1381. Thurston T., b. Sept. 29, 1832, m. Harriet Chase of Wilmot, N. H. Three children. He d. Aug. 24, 1868.

1382. Sarah T., b. Oct. 16, 1835, m. 1858, Austin Todd of New London, N. H. No children.

1383. Hannah T., b. Feb. 21, 1838, m. 1859, Joseph A. Noyes of Franklin, N. H. Son, Joseph F., b. 1861.

1384. Stephen T., b. May 9, 1840, m. 1863, Ann Folsom, Waterville, Me. No children.

1385. Maria A., b. Aug. 18, 1842, m. in 1859, Sylvander French of New London, N. H. Four children.

1386. Charles E., b. Dec. 13, 1846, d. September 4, 1848.

VI. KEYES, MARCUS (1376), m. in 1836, Maria Winch of Fitchburg, Mass. She was b. Aug. 31, 1819, and d. Nov. 1866. Marcus d. Jan. 2, 1873.

### CHILDREN.

1387. Helen M., b. March 2, 1838, d. March 30, 1838.

1388. Marcus W., b. Jan. 22, 1840.

1389. Stephen F., b. March 2, 1842, in Chelmsford, Mass.

1390. Mary Elizabeth, b. Feb. 16, 1849, in Chelmsford, m. L. B. Caswell of Athol, Mass., Jan. 2, 1877.

VII. KEYES, MARCUS W. (1388), m. 1859, Hannah Pierce of Lowell, Mass. He enlisted in the U. S. service in 1861, served in 26th Regiment, Company C., Massachusetts Volunteers, wounded in the knee at Cedar Creek. Painter in Methuen, Mass.

### CHILDREN.

1391. Ella M., b. Feb. 4, 1860, d. 1876, July 11.

1392. Alice B., b. 1865.

1393. Linsey W., b. 1869.

VII. KEYES, STEPHEN F. (1389), m., Oct. 26, 1865, in Lowell, Mass., Evelyn Hill, b. Jan. 19, 1841, of Wells, Me. He enlisted as a private Aug, 1862, to recruit Company B., second Mass. Inf. Vols; was promoted to Corporal and discharged May, 1864. Admitted to the Suffolk Bar 1874, in Boston,

Mass., where he has since practiced law.   Res. Melrose, Mass.
Office 33, Room 5, School St., Boston.

CHILDREN.

Born in Melrose.

1394. Frank Forrest, b. Oct. 30, 1868.
1395. Ward, b. Sept. 3, 1872, d. Jan. 25, 1877.
1396. Starr, b. Sept. 10, 1874.

VI. KEYES, JONAS (1377), m. 1842, Esther Wright of
Acton, Mass.  Settled in Pelham, N. H.  Farmer and Nursery-
man.

CHILDREN.

1397. Ellen A., b. Nov. 10, 1843, d. April 2, 1867.
1398. Edwin A., b. Oct. 7, 1844, m. 1871, Elizabeth Simpson
of West Concord, Mass.  Dau.,
    Esther M., b. October 15, 1875, d. young.
1399. Clara A., b. Nov. 27, 1845.
1400. Flora Emma, b. Nov. 3, 1847, d. May 27, 1855.
1401. George Henry, b. July 9, 1849, d. Oct. 1, 1849.
1402. Ella Frances, b. Sept. 15, 1851.
1403. Frederic A., b. Nov. 19, 1852.
1404. Winthrop B., b. Sept. 18, 1855.
1405. Milan C., b. Jan. 2, 1862.

VI. KEYES, STEPHEN (1378), s. of Jonas, m. Feb. 5,
1860, Amelia Canaday of North Carolina, settled near Wilmington, N. C. Was a teacher. Has since been County Commissioner,
&c., in that State.

CHILDREN.

1406. Sallie E., b. June 20, 1860.
1407. John F., b. Sept. 17, 1865.
1408. William F., b. June 20, 1867.
1409. Stephen T., b. Jan. 5, 1869.
1410. Mary J., b. Dec. 17, 1872.

V. KEYES, JOASH (1288), 6th and youngest s. of Issacher,
m. 1812, Mary Ann LeGross of Westford, b. 1787.  He was a

Farmer, settled in Westford, lived there eighteen years; was 3 years in Acton, and finally removed to Chelmsford. Capt. Joash Keyes d. in Chelmsford, July 2, 1853.    Mary Ann, his wife, d. May 28, 1873.

### CHILDREN.

1411. Zoa Ann, b. Dec. 27, 1813, m. George Bulmer of Lowell, Mass.  Children, Geo W., b. Sept. 13, 1855.; Olive E., b. Jan. 17, 1857.; Mary L., b. Sept. 29, 1859.; Sarah K., b. July 25, 1861.

1412. Mary Ann, b. July 12, 1815, m. Asa G. Farwell of West Chelmsford.  Res. Fitchburg, Mass.  Children, Isidora F., b. Jan. 4, 1848.; Kate, b. Aug. 7, 1850, d. June 18, 1873.; Frank, b. June 18, 1852.

1413. Frank, b. June 17, 1817, d. Aug. 3, 1820.

1414. Aaron, b. Jan. 14, 1819.

1415. Moses, b. May 10, 1821, m. Martha Aldrich of N. Y., who d. 1865.  No children.  Printer in Lowell, Mass.

1416. Joshua, b. Nov. 6, 1823.  Res. California, unm.

1417. Maria, b. Sept. 9, 1825, m. Amos Green of Lowell, Mass. Children:   Ellen M., b. June 28, 1855.; Winfield S., b. Nov. 15, 1857.; Jessie, b. Jan. 21, 1863.; Anna, b. December 6, 1869.

1418. Shepherd, b. March 29, 1827.  Farmer and Miner, living in St. Lawrence County, N. Y., unm.

1419. Daniel, b. June 6, 1829, d. May 10, 1843.


VI. KEYES, AARON (1414), m. 1837, Mary Winch of Fitchburg, Mass., and first settled in Salisbury, Litchfield Co., Conn., afterward moving to Norfolk.  He d. in New Haven, at the house of his daughter, Mrs. Dewell, and his remains were taken to Norfolk for interment.

### CHILDREN.

1420. Elizabeth M., b. March 8, 1839, m. James D. Dewell, wholesale Grocer and Tea dealer, in New Haven, Conn., about 1860.  Has six children, the eldest Jessie, b. July 18, 1861.

1421. Daniel A., b. July 14, 1841.

1422. Cassius C., b. Jan 5, 1843, m. in Geneva, N. Y., Emma L. Dibble.  Chil. May and Grace, the latter dec.  Cassius C.

Keyes d. Jan. 1875, and his family res. in Des Moines, Iowa.

1423. Charles K., b. 1845, served in the late war about two years and d. at Fairfax Court House, Va, 1863.

VII. KEYES, DANIEL A. (1421), m. in Norfolk, Conn., Frances R. Canfield, b. Nov. 29, 1844, at Norfolk, Conn. Clerk in Providence, R. I., of Mutual Life Insurance Company, N. Y. He was in the late war, enlisted in the 5th Conn. Vols. Co A., July 22, 1861, and served three years.

CHILDREN.

1424. Adella Canfield, b. Feb. 26, 1867, at Norfolk, Conn.
1425. Lena Canfield, b. Sept. 28, 1874, at Norfolk.

IV. KEYES, URIAH (1271), youngest s. and 8th child of Zechariah, m. 1774, Hannah Livingstone.

CHILDREN.

b. some in Chelmsford, others in Ringe, N. H.
1426. William, b. Oct. 22, 1775, in Chelmsford.
1427. Hannah, b. Aug. 21, 1778.
1428. Anna, b. July 21, 1780.
1429. Polly, b. Aug. 18, 1781.
1430. Levi, b. June 30, 1783, d. of spotted fever, 1814.
1431. Josiah, b. July 14, 1785, No children.
1432. Sally, b. June 27, 1787.
1433. Dorcas, b. May 17, 1789.
1434. Amial, b. Jan. 4, 1790, d. of spotted fever, 1814.
1435. Dolly, b. Sept. 26, 1792.
1436. Lydia, b. April 7, 1794.
1437. Reuben, b. Nov. 2, 1796, m. and had one daughter. Lived in Brooklyn, N. Y.
1438. Aaron, b. Nov. 6, 1798. Still living in Norwich, Vt. No children. Was in the war of 1812, draws a pension.

V. KEYES, WILLIAM (1426), m. March 19, 1799, Mercy Whitney of Winchendon, Mass.

CHILDREN.

1439. William, Jr., b. Nov. 26, 1799, m. Sally Tacrits of Plymouth, N. H., d. Dec. 1835. No children.

1440. Stillman, b. March 25, 1802, m. 1826, Nancy Washburn of Woodstock, Vt. Res. Norwich, Vt. No children.

1441. Ira, b. July 10, 1805, m. 1850, Irena Stearlin of Woodstock. They had two dau. and one s. The s. and one dau. dec. Ira d. Oct. 1842.

1442. Asahel, b. Feb. 14, 1808, in Cavendish, Vt.

1443. Jacob, b. Nov. 24, 1810, m. Almira Morgan, had a son and dau. The son d. in the army. The dau. Nancy, m. Justin Taylor of West Windsor, and res. at last account in Dexter, Me.

VI. KEYES, ASAHEL (1442), m. Aug. 9, 1829, Mary Smith of Woodstock, Vt. Res. Strafford, Vt.

### CHILDREN.

1444. Lucy M., m. William Stone, res. Northfield, Vt.

1445. Asahel, Jr., b. Oct. 18, 1836, m. Harriet Dinsmore of Washington, Vt., now of North Tunbridge, Vt. No children.

1446. Mary L., m. Leonard Warren. Res Chester, Vt.

1447. Reuben, b. March 24, 1839, m. Susan Morgan of Claremont, N. H. Res. Weathersfield, Vt., where he d. July 23, 1873.

### CHILDREN.

1448.        Orin.

1449.        Willie.

1450. Alonzo B., b. Oct. 7, 1840, m. Abbie M. Knowlton of Stockbridge, Vt. He d. in Northfield, Vt., Aug. 31, 1868.

### SON.

1451.        Alonzo A.

1452. Laurinda M., b. Dec. 1, 1844, m. Franklin B. Lewis of Claremont, N. H. Res. Strafford, Vt. Two boys.

1453. Abbie F., b. July 6, 1851, m. Warren Franklin.

Here ends the record of Moses Keyes, son of Solomon of Chelmsford, Mass.

II. KEYES, JOHN (11), youngest s. of Solomon and Frances, was b. in Chelmsford, Mass., his birth there recorded. We first hear of him in Marlboro, Mass., where is recorded the birth of his children. He probably moved to Shrewsbury about 1720, and was one of the founders of the church there.

"He m. Mch. 11, 1696, Mary, dau. of Gersham and Hannah (Johnson) Eames. Gersham Eames d. in Watertown, Mass., Nov. 25, 1676, and Mary was b. four months after her father's death. Her mother subsequently m. a Ward, and became the mother of Col. Nahum Ward. In Aug. 1723, a carpenter by the name of Ebenezer Bragg, was building a house for John, then Capt. John Keyes, in Shrewsbury. On the night of the 7th, the house being nearly finished, was burned, as also the old one near it in which Major John was then residing. Six persons were sleeping in the new house. Three sons of Capt. Keyes, and two of Bragg's apprentices were burned, and Bragg saved himself by jumping from the window. John, usually known as the famous Major John Keyes, lived with his wife 72 years. Their son-in-law, Daniel Rand, m. Martha Bruce for his 2nd wife, was m. by Major John who had then passed his 85th year, and afterward lived with his father-in-law. His farm was subsequently known as the Rand farm, and was purchased by Col. Joseph Henshaw of Rand or his heirs. Maj. John d. Mch. 31, 1768. Mary, relict of Maj. John d. April 16, 1772, aged 95 years and one month."

#### CHILDREN.

1454. Gersham, b. Mar. 1, 1698.

1455. Mary, b. Oct. 24, 1700, m. Daniel Rand in Marlboro, Mass., Jan. 18, 1720. Rand lived in Shrewsbury, and was one of the founders of the church there.

#### CHILDREN.

Mary, b. Oct. 12, 1721, dec.; Solomon, b. Mch. 13, 1723, the first baptism in Shrewsbury church; Mary; Thankful; Sarah; Phebe, b. Jan. 1, 1733, m. Samuel Bigelow, June 1755; Rezina; Daniel; Levina, dec. Levina, m. John K. Wetherby.

1456. Solomon, b. Aug. 30, 1703.

1457. Hannah, b. July 9, 1706. m. 1st Gersham Flagg. m. 2nd Lieut. Eleazer Taylor.

1458. Thankful, b. May 24, 1709. m. Jonas Keyes Aug. 20, 1731. Chil. Olive or Alice, bap. May 27, 1733, and Rachel, b. April 17, 1735, sup. to have m. Thomas Miles, 1767.

1459. John, b. Apr. 30, 1712.

1460. Sarah, b. Mch. 5, 1715. m. Joshua Wilder, 1731. Chil. Rosina, b. July 1, 1732. Probably d. young. John, bap. Dec. 4, 1748.

1461. Stephen, b. Apr. 2, 1718.

III. KEYES, GERSHAM (1454), eldest s. of Maj. John, and the only one of his sons who survived the fire, m. 1718, Sarah———— and was living in Shrewsbury, on house lot No. 15, in 1729. His wife joined the church there 1727. After the birth of his children, says the record, "Gersham removed to Boston and became a wealthy merchant." Gersham afterward removed to Virginia and established a ferry, still called Keyes Ferry, on the Shenandoah river, near Charlestown, Jeff. Co. The ferry was then half a mile below its present site, opposite Sheler's Spring, now Keyes Switch. There are no data to fix the time of Gershams removal to Virginia, but in 1755, when Braddock with his force crossed the Shenandoah, he was living there, and from him supplies were bought for Braddock's army. The descendants still preserve a letter, relative to the survey of the 'Keyes Ferry tract,' which we here insert, as showing the extent of that tract, and as every item relating to the father of his country must be interesting.

M Vernon 26th March 1762

Mr Keyes.

Your letter of the 18th Feb'y was delivered to me at our last court, by Mr Ramsay. In regard to the Warrant which you enquiro after, I can only repeat what I have often done before that it must have been returned with the others to the Proprietor's office, if I ever had such a one, but since it is not to be found there, I shall at your request declare all I remember concerning it, which is this, that there was a Warrant directed to me for surveying you (I think) four hundred acres of Land, either at or about your Ferry, which then stood lower down the river; but who it was to join on, or what was the reason of not executing it I cannot absolutely recollect; this I perfectly well know, that I did make you a survey at some place near to where your Ferry then stood, but I think it was in consequence of another Warrant, and that I have had such a Warr't as you ask after in my Possession and moreover that it was not executed owing to some dispute between Col. Fairfax and yourself.

I am Sir

Yr. Hble Servt.

Go WASHINGTON.

Superscription.

To

MR. GERSHAM KEYES,

In

Frederick.

Recommended to )
the care of
Mr. Ramsay. )

### CHILDREN OF GERSHAM.

1462. Frances, b. Dec. 5, 1719.
1463. Humphrey, b. Aug. 29, 1721.
1464. Lucretia, b. Aug. 18, 1723.
1465. Lavina, b. Feb. 16, 1726.
1466. Elizabeth, b. Apr. 4, 1728.

IV. KEYES, HUMPHREY (1463), was a Sea Captain, m. in New England, probably in Boston, Marcella Wade, had two sons, was wrecked off the coast of Turkey, and taken captive by the Algerines. He escaped and returned home after some years, to find that his wife supposing him dead had married another, with whom she passed the remainder of her life. After her death, Capt. Humphrey m. in Virginia, Sarah Hall, b. 1745, consequently ten years old at the time we first hear of Gersham at his ferry on the Shenandoah. Her three brothers were the founders of Halltown, in Jefferson Co., and in "notes on Jefferson Co. Va.," printed in Va., 1857, we find that "Sarah lived with her parents in a little dale near a fine orchard, at the foot of the hill where Rion Hall now stands." The same record states that Capt. Humphrey Keyes was proprietor of Keyes

28

Ferry in 1775. Capt. Humphrey d. April 19, 1793, so says an old family record, now in possession of Jno. T. Keyes, Bristol, Tenn., which record gives also the birth of John, s. of Humphrey.

### CHILDREN OF CAPT. HUMPHREY AND MARCELLA.

1467. "John Keyes, Sen., s. of Humphrey Keyes, was born in Mistick, near Boston, N. E., in the year 1752, Sept. the 25."

1468. Frank, 2d son, was a lawyer, had but one arm, supposed to have settled in Baltimore, Md., and had seven children.

### CHILDREN OF CAPT. HUMPHREY AND SARAH.

1469. Gersham.

1470. Thomas.

1471. Humphrey, supposed to have lived in Greenbrier Co. Va.; no descendants now to be found there.

1472. Mrs. White, who removed to Ohio.

1473. Mrs. Pyles, removed to Ken.

1474. Mrs. Humphreys, wife of David Humphreys.

1475. Eliza, b. 1773, who m. Capt. George North.

1476. Mrs. O'Bannon, wife of Capt. Jno. O'Bannon.

V. KEYES, JOHN (1467), eldest s. of Capt. Humphrey, m. Jan. 27, 1773, in Virginia, "Louisa," or Luvica Talbott, niece of Mr. Monroe. She was b. near Alexandria, Virginia, Apr. 20, 1756. Capt. John Keyes settled near Alexandria, moved thence to the vicinity of Blountsville, Sullivan Co., East Tenn., and finally to Athens, Limestone Co., Alabama, where he d. Feb. 13, 1839. Luvica, his wife, d. Nov. 6, 1836.

### CHILDREN.

1477. Francis, b. Sept. 25, 1775.

1478. Amelia, b. Nov. 13, 1777. m. Samuel Meek, Aug. 14, 1798.

1479. Marcella, or Mercy, b. Oct. 13, 1779. m. Dr. Clemens, July 4, 1805.

1480. "Saley," or Sarah, b. Aug. 9, 1781. m. Daniel Hughes, Jan. 26, 1802.

1481. John, b. Dec. 9, 1783.

1482. Harvey, b. July 31, 1786. m. Salley Greever, Sept. 1, 1807. He located in Smith Co., Virginia, and d. not long after the war without issue.

1483. Elizabeth, b. Sept. 9, 1789. m. Charles Meek of Limestone Co. Ala., Oct. 8, 1806, and d. Feb. 7, 1839, leaving a large family.

1484. George, } b. Nov. 18, 1792.
1485. Washington, }

1486. Nancy, b. Feb. 2, 1795, d. Feb. 4, 1806.

1487. Charlotte, b. Apr. 24, 1797. m. John Cowen, Jan. 20, 1820, d. April 1, 1826.

1488. Matilda, b. Apr. 9, 1799. d. May 4, 1803.

1489. Mary, b. March 29, 1801.

1490. Louisa, b. April 2, 1803. m. 1st Micajah Thomas; m. 2d, Mr. Bradford, res. Denver, Col. Three dau. and s. William.

VI. KEYES, FRANCIS (1477), eldest s. of Capt. John, m. Oct. 5th, 1801, Mary Meek, emigrated to Mo. from Virginia, accompanied it is said, by some of his sisters, and lived in Morton, Ray Co., Mo.

CHILDREN.

1491. James Harvey, b. 1802, in Abington, Washington Co., West Virginia.

1492. Joseph, m. his cousin Bettie Keyes.

1493. William, d. in Miss., about 1865, unm.

1494. John, has lived in Mo. since the war.

1495. George, res. in Mo.

1496. Frank, d. about 1855, in Mo.

There were also three dau.

VII. KEYES, JAMES H. (1491), m. 1st Elizabeth Hall of Mooresville, Limestone Co. Ala.; 2nd Elizabeth Ward, near Aberdeen, Miss. Capt. J. H. Keyes moved to Alabama, afterward to Monroe Co. Miss. He d. in 1865. Elizabeth his wife, d. 1864, both near Helena, Ark.

CHILDREN.

1497. Ann M., b. June 21, 1835, near Athens, Ala.

1498. Jane, m. 1st Liberty Norwood, Miss.; m. 2d James Goode, Ark.

1499. Bettie, m. Hampton Jones, res. Ark.

1500. Cornelia, unm. Res. Simmons Bluff, Tenn.

### CHILDREN BY SECOND MARRIAGE.

1501. Emma, m. Mr. H——

1502. Lal, m. M. Mathews.

1503. John.

1504. Joseph.

These two sons were children when their father d. The family were living near Helena, Ark., at last accounts.

VIII. KEYES, ANN M. (1497), removed to Miss., with her father's family, was educated in Athens, Ala., and m. in Huntsville, Ala. Jan. 12, 1853, S. S. Preston, then a resident of Huntsville. Mr. Preston was b. near Liberty, Bedford Co., Virginia, Nov. 22, 1827. Res. Simmons Bluff, Tenn.

### CHILDREN.

James Harvey Keyes, b. Jan. 24, 1855, graduate of the medical department of the Vanderbilt University, 1879. John, b. Nov. 6, 1856; Laura, b. Apr. 10, 1861; Stephen S., b. May 1, 1863; Ella, b. July 17, 1865; Alice, b. July 18, 1867; Mattie, b. Sept. 16, 1870.

VI. KEYES, SARAH, (1480), m. Daniel Hughes, Jan. 26, 1802. Chil. James H., of Lenoir, N. C.; John K., and a dau. Ellen, perhaps others. T. W. Hughes, s. of James H., graduated at Maryville Coll. Tenn., 1859, and at Union Theo. Sem. N. Y., 1862. Now principal of Liberty Hall Institute, Washington Co. Va.

James P. Snapp, son of Ellen Hughes, who m. Jacob K. Snapp, graduated at Emory and Henry Coll. Va., about 1853, res. in Tenn.

VI. KEYES, JOHN Jr. (1481), second s. of Capt. John, m. Catharine Greever, Dec. 30, 1806, had eleven children, and d. July 17, 1864. Catharine, his wife, d. June 20, 1842.

## CHILDREN.

1505. William G., b. Feb. 1, 1808. Res. Caney Branch, Greene Co., Tenn.

1506. Nancy, d. at six years.

1507. John Talbott, b. Sept. 20, 1811.

1508. Elizabeth. Res. in Canada.

1509. Washington, d. in Cumberland Co. Tenn., Feb. 13, 1838.

1510. Campbell. Res. in Canada.

1511. Robison. Res. Cumberland Co., Tenn.

1512. Joseph Clemand. Res. Walker Co., Ga.

1513. Alpheus. Res. Gentry Co., Mo.

1514. Hiram, d. in Gentry Co., Mo.

1515. Martha. Res. in Canada.

VII. KEYES, WILLIAM GREEVER (1505), moved with his father and mother from Washington Co. Va., to Hawkins Co. Tenn., where he m. Emmeline Wright, and had one son, then moved to Greene Co. Tenn., where Emmeline d. Sept. 21, 1859. William Keyes m. 2d, Nov. 29, 1868, Harriet, dau. of Charles Cook, by whom he has 2 s. and a dau.

VIII. KEYES, THOMAS LILBURN, s. of William G. and Emmeline (Wright) Keyes, was b. Sept. 17, 1833, m. Sept. 25, 1859, Elizabeth Nease, of Cocke Co. Tenn. They have 4 chil.: Cyrus Hannibal, William Perry, Sarah Emmeline, and Sabiana Bell.

VII. KEYES, JOHN T. (1507), m. Lucy Josephine Childress. She was b. April 23, 1819, and was niece of Gen. Edmund P. Gaines. Col. John Keyes has in his possession the old family Bible, bequeathed by Capt. John, to the oldest John in the family successively, from which book, many records relating to this family have been taken. Res. Bristol, Tenn.

## CHILDREN.

1516. Mary Virginia, b. Feb. 12, 1844.

1517. Theora Behethaland, b. Sept. 28, 1845.

1518. Letitia Catharine, b. Mar. 13, 1847, d. Nov. 2. 1857.

1519. Martha Elizabeth, b. Sept. 2, 1848.

1520. Geo. Alphius, b. May 27, 1850, d. June 30, 1858.

1521. John Mathew, b. Dec. 4, 1851, d. Dec. 10, 1857.

1522. Letitia Gaines, b. Nov: 10, 1854, d, Jan. 19, 1878.

VI. KEYES, GEORGE (1484), 4th s. of Capt. John, was b. in Washington Co., Virginia. Early in life he and his brother Washington removed to Limestone Co. Ala., and there merchandised and planted in company. He served at one time as Captain of a volunteer company under Gen. Jackson, and later was elected and served as General of the brigade of militia in his military district in Ala. He m. in Sullivan Co. Tenn., Nov. 16, 1820, Nelly, dau. of Robert and——— (Crockett) Rutledge, and the young couple made the trip to Ala. on horseback. Robert Rutledge was son of William Rutledge of County Tyrone, and Nelly Gamble of County Cavan, Ireland, and grandson of George Rutledge. George Keyes d. in Limestone Co., June 13, 1833. Nelly, his wife was b. Mar. 1st 1799, and d. Oct. 22, 1834.

CHILDREN.

1522. Wade, b. in Mooresville, Limestone Co. Ala., Oct. 10, 1821.

1523. Martha Louisa, b. in Limestone Co. Sept. 23, 1823.

1524. John Washington, b. in Athens, Ala. Nov. 25, 1825.

1525. Jane Charlotte, b. in Limestone Co. Nov. 16, 1827.

1526. George Presley, b. in Athens, Ala. Sept. 8, 1829.

1527. Buran, b. in Limestone Co. Jan. 1, 1832, d. in Morgan Co. Ala., June 29, 1848.

VII. KEYES, WADE (1522), was a student at the University of Virginia, in the sessions of 1837—8. He left the senior classes during the session of 1838—9 on account of ill health and deaths in the family. He studied law with William Richardson, Esq., subsequently joining a law class taught by Hon. Daniel Coleman, and finally graduated in the law department of Transylvania University, at Lexington, Ken. In 1842, he sailed from N. O. to Genoa, traveled on the continent, and in

England and Ireland, returning in the Autumn of 1843; removed to Florida in 1844, and practiced law in Marianna, Jackson Co., in that state. While residing there he published two legal volumes which attracted much attention. In 1851, he returned to Alabama and commenced the practice of law in Montgomery, then the capitol of the state. He was elected Chancellor of the southern Chancery Division of the state, 1853, and held the office six years. Says a southern paper: "He made a splendid reputation as a Chancellor, and established himself among the foremost chancery lawyers of the day." During his chancellorship, he organized a law class at Montgomery, and the school was subsequently organized as the Montgomery law school, and made the law department of the University at Tuscaloosa. In 1861, while 1st Lieutenant of a volunteer company, in a fort in Mobile Bay, he was appointed Assistant Att'y. Gen. of the Conf. Gov't, and during the existence of that Gov't. continued in the Department of Justice, either as assistant or acting Attorney General. After the war he returned to Ala. to his profession. When the Act was passed for codifying the laws of Alabama, he was appointed by Gov. Houston one of the commissioners, the late Judge F. M. Wood being his associate. May 16, 1848, he m. Alice Wharton, dau. of Gen George Whitfield, then of Leon Co., Florida, earlier of Lenoir Co. N. C., and g. dan. on the mother's side of William Blackledge, who d. in Philadelphia while a member of the Continental Congress from the old North State. She was great grand dau. on the father's side of Gen. Nathan Bryan. Judge Wade Keyes d. suddenly, in Montgomery, Mar. 2, 1879.

### CHILDREN.

1528. Louisa Blackledge, wife of Norman G. Kittrell, a lawyer of Galveston, Texas.

1529. Nelly Rutledge.

1530. Mary Whitfield.

There were five children who d. in infancy.

VII. KEYES, MARTHA LOUISA (1523), m. Henry C. Jones, Oct. 13, 1844. Mr. Jones has been several times in the

Legislature, was a member of the Conf. Congress, and is now States Attorney for his Judicial Circuit.

### CHILDREN.

William Stratton, d. from a wound received as a Confederate soldier, in the fight at Franklin Tenn.; Bertha, m. Melville Allen, Marion Co. Ala.; George P., Lawyer, Lauderdale Co. Ala.; Ellen Rivers; Henry C.; John K.; Jennie Keyes; Martha Bolling; Robert Young; Wade Keyes.

VII. KEYES, JOHN WASHINGTON (1524), "entered La Grange College, Ala. Jan. 1842, whence he was suspended 1843, for fighting. Returning home he studied medicine, attended medical lectures in Louisville, Ken., and commenced the practice of medicine in partnership with Dr. Welch, in Somerville, Alabama." On the 4th of Nov. 1846, he m. Julia L., eldest dau. of Prof. Nicholas Marcellus, and Caroline Lee Hentz, in Tuskegee, Ala. They have had 15 children, whose names we have not received. In 1849, he studied in Cincinnati and 1850 took the degree of Dr. of Dental Surgery, from the Ohio Dental College, and the degree of Dr. of Medicine, from the Medical College of Ohio. Dr. Keyes was for a time in Florida, and in 1857, removed to Montgomery, Ala., devoting himself to the practice of Dentistry, to the literature of which profession he was an occasional contributor.

He was in the Conf. army at Mobile, in Co. A., 1st Battalion of Hilliard's Legion, and as surgeon of 17th Ala. Reg. He also acted as surgeon in St. Mary's Hospital in Montgomery, and elsewhere. The citizens of Montgomery presented him with a fine horse as a mark of esteem. After the war he went to Brazil, returned, and in 1873 bought lands in Calhoun Co., Florida, and engaged in the culture of the orange. Dr. Keyes is six feet tall, weight 180, with great physical strength, as may be seen from the fact of his having captured a shark eight feet in length without the aid of men or weapons.

VII. KEYES, JANE C. (1525), m. John D. Rather, Jan 26, 1843. He is a lawyer, has been Circuit Judge, Speaker of the

House of Representatives, President of the Senate of the General Assembly of Alabama, and member of the Constitutional Convention of 1875. Has also been President of the Memphis and Charleston R. R. Company. Res. Tuscumbia, Colbert Co. Ala. Mrs. Jane C. Rather d. 1853.

### CHILDREN.

George T., connected with the R. R. Memphis and Tennessee; Silas P., lawyer, Decatur, Ala.; Eldon Rutledge, res. Tampa, Florida.

VII. KEYES, GEORGE P. (1526), graduated at La Grange College, Ala., at the age of 18, receiving the degree of A. B. Edited the Athens Alabama Herald, afterwards removing to Montgomery, where for twelve consecutive years, he was Register and Master in the Chancery Court. He was in the southern army during the late war, with Col. Bibb's company at Fort Morgan as its first Sergeant, and in the Alabama Legion during the celebrated campaign into Kentucky. After having been discharged on account of ill health, he commanded a battalion of Home Guards. He is now connected with the editorial department of the Montgomery Daily Advertiser, and occasionally indulges in writing verses, some of which have been popular among his friends. He m. 1859, Fannie L. Gayle, who d. May 1, 1876, leaving a dau. about ten years of age.

VI. KEYES, WASHINGTON (1485), s. of Capt. John, and twin brother of George, m. Elizabeth Williamson of Columbia, Maury Co. Tenn. Her mother was a Hunter, of North Carolina, nearly related to the Hintons of Raleigh. Col. Harney Walker, A. O. P. Nicholson, and Dr. A. Voorhies of Columbia, were her cousins. Col. Washington Keyes was a merchant, was very popular during his life and lamented at his death, which occurred Feb. 13, 1838.

"Died, near Quincy, Florida, on Tuesday the 13th of Feb. last, Col. Washington Keyes, late cashier of the branch of the Bank of the State of Ala., at Decatur, of Pulmonary affection, with which he had been affected several years. He was b. in Washington Co. Va., Nov. 18, 1792, and at an early age removed thence to East Tenn., where he res. until 1818, or '19. He thence removed to Limestone Co. Ala., where he lived until his residence in this place (Decatur), whence he went to Florida for the benefit of his health. In the death of Mr. Keyes this community mourns the loss of one of its most worthy citizens, and Alabama one of her ablest and most efficient financiers. Mild and unassuming in his manners, and pleasant in his address, he possessed the friendship and esteem of all who knew him." Col. W. Keyes, also his sons William and Frank were Masons.

### CHILDREN.

1531. William McCord, b. about 1824.
1532. Laertes John, d. Mar 7, 1861. unm.
1533. Antoinette, d. at 15 years.
1534. Albert Green.
1535. Bettie, b. Mar. 20, 1834.
1536. Francis W., b. July 28, 1836, in Decatur, Ala.

VII. KEYES, WILLIAM Mc. C. (1531), engaged at 19 in the study of the law, passed his legal examination, and removed to Houston, Chickasaw Co. Miss., intending to settle there. But on the breaking out of the Mexican war, he was chosen leader of a company, and commanded the post at Tampico, at which place and elsewhere in that war, he distinguished himself by his bravery. On one occasion he was presented by Gen. Taylor to a large Assembly of the citizens of N. O., and complimented by him in the highest terms. At the close of the war he devoted himself to his plantation, at the same time studying many hours each day, and acquiring several of the modern languages. "But he brought home with him, the seeds of that insidious disease which ultimately caused his death." He d. one year after his return, at the age of 25, unm.

VII. KEYES, ALBERT G. (1534), was educated at the Univ. of Miss. at Oxford. In the late war, he belonged to the 28th Miss. Reg. of Cavalry, was wounded in the charge through Franklin, Tenn., under Van Dorn, was taken to the hospital in Nashville, Tenn., and d. there May 23, 1863. He left a dau. whose death occurred soon after his own.

VII. KEYES, BETTIE (1535), m. 1st Aug. 1851, her cousin Joseph M. Keyes, a merchant of N. Orleans, and had four chil; Bella and Lillie, and two boys who d. in infancy. Bella m. Frank Andrews of Warsaw, Franklin Parish, La., and has one child. Lillie is the wife of Charles W. Hunter, Bolivar Co., Miss. dau. Keysey, three years of age. Col. Jo. Keyes d. July, 1857. In 1864, Bettie m. 2nd, Mr. A. M. Hunter of Clairborne Co. Miss. He was killed (through mistake), May 20, 1872. Bettie m. 3d, May 12, 1878, Judge William Chambers of Chambers Co. Texas, where she now resides.

"Claxton, Remsen and Haffelfinger of Philadelphia, have published a book in which will be found the name of Mrs. Bettie Keyes Hunter, among the living Female Writers of the South." Her poem, "Death in Prison," written upon the death of her brother in hospital prison, was extensively copied by the press, and others have been republished in the London Times. She has now a vol. of poems nearly ready for the press. She is spoken of as having been, after the death of her parents, the "good angel" of her brothers, making for them a happy home, encouraging them to all that was noble and good. Col. Jo. Keyes, and Judge Chambers were masons, and Mrs. Chambers has herself taken two degrees.

VII. KEYES, FRANK W. (1536), graduated at the Univ. of Miss. Oxford, was in the 20th Miss. Reg. Infantry, was made Capt. taken prisoner with Floyd's Brigade at Ft. Donnelson, and remained in prison at Sandusky, Isl., seven months, afterwards exchanged. A southern paper of that period speaks of him as "the youngest of a noble family of brothers, who moved into Carroll Co., a few years before the war, all whole souled and generous, and superior to every thing mean, sorded or base." The same paper speaks of him as a "splendid soldier." After the war Capt. Keyes returned to Carrollton to the practice of Law. He was chosen delegate to the Baltimore Convention after the war, and during the administration of Gov. Alcorn, was Prosecuting Attorney for his District. Capt. Keyes m. 1st, 1860, Mary dau. of Col. Griffith of Baltimore, Md., who d. Apr. 13, 1861. He m. 2d, Claudine Griffith, (sister of his first wife), Sept. 1864. He d. after a short illness, Oct. 1st, 1875, and his wife d. the 12th day of the following March, 1876.

### CHILDREN.

1537. Francis Williamson, Jr., b. Oct. 14, 1865, at York, Penn.

1538. William Stuart Parrott, b. Sept. 3, 1867, at Carrollton, Miss.

1539. George Griffith, b. Dec. 1, 1869, at Carrollton.

1540. Louis Parrott, b. April 15, 1872, at Carrollton.

These sons of Capt. F. W. Keyes, now res. with their mother's sister, Mrs. Peter Bentz, in York, Penn.

VI. KEYES, MARY (1489), dau. of Capt. John, m. June 30, 1820, John M. Richardson. Mary m. 2d, Mr. Redus, who dec. She now res. with her son J. W. Richardson in San Antonio, Texas.

### CHILDREN OF MARY AND J. M. RICHARDSON.

Harriet L., b Dec. 21, 1820, m. Dr. Yarborough, d. Dec. 1855; Margaret J., b. June 6, 1823, d. June, 1851; William J., b. Oct. 11, 1825, d. Sept. 30, 1852; George W., b. May 12, 1828, d. July 22, 1851; Louisa, b. Nov. 12, 1831, d. Oct. 12, 1848; John B., b. Apr. 28, 1833, during the war, was an officer of the Washington Artillery, (Conf.) now res. in N. O. Edward S., b. Dec. 30, 1835, d. Apr. 22, 1841; James W., b. Aug. 22, 1842, res. in San Antonio, Tex.

V. KEYES, GERSHAM (1469), eldest s. of Capt. Humphrey and Sarah Hall, m. 1st Susan Wood, who d. early and left one son, Humphrey. By a 2d marriage he had two sons, and one son by a 3d marriage.

### CHILDREN.

1541. Humphrey, b. about 1792.

1542. John, d. in Charlestown, Va., in the winter of 1878, unm.

1543. Robert, Res. Fort Worth, Texas.

**1544. Thomas W.,** Res. St. Joseph, Mo.

These two brothers moved West many years since, and nothing is now known of them.

## VI. KEYES, HUMPHREY (1541), eldest s. of Gersham,

m. 1st, Miss Yates, who d. leaving no children. Humphrey m. 2d 1833, Jane H. Brown, a neice of Gov. Brown of Florida, and res. in Charlestown, Jeff. Co. W. Va. Humphrey Keyes d. Sept. 1875. Jane his wife d. March, 1879, in Charlestown.

### CHILDREN.

**1545.** Susan Wood, m. 1860, Rev. C. E. Ambler (Episcopal), who about 1876, d. leaving five children, who, with their mother res. in Charlestown.

**1546.** Margaret, now res. in Charlestown, West Va.; has given many particulars of this branch of the family.

## V. KEYES, THOMAS (1470), s. of Capt. Humphrey and Sarah.

"On the map of Jefferson Co. Va., in the eastern part of school Dist. No. 16, will be found a place designated as Rose Valley. A spring, also marked on the map, commences in that valley, and after meandering gently through a number of meadows, and receiving other rivulets, enters into the Shenandoah. This streamlet, nameless on the map, has been sometimes called the Douglass Branch, from William Douglass, a venerable old gentleman, with snow white locks, fair topped boots and beaming face. Along this branch or stream dwelt various families well known to the dwellers in that neighborhood, the Rutherfords, the Andersons, the Gardners, the Ridenours, &c. Still descending the stream toward its outlet, passing the Brown and Burnett homesteads, the last house we come to before reaching the Keyes Ferry tract, is the place where the late Rev. Thomas Keyes resided, the little stream coursing through his meadow almost in a crescent. At that day circuit preachers of the Meth. Epis. Chh. regularly preached at his house and held class-meeting once a fortnight on week days. A portable pulpit with long rows of benches, occupied the back porch, the whole length of the hospitable old

mansion, and these were all brought into the largest room of the
house on preaching days. Rev. Thomas Keyes was himself a
local preacher and if the preacher failed to arrive, he preached
the sermon and led the class himself. The old homestead church
of Mr. Keyes, was for pioneer work. The growing congregations
of Charlestown and Harpers Ferry, each about four miles dis-
tant, gradually rendered it unnecessary to keep up public wor-
ship at this rural spot. The place, known as Rose Hill, was
afterward occupied by Isaac Chapline, who married the widow
of Rev. Thomas Keyes. The place was originally a portion of
the Keyes Ferry Tract, but was set off to the Rev. Thos. K.,
on a partition of the domain among the heirs of Humphrey, son
of the 1st Gersham."—*Charlestown, W. Va., Paper.*

V. KEYES, ELIZA (1475), was b. at Keyes Ferry, and m.
1794, at Halltown, at the house of one of her uncles, Capt.
George North, as his 2d wife. She had nine children, "who
partook of the restless, roving disposition of her seafaring father
and military husband, and are scattered through half the States
of the Union to S. America and foreign lands." Capt. North removed about 1790, to Va., from Chester Co. Pa. He res. ten
years or more on the Potomac, one mile above Harpers Ferry, in
1801, removed to Mt. Jefferson, a farm of 400 acres, then to
Charlestown, then to the neighborhood of Alexandria. The
mother of Capt. North was a Swedish lady, Lydia Rambo, who
inherited a share in the old Swedish church in Philadelphia,
which share is now held undivided by all her descendants. Capt.
North inherited from an older brother, Col. Caleb North, his
sword, a pair of pistols used by a progenitor at the Boyne water
about 1690, and a black charger which had borne him at the
head of his troop on many a hard fought field, especially at
Monmouth, in which battle it is supposed that seven of the
brothers participated, and concerning which it is said that there
is in the family an autograph letter of compliments from Washington himself. The eldest son of Capt. North and Eliza
was named William Darke, from Gen. Darke, between whom
and Capt. North there was a warm friendship, and the 2d son,

owns the golden epaulets, a present to his father from the old General. Capt. North d. at his home in Fairfax Co. Dec. 30, 1814. Mrs. Eliza North was living in Charlestown in 1857, in her 83d year, in "good health and of sound mind," and from her many of these facts were learned.

Here ends the record of John Keyes, son of Solomon, of Chelmsford, Mass.

The following record was found by Danforth Keyes, Esq., now of Warren, Mass., in an old English Bible which had formerly belonged to his grandfather, Col. Danforth Keyes.

It is probable that had the persons mentioned in the list been born, or lived in this country, we should have found some of their descendants. Not having done so, we conclude them to be relatives of the family, of whom we know nothing, born in England or Scotland.

"Thomas, son to Jonathan and "Rebaca," Born Jan. 30th, 1683.

| | | |
|---|---|---|
| Danforth, | Born | Mar. 17, 1686. |
| Jonathan, | " | Mar. 22, 1689. |
| Elizabeth, | " | Aug. 31, 1690. |
| Samuel, | " | Sept. 16, 1692. |
| Nicholas, | " | Aug. 17, 1695. |
| Jacob, | " | Feb. 6, 1698. |
| Sarah, | " | Aug. 18, 1700. |
| John, | " | June 3, 1703." |

# PART THIRD.

---◆━◆---

COMPRISING FAMILIES OF THE NAME OF KEYES
WHOSE DESCENT FROM ROBERT OR SOLOMON
IS NOT CERTAIN, ALSO OTHERS OF THE
NAME, OF LATER ARRIVAL IN
THIS COUNTRY.

## IV. STEPHEN KEYES.

It is recorded in Chelmsford, Mass., that Stephen Keyes and Anna Robbins, were m. in 1706, by Jon. Tyng, Esq., and that Stephen was one of the town committee in Chelmsford, in 1714. This is all we know of his history. He may have been s. of the elder Joseph, who with his brother Sol. settled in Chelmsford, 1664—5. The prevalent tradition is, that whereas, Sol. had a large family and numerous descendants, Joseph has had few, or no representatives among the Keyeses of later days. Stephen may have been his son. I find no record of the death of Joseph in Chelmsford. Probably he removed to some other locality, where Stephen, (if his son) was born, and where both father and son died. I incline however to the theory that Stephen was oldest son of Elias of Sudbury, and grandson of Robert of Watertown, and with the exception of Joseph, I know no other parentage he could have had, in the line of Robert or Solomon, who have been supposed father and son, and who undoubtedly were family connections.

CHILDREN OF STEPHEN AND ANNA.
Recorded in Chelmsford.

1. Phebe, b. Dec. 10, 1706.
2. Anna, b. Dec. 29, 1707.
3. Jonas, b. Aug. 3, 1709. Sup. m. Thankful, dau. of Maj. John Keyes.
4. Robert, b. Sept. 21, 1711.

V. KEYES, ROBERT (4), s. of Stephen and Anna, m. in Shrewsbury, Dec. 24, 1740, Martha, dau. of Asa and Martha (Eager) Bowker. The birth of all Roberts children but the last is recorded in Shrewsbury, the two last names being found in Princeton, Mass. Robert removed to Princeton, Mass., and settled on Wachusett Mt. Among the most thrilling tales of pioneer life, is that of the loss of his little dau. Lucy, who while playing on the mountain, with her brothers and sisters, probably strayed away, and was missed from the band of children on their return home. The neighbors collected, and search was made;

she was never found, and the minds of the parents were long distracted with visions of a terrible death by wild beasts, starvation, or the unknown dangers of the forest. The death-bed confession of a former resident of Princeton, revealed the fact of her murder, on account of some business trouble with Robert.

Robert d. in Princeton, Mar. 1, 1795. Martha his wife, d. Aug. 9, 1789.

### CHILDREN.

5. Stephen, b. Jan. 19, 1742, d. Dec. 20, 1748.
6. Jonas, b. Dec. 24, 1743.
7. Martha, b. Dec. 6, 1745.
8. Anna, b. June 21, 1748.
9. Lucy, b. Aug. 15, 1750.
10. Phebe, b. July 31, 1752.
11. Abraham, b. Mar. 10, 1755.
12. Mary, b. July 19, 1757, at Wachusett.
13. Solomon, b. June 28, 1762, at Wachusett.
14. Martha, b. Sept. 1764,

VI. KEYES, SOLOMON (13), s. of Robert, m. Oct. 2, 1796, Betsey Rand of Weston, Mass. Sol. d. Feb. 29, 1808. Betsey, his wife d. Dec. 25, 1808.

### CHILDREN.

15. Stephen, b. Feb. 20, 1797, moved to the State of N. Y., about 1826 or '28.
16. Lucinda, b. Sept. 14, 1798, m. Rev. Samuel Everett, (Bap.)
17. Phebe, b. Dec. 11, 1800.
18. Lucretia, b. Oct. 19, 1802.

## OLIVER KEYES.

IV. KEYES, OLIVER m. Rebecca Patterson, Nov. 13, 1727. Children recorded in Shrewsbury. Barry's history of Framingham notices that Oliver Keyes of that town was a soldier under Col. Buckminster. We have no record of his parentage, but it is probable that Oliver and Eli were younger sons of Elias, son of Elias of Sudbury, and g. g. sons of Robert of Watertown.

## CHILDREN.

19. Lydia, b. Feb. 25, 1729.
20. Titus, b. Jan. 24, 1731.
21. Joanna, b. Apr. 16, 1733.
22. Orin, b. Sept. 14, 1735, d. 1736.
23. Stephen, b. Feb. 8, 1738.
24. Sarah, b. Apr. 6, 1740, d. 1745.
25. Elizabeth, b. 1742, d. 1745.
26. Esther, b. 1745, d. 1745.
27. Abijah, b. 1746.

V. KEYES, TITUS (20), eldest s. of Oliver, m. Esther Perham of Upton, Mass., 1757. son. Oren, b. Mar. 23, 1758.

V. KEYES, STEPHEN (23), 3d son of Oliver, m. Elizabeth Ward, and lived in Charlemont, later in Conway, Mass. Stephen "Kies" of Conway, m. widow Molly Cross of Ashfield, Mass., Oct. 3, 1799. He was admitted to the church, (Cong.) in Ashfield, Dec. 14, 1800, and his death rec. there, Feb. 17, 1812.

### CHILDREN.

28. Levinah, b. July 6, 1760.
29. Elizabeth, b. Oct. 3, 1762.
30. Calvin, b. Mar. 17, 1765, in Lancaster, Mass.
31. Gerrish, b. July 2, 1767.
32. Lydia, bap. Oct. 4, 1772, in Ashfield, Mass.
33. Nabby, bap. July 9, 1775, in Ashfield, Mass.

VI. KEYES, CALVIN (30), s. of Stephen, m. Reliance Tolman of Deerfield, Mass., Feb 22, 1785. He was a clergyman, (Bap.) lived for a time in Ashfield, mostly in Conway, Mass., and d. there some years since.

### CHILDREN.

34. Calvin, b. Dec. 6, 1785.
35. Luther, b. Sept. 10, 1787, d. in infancy.
36. Reliance, b. Aug. 11, 1788.
37. Lydia, b. May 28, 1790.
38. Phila, b. Apr. 22, 1792, dec.

39. Luther, b. July 9, 1794. Went to Penn., forty years ago.

40. Rhoda, b. May 19, 1796, m. George Barrows, res. Ashfield, Mass.

41. Joel, b. Aug. 11, 1798. Always lived in Conway.

42. Nancy, b. May 1, 1800, d. in South Ashfield, 1877.

43. Mary, b. Mar. 16, 1803.

44. Elmira, b. June 23, 1806.

45. Clarissa, b. June 22, 1808, m. a Childs, res. Conway.


VII. KEYES, CALVIN Jr. (34), m. Jemima Hillman of Martha's Vineyard, about 1809, d. about 14 years ago, in Winchester, Mass., of paralysis, at the house of her son. Calvin lived in Conway, later in Charlemont, Mass., and d. there 1874.

### CHILDREN.

46. Love, b. 1810, m. in Clarksburg, Mass., Oren Cook, eight chil. three boys, one of whom d. in the army.

47. Laura, b. 1812, m. Ephraim Leonard, who d. 1878, no chil.

48. Seth, b. 1814, m. Mila Ann Smith, two dau. He d. in Charlemont, 1874.

49. Luther, b. 1816, in Charlemont.

50. Levi, b. 1818. Has an adopted son. Res. near Ogdensburg, N. Y.

51. Susan, b. 1820, m. Write More. Five chil. Res. Athol, Mass.

52. Lorenzo D., b. Oct. 17, 1822.

53. Lewis Hart, b. Apr. 14, 1824, m. Marissa Davis, res. Athol, Mass., three dau.

54. Electa, b. May 1826, m. Charles Upton, four chil. two dec. Res. Charlemont, Mass.


VIII. KEYES, LUTHER (49), m. Rosaline Courser, has a farm of a hundred acres in Rowe, Mass., where he res.

### CHILDREN.

55. Oscar, res. Pittsfield, Mass.

56. Delia.

57. Emma.

58. Charles. dec.
59. Lydia, m. res. in Rowe, Mass.
60. Luther, res. Rowe.

VIII. KEYES, LORENZO D. (52), m. Jan. 1850, in Ber-
nardston, Mass., Velonie P. Day. Farmer. Res. Brattleboro, Vt.

### CHILDREN.

61. Albert Arthur, b. Oct. 1852, m. Carrie Emerson, who d.
1877. Three chil. of whom only Lilla survives. Res. Brattleboro, Vt.

62. Willis, b. Oct. 14, 1854, m. Emma Aldrich of Worcester,
Mass., dau. Daisy and a s. not named. Res. Brattleboro, Vt.

63. Etta, b. April 14, 1856, m. Clifton Haynes, son Roy. Res.
Marlboro, Vt.

VII. KEYES, JOEL (41), m. Apr. 26, 1828, Hannah L.
Porter, who d. Sept. 16, 1876, aged 69. Res. Conway, Mass.

### CHILDREN.

64. Sylvester W., } d. in infancy.
65. Miranda J., } d. at two years.
66. Christopher C., b. Oct. 5, 1829, m. Sophronia Smith. 2 s.
3 dau. Res. Northampton, Mass.

67. James P., b. July 2, 1831, m. Jane E. Abercrombie. Has
3 sons. Lives on the old homestead in Conway.

68. Wealthy R., b. Mar. 31, 1833, m. William Rhood. Has 2
s. and 2 dau. She d. Feb. 22, 1872.

69. Miranda J., b. June 2, 1838, m. Alvin B. Stone. Has 10
chil. Res. Claremont, N. H.

70. Viola, b. Apr. 4, 1839, m. Rodney Blodgett. Has 2 s.
and a dau. Res. Greenfield, Mass.

71. Joel, Jr., b. Jan. 28, 1841. m. Sarah D. Brown. Has 2 s.
Res. Conway, Mass.

72. Fidelia, b. June 12, 1844. m. Stephen Smith, has 1 dau.
Res. Greenfield, Mass.

73. Simeon P., b. Sept. 12, 1847. m. Frances Allen. Has 4 s.
and 1 dau. Res. Conway.

74. Sylvester P., b. Nov. 12, 1849, unm. Res. St. Louis, Mo.
75. Dwight A., b. Aug. 5, 1855, unm. Res. Conway.


## ELI KEYES.

IV. KEYES, ELI perhaps s. of Elias, (No. 10, of part 1st),
m. Mary Wheelock, 173—, and res. in Shrewsbury, Mass.

### CHILDREN.

76. Eli, b. Mar. 24, 1733.
77. Nathaniel, b. Sept. 6, 1739. Was in Jaffrey, N. H., 1801.
78. Ebenezer, b. July 15, 1741.
79. Mary, b. Oct. 24, 1743.
80. Ezra, b. Jan. 24, 1750.


V. KEYES, ELI Jr., (76), m. Hannah Howe, 1762. His
name found in Jaffrey, N. H., in 1795—'6, and 1803.

### .CHILDREN.

81. Ezra, b. Jan. 27, 1763, in Holden, Mass.
82. Daniel, b. Nov. 17, 1764.
83. Azubah, b. June 5, 1767, m. a Whitney, res. Winchendon,
Mass.
84. Abigail, m. a Sawyer, moved to Vt.
85. Sally, m. a Willard, lived in Harvard, Mass.
86. Nathan, had sons, Josiah, Everett and Silas. It is said
that Nathan moved to Vt., or N. Y.


VI. KEYES, EZRA (81). At the age of 16, enlisted, and
served in the Rev. army, m. Dec. 1792, Hannah ———, b. Aug.
13, 1770, moved to Readsboro, Vt., where his children were b.
and where he died.

### CHILDREN.

87. Eli, b. Aug. 19, 1794. Removed to N. Y. State.
88. Sally, b. Nov. 2, 1795.
89. Ruel, b. June 22, 1797.
90. Hannah, b. Feb. 17, 1799.
91. Polly, b. Jan. 4, 1801.
92. Ezra, b. Oct. 14, 1802.

93. Henman, b. Dec. 11, 1804.   Res. Pittstown, N. Y.

94. Daniel, b. Mar. 28, 1807.

95. Nathan, b. Oct. 8, 1809.   Removed to N. Y. State.

96. Azubah, b. July 26, 1813.   Res. E. Bennington, Vt.

97. Lorton, b. July 19, 1816.   Res. South Pownal, Vt.   m. No chil. living.

VII. KEYES, RUEL (89), m. went to N. Y., about 1823, settled in Chatauque Co., d. in Jamestown, N. Y., Dec. 22, 1870.

### CHILDREN.

98. Alfred, b. in Chatauque Co., sup. now living there.

99. Mary Ann, m. a Kimberly.

100. Mara, m. a Blanchard.

101. Lyman B., b. in Chatauque Co., Aug. 1830, m. Sept. 16, 1868.   one dau., three years.   Res. Bennington, Vt.

VII. KEYES, EZRA Jr. (92), m. Apr. 1, 1830, Elizabeth ———, b. Feb. 25, 1808.   P. O., South Walpole, Mass.

### CHILDREN.

102. Joann E., b. Feb. 28, 1831.

103. Nancy C., b. June 1, 1833.

104. Warren C., b. Apr. 4, 1835, in Dover, Mass.

105. Hannah E., b. June 12, 1837.

106. Abbie F., b. Mar. 4, 1842.

107. George R., b. Nov. 9, 1845.

108. Alvin L., b. June 16, 1849.   m. Jan 22, 1873, Ella M. Carroll.   s. Lester C., b. Oct. 17, 1875.

VIII. KEYES, WARREN C. (104), m. Nov. 27, 1855, in Newton, Mass., Dorcas A. Tefft, who was b. in Pawtucket, R. I., Dec. 10, 1839.   Res. Worcester, Mass.

### CHILDREN.

109. Fred W., b. Feb. 16, 1857, in Foxboro, Mass., d. Nov. 27, 1857, in Ill.

110. Anna E., b. Aug. 13, 1858, in Delavan, Ill.

111. Charles E., b. Oct. 28, 1860, in Boston, Mass.

112. Herbert W., b. Dec. 14, 1862, in Boston.

113. Ida F., b. Mar. 2, 1864, in Boston.

VI. KEYES, DANIEL (82), 2d s. of Eli, Jr., m. Jedidah
Sawyer, b. Jan. 16, 1767, d. Feb. 14, 1850.  He moved from
Lancaster to Princeton, Mass., 1809, and d. Dec. 4, 1826.

### CHILDREN.

114. Roxie, b. May 18, 1793.

115. Sarah, b. July, 1795, d. 1856, unm.

116. John, b. Dec. 1797, d. Jan 23, 1845, s. John.

117. Mary, b. July, 1801, m. 1823, E. N. Hager.  Res. Sterling, Mass.

118. Lucinda, b. Jan. 16, 1804, d. 1859, unm.

119. Martha, b. July 13, 1808, 2d wife of Silas Keyes, see
appendix.

120. Charles, b. May 7, 1811, d. May 24, 1839, unm.

## WILLIAM KEYES.

I. KEYES, WILLIAM, and Mary his wife, lived in Bolton, and in Harvard, Mass., where he was assessor in 1755.  We
know  nothing of his ancestry but may suppose him to be an
original emigrant from Great Britain, or possibly a son of Dea.
John, No. (11), of part 1st.  In the absence of proof as to his
ancestry, we make him of the first generation in this country.

### CHILDREN.

121. Nathan, b. 1737, in Bolton, Mass., d. Mar. 3, 1739.

122. Nathan, b. 1740.

123. Timothy, b. 1741.

124. Solomon, b. 1744, d. Mar. 19, 1745.

125. Mary, b. 1746.

126. William, b. 1752.  Rec. in Harvard, Mass.

II. KEYES, NATHAN (122), of Harvard, m. Zuriah Greenough of Marlboro.  Published July 16, 1763.

### CHILDREN.

127. Willis, probably the eldest son.  Rec. in New Marlboro,
Mass.

128. Thaddeus, b. Aug. 23, 1767.

III. KEYES, WILLIS (127), m. Sarah——— about 1786,
and rec. in New Marlboro, Mass.

### CHILDREN.

129. **Mary,**
130. **Martha,** b. Aug. 17, 1787. dec.
131. **Clarissa,** b. Aug. 1789. d. young.
132. **Sarah,** b. Sept. 25, 1792.
133. **William,** b. May, 1798.
134. **Lucinda,** b. Jan. 11, 1801.
135. **Sidney Willis,** b. Apr. 25, 1806. d. young.
　　　Also a son not named, b. 1796.

IV. KEYES, WILLIAM (133), s. of Willis, m. Abigail Smith. He d. Sept. 6, 1867.

### CHILDREN.

136. James, m. Abigail Rhoades, and lived on the farm on which his father and grandfather lived. He has two children living,
137. 　　　　William.
138. 　　　　Mary.
139. Charles, d. at 18 years of age.
140. Sarah, d. at 13.
141. Edgar, m. Jane Huntley and had two s,
142. 　　　　Frank.
143. 　　　　Ezra.

III. KEYES, THADDEUS (128), 2d s. of Nathan, m. 1st Hulda Spelman; m. 2d Tamar Smith. Res. New Marlboro, Mass. He d. there Mar. 12, 1756.

### CHILDREN.

144. Albert, b. June 10, 1795. Lost at sea. Unm.
145. Willis, b. Oct. 22, 1796.
146. Lucius, b. Nov. 2, 1797.
147. Lester, b. Mar. 22, 1801. m. 1st Lucy Smith; m 2d Lucretia Davis, no chil. Res. Southfield, Mass.
148. Paulina, b. June 29, 1803. m. Peter Smith. dec.
149. Dennison N., b. Sept. 29, 1805.
150. Emmeline S., b. Jan. 9, 1808. m. John Morse. Two sons. Res. Monterey, Mass.
151. Salmon G., b. Dec. 1810. m. Mary Smith. No chil. Res. Southfield, Mass.

152. Angeline, b. Apr. 11, 1818, d. about 1838, unm. Dau. of 2d marriage.

IV. KEYES, LUCIUS (146), m. Sarah Segar. Res. New Marlboro, Mass.

### CHILDREN.

153. Burton, b. Dec. 3, 1825.
154. Homer, b. June 25, 1827.
155. Huldah, b. Apr. 17, 1828.
156. John S., b. Aug. 5, 1832.
157. Oliver, b. Sept. 15, 1834.
158. Sarah, b. Apr. 20, 1836.

IV. KEYES, DENNISON N. (149), m. Emmeline Marshall. He res. in Southfield, Mass., and d. Apr. 18, 1879.

### CHILDREN.

159. Mary A., b. Sept. 28, 1830.
160. Dorrance B., b. Aug. 4, 1832. m. Emmeline Hadsel. Res. Southfield, Mass.

### CHILDREN.

161.        George.
162.        Charles.
163. Marshall, b. Oct. 27, 1835. Killed at the 2d battle of Bull Run.
164. Lorren P., b. Jan. 6, 1838. m. Sarah Rhodes, Sept. 8, 1862. Res. Southfield, Mass.

### CHILDREN.

165.        John H., b. Dec. 24, 1865. d. Oct. 9, 1878.
166.        Howard L., b. Apr. 6, 1868.
167.        Edward Z., b. Oct. 10, 1870. d. Oct. 5, 1878.
168.        Arthur P., b. May 5, 1874.

Dennison had also two children, Henry and Helen, twins, b. Aug. 23, 1842.

## WILSON KEYS.

I. KEYS, WILSON, was b. in 1718, and according to a descendant, emigrated from Scotland, where the name was Mc Kies. His wife Sarah H., was b. 1729, and d. Oct. 2, 1821.

Wilson d. Apr. 5, 1800. The dates are found on grave stones, in West Killingly church yard.

### CHILDREN.

169. Nathaniel, b. May 7, 1759, in Killingly, Conn.
170. Ebenezer.
171. Wilson, b. 1765.

II. KEYS, NATHANIEL (169), m. Anna——, b. Mar. 21, 1758, and lived in Killingly. His name on the record spelled Keys. About 1808, removed to Elmira or Palmyra, N. York.

### CHILDREN.

172. John Hutchinson, b. Mar. 5, 1881.
173. Lucy, b. Oct. 20, 1783.
174. Archibald, b. Apr. 9, 1788.
175. Harden, b. Feb. 6, 1793.
176. Nathaniel, b. May 21, 1795.
177. Joseph Lyman, b. Aug. 29, 1797.
178. Ronitoma, b. Jan. 16, 1799.

III. KIES, ARCHIBALD (174), lived in Killingly, and d. about 1852.

### CHILDREN.

179. Horace A., b. about 1814. Farmer in Killingly, spells his name Kies.
180. John, d. young.
181. Eleizer T., studied medicine. Present res. unknown.
182. Lyman. Farmer in South Killingly.
183. Archibald, is, or was, a clergyman, and went West.

II. KEYS, WILSON Jr. (171), m. Betsey ——, who d. 1829. Spelled his name Keys. He d. Jan. 3, 1825, and was buried in Killingly.

### CHILDREN.

184. Marvin, b. June 4, 1798.
185. Prentiss. Farmer in Killingly. s. Leonard.
186. William Wilson. Farmer in Killingly.
187. Knight, d. when a young man.
188. Phila, m. a Davis.

189. Mary, m. a Phillips, and removed West.

190. Eliza, m. a Bump, and removed to Michigan.

191. Harriet, m. a Cooper, removed to Iowa.

192. Almira, d. at 18 years of age.

III. KEYS, MARVIN (184), m. 1823, Frelove Buck. Was a farmer in Killingly.

### CHILDREN.

193. William Knight, b. Dec. 22, 1823.

194. Henry, b. Mar. 15, 1825. Clergyman. Removed to Troy, Iowa, where he d. 1855.

195. Geo. Whipple, b. 1828, merchant in Norwich, Conn.

196. Welcome, b. 1831, d. 1850.

197. Marietta, d. an infant.

198. Ahira Z., b. 1834. Farmer in Killingly.

199. Lydia Melissa, b. 1836, m. a Vaughn, d. 1869.

IV. KIES, WILLIAM K. (193), m. Maranda, dau. of Joshua Young of Killingly. Res. West Killingly, Conn.

### CHILDREN.

200. Adaline, b. Feb. 12, 1851, m. A. Stearns.

201. Marietta, b. Dec. 31, 1853.

202. Alice Melissa, b. July 24, 1856, m. a Davis.

203. Ellen Maranda, b. Aug. 11, 1858, m. a Burton.

204. Julietta, b. Dec. 31, 1863.

There is a John Kies, now living in Killingly, s. of Ambrose dec., and grandson of William, also dec., both of whom lived in Killingly, ancestry unknown, unless they are descendants of Ebenezer, s. of Wilson, (170.) There is also a family of Kies now living in Clinton, Mich., who emigrated from Killingly. The father Alpheus, went a long time ago from Conn., to Caledonia or Moravia, Cayuga Co., N. Y. He claimed to be a cousin of Edward, s. of Solomon and Sarah Keyes of Ashford, Conn. A dau. of William Kies, (193), says the name has been spelled Kies but a short time.

## DANIEL KEYS.

I insert here the family of Daniel Keys, as he was one of the Killingly families, and it is not improbable that he was a descendant of Wilson Keys, Sen. The names however are not similar, but resemble those of the Solomon families.

I. KEYES, DANIEL, was born Apr. 13, 1755, and m. Dec. 5, 1779, Abigail Hutchins, in Killingly. They moved to Waterville, Oneida Co. N. Y., June 1806, where Daniel d. Apr. 15, 1825. Abigail d. Feb. 14, 1840.

### CHILDREN.

205. Hannah, b. Oct. 2, 1780, d. June 4, 1832, unm.

206. Ezra Hutchins, b. Dec. 27, 1781.

207. Pardon, b. May 22, 1783.

208. Clarissa, b. Sept. 27, 1785, m. Jan. 21, 1810, J. Bunce, and d. about 1840, leaving three children, Mary, Clara and Sidney A., who was a prominent man, and member of the N. Y. Legislature in 1871. He d. 1876.

209. Shubael, b. May 2, 1789.

II. KEYS, EZRA H. (206), m. Mar. 28, 1805, Almy Spaulding.

### CHILDREN.

210. Horatio Nelson, b. Dec. 23, 1805, at Killingly, Conn.

211. Abigail H., m. May 15, 1832, O. Moffitt, and d. Dec. 16, 1832, leaving two sons.

212. Clarissa, d. unm.

213. Eliza A., d. unm.

Mrs. Alma Keys, wife of Ezra, d. Aug. 19, 1814. Ezra m. 2d, June 4, 1815, Martha Hall, who had three children.

214. Rebecca, d. unm.

215. Hiram E., d. about 1835, unm.

216. Elisha D., m. Nov. 12, 1849, Fidelia Day, who d. Apr. 2d, 1871, leaving two dau. Elisha m. 2d, Feb. 24, 1874, Mrs. A. Dewey. Res. Holley, N. Y.

Mrs. Martha Keys, wife of Ezra, d. Apr. 10, 1838, and Ezra m. Apr. 15, 1839, Mary Blake, who d. Apr. 29, 1861. Ezra d. at Holley, Feb. 12, 1864.

III. KEYS, HORATIO N. (210), m. May 15, 1832, Marietta Beebe. Res. Holley, N. Y., where he has been P. M., and Deacon in the congregational church.

### CHILDREN.

217. Daniel Hutchins, who m. Nov. 28, 1861, Emily R. Wood, res. in Cleveland, O., and has two children.

218.      Dodd N., aged 13.

219.      Kitty, aged 11.

220. Amy Spaulding. Teacher in Cleveland.

221. Marietta Beebe, d. July 23, 1836, aged 15 weeks. Marietta, wife of Horatio, d. Apr. 30, 1836, in her 27th year. Horatio m. Jan. 15, 1837, Alethea Beebe, sister of Marietta.

222. Paphyrus B., b. Jan. 4, 1838, was Capt. of a company of 100 days men in the last war. Res. Bloomington, Ill.

223. Marietta, b. June 24, 1839, m. Jan. 16, 1862, T. Fitch Harwood. They have four chil. Res. Bloomington, Ill.

224. Ezra, b. Apr. 22, 1841. Killed at the battle of Fredericksburg, Dec. 13, 1862.

225. Harlan Page, b. Apr 22, 1843, m. Aug. 27, 1868, Mary Winchester. Res. St. Johns, Mich.

### CHILDREN.

226.      Ezra, aged nine years.

227.      Stephen, aged seven years.
         and three daughters.

228. Berton, b. Feb 10, 1845. Res. Holley.

229. Clarissa, b. Feb. 14, 1847, d. July 22, 1862.

230. Sarah Louvira, b. Sept. 23, 1849, m. J. Q. Pierce, June 1, 1874. Res. St. Johns, Mich. One son.

231. Silas Day, b. July 25, 1851, m. Sept. 12, 1875, Mary Maxon.

232.      Son Dwight B., Res. St. Johns, Mich.

233. Eliza Frances, b. Apr. 27, 1853. Res. Cleveland, O.

234. Horace Nelson, b. Aug. 8, 1858. Res. St. Johns, Mich.

235. Willie Aram, b. July 25, 1860. Res. Holley.

II. KEYS, PARDON (207), m. March 1, 1810, Clarissa Wells, and d. Aug. 26, 1833.

### CHILDREN.

Jane S., and Harvey S., both married, Milton, Caroline, Clara, Elisha, Daniel and Catharine. Sup. living in Mich.

II. KEYS, SHUBAEL (209), m. Apr. 19, 1811, Betsey Wattles, and had five children. He was m. three times, and d. 1864 or 5.

### CHILDREN.

Harriet Ann, dec., Shubael Sherman, Sally M., Mary, James, Cornelia. Sons sup. to res. near Munsville, N. Y.

## PETER KEYES.

I. KEYES, PETER lived in Plymouth, N. H., afterwards in Strafford, Vt. They also lived in Bethel township, Vt. Peter was in the Rev. war. m. Rhoda Durkee, and d. at the age of 93.

### CHILDREN.

236. Sarah, b. Aug. 4, 1782, in Plymouth, N. H.

237. Peter, b. June 15, 1784. m. Feb. 17, 1807, Nabby Beedy. He d. at 80.

238. John, b. Mar. 20, 1786. Now living near Meadville, Penn.

239. Rhoda, b. Jan 7, 1788.

240. Polly, b. July 27, 1790. m. Oct. 13, 1811, Sephas White of Pittsfield, Vt.

241. William, b. Sept. 17, 1792. d. in infancy.

242. William Durkee, b. Oct. 23, 1794.

243. Elizabeth, b. Jan. 16, 1797, in Strafford, Vt. m. a Cady.

244. Lovina, b. Sept. 6, 1799. m. a Benjamin.

245. Ama, on record, or Apey, according to descendants, b. Sept. 18, 1801.

246. Thomas Jefferson, b. Dec. 4, 1803. Now living near Olean, N. Y.

247. Henry Hammond, b. Mar. 27, 1806. Res. Wis. or Mich.

II. KEYES, WILLIAM D. (242), m. Sept. 3, 1816, in Strafford, Vt., Lydia, b. July 1801, dau. of John Evans, of Strafford. He moved first about 1817 to Eagle, Wyoming Co. N. Y., and in the fall of 1835, to Chatauque Co. N. Y., where he d. Aug. 1874. Lydia, his wife now lives in Westfield, Chatauque Co. William was in the war of 1812.

### CHILDREN.

248. Sidney W.; b. May 24, 1818. Now living in Waupun,

Fond du Lac Co. Wis.

249. Chauncey, b. Nov. 14, 1819, res. in Mayville, Chatauque Co., N. Y.

250. Benjamin S., b. Sept. 18, 1828, was surgeon in Finly General Hospital at Washington, where he died, Sept. 22, 1863.

251. Alvah Evans, b. Aug. 2, 1825.

Also four dau. of whom we have only the name of Rhoda.

III. KEYES, A. E. (251), received an academic education and is a graduate of two Med. Colleges; Berkshire Med. College of Mass., and the Homeopathic Med. College, Philadelphia, Penn. He m. 1st, May 12, 1846, Mary, dau. of Samuel Brown, formerly of Herkimer Co. N. Y. Mary d. June 5, 1865. They had two sons and two dau., the latter married to brothers of the name of Graham. The sons d. at the ages of 5 and 24. Dr. Keys m. 2d, Annis B., dau. of James K. Neiler, of Philadelphia, Penn. Dr. Keyes was surgeon in the late war from Aug. 1861, to Sept. 1863. He res. in Mansfield, O., and has one son.

252.          Stephen B., b. about the year 1868.

## ROGER KEYS.

I. KEYS, ROGER and his wife Sarah Adair, were from Ireland, in the year 1730, and settled in Old Virginia, i. e., East of the Blue Ridge, in what is now Augusta Co. A descendant thinks they removed to Va., from Penn. Roger was a weaver by trade, and an "old fashioned Irish Presbyterian."

### CHILDREN.

253. John, said to have been much older than his brothers.

254. Margaret, m. George McCawder. Their chil. John, who m. Elizabeth Trotter, George, Francis, Roger and Sally.

255. Sarah, m. Thomas Hammond. Chil. William, Thomas H., Samuel H., Sally, Betsey and Rachel.

256. Benjamin.

257. Samuel.

II. KEYS, JOHN (253), eldest s. of Roger, m. Nancy, and had two                         SONS.

258. James, b. 1762. He may not have been eldest son.

259. John, who had a s. John, and perhaps other chil.
There were also ten dau. of John, (253.)

III. KEYS, JAMES (258), who was wounded at the battle
of King's Mountain, in 1781. He lived in Washington Co. Va.
and d. there about 1840.

### CHILDREN.

260. John, moved to Rutherford, Tenn.
261. Robert, dec. Family now living in Bristol Tenn.
262. Samuel, d. in Mo., several years since. Son,
263.        Rev. James Keys, of Liberty Hall Ins. Glade
         Springs, Washington Co. Va.

II. KEYS, BENJAMIN (256), 2d s. of Roger, m. Betsey
McCord, and had eight chil., who all lived and d. in Washington Co. Va.

### CHILDREN.

264. James.
265. Roger.
266. Betsey.
267. John, b. Feb. 10, 1793.
268. Robert.

III. KEYS, JAMES (264), m. Margaret Doran. He had
six             SONS.

269. John.
270. Alexander D.
271. Benjamin.
272. Robert W.
273. James.
274. David L.

III. KEYS, ROGER (265), m. Susan Berry, and had four
SONS.

275. Benjamin.
276. George B.
277. Samuel.
278. John.

III. KEYS, JOHN (267), m. Martha Buchanan, and had three s. He d. Oct. 31, 1828.

### SONS.

279. Robert, b. about 1824. m. 1st Isabel Jane Lowry, who had five children, all dec. but one dau. Emma, who m. A. T. Barrow of Abingdon, Va. Robert m. 2d, a Miss Mayer, g. dau. of Geo. Selby, of Bennington, Vt.

280. Andre.

281. John.

III. Robert (268), m. Mary Buchanan, and had two

### SONS.

282. John.

283. Benjamin.

II. KEYS, SAMUEL (257), youngest s. of Roger, m. Esther Lyle, and settled at or near Timber Ridge, Rockbridge Co. Va., in sight of the Blue Ridge, and near the Natural Bridge, which gave the name to the County. Samuel Keys, Esq., was at the time of his death, High Sheriff of Rockland Co. Not long after his death his widow and family moved to Ohio, and settled in Highland County. They belonged to old Scotch Presbyterian stock, two sons of Samuel being elders in the church, and all holding strong anti-slavery views. Mrs. Esther Keys d. at about 70. Samuel Keys, Esq., d. Mar. 1803, in Rockbridge Co. Va.

### CHILDREN.

284. John.

285. William, b. 1778.

286. Samuel.

287. Andrew R., b. 1786.

288. Jane, m. Hugh Rogers. Chil. Andrew R., Joseph and Amanda.

289. Betsey, m. Hugh Hills. Chil. Samuel and Joseph.

290. Polly, m. Samuel Ramsey. Chil. George and Joseph, and four dau.

291. Martha, m. William Jones. Chil. Calvin and James.

III. KEYS, JOHN (284), eldest s. of Samuel, was Captain in the war of 1812. He m. in Va., Polly Smiley, and emigrated with his mother and family to Ohio.

#### CHILDREN.

292. Samuel.
293. John.
294. Susan.
295. Calvin.
296. Reid.
297. Hugh Y.

III. KEYS, WILLIAM (285), 2d s. of Samuel, m. in Rockbridge Co. Va., Nov. 18, 1802, Margaret, dau. of Mathew Donald, who m. a widow Thompson, neé Lyle. He came to America about 1774, and settled in Rockbridge Co. He was descended from the McDonald's of Scotland, sup. descendants of some of said Clan, who escaped from the massacre of Glenco. Samuel and Margaret were m. by Rev. Dan. Blair. They moved to O., in the fall of 1805, and settled on Fair Creek, Highland Co., and to Hillsboro, O., Sept. 1811. William was in the war of 1812 and '13, was appointed Colonel and raised a regiment for scouting on the Anglaise and Maumee Rivers, to protect Gen. Harrison, at Ft. Meigs. For Many years he was Auditor, Justice and Mayor in Ohio, until in 1862 or '3, he was stricken with paralysis.

Col. William Keys d. in Princeton, Ind., Feb. 1, 1864. Margaret d. Mar. 16, 1846. Age 71.

#### CHILDREN.

298. Samuel Addison.   dec.
299. William Lyle.
300. James Madison, b. Sept. 19, 1810.
301. John Milton.
302. McDowell, d. in infancy.

IV. KEYS, SAMUEL A. (298), m. Jane Jolly.

#### CHILDREN.

William, James, Theodore, Milton, Elizabeth, Tamsia.

IV. KEYS, WILLIAM LYLE (299), a natural artist and musician, grad. at Washington Coll., at Lexington, Va. Studied medicine, then grad. at Andover, Mass., Theological Sem., but on account of ill health did not preach, or practice medicine. He married but had no children, and is now dead.

IV. KEYS, JAMES M. (300), m. June 12, 1832, Catharine Bethel Hand, b. in Hillsboro, O., Mar. 31, 1817, d. 1864. He m. 2d a sister of his first wife. They were dau. of Dr. Jasper Hand, Surgeon General of the U. S. Navy. It is related that being at a ball in Philadelphia, given in honor of the English Admiral, the patriotic feelings of Dr. Hand were aroused by seeing the English Crown, placed above the American Eagle, and he drew his Navy pistol, and knocked the crown from its superior position, on which account he was cashiered. The father of Dr. Hand was Brig. Gen. Edward Hand, prominent at the Battle of Trenton, and descendants describe having seen many trophies of that field, in his possession. J. M. Keyes has been since early youth in positions of public office, for 16 years was Deputy Auditor, Clerk and Treasurer. Now recorder of Deeds for the County. Res. Princeton, Ind.

### CHILDREN.

303. Jasper Hand, b. Feb. 6, 1836, in Hillsboro, O., m. Amanda King, has six chil. He is Editor and Publisher of a paper in Northern Ind.

304. Henry Brien, b. Nov. 4, 1837, has been traveling in Europe since the Paris Exposition, in 1866 or '7, where he received a medal as Aerial performer on the Trapese. m. in Berlin, Prussia.

305. William Lyle, b. Mar. 12, 1839. Studied medicine, held a position in the Miss. Fleet, in the late war, where he contracted disease of which he died.

306. Jane Ann, b. Dec. 30, 1841, m. Wm. H. Evans of the Princeton Dem. She has dec.

307. Kate, b. Mar. 17, 1844, m. Gilbert R. Stormont, Editor and proprietor of the Princeton Clarion.

308. Donald McDowell, b. May 22, 1855, foreman in the office of the Clarion.

Five other chil. have dec.

IV. KEYS, JOHN MILTON (301), was ornamental painter and gilder, and d. 1864. He m. his cousin Sarah. Chil. William, now in Oregon, James, Kate, Martha and Frank.

III. KEYS, SAMUEL (286), 3d s. of Samuel, m. Jane Morrow, after his removal to Ohio.

### CHILDREN.

309. John Morrow.
310. Samuel, now living in Hillsboro, Ohio.
311. William P. Probably res. in Hillsboro.
312. James.
313. Ester, m. a Lowman.
314. Betsey, d. single.
315. Martha, m. Milton Keys. Probably the Sarah mentioned under head of 301.

IV. KEYS, JOHN M. (309), m. Sarah Lowman. Res. Douglass, Ill. Removed to Ill, 1837.

### CHILDREN.

316. Samuel, b. Oct. 26, 1844. P. M. in Douglass.
317. Mary J., b. May 24, 1847.
318. G. N., b. May 9, 1849.
319. William D., b. June 2, 1851.

III. KEYS, ANDREW R., (287), 4th s. of Samuel, emigrated to Hillsboro Co. O., in 1805. He m. Nancy Hill, in Ohio.

### CHILDREN.

320. William H., b. 1812, now living in Berryville, Hillsboro Co., Ohio. He m. Dec. 9, 1841, Maria Springer.

### CHILDREN.

321. Ira S., b. Dec. 25, 1842.
322. Albert N., b. May 30, 1844.
323. Cynthia I., b. Feb. 27, 1846.
324. Nathan A., b. Nov. 17, 1847.
325. John W., b. July 22, 1849, d. in Kansas, 1870.

326. Frank H., b. Feb. 3, 1851.

327. Robert L., b. Dec. 16, 1852.

328. Oscar D., b. Aug. 27, 1854.

329. Sylvester M., b. Aug. 7, 1856.

330. Olive C., b. Mar. 28, 1858.

331. Edwin W., b. Oct. 3, 1860.

332. Charles E., b. Feb. 24, 1864.

333. Hettie M., b. Nov. 9, 1866.

Only two of these sons married. There are three g. chil. Andrew R., had a number of dau. but no other s. who lived to maturity.

About 1789 or '90, four brothers by the name of Keys, settled in East Bloomfield, N. Y. The date not certain, but the town was settled 1789, and some of them were there in its earliest days. Their descendants represent them as emigrants from the town of Pownal, Vt. From the recurrence of the names John and Benjamin, it is probable that they were children of John, s. of Roger, of whose children we know nothing.

### NAMES OF THE BROTHERS.

334. Henry.

335. John.

336. William, res. in Batavia, Genesee Co. N. Y. s. Chauncey.

337. Benjamin.

III. KEYS, HENRY had seven chil. He d. of Epidemic fever, 1813.

### CHILDREN.

338. William, had a large family, and lived in East Bloomfield, N. Y.

339. Charles, d. of Epidemic fever within a week of his father's death.

340. Nathaniel, d. of brain fever about 1813, at 21 years.

341. Lyman.

The dau. were Olive, Polly and Mahala.

IV. KEYS, LYMAN (341), m. Hannah Francis, was in East Bloomfield about 1814, soon after removing to Niagara Co. N. Y.

Lyman, was in the war of 1812, d. Sept. 18, 1828. His widow removed in 1836 to Mich. where she d. Jan. 5, 1866.

### CHILDREN.

342. Charles H., dec.

343. Orlando, dec.

344. Nathaniel, dec.

The dau. were Mahala, perhaps Mary; Julia, Rebecca. Julia who m. Silas Carney, res. Climax, Mich., and dec. Mary, m. Mr. Crowhurst, res. Kalamo, Mich.

III. KEYS, JOHN (335), was in E. Bloomfield, with a surveying party, among whom was Thaddeus Keys, as early as 1789. He had a large family, and left the town about 1815, with his two sons. Nothing more is known of them.

346. John.

347. Milton.

III. KEYS, BENJAMIN (337), m. Pamela Fellows, lived for a time in Sheffield, Mass., as is shown by a record of birth of part of his children. He followed his brothers to East Bloomfield, N. Y., about the year 1800, where he d. about 1804. Says Mr. H. Munson, a resident of E. Bloomfield and a connection: "The name of Benj. Keys, should be held in grateful remembrance, for his gift of a piece of land to the town for a public green, containing five or six acres, which was used many years for a Military parade ground and for like purposes, but now planted out to trees, making one of the most beautiful Parks in Western N. Y., in the centre of which is erected a 6,000 dollar monument, to the memory of the soldiers who lost their lives in the late war."

### CHILDREN.

348. Julius, b. April 14, 1780, in Sheffield, Mass.

349. Rhoda, b. Mar. 5, 1782. Probably dec. young.

350. Harriet, b. Dec. 18, 1784.

351. Julia, b. Mar. 18, 1787.

352. Harry, b. June 14, 1789.  d. Mar. 23, 1791.

353. Harry, b. May 21, 1791.  Probably dec. young.
These six chil. rec. in Sheffield.  There were others of whose birth we have no record.

354. Roderic, m. lived in E. Bloomfield until after the death of his mother.  Had a dau.  Nothing now known of him.

355. Frederic, went to Mich.  Probably dec.

356. John, went to Mich.

357. Orlando, b. May 15, 1797, in E. Bloomfield.

358. Douglass, b. 1799, d. in E. Bloomfield, unm.

359. Julia.

360. Delora.

361. Maria, b. after her fathers death.


IV.  KEYS, JULIUS (348), eldest s. of Benj. m. in E. Bloomfield, about 1807, a Miss Munson, lived in the town of Clarence near Buffalo, till about 1812, when he returned to E. Bloomfield. He was Brigade Maj. under Gen. Van Rensalaer, in the war of 1812.  He was drowned by the capsizing of a boat in Sandusky Bay, O., in 1837.

### SON.

362. Jared Bradley, b. 1815, in E. Bloomfield, N. Y.  Settled in Sandusky, O., in 1829, moved to Ill. 1839, and returned to Sandusky 1847.  He m. 1833 in Sandusky, Arvilla Knapp, who moved from Stockbridge, Vt., in 1819.  Both now living.

### CHILDREN.

363.          Charles M., b. 1840, in Tazewell Co. Ill.  He served through the war, in the 8th Ohio Vols., and in the 123d Ohio Vols., and witnessed the surrender of Lee at Appomattox. In 1873 he m. Emma A. Quimby.  No chil.  Res. Sandusky, Ohio.

364.          Thomas Julius, b. 1842, in Ill., served in the war in the 123d Ohio Vols., m. 1871, in Sandusky, Libbie Wood. Res. Blissfield, Mich.  Two chil.

365.          Worthy.

366.          Ralph.

IV. KEYS, ORLANDO (357), m. Sept. 21, 1821, Nancy, dau. of Briant and Martha (Seymour) Stoddard. He d. of consumption June 29, 1828, at his mother's house in E. Bloomfield. Mrs. Keyes, after the death of her husband supported herself by teaching; lived in Binghamton, N. Y., then moved West and lived in De Kalb, Ill. Then moved with her daughter-in-law to Solomon City, Kansas, where she d. Aug. 18, 1867.

### CHILDREN.

367. Martha Elizabeth Seymour, b. in Sandy Creek, Monro Co. N. Y., Oct. 18, 1822, d. at Smithboro, Tioga Co. N. Y., Dec. 29, 1852.

368. Andrew Jackson, b. at Sandy Creek, Aug. 27, 1824. He m. Nov. 8, 1847, Susan, dau. of Dr. Calvin and Susan (Williams) Leet. She d. Feb. 11, 1849. She had one child who d. young. Andrew m. 2d June 15, 1853, in Marengo, Ill., Mary M. Coolidge, b. in Erie Penn. Jan. 7, 1838. He was a locomotive driver and was killed at De Kalb, Ill., by the bursting of the boiler of his locomotive, Sept. 30, 1856.

### CHILDREN.

369.     Ella Susan, b. April 8, 1854, at De Kalb.

370.     Charles Joseph, b. April 7, 1855, at De Kalb.

## PLYMOUTH RECORD.

In Plymouth, Mass., is found the rec. of marriage of

371. Benjamin Keys and Polly Norris, in 1796. Also of

372. Oliver Keys and Lydia Bagnell, Sept. 1, 1796. The m. of the latter celebrated by Rev. Dr. Chandler Robbins. Oliver was sup. to have been lost at sea. Oliver and Benj. may have been descendants of Roger.

### CHILDREN OF BENJAMIN AND POLLY.

373. William, b. July 7, 1798.

374. Benjamin, b. Apr. 6, 1801.

375. Samuel Norris, b. May 17, 1805.

376. Jane Williams, b. Nov. 24, 1808.

377. Oliver, b. Feb. 12, 1811.

### CHILDREN OF OLIVER AND LYDIA.

378. Lydia, b. Dec. 6, 1798. d. at Plymouth, about 1875.

379. Oliver, b. Aug. 14, 1799.

380. William Shurtleff, b. Sept. 24, 1801.   Lost at sea.

## JAMES KEYS.

381. KEYES, JAMES came from the North of Ireland about the year 1750, and settled in Chester Co., Penn.   He had one son,

382. Richard, b. 1760, who at the age of 19, became a Lieut. in the Rev. Army.   He afterward m. Mary, dau. of James Bayley, also from the same part of Ireland.   After Richard's marriage, he lived at Anderson's Ferry, or Marietta, on the Susquehanna, then at Maytown, and in 1801, moved to Baltimore, Md.

### CHILDREN.

383.        John Finley, b. Apr. 27, 1786, in Maytown, Lancaster Co. Penn.

384.        James, who settled in Cincinnati, and d. 1826, leaving one daughter.

385.        Bayley, who lived and died in Baltimore, leaving a large family of sons and daughters.

KEYS, JOHN F. (383). The "Biographical Encyclopedia of Ohio, of the 19th century", has given the above particulars of the ancestry of John F. Keys, with the mention of the removal of his father to Baltimore, where in 1801, at the age of 15, the subject of this sketch began his course as a business man in a shipping and commission house.

"In 1809, he was sent to the West Indies on business of great importance to his house.   Executing this commission satisfactorily, he returned to Baltimore, and in August of the following year was married to Margaret Barr, sister of Major Wm. Barr. In December of the same year he moved to Cincinnati. Remaining but a few months, in the Spring of 1811 he took up his residence in Chillicothe.   There the mercantile house of Barr and Keys was formed and carried on an extensive and successful business until 1815, when he again returned to Baltimore, and became a member of the firm of Barr, Keys and Welsh. But finding it to his taste and advantage, in 1817 he returned to

Cincinnati, with a view to making it his permanent home. And there he did, indeed, remain for nearly fifty years, only a few years before his death residing at Glendale.

During the greater part of that long period he was actively engaged in business, and was thoroughly identified with all the best interests of the city. He came to Cincinnati when it was without the pretensions of a city, being but a village. In 1818, he himself built the first three story brick house ever erected in that city. This building stood on the South side of Pearl street. He also built, and for many years occupied, the frame mansion at the foot of Vine street hill, now a part of the McMicken estate, and constituting a part of the McMicken University grounds. This was then in the woods and far beyond the village or town limits. Few men were so long uninterruptedly concerned in the growth and business of the city as Mr. Keys, and doubtlessly no man ever lived more in the confidence and esteem of the people of Cincinnati.

Soon after his location in Chillicothe he was elected Ruling Elder in the Presbyterian church of that place. This position he filled in the various churches with which he was connected until his death.

His family relations were like those of his church and society at large, of the most exemplary character. Four of his family of eight children are living at Cincinnati, and are known as worthy followers of their universally esteemed christian father. At his home in Glendale, on the 19th of May, 1865, this Christian pioneer passed away, with the words upon his lips, "may the Lord not long delay his coming."

CHILDREN OF JOHN F., AND MARY BAYLEY KEYS.

386. Richard Wilson, b. Oct. 15, 1815, in Chillicothe, O., now living in Glendale.

387. Samuel Barr, b. Aug. 15, 1823, in Cincinnati. Graduated at Hanover, 1844, studied law, and was admitted to the bar, 1847. Res. Cincinnati, O. We have from him an anecdote of Gen. E. D. Keyes of the late war, which although not strictly in place, we insert, having received it too late for its proper place in the notice of that officer.

· "In 1864, in Washington City, Maj. Gen. Keyes of the U. S. Army, (to whom I was introduced by Sec'y Chase,) asked me in a joking way, why he preferred *his* name to *mine*. And when I gave it up, the gallant old soldier "with a wink and a smile," said, because I can spell my name with more *Ease*. (ee.)

Samuel B. Keys has one son.

388.　　John B., b. Dec. 6, 1855, who graduated at Harvard 1877, and is now connected with the printing and publishing house of W. Baldwin and Co., Cincinnati.

## JOHN KEYS.

389. KEYS, JOHN was an original Irishman, was of old Presbyterian stock, moved from near Abington, Va., to Chester Co., So. Carolina, and d. there 1820. He had two sons.

390. Charles, who moved with his family to Georgia.

391. George, m. a Miss Patterson, removed to Wilkes Co., North Carolina, and d. 1847. The wife of George was neice of Robert Patterson, L. L. D., of Philadelphia, Brigade Major in the Rev. war, Prof. of Mathematics in the Univ. of Penn. 1779, then Vice Provost. Appointed director of the Mint of the U. S. in 1805, d. 1824. *Encyclopedia of Religious Knowledge.*

### CHILDREN OF GEORGE.

392.　　John, now living at Stony Fork, Wataugo Co., N. Carolina.

393.　　Hiram, now living at Stony Fork, Wataugo Co., N. Carolina.

394.　　Charles, emigrated to Princeton, Ind. 1833, where he now res. He has one son who res. in Texas.

## SAMUEL KEYES.

395. A Samuel Keyes removed from Hartford, Conn., to Pownal, Vt., about the year 1800. His father's name supposed to be Samuel, but further than that, his ancestry is unknown. Name of his wife, Alexa. He moved to Ohio with part of his family, and nothing more is known of him.

### CHILDREN.

Elihu, Samuel, Seth, Oren, (he was sheriff somewhere in Ohio), Josiah, Jesse and dau. Elexa.

396. KEYES, SETH s. of Samuel, did not accompany the family to Ohio. He m. Esther Morgan and d. by drowning, 1818.

CHILDREN.

397. Hiram.

398. Anna.

399. Joseph, located in Vt., probably in Pownal, dec.

400. Horatio, located in Ohio, and d. there.

401. Samuel, b. Jan. 28, 1812.

KEYES, HIRAM (397), s. of Seth, located in Vt., and has dec. Had four sons.

402. Samuel, recently a merchant in North Adams, now residing in Terre Haute, Ind.

403. Horatio, res. Terre Haute, Ind.

404. Henry.

405. Seth.

KEYES, SAMUEL (401), res. in Pownal, Vt., from 1861 to 1866, when he removed to Bennington, where he now res. He was Post Master in Pownal, under Buchanan. He has been Justice of the Peace, for ten or fifteen years in Bennington, Appraiser of Real Estate, Village Trustee, and Moderator at town meetings in that place. Also has been Merchant, Farmer and boss Mason. He m. Nov. 4, 1835, Susan Bannister.

CHILDREN.

406. Albert R., b. Jan. 13, 1838, is m. has two chil. Res. Bennington.

407. Delia A., b. Mar. 24, 1840. m. two children.

408. Susan C., b. July 13, 1842.

409. Catherine E., b. Oct. 14, 1844. m. two children.

410. Samuel J., b. Apr. 24, 1849. m. two children.

411. Andrew S., b. Dec. 2, 1854. Graduated at Williams Coll. 1877, and was one of the Class Orators. Was in the class of 1879, at Columbia Law School. Now res. in Bennington, Vt.

## SAMUEL KEYES, OF MILTON, MASS.

The following intentions of marriage are taken from the Leicester, Mass. records.

412. Samuel Keyes of Shrewsbury, and Hepsibah Green of Leicester, Oct. 6, 1733.

Samuel Keyes of Leicester and Hannah Culivier of Milton, May 6, 1739.

Samuel was m. according to Milton, Mass. records, to Hannah "Gulliver," May 29, 1739.

Nothing is known of the ancestry of the Milton family. Samuel may be a descendant of the Samuel Keies, b. 1628, m. at Salisbury, 1656, and associated with John Williams in Boston, Sept. 10, 1667, in witnessing the will of Robert Meere.

### CHILDREN OF SAMUEL AND HANNAH.

413. Nathaniel, b. Mar. 16, 1739, m. Abigail Vose, 1762. Chil. Abigail, b. sept. 28, 1765, d. an infant, and Eunice, b. May 7, 1767. Nath. d. Oct. 28, 1811, record in Milton.

414. Elisha, b. April 19, 1743.

415. John, b. Oct. 25, 1744.

416. Samuel, b. Nov. 16, 1746.

417. Hannah, b. Dec. 26, 1748, m. Elijah Horton, 1767.

418. Elijah, b. Nov. 9, 1750.

KEYES, SAMUEL Jr. (416), m. Thankful Hunt, 1762. He was undoubtedly s. of Samuel and Hannah, but was, as will be seen, only sixteen at the time of his marriage.

419. Phebe, b. Dec. 23, 1762.

420. Tryphena, b. Nov. 26, 1764.

421. Susanna, b. Aug. 8, 1767.

422. Elizabeth, b. Mar. 2, 1770.

KEYES, ELIJAH (418), m. Grace, his eldest child, b. in Milton, after which he appears for a time in Mason, N. H. Lt. Elijah Keyes was taxed in Mason, 1779, '80, '81, '82 and '83.

### CHILDREN.

423. Lemuel, b. June 14, 1778, in Milton, Mass.

424. Lydia, b. Nov. 6, 1779, in Mason.

425. Elisha, b. April 19, 1781.

426. Bathsheba, b. July 2, 1783.

## HUGH KEYES.

KEYES, HUGH was b. in Ireland. His father was a

Scotchman, who emigrated to Ireland about 1730, and settled near the city of Armagh, where the family lived until the removal to this country, and where it is supposed many of the connections still remain. Hugh d. at about 90.

SON.

427. Thomas, b. lived, and d. at the age of 30, near Armagh.

SON.

428.          James, b. 1819, at Armagh, came to this country about 1843, settled in Waddington, St. Lawrence Co. N. Y., where he now res.

SON.

429.          Sam. H., now living in Ogdensburg, N.Y.

# APPENDIX TO PART FIRST.

V. KEYES, SIMON, Sen. (97 of Genealogy), m. Sept. 5, 1766, Lucy Wheeler, who d. Apr. 26, 1801. Simon, Sen., d. Oct. 29, 1802.

### CHILDREN.

1. Simon, b. Aug. 25, 1767.
2. Lucy, b. Aug. 15, 1769, m. Artemus Childs.
3. Phebe, b. Aug. 28, 1771, m. Samuel Sheldon, Jr.
4. Abijah,  } b. June 30, 1773, in Wilton, N. H.
5. Solomon,}

Solomon settled in the vicinity of Farmington, Me. A son, perhaps Simon, lived in Grafton, Mass., 1853.

6. Abigail, b. Oct. 14, 1775, m. Amos Lawrence.
7. Thomas, b. Aug. 7, 1777, d. July 23, 1801.
8. Sally, b. Dec. 30, 1780, d. July 2, 1801.
9. John, b. Mar. 2, 1783, d. Mar. 8, 1801.
10. Jeduthan, b. Mar. 26, 1785.
11. Ezra, b. July 26, 1787, d. May 28, 1801.
12. Hannah, b. Aug. 19, 1789, m. John Simons.
13. Eber, b. Feb. 15, 1792, d. in Troy, of consumption, 182—. Married, but no children.

VI. KEYES, SIMON, Jr. (1), eldest s. of Simon, Sen., m. Hannah Hosmer, and settled in Wilton, N. H. For all we know of this family, see page 12. The record there is erroneous, as will be seen. It was Simon (109 of Gen.) who m. Hannah Hosmer, and his mother was Lucy Wheeler, according to record. The names of the children also are uncertain, with the exception of Solomon.

VI. KEYES, ABIJAH (4), s. of Simon, m. 1798, Sarah Abbot, b. Oct. 12, 1775. They lived in Wilton until 1811, then moved to Pelham, N. H., and passed there the remainder of their days. He was a farmer. He d. Dec. 25, 1844. Sarah his wife d. at the home of her son Nath A.,Feb. 17, 1854.

### CHILDREN.

14. Abijah Wheeler, b. Oct. 5, 1799.

15. Solomon, b. Nov. 10. 1800.

16. Sally, b. Oct. 14, 1802, m. Silas Tupper, Nov. 11, 1824. d. June 1827, in Barnard, Vt. 2 chil.

17. Polly, b. Feb. 3, 1804, accidentally scalded to death at 2 years.

18. Nathaniel A., b. Dec 26, 1807. The Dartmouth record has 1808.

19. John Calvin, b. Feb. 3, 1814, d. Aug. 5, 1818.

20. Polly, b. Nov. 13, 1820, d. Jan. 10, 1841.

VII. KEYES, ABIJAH W. (14), s. of Abijah Sen., m. Martha C. Butler, of Hudson, N. H., May, 1841. He moved with his father to Pelham, 1811. Martha his wife, d. Aug. 23, 1849. Abijah is a farmer and res. in Pelham.

### CHILDREN.

21. Calvin Abbot, b. Apr. 17, 1842, m. Lucina Stephens, of Nashua, N. H. No chil. Calvin d. in Nashua, 1874.

22. Charles W., b. Aug. 23, 1843. Went west 20 years ago.

23. Abijah, b. Apr. 15, 1848, d. 1849.

VII. KEYES, SOLOMON (15), s. of Abijah Sen., m. 1826, Eliza Todd, d. 1866, in Crystal Lake, Ill., "where he was an early settler, and struggling through the hardships of pioneer life, did much for the educational and religious interests of the neighborhood, contributing liberally toward the same."

### SONS.

24. Edward.

25. Nathaniel A.

26. R. Kimball, who d. 1858.

VII. KEYES, NATHANIEL A. (18), s. of Abijah, Sen., graduated at Dartmouth, 1835, studied Divinity at Andover

one year in the class of 1838, and finished at Lane Theo. Sem.
Walnut Hills, O. He was ordained a missionary at Pelham, N.
H., Aug. 9, 1839, sailed for Beiroot, Syria, Jan. 24, 1840, and
arrived the following April.

"During his missionary life he travelled considerably in the
Holy Land, made some valuable discoveries, and published an
interesting series of letters in the N. Y. Evangelist. On account
of ill health he returned 1844, and preached at Charlemont, and
at South Royalston, Mass. Finding the winters too severe, he
accepted a call to Lancaster, Penn., where he remained until
his removal west, in the fall of 1855. He was pastor elect at
Griggsville, Ill., and d. suddenly of Pneumonia, Mar. 30, 1857,
while engaged in removing thither. An elegant mural tablet
has been erected to his memory in St. Pauls church (German
Reformed) Lancaster, Penn., of which he was the first Pastor.
A portion of the inscription reads: "Eminently devoted and
beloved as a missionary, pastor, husband, parent and friend.
His best epitaph is written on the hearts of those he labored to
bless. They that turn many to righteousness shall shine as the
stars forever." Rev. Mr. Keyes m. Sept. 26, 1839, Mary Pette-
grew, of Weathersfield, Vt., who descended on her mothers
side from John Alden of the 'Mayflower.'"

### CHILDREN.

27. Mary E., b. in Jerusalem, July 24, 1840, d. in Mt. Leba-
non, Syria, June 13, 1841.

28. Edward Abbot, b. in Beiroot, June 26, 1842, d. July 1st
of the same year.

29. Harriet Louisa, b. in Beiroot, Feb. 1, 1844.

30. Helen C., b. in Charlemont, Mass., June 2, 1846.

31. Samuel A., b. in Lancaster, Penn., Oct. 8, 1849, d. Oct.
22, 1849.

VI. KEYES, JEDUTHAN (10), s. of Simon, Sen., m. Apr.
25, 1806, Susan, dau. of Nath. Abbott, of Concord, N. H.
Susan d. Apr. 26, 1814, in Oxford, N. H., aged 29. Jeduthan
m. 2d 1814, Sarah Abbott, sister of his first wife. He removed
about 1830, to Boonville, Oneida Co., N. Y., where he d. Jan. 2,
1841.

The record of the children of his 1st wife, on page 12 of the Genealogy is correct. Ezra W. (116), m. a Miss Merrill, and had 2 sons. He had also a son by 2d marriage. Ezra lived in Warren, N. H., and d. there about 1876. Albert (117), lived and d. in Boonville, N. Y. He m. a Miss Potter, and had 2 s.

### CHILDREN OF JEDUTHAN BY 2D MARRIAGE.

32. Daniel W., m. Jane Steel, had one dau. Res. Forestville, Conn.

33. Mary, m. Jan. 5, 1839, Morgan North, in Boonville, N. Y., and has 3 sons, Wayne, Merton and Charlie. Res. Princeton, Ill.

34. Maria, m. Thomas Fetterly, res. in Monroe, Wis.

35. Martha, m. Charles Swift, res. Eu Clare, Wis.

VII. KEYES, DAVID A. (119 of Gen.), b. in Haverhill, N. H., m. Feb. 17, 1836, Julia J., dau. of Salmon Gridley, b. in Farmington, Conn. Mar 3, 1815, d. in Unionville, Conn., Feb. 1, 1855. David Abbot Keyes res. in Unionville, Conn.

### CHILDREN.

36. Cornelius A., b. Mar. 12, 1837, d. Aug. 6, 1840.

37. Mary Elizabeth, b. Apr. 8, 1839.

38. D. Dwight, b. Feb. 23, 1841, d. May 14, 1864.

39. Albert C., b. Mar. 18, 1842, d. Sept. 28, 1842.

40. Julia M., b. Jan. 13, 1844.

41. Cynthia Bull, b. June 8, 1845.

42. Salmon G., b. Apr. 15, 1849, d. Aug. 1, 1868.

43. Martha J., b. Mar. 7, 1850.

44. John B., b. Apr. 25, 1851.

45. William Henry, b. Nov. 30, 1854, d. in infancy.

VII. KEYES, DAVID C. (133 of Gen.), s. of Rev. John, and Lucy Keys, m. May 26, 1836, Clementine Nichols, at Waynesburg, Wayne Co., O. David Keyes M. D., d. in Oakland, Alameda Co., Cal., Mar. 27, 1865.

### CHILDREN.

46. Adelaide A., b. June 22, 1837, at Jackson, Wayne Co., O.

47. John N., b. Mar. 14, 1840, at Newport, Ky.

48. Mary J., b. Dec. 1, 1842, at Congress, Wayne Co., O.
49. Lucy C., b. Feb. 1, 1846, at East Cleveland, O.
50. Merlin, b. Nov. 3, 1848, at Salem, O.

VIII. KEYES, ADA A. (46), m. Jan. 3, 1857, Henry S. Hill, at Elmwood, Peoria Co., Ill. Res. Peoria. Chil. Irene, b. Oct. 25, 1857, Mabelle A., b. May 17, 1869, at Peoria.

VIII. KEYES, MARY J. (48), m. Sept. 24, 1862, D. G. Voorhies. Chil. Josie A., b. Sept. 30, 1867, at San Francisco.

VIII. KEYES, LUCY C. (49), m. June 6, 1867, in San Francisco, William V. Kingsbury, her cousin. Chil. Mary C., b. July 2, 1868, at Susanville, Cal.; Willie V., b. Aug. 3, 1870, at Oakland, Cal.; Ray W., b. Mar. 25, 1873, at Oakland ; Ivy, b. Sept. 7, 1876, at Oakland.

VII. AMOS EDWIN (181 of Gen.), s. of Susanna (Keyes) and Peter Kendall, b. June 30, 1816, m. May 17, 1837, Mary Mason, of Princeton, Mass. No chil. Res. N. Y. City.

VII. KEYES, PETER KENDALL (186 of Gen.), s. of Amos, has only one son,
51. Herbert L., who is m. and res. in N. Y. City.

#### CHILDREN.

52.         Florence.
53.         William.

VII. KEYES, EZRA SAWYER (187 of Gen), s. of Amos, m. May 30, 1844, Abigail Florella Beaman, b. Aug. 2, 1823, d. May 4, 1876.

#### CHILDREN.

54. Myra Cordelia, b. Jan. 17, 1847, d. Nov. 18, 1865.
55. Atwood Beaman, b. Oct. 30, 1850, m. Nov. 26, 1872, Ella Sabia Hastings, b. July 1850, dau. Mary Florella, b. May 6, 1874.
56. Luna Florence, b. Dec. 27, 1857.

57. Chester Delano, b. Sept. 20, 1861.
58. Fannie Augusta, b. June 20, 1863.

VII. KEYES, CHARLES N. (189 of Gen.), s. of Amos, m. May 10, 1854, Anne E. Parker.

### CHILDREN, BORN IN PRINCETON, MASS.

59. Willie Harwood, b. June 9, 1856.
60. Minette Frances, b. Sept. 7, 1858.
61. Emma Dora, b. Mar. 26, 1860.
62. Andrew Augustus, b. Nov. 20, 1861.
63. Melville Warren, b. Oct. 28, 1866.
64. Kendall Grant, b. Dec. 27, 1868.
65. Charles Edwin, b. Apr. 5, 1870.
66. Freddie Herbert, b. June 26, 1874.
67. Daisy M. Roseanne, b. June 30, 1877.

VI. KEYES, SILAS (226 of Gen.), s. of Ephraim, m. 1st, 1821, Julia Brooks, of Princeton, Mass. He d. July 3, 1877, in Princeton, Mass.

### CHILDREN.

68. Augusta, b. Aug. 5, 1824, m. 1845, G. S. Beaman, and had 2 sons and 1 dau. Res. Worcester, Mass.
69. Joseph, b. 1825, d. 1827.
70. Adeline, b. May 31, 1827, m. 1849, Laban Cushing. Has 3 dau. Res. Fitchburg, Mass.
71. George, b. Nov. 27, 1832, d. 1835.
72. Emily S., b. Apr., 1834, m. William Baker, 2 sons and a dau. Res. Nelson, N. H.
73. Julia B., b. May 14, 1836, m. 1863, J. W. Lawrence. Has 3 dau. Res. Roxbury, N. H.

Silas, m. 2d, Oct. 20, 1836, Martha, (119 of 3d part) dau. of Daniel Keyes.

74. George, b. Oct., 1838, killed 1864, at Petersburg, Va.
75. Sarah S., b. Aug., 1840, m. 1862, Edwin Keyes, s. of Moses. Has had 2 chil. Harry, d. in infancy, and Murray, b. Sept. 27, 1870.
76. Charles Howe, b. Aug. 29, 1842.

77. Joseph H., b. Oct., 1844, d. in Fitchburg, Mass., 1872, s.

78.  Joseph, now in Greenville, N. H.

79. John, Jr., b. 1847, d. 1878, unm.

80. Henry F., b. Dec. 19, 1849, living in Princeton, on the old Ephraim Keyes place, unm.

VII. KEYES, CHARLES H. (76), lived for a time in Fitchburg, Mass., where he m. Dec. 24, 1763, Lucinda Huntley, and Sept. 25, 1865, removed to Dixon, Ill. Lucinda, his wife d. May, 1867, leaving no children. Mar. 30, 1869, he m. 2d, Annie Chiverton. Mr. Keyes is a Photographer in Dixon and Alderman of the 4th ward in that place.

### CHILDREN.

81. Amy Louisa, b. Dec. 13, 1871.

82. Annie Lena, b. Apr. 11, 1874, d. Nov. 17, 1878,

83. Charles Edwin, b. June 9, 1876.

A David Keyes, s. of Robert Keyes, b. 1753, removed from Mass., to Middletown, Vt., date of removal uncertain, and ancestry unknown to descendants.

In Sheffield, Mass., is the following record :

84. "David Keyes, s. of Robert, and that which wife Azubah bare to him, was born, Aug. 28, 1763.

85. Elizabeth, dau. of above, b. Oct. 20, 1754.

86. Hannah, b. Sept. 26, 1756.

87. Phebe, b. Aug. —, 1759.

88. Mary, b. Mar. 5, 1767, d. May 10, 1769.

89. Jane, b. June 22, 1769."

Robert, father of David was probably (239 of Gen.) and s. of Elias. It seems probable, from the names Robert, David and Azuba in that family. Also, because we have in no other place found Roberts descendants. It is supposed by those most familiar with the records, that 1763, given as the date of David's birth at Sheffield, should read 1753, which was the date of birth of David of Middletown, Vt. The Town Clerk of Sheffield says : "I am of the opinion that it is an error, as all the births that follow are in chronological order, and if this was 1753 instead of 1763 the dates would all harmonize. I have examined the record of quite a number of families recorded in this town, and this is the only instance where the date is in any manner reversed, but follow strictly in order of time."

### CHILDREN OF DAVID.

90. Robert, b. Sept. 6, 1783.

91. Tolman, went west, and dec. Descendants scattered through the west.

92. Stephen, b. 1790.'

93. Hiram, went west, and dec. Descendants still living.

94. Lyman, b. 1796, lived in Middletown, Vt. He d. Jan. 23, 1833. He had one son,

95.       Jonas, C., who left home when young. Present res. unknown. The dau. were Sally, Azuba and Polly, who d. in Middletown, and Emmeline, who removed to the west.

KEYES, ROBERT (90), eldest s. of David, m. in Middletown, Dec. 4, 1806, Sally Scribner, b. Nov. 26, 1781. He then removed to Poultney, Vt., and in the Autumn of 1823 emigrated to Ohio, and entered a tract of land in the north-western part of Knox Co., which was a part of the Walnut Ridge. He cleared the land and lived on it until his death, Dec. 22, 1870, aged 87 years, 3 months and 16 days. "He was a strong, hardy man, an upright honest citizen, and a member of the Baptist church, 60 years." His wife d. Feb. 27, 1864.

### CHILDREN.

96. Harriet, b. Dec. 24, 1807, m. Mar. 6, 1832, Niles Strong. She d. in Iowa, Nov. 9, 1869. Her husband is yet living.

### CHILDREN.

97.       William Cristie, now living.

98.       Sarah D.,     "    "

99. Elvira, b. Aug. 10, 1810, m. Nelson Strong, d. June 30, 1852, in Ohio.

100. Louisa, b. Mar. 3, 1814.

101. Elizabeth, b. May 8, 1817.

102. Robert S., b. July 22, 1823.

KEYES, LOUISA (100), m. Oct. 6, 1838, William Lyon, both now living in Ohio.

### CHILDREN.

Newton, b. Aug. 30, 1839; Marian, b. Mar. 29, 1842; Mary, b.

Feb. 6, 1844 ; Clotilda, b. Dec. 14, 1846 ; Araminta, b. July 17, 1850 ; Myrta, b. Dec. 31, 1853 ; Hattie, b. Nov. 28, 1856.

KEYES, ELIZABETH (101), m. Oct. 1, 1839, Joseph Denman.

CHILDREN.

Harriet C., b. Aug. 27, 1841 ; Wilson K., b. Oct. 29, 1843 ; Sherman N., b. July 3, 1846 ; Oscar S., b. Mar 31, 1849 ; Sarah Louise, b. Aug. 25, 1852 ; Viola A., b. Feb. 9, 1854 ; Elina Elvira, b. Oct. 22, 1856 ; Adda, b. July 8, 1861.

KEYES, ROBERT S. (102), m. June 25, 1848, Mary Hull.

CHILDREN.

103. Elmore Leroy, b. April 19, 1848.
104. Burton, b. Nov. 2, 1851.
105. Elvina, b. July 15, 1849.
106. Lewis, b. Feb. 28, 1853.
107. Monroe James, b. May 5, 1855.
108. July A., b. Apr. 11, 1858.

MONROE, JAMES (107), graduated at ——— College, and is a licensed preacher of the M. E. Church. At present, merchant and Post Master in Levering, Knox Co., Ohio.

KEYES, STEPHEN (92), m. Polly Waldo, in Middletown, Vt. He lived in Middletown, and d. there Dec. 28, 1865.

CHILDREN.

109. Harley L., b. 1813, lived in E. Rutland, Vt., d. Mar. 1878. He had one dau.
110.            Laura C., who res. in West Rutland.
111. Mary Ann, b. 1814, d. Oct. 31, 1848.
112. Sally Maria, m. L. B. Adams. Present res. Castleton, Vt.
113. Isaac B., b. 1822, d. June 15, 1862. He had a dau. who d. in infancy. His widow now living in Spencerport, N. Y,
114. Annis J., b. 1827, d. Jan 13, 1842.
115. Lovisa, d. in Poultney, about 1866.
116. David H., b. Aug. 11, 1833, in Middletown, Vt. He lived on the farm where he was born, until he was 15, afterward in Middletown village and Poultney. He was a merchant until his store was destroyed by fire, in 1862. The following Autumn he removed to Chicago where he has been successful in business, and where he now res.

VI. KEYES, CHARLES ancestor of the family given below, was born in Bolton, Mass., about 1760 or '61, and lived in Boston or Roxbury. He was in the Rev. war, emigrated to New York State and later to the city of that name. His descendants remember him as a Christian and a patriot, taking much pride in the growth of Boston while resident there. A number of brothers and sisters lived in the city or vicinity. He m. Dorothy Overlaugh, a lady of New Jersey. Charles Keyes was undoubtedly 278, of the Gen., the son of Joseph, and grandson of Mathias. The dates of birth correspond, and the names are repeated to the 3d generation.

### CHILDREN.

117. David, b. Jan. 5, 1789.
118. John Banker, b. 1791, in N. Y., city.
119. Dorothy, m. Charles Place, settled in N. Y., city.
120. Elizabeth, m. a Mr. Miller, settled in N. Y.
121. Hannah.

VII. KEYS, DAVID (117), eldest s. of Charles, m. Lavinia West, b. Nov. 22, 1793, or according to another, 1799. He res. in N. Y., and d. there April 29, 1866. Lavinia, his wife d. July 3, 1835. David spelled his name Keys, and his descendants follow his example.

### CHILDREN.

122. Angeline, m. Ezra M. Stratton, Editor in N. Y. They have two sons, of whom one was lost at sea, and two dau. Res. 325, E. 18th St., N. Y., city.

123. Jane West, m. 1st Rev. Elijah Crawford, (M. E.) of the N. Y. Conference. She m. 2d Mr. Van Vleck, of Kingston, N. Y., and has dec. No chil.

124. Lavinia, b. Dec. 4, 1817, m. Oct. 28, 1848, Elliott Eaton Lapham, who has dec. She has two

### CHILDREN.

125.         Elijah Crawford, b. Sept. 2, 1849.
126.   '      Emma Josephine, b. Jan. 18, 1853.
127. Charles Christopher.
128. David, b. Dec. 12, 1820.
129. Mathew, d. unm.
130. John, b. May 5, 1824.
131. William E., b. Jan. 27, 1828.
132. Jesse Goodsell, b. Aug. 6, 1831.
133. Hannah, m. Edgar Hudler, who dec. Res. N. Y., city.

VIII. KEYS, CHARLES C. (127), "was educated under private tutelage, and began preaching before he was 20, at Woodbury, Conn. In 1858, after 23 years of earnest work in the ministry, he retired from his pastoral labours. He was a member of the N. Y. Conf., of the M. E. church." Rev. Dr. Keys m. Elizabeth Schureman, res. in N. Y., and d. there about 1876.

CHILDREN.

134. Gilbert Schureman, b. Feb. 14, 1839, at Hyde Park, N.Y.
135. Mary Lavinia, living in N. Y., unm.
136. Elijah Crawford, res. N. Y., city. Four chil.
137. Charles Griffen, m. at New Haven, Conn., 1878, Josephine A., dau. of G. W. Goodsell, of N. H. Res. N. Y., city.

IX. KEYS, GILBERT S. (134), graduated at Wesleyan University, Middletown, Conn., was admitted to the Bar in N. Y., city, removed to San Francisco in the Spring of 1868, where he is merchandizing. Firm of Dempster & Keys. He m. Nov. 16, 1865, Theresa Catharine Weeks, at Cooperstown, N. Y.

CHILDREN.

138. Clinton Weeks, b. Oct. 7, 1869, in San Francisco.
139. Gilbert Winslow, b. Sept. 14, 1878, in N. Y., d. there Jan. 27, 1879.

VIII. KEYS, DAVID Jr. (128), m. June 20, 1843, Mary Anne De Forest. He is a Dentist, lived for a time in Danbury, now in Saugatuck, Conn.

CHILDREN.

140. Margaretta Crawford, b. Mar. 29, 1844, m. Sept. 10, 1867, Philip Gerard Sanford.
141. Alfred De Forest, b. Mar. 9, 1848, m. Dec. 29, 1874, Nettie R. Scobie.

VIII. KEYS, JOHN (130), m. Nov. 5, 1851, Sarah Elizabeth Jenkins. He had a Cooperage establishment in N. Y., from which he has retired. Res. N. Y., city.

CHILDREN.

142. Sarah Cornelia, married.
143. John Edwin, married.
144. George Albert, unm.

VIII. KEYS, WILLIAM E. (131), m. Feb. 20, 1854,

Eleanor Sarah Logan. Retail coal merchant. Res. 45, E. 59th
St., N. Y., city. CHILDREN.

 145. William E., b. July 18, 1855.
 146. Eleanor Estelle, b. Jan. 22, 1859.
 147. Edward G., b. Aug. 20, 1862.
 148. Albert L., b. Jan. 4, 1865, d. Mar. 1, 1871.
 149. Arthur Logan, b. Apr. 16, 1868, d. Mar. 19, 1871.

VIII. KEYS, JESSE G. (132), m. Dec. 23, 1853, a Miss Anderson, who dec. and he m. her sister. Cooperage, 268, Cherrry St., N. Y., city. CHILDREN.

 150. William Anderson, b. Apr. 13, 1857.
 151. Jesse Stanbury, b. June 16, 1860.
 152. Charles Harrison, b. Oct. 29, 1864.
 153. Mary Louisa, b. Apr. 27, 1869.

VII. KEYES, JOHN B. (118), 2d s. of Charles, d. 1875. We insert the following notice of his death, from a paper of that date. "A VETERAN GONE.—On Wednesday last, Mr. John B. Keyes, a veteran of the war of 1812, died at his residence, No. 237, Schermerhorn street, Brooklyn, at the advanced age of eighty-four years. Mr. Keyes was born in New York, and for many years carried on a prosperous mercantile business in this city. Thirty-five years ago he went to Brooklyn and engaged in business in that city. Shortly after going to Brooklyn he founded the De Kalb Avenue Methodist Episcopal Church, which is now one of the most wealthy organizations in the city of Churches. Mr. Keyes' funeral will take place from the church of which he was the founder, on Sunday next, and will be attended by the surviving veterans of 1812."

CHILDREN.

 154. John Allaire, now in San Francisco.
 155. Sarah Jane, dec.
 156. Seth Crowell, d. in infancy.
 157. Seth Crowell, b. Feb. 9, 1821.
 158. Dorothea, dec.
 159. William Edgar. Res. Brooklyn, N. Y.
 160. David Allaire. Res. Brooklyn, N. Y.
 161. Eliza. Res. N. Y., city.
 162. Mary Ann. Res. N. Y., city.
 163. Samuel. Res. Brooklyn, unm.

VIII. KEYES, SETH C. (157), m. and res. in Boston, where his children were born. He was for a time in Danbury, Conn., now res. in N. Y., city. Has been Clothing merchant and farmer, and is now a Carriage merchant, 372 and 374, Broome St., New York. Firm, Keyes & Wilson. Trademark, A. S. Flandrau & Co. Most of the other children of John B. Keyes, (118), are married and have children and grandchildren, whose names we have not obtained.

VI. KEYES, SALMA (301 of the Gen.), was b. in Worcester Co. Mass., probably in Shrewsbury, ran away from home when a boy, and enlisted in the Rev. Army, in which he served three years. After the close of the war he worked in various places as carpenter and mill-wright. In the year 1790, he settled in Rockbridge Co. Va. He m. Dec. 31, 1795, Polly Andrews, a native of Va., but of Irish Presbyterian ancestry, and began housekeeping about three miles from Lexington, Rockbridge Co. There, the two eldest chil. were born. About the year 1800, Salma purchased some mill property between Staunton and Richmond, in Albermarle Co., where in the beginning of Jefferson's Administration a new Post Office was created, called 'Keyes Mills,' and Salma Keyes appointed P. M. He received a letter from his brother Ebenezer in 1805, the last he ever heard from his N. E. relatives. He seems to have been prospered in business, during his residence there, and five more chil. were added to his family. But his strong dislike to the institution of slavery, prompted his removal to Ohio, in 1810, and in October of that year with such part of his property as he could transport, packed in two wagons, started for the 'far West.' A rougher road was hardly ever passed by wagons, over mountains and through valleys, until the head of the Kanawha river was reached. There one team was left and part of the goods stored, which were carried on by water the following summer. The family pushed on with one team to the mouth of the Sciota river, in Sciota Co. O., rented a field, and moved into a cabin sixteen feet square, where they passed the winter. They endured great hardships for a time, as did others around them, in reclaiming the wilderness, and making a home. This was particularly hard for the mother, who had been used to all the comforts of a well ordered Virginia farm house. But they had escaped the surroundings of slavery, and after a time bought a farm, and were prospered until 1814. At that time Salma went to Ill., and Ind., prospecting, in which latter State he d. Aug. 1814. Mrs. Keyes kept her family together until 1821, when it being a 'sickly year.' she and her son Andrew died.

### CHILDREN.

164. John, b. 1797. Took to the river before his father's death, and followed keel boating. Went to St. Louis, where he married. He had no chil. and his wife died early. He went to Cal. with the first overland train, and subsequently d. there.

165. Polly, or Mary, b. 1799, m. Feb. 1819, Levi Sikes, had three sons, and five daughters, all m. and settled in the vicinity of Portsmouth, O.

166. James, b. 1801, m. April 1831, had two dau. who d. young, and two sons. He res. in Portsmouth, O., and from him we have obtained the above history of Salma Keyes, who had long been lost to his family. He is under the impression that his father had a brother Jonathan. There is an impression among the Maine people, that there was another son, although they call him Thomas. James thinks Solomon must have d. young, as he has no recollection of hearing any mention of him, by his father. SONS.

167.  Thomas, res. in Col., unm.
168.  Milford, res. in Portsmouth, O. A printer, unm.
169. Robert, b. 1803, followed steamboating. In 1863, was pilot on one of the Government Gunboats, and ran the gauntlet at the seige of Vicksburg. He m. and lived in St. Louis, Mo., until his wife died. No chil. He d. at Baton Rouge, shortly after the surrender of Port Hudson.

170. Andrew, b. 1805, d. young, unm.

171. Elizabeth, or Betty, b. 1807, m. 1825, Philip Hayward. Betty d. 1826, leaving a dau., who m. John H. Noel. P. O., Portsmouth.

172. William, b. 1809, d. young, unm.

173. Thomas, b. 1813, in Ohio, m. in Cincinnati, removed to St. Louis, Mo., and raised a large family, mostly girls. He had two SONS.

174.  Henry, d. young.
175.  John, b. about 1854, now probably in St. Louis.

# APPENDIX TO SECOND PART.

VII. KEYES, LARNARD (191 of Gen.), m. Charlotte
————. He d. July 13, 1871.

### CHILDREN.

1. Winslow S., b. Feb. 27, 1832, m. Jan. 29, 1860, Catharine
H. Harding. Res. West Peterboro, N. H.

### CHILDREN.

2.        Frank W., b. Dec. 4, 1860.
3.        Katie L., b. Oct. 17, 1864.
4.        Gertrude H., b. Mar. 23, 1866.
5.        Karl S., b. May 21, 1878. (Probably 1868.)
6. Diantha, b. Mar. 19, 1839, m. Oct. 13, 1874, John F.
D'Orsay.
7.        Dau. Edith M., b. June 27, 1875.

VI. KEYES, SAMUEL W. (288 of Gen.), b. 1786, d. Feb.
17, 1851.

VI. KEYES, STEPHEN S. (289 of Gen.), b. Mar. 11, 1787
at Manchester, Vt. m. May 25, 1829, Deborah Sherman Barlow. He d. Nov. 19, 1866. They had nine chil. of whom
five lived to maturity.

### CHILDREN.

8. William, b. Dec. 29, 1831, m. Jan. 16, 1868, Lucy M.
Haskins. Dau. Lillian Wood, b. Sept. 21, 1873, d. Mar. 23,
1876. William Keyes is a Lawyer, res. Highgate, Vt.

9. Stephen, b. Mar. 1, 1837, m. May 7, 1873, Emma J. Cas-
sons. Res. Utica, Winona Co., Minn.

10. Elizabeth Sheldon, b. Mar. 7, 1839, m. Dec. 2, 1864,

Jacob M. Smalley, who dec. Mrs. Smalley has three chil. Res. Green Bay, Wis.

11. Helen, b. Feb. 14, 1842, d. May 12, 1864.

12. Laura Barlow, b. Dec. 11, 1851, m. Sept. 24, 1872, Myron P. Skeels. Two chil. Res. Green Bay, Wis.

Stephen, Helen, Elizabeth and Lucia W., d. in infancy.

VI. KEYES, ELIZABETH (292 of Gen.), b. 1792, d. Aug. 11, 1838.

IV. KEYES, SAMPSON, Sen. (21 of Gen.), 3d. s. of Elias and Mary, m. Abigail Brooks, of Ashford, Conn., lived in Ashford, and d. by drowning. Of his children, whose names have been given in the Gen., Zachary was a surgeon in the army, and d. of small pox, on board of a British prison ship, where he was a prisoner. Olive, m. a widower by the name of Weeks, lived and died not far from Utica, N. Y. No chil. Abigail m. a Mr. Hall, had children and lived somewhere in Vt. Avis, m. a Mr. Bullard, res. near Boston, had 16 chil.

Antoinette (327 of Gen.), dau. of Clarissa (Keyes) Paige, m. 1st, George Smith, 1825, who d. at Fort Johnson———Co., N. Y. Aug. 1828. Her dau. Mary, was b. 1827, m. in Schenectady, 1847, B. T. Potter, a Lawyer, who d. Mar. 18, 1870. Mrs. Smith m. 2d, Judge Platt Potter, in 1836.

V. KEYES, JOHN (306 of Gen.), was married to Mercy Scott, 2d wife (says the record at Farmington, Conn.) by Rev. Noah Porter, D. D.

VI. KEYES, ELNATHAN (315 of Gen.), m. Jane Fellows of Sheffield, Mass., two of whose sisters m. gentlemen by the name of Penfield, (for whom the town of Penfield, near Rochester, N. Y., was named.) Another m. Judge Edwards of N. Y., city. His granddaughter writes: "I remember my grandfather as being a grand looking old man, full of life and animation, very genial and well educated, and very attractive to all young people who called him uncle Ell. I remember he had some hobbies such as liking to arrange the wood across the fire, always taking bread and milk for his last meal, thinking the Indians were very badly treated, a constant student of the Bible, and holding liberal views of religion." His son, John Fellows Keyes, (328 of Gen.), had two dau. one of whom, Jennie, res. with her uncle by marriage, Judge Edmonds, until her marriage with a Mr. —— Hamilton, a Lawyer in N. Y., city, 94 Lexington Av., office 120, Broadway, room No. 50.

The youngest dau. Mary, m. Mr. Zust, office 53, New St., N. Y. city.

CHARLOTTE (KEYES) WILSON (331 of Gen.), d. 1836, through the blunder of a physician in giving her arsenic.

The two eldest sons of Cyrus Kyes, were Samuel Proctor (391 of Gen.), and Rollin Headly, which name should be in place of Marcus, 392.

VIII. KYES, WILLIAM E. (394 of Gen.), m. Jennie Stacy, July 16, 1866. His brother, Benton D., m. Alace Burras.

VII. KEYES, ERASTUS (388 of Gen.), d. about 1855. He left two dau. Ellen and Mary, res. in Hudson, Mich.

VII. KYES, SAMUEL (389 of Gen.), d. about 1875.

CHILDREN.

13. Cyrus J.
14. Franklin.
15. Leverett.
16. James.
17. Eliza Keesler.

VI. KEYES, STEPHEN (431 of Gen.), s. of Sampson, Jr., probably d. young, as the descendants know nothing of him. His birth however was on record.

VI. KEYES, PEGGY OR MARGARET (432 of Gen.), b. 1792, m. Job Pitts. She d. in Hartford, July 26, 1855.

VI. KEYES, SARAH B. (433 of Gen.), b. 1793, m. Joseph Burnham of Ashford, Conn., lived in Tolland, Conn. many years, then in Hartford. Her husband d. July 27, 1841, age 59. Mrs. Burnham res. with a son in Neantic, Conn.

### CHILDREN.

18. Joseph D., m. 1st, Amanda Blauvett, of Ramapo, N. Y., who d. Jan. 24, 1859. Dau. Sarah C., who m. Wallac Tracy, res. Hartford; Charles and two dau. who d. early. Joseph m. 2d, Catharine Dow of Ashford. Chil. Harry, Philip and Bessie. Res. Hartford, Conn.

19. George, married, has children and res. in Placerville, Cal.

20. Albert A., m. Sarah Williams of Norwich, Conn. Chil. Albert, Leonard, Joseph, Mary dec. Another Mary, res. Neantic.

21. Charlotte E., m. Edward Williams of Brooklyn, Conn., d. Sept. 1876. Dau. Lucy, b. about 1869. Res. Hartford.

22. John H., m. Estelle Terre, Dec. 20, 1866, who d. Jan. 25, 1876. No chil. Col. John H. Burnham is Post Master in Hartford, Conn.

VI. KEYES, PENELOPE (434 of Gen.), b. 1795, m. Ira Peck of Farmington, Conn. They lived in Marion, Ga. many years, then returned to Hartford, where Mrs. Peck d. Mar. 22, 1869. Her husband d. July 4, 1870.

### CHILDREN.

23. Henry Keyes, b. May 12, 1824, in Ashford, Conn., m. Oct. 31, 1867, Frances B. Johnson, d. Aug. 22, 1877. No chil.

24. John, b. Oct. 19, 1825, d. Nov. 13, 1825.

25. Cornelia C., b. Aug. 24, 1827, res. Hartford. unm.

26. Amanda E., b. Oct. 16, 1829, d. July 5, 1831.

27. Ira H., b. Apr. 16, 1832, d. Nov. 26, 1876. unm.

28. Mary J., b. Mar. 25, 1834, m. Giovanni Danesi of Turin, Italy, June 14, 1873. No chil.

29. William H., b. Mar. 14, 1836, d. July 2, 1837.

30. William H., b. Apr. 19, 1838, m. Dec. 11, 1862, Georgie C. Roberts of Hartford. Res. Hartford. Seven chil.

31. Caroline, b. Oct. 3, 1840, in Marion, Ga., m. May 20, 1862, Henry A. Redfield of Essex, Conn. Has one son. Res. Hartford.

VI. KEYES, HENRY C. (436 of Gen.), eldest son by second

marriage, m. Louisa Perry of Twiggs Co. Ga., and res. in Columbus, Georgia.

### CHILDREN.

Lucia, Mary, Eunice, Lavinia, Lucy and Dent.

VI. KEYES, JOHN (435 of Gen.), 2d son by 2d marriage, m. Sophia Whiting of Ohio, and moved to Iowa. He d. there about 1872. He left a dau. Cornic Peck, aged about 9 years.

A speech of Judge Elias Keyes (438 of Gen.), on the Cumberland or National Road, may be found in a newspaper printed in Washington, and now in possession of Charles Morgan, of Rochester, Vt. H. D. Morgan, of Stockbridge, Vt., has his photograph.

VI. KEYES, EDWARD, Jr. (496 of Gen.), m. Oct. 17, 1821, Mary Hughes, b. Sept. 21, 1802. (The name so spelled by Mrs. Keyes, while other members of the family leave out the e.) They moved to La Salle Co. Ill., Oct. 1830. Mrs. Keyes m. 2d, Alonzo Walbridge, who dec. She res. in Marseilles, Ill., on the homestead. Of the children, Sarah M. was b. Mar. 12, 1826; Roxy E., b. Nov. 1831, d. Jan. 5, 1850; Esther, b. July 1, 1834, d. May 20, 183–, Sarah M., m. May 3, 1846, William Johnson.

### CHILDREN OF SARAH AND WILLIAM JOHNSON.

32. Anna, b. Jan. 15, 1852. Res. Pontiac, Liv. Co. Ill.

33. Isabella, b. July 27, 1857, m. a Denis. Res. Buckley, Iroquois Co. Ill.

34. Emily, b. Oct. 16, 1859. Res. Odell, Liv. Co. Ill. We understand they have also a son, who is a physician.

VI. KEYES, SARAH (497 of Gen.), m. Senator Upham of Vt., who d. in Washington, D. C., of small pox.

IV. KEYES, SIMEON (probably 613 of Gen.), m. Abigail Ward, of Sutton, Mass., Dec. 18, 1781. Record in Sutton.

V. KEYES, PHEBE, dau. of Asa (638 of Gen.), was without doubt, the one of Asa's dau. who married Thomas Lincoln, instead of Anna, as stated in Gen. The father of Thomas was Seth, b. in Rochester, Feb. 10, 1725, descended from one of the first settlers of Hingham, Mass. He married Oct. 19, 1751, Lucy Paige, b. in Hardwick, Mass., Feb. 22, 1734.

35. Otis, s. of Thomas and Phebe (Keyes) Lincoln, was born in Western, (now Warren,) Mass., June 24, 1787, m. Sarah Slosson, b. Aug. 2, 1796, and settled in Newark Valley, N. Y. "He was an active, energetic, enterprising man, engaged in farming, milling, lumbering, trading and manufacturing, and more than any other man has contributed to the advancement of the village of Newark Valley." Sarah, his wife d. Mar. 28, 1844. He m. 2d, Mrs. Mary (Hayes) Pearsoll, who survives him. He d. Dec. 7, 1863. Otis and Sarah rest in Hope Cemetery. They had 12 children. Among them.

36. William Slosson, 1st child, was elected to Congress from 26th Cong. Dist. of N. Y. Res. since 1867, in Washington, D. C. A Lawyer.

37. Charles, 5th child, a druggist of Owego, N. Y.

38. George E., a trader of Painesville, Ohio.

39. Helen Maria, m. June 8, 1853, D. Williams Patterson, s. of Chester and Mary (Elliott) Patterson, "Dentist by profession, farmer and genealogist by practice." Res. Newark Valley.

V. KEYES, SALLY (692 of Gen.), m. William Tufts, July 1, 1807, and d. May 26, 1860. William Tufts d. at New Braintree, July 21, 1824, aged 77.

### CHILDREN.

40. Danforth Keyes, b. July 5, 1808, at New Braintree, m. Sept. 24, 1835, Hannah Mathews. He d. at New Braintree, Aug. 31, 1853.

### CHILDREN.

41. Willie, b. June 11, 1839, d. Mar 28, 1840.

42. George, b. Oct. 17, 1840. He entered Yale college which he was obliged to leave on account of ill health after two years of study, and is now a merchant and a prominent man in New Braintree.

43. James, b. Apr. 23, 1810, d. Oct. 2, 1862.

44. Sally Cutler, b. Aug. 8, 1812.

45. **Washington**, b. Oct. 16, 1814, m. June 4, 1858, Harriet A. Sanford, of Brookfield, Mass. who dec. He has lived in Brookfield 38 years, and for 30 years of that time has been agent of the Boston and Albany R. R., Town Clerk ten years, Town Treasurer and Selectman. Was also in the State Senate of 1875. His sister res. with him.

VI. RENSALAER, READ (697 of Gen.), was son of Nathaniel Read, g. s. of Maj. Reuben Read of Warren, Mass., and g. g. s. of Capt. Nath. Read of the same place. Capt. Nath. was son of Thos. Read, g. s. of Thos. Read, and g. g. s. of Thomas Read, the three last being of Sudbury, Mass.

46. Hannah B., dau. of Rensalaer Read, m. Alanson Read, and had a son,

47. Alanson H., now res. in Chicago, spells his name Reed. The 9th generation from the 1st Thos. of Sudbury. "A. Reed and Sons, Reed's Temple of Music, 191 and 193, State St., Chicago."

IV. KEYES, DANIEL (786 of Gen.), s. of Zebediah and Mary, was b. June 4, 1741.

IV. KEYES, ZEBEDIAH s. of Zebediah, (18 of Gen.), b. May 17, 1746. Brother of Dan. John and Sol.

IV. KEYES, JOHN (788 of Gen.), b. June 7, 1749.

IV. KEYES, SOLOMON (789 of Gen.), b. July 18, 1752.

We know almost nothing of this family with the exception of Daniel, who, as will be seen by referring to Gen., married Abiel, or Abial. A stone in the old cemetery in Keene, N. H., bears this inscription: "Widow Abial, mother of Z. Keyes, d. Aug. 19, 1807, aged 78 years." Although this makes Abial 12 years older than her husband, there seems little doubt that the "widow Abial," was the widow of Daniel Keyes (786 of Gen.), and that she had named her son for his grandfather and uncle. She had five dau. and Zebadiah the only son, is supposed to be the youngest of the family.

48. Zebadiah, b. 1776, d. Sept. 16, 1859. He is supposed to have settled in Keene before 1803.. He had 9 chil. and a number of his descendants still reside there; among them, his grandson, Francis E. Keyes.

The numbers included in parenthesis for the remainder of part 2d, refer to the Gen.

III. KEYES, JOSEPH, JR. (792), s. of Joseph, d. June (or July) 11th, 1744.

IV. KEYES, JONATHAN (794), was b. June 20, 1721, d. 1781.

VI. KEYES, JONAS (819), was b. Nov. 13, 1782. We have no record of his marriage, but he did not marry Sally Read, as supposed in Gen. Sally P. Read was wife of Jonas (1287), s. of Issacher.

KEYES, ANN (831 of Gen.), who m. Lyman Smith, has

### CHILDREN.

49. Charles L., who is m. and res. in Pepperell, Mass.
50. George L., res. E. Pepperell.
51. Mary, married, res. Hudson, N. H.
52. Martha, married, res. in Pepperell.

KEYES, GEORGE H., s. of Liberty (858), b. 1855, res. in Omaha, Neb.

KEYES, LUCY E., dau. of Edward (862), m. Nov. 28, 1870, Charles J. Miller.

53. Abigail, dau. of Moses, Jr. (920), omitted in the list of his children, b. May 18, 1736.

V. KEYES, ABEL (950,) s. of Daniel, b. Sept. 11, 1773.

KEYES, ELECTA (960), had only one dau. Mary Jane. The other two, were children of another marriage.

Mrs. Sarah Keyes, wife of Asa (955), b. June 28, 1791, d. Oct. 29, 1859, in Brattleboro, Vt.

VIII. KEYES, JOEL P. (989), s. of L. M. Keyes, was b. in Ill., learned Fagineering, and ran on the Ill. and Miss. rivers two seasons. Nov. 11, 1861, enlisted into 46 Ill. Inf. At Ft. Donaldson he distinguished himself and received much praise, and later the commission of 1st Lieut. He was twice assigned to the command of a Battallion of Artillery, was also at Pittsburg Landing, Hatchee and other battles. He served through the war, then went into the cotton business in Miss. and La., and made a fortune of nearly $75.000 which the army worm lost to him. Later, the 29th of Feb. 1872, he m. Mary S. Fairley of Princeton, Mo. Present res. Cameron, Mo.

### CHILDREN.

54. Ida May, b. Dec. 11, 1872, in Princeton, Mo.
55. Alta Dale, b. Mar. 18, 1875, in Princeton, Mo.
56. Ella Nora, b. Sept. 26, 1877, in Cameron, Mo.

KEYES, STEPHEN (1125), was a soldier in Rev. war.

VI. KYES, LABAN (1131), changed the spelling of his name either from fancy or want of early education.
Bridget, wife of Ephraim Keyes (1121), d. June 14, 1839.

KEYES, LEWIS (1170), b. Feb. 16, 1800.

KEYES, JAMES (1162), d. Mar. 27, 1841.

KEYES, HENRY (1172), m. 2d, Mrs. Mary Albee.

VI. KEYES, BENJAMIN (1225), m. 1818, Mehitable Bickford of Campton, N. H. Lived in Plymouth, N. H., and Barton, Vt., and d. in Brookfield, Mass., Jan. 20, 1858. His widow now in Brattleboro Lunatic Asylum.

### CHILDREN.

57. Sherburn, d. in Brookfield, Mass.
58. Sylvester, res. Natic, Mass.
59. Caroline, m. Roswell F. Fisk, res. in Barton, Vt.

VI. KEYES, ABEL (1226), m. a widow Abels. Had two sons and one dau. The eldest s. Marquis, now res. in Paton, in the village of Mansonville, Canada, also the dau. Ezra, 2d son lives in Wis. Abel Keyes d. in Paton about 1858, and was buried on his farm.

60. **Franklin Keyes,** s. of Sewell (1228), sup. res. in Concord, N. H. The names of Sewell's dau. were Maria, Esther, Eliza, Augusta and Martha. It is supposed that Augusta m. William M. Lee of Lowell, Mass.

Frank Keyes (1253), s. of Veranus, received an injury in the late war which lost him the use of his lower Fibs. Res. Portsmouth, N. H. His sister Ellen, (perhaps instead of Susan Elizabeth), m. Andrew Varnum. Flora M. ., Sept. 21, 1846, m. Arthur Porter, res. North Adams, Mass.

**KEYES, JONATHAN F.** (1248), m. Nov. 1831, Mary Wood of Francestown, N. H.

IV. **KEYES, ISSACHER** (1270,) was b. according to the record in Chelmsford, July 3, 1747. According to descendants, August 10th, 1747.

This name is recorded Issacher, some of descendants write it Issachar.

**KEYES, PRISCILLA** (1283), m. James Baldwin, in 1798.

**KEYES, CALVIN** (1345), m. Lucy A. Mooar.

**KEYES, MARCUS C.** (1358), was wounded at Petersburg, Va. He m. Corinda Dunham.

**KEYES, MARY O.** (1364), m. J. F. Niles.

Since printing appendix to 2d Part we have received the following:

V. **KEYES, ZEBADIAH** (48 of App. to 2d part), m. Sybel Dunn. One of the sisters of Zeb. m. a Breed, and was living in Lowell, Mass., a few years since. Another m. a Locke, another a Lawrence.

#### CHILDREN.

61. Almira, b. in Keene N. H., Jan. 17, 1803, m. John Colony.

62. Elbridge, b. Dec. 13, 1804.

63. Harriet, b. Nov. 8, 1807, m. Nat. Evans.

64. Fanny, b. Jan. 2d, 1810.

65. Charles, b. Feb. 17, 1812.

66. Sally Ann, b. Jan. 3, 1814.

67. Susan Butterfield, b. Aug. 8, 1816, m. Harvey A. Bill, Keene, N. H.

68. Francis Hartwell, b. Sept. 24, 1818.

69. Hannah, b. Feb. 26, 1821, m. George Perham, of Nashua.

VI. KEYES, ELBRIDGE (62 above), s. of Zebediah, m. Martha Wyman Rugg, of Lancaster, Mass.

### CHILDREN.

70. Francis Elbridge, b. July 10, 1832.

71. Ephraim Wyman, b. 1834, d. Mar. 23, 1835.

Martha W. wife of Elbridge, d. Dec. 22, 1837, aged 29, years. He m. 2d, Mary Wilder Campbell, who d. in Concord, N. H., Sept. 10, 1878. Elbridge d. Dec. 15, 1864.

VII. KEYES, FRANCIS E. (70 above), s. of Elbridge. m. Oct. 3, 1853, Ellen Rebecca Davis, of Keene, N. H.   F. E. Keyes is a merchant of Keene.

### CHILDREN.

72. Willis Sherwood, b. Dec. 26, 1854, d. Feb. 12, 1859.

73. Mary Augusta, b. Aug. 5, 1856, d. Feb. 14, 1859.

74. Herbert Willis, b. Jan. 3, 1859.

75. Martha Rebecca, b. Aug. 7, 1861, d. Apr. 11, 1862.

76. Fannie Ellen, b. Sept. 23, 1863.

77. Grace Louise, b. Oct. 27, 1868.

VII. KEYES, CHARLES, (65 above), s. of Zeb., m. Feb. 22, 1843, Elizabeth E. Richardson, of Rochester, Vt., and d. May 28, 1874.

### CHILDREN.

78. Mary Ellen, b. June 3, 1846, d. Apr. 13, 1852.

79. Charles Edward, b, Aug. 19, 1849.

80. Hannah Perham, b. Oct. 26, 1851.

81. Clara Mabel, b. June 26, 1854.

82. George Harvey, b. Mar. 26, 1863.

VIII. KEYES, HANNAH P. (80 above), dau. of Charles, m. Aug. 21, 1872, Jonas Fred Whitcomb, of Keene.

### CHILDREN.

83. Jonas Fred, Jr., b. May 16, 1873.
84. Hannah, b. Feb. 16, 1875.
85. Charles, b. May 28, 1877.

Washington Tuffs, (45 of App. to 2d part), m. Harriet A. Sanford, June 4, 1846.

Mrs. Tuffs, d. Oct. 3, 1858, aged 36 years.

V. KEYES, HUMPHREY, (1471 of Gen.), m. a Fawcet (or Faucet) lived for a time at Keyes Ferry, then in Greenbrier Co., Va.

### CHILDREN.

86. Joseph, b. at Keyes Ferry, Jeff. Co., Va.
87. Thomas.
88. Isaac, Captain in the war of 1812.
89. Lucretia.
90. Phebe.

VI. KEYS, JOSEPH, (86 above), s. of Humphrey, married, lived for a time in Monroe Co. Va., moved to Greenbrier Co., about 1840, and d. some years since. They write their names Keys.

### CHILDREN.

91. Thomas B., b. May 30, 1829.
92. John.
93. Isaac, was in the Rebel army, taken prisoner, and carried to camp Chase, where he d.
94. Gersham, m. a Miss Hosapple. One child, a daughter. Res. White Sulphur Springs, Va.
95. Lucretia.
96. Phebe.
97. Charlotte, m. a Perry. Six chil.
98. Arabella, m. David Alpaugh.

### CHILDREN.

David, Thomas, Mary Ann, Lucretia, Bettie, Catharine,

Josephine, Denslia.   Res. White Sulphur Springs, Va.
99. Betsey, m. a Myers.

#### CHILDREN.

Joseph, George, Annie, Sarah.

VII. KEYS, THOMAS B. (91 above), s. of Joseph, m. Aug.
4, 1868, Anna Cadwell. They have had a dau. dec. also a son,
100. Jacob, now living.

VII. KEYS, JOHN (92 above), s. of Joseph, m. a Miss
Mapie (or Massie), by whom he had a s. and dau. He m. 2d, a
Miss Pine, and had six chil. Res. White Sulphur Springs.

#### CHILDREN.

James, Joseph, Humphrey, Gersham, Araminta, Elvina.

# APPENDIX TO THIRD PART.

VI. KEYES, LUCY (9 of Gen.), dau. of Robert and Martha. The lost child. "The main facts of the child's mysterious disappearance are briefly told in "Whitney's History of Worcester Co.," published in 1795, and copied almost verbatim into both Russell's and Hannford's Histories of Princeton. The story is also alluded to in a poem written by Prof. Erastus Everett, for the Princeton Centennial Celebration, in 1859.—It was in 1751, that Robert Keyes commenced his pioneering on the slope of Wachusett. The Keyes family was the fourth that settled in Princeton, and the parents were about forty years old, when Robert commenced hewing out for his family a home on the Eastern slope of Wachusett Mountain, in ye township of Princeton, in ye countie of Middlesex, * and Colonie of Mass. Bay. The disappearance of the child occurred in 1755. The next morning after her disappearance, it was observed that the mother's hair had turned from black to gray, and in less than two weeks it was white as snow." The neighbours collected, and by the third day the story had spread, and thousands were on the ground, from Lancaster, Worcester and Barre, and other towns in the vicinity, eager to join in the hunt. The mother became insane, and the father travelled far and long, tracing rumours, often wild and always baseless, and both went down to their graves without a ray of light upon the fate of their lost child.—"Half a century passed away and there lies upon his deathbed, at Deerfield, N. Y., a wretched old man, suffering untold agonies of body and mind. A minister is sent for, and John Littlejohn confesses, that he was the murderer of the dau. of Dea. Robert Keyes, with whom he had a quarrel, about the boundary of their farms." The story of "The lost child, a true tradition of Wachusett Mountain," has been written in an interesting and graphic manner, by William T. Harlow, and printed in "Old and New."

* The northern part of Worcester Co., was originally included in Middlesex.

VII. KEYES, STEPHEN (15 of Gen.) s. of Solomon, sup. m. a Jennison, in Princeton, before going to Michigan. He returned East, as far as Norwich, N. Y., where he d. about 1869. The birth of one child recorded in Princeton.

1. Rosine Elizabeth, b. Aug. 16, 1832. He had also,
2. Stephen (16 of Gen), and several other daughters.
3. S. P. Everett, s. of Rev. Sam. and Lucinda (Keyes) Everett, now res. in Colerain, Mass. Parents dec.

The following record of Nathan Keyes' descendants was collected by Mrs. J. Josephine Waid of Monmouth, Ill.

VI. KEYES, NATHAN (86 of Gen.), s. of Eli, was b. July 17, 1774. A descendent says, "I lived in a town called Notown, afterward called Princeton." Nathan however was not born until sixteen years after Princeton was incorporated. West Princeton may be the locality referred to. Nathan m. 1st, Sally Duncan, and had one son. He m. 2d, Nabbie Phelps, who was b. May 2d, 1778, and d. Nov. 12, 1851. He moved from Mass. to N. Y., State, about 1819, lived in De Kalb, St. Lawrence Co., and d. there, Feb. 20, 1860, at the house of his son Josiah R. Keyes.

### CHILDREN.

4. Luther, b. July 2, 1803.
5. Josiah Richardson, b. Aug. 18, 1806.
6. Betsey H., b. Jan 27, 1809.
7. James, b. Aug. 14, 1811.
8. Everett, b. Mar. 12, 1815.
9. Nathan, b. Aug. 11, 1817.
10. Samuel, b. May 5, 1819.
11. Sally, b. Mar. 30, 1825. d. in infancy.

VII. KEYES, LUTHER (4), s. of Nathan, had five children. Ezra, Esther, Emily, Luther and Warren. Emily m. a Hastings, and res. in Ill.

VII. KEYES, JOSIAH R. (5), s. of Nathan, m. Sally Slayton, Nov. 28, 1850, and d. Apr. 25, 1875. Res. DeKalb, N. Y.

SON.

12. Albert Richardson, b. Jan. 9, 1852, m. Feb. 15, 1877, Kattie J. Sinett. Res. De Kalb, N. Y.

CHILDREN.

13.        Benjamin F., b. Sept. 6, 1878.
14.        Willie E., b. Sept. 22, 1879.

VII. KEYES, BETSEY H. (6), dau. of Nathan, m. Sept. 12, 1830, George Lord.

CHILDREN.

Laberna, Charles, Rosaltha, Nabby and Sally, twins, and William. The first and last have dec.

VII. JAMES (7), s. of Nathan, m. Mar. 12, 1833, Sally Peters, b. in Vt., Aug. 17, 1814. Has. res. in various places, and in late years has been a preacher of the Gospel. Present Res. Montague, Muskegon Co., Mich.

CHILDREN.

15. Horace H., b. Mar. 9, 1834, in St. Lawrence Co., N. Y.
16. William E., b. Feb. 4, 1836, in St. Lawrence Co., N. Y.
17. Abagail C., b. Mar. 12, 1838, in St. Lawrence Co., N. Y.
18. Martha E., b. Feb. 4, 1840, in St. Lawrence Co., N. Y.
19. Olive L., b. May 26, 1842, in St. Lawrence Co., N. Y. unm.,
20. James A., b. Jan. 12, 1845, m. Have not names of chil.
21. Celia I., b. June 6, 1852, in Harrisburg, Lewis Co., N. Y. unmarried.

VIII. KEYES, HORACE H. (15), s. of James, graduated from————College. Is a preacher (Bap.) He married and had three

CHILDREN.

Edward Chapman, Mattie E., Abbie R.

VIII. KEYES, WILLIAM E. (16), m. Nov. 24, 186—, S. Wudellen Salmon.

CHILDREN.

22. Willie W., b. Dec. 20, 1867.
23. Hillie Humphrey, b. Jan. 5, 1870.
24. Harry, b. Dec. 15, 1871. d. Feb. 1873.

VIII. KEYES, ABIGAIL C. (17), m. Oct. 14, 1862, Albert Antrim.

### CHILDREN.

Fred S., Grove W., Mattie B.

VIII. KEYES, MARTHA E. (18), m. Apr. 13, 1864, J. M. Weatherwax.

### CHILDREN.

Clyde B., Jay G., Jessie W., L. Fern, Cliffe M.

VII. KEYES, EVERETT (8), s. of Nathan, m. Jan. 9, 1838, Jane A. Ames. All their children but the youngest, b. in St. Lawrence Co., N. Y. Everett with his family returned to Mass. about 1853. Having been unfortunate in business, he sought and found occupation for his large family in the cotton mills in (probably) Oakdale, and were prospering, when they were seized with Typhoid fever, which went through the family of twelve, commencing with Rosana the 8th child, and ending with "Sir Isaac Newton," the eldest, who died. Everett Keyes, d. of the fever Feb. 21, 1857. After his death and the recovery of the remainder of the family, they returned to N. Y., State. Subsequently, Mrs. Keyes removed to Napolean, Henry Co. O., where her sons joined her after the war. Mrs. Keyes, after 22 years of widowhood, m. F. O. Jones, in Howard City, Mich., in which place three of her children had settled.

### CHILDREN OF EVERETT AND JANE.

25. Sir Isaac Newton, b. Feb. 12, 1839, d. July 14, 1857.

26. J. Josephine, b. Oct. 3, 1840.

27. Mittie M., b. June 8, 1842.

28. Elizabeth A., b. Dec. 11, 1843.

29. Everett A., b. Apr. 6, 1845.

30. Lucius J., b. Oct. 5, 1846.

31. Cautious M., b. May 30, 1848, m. and res. in Howard City, Mich.

32. Rosana M., b. June 29, 1850, d. June 1, 1872.

33. Benjamin F., b. Sept. 6, 1853.

34. Leslie W., b. Oct. 5, 1855. Entered college; not graduated. Studying medicine.

VIII. KEYES, J. JOSEPHINE (26), m. in Richville, N. Y., May 12, 1863, Dr. A. J. Waid. Dr. Waid was b. in Gouverneur, N. Y., studied Dentistry in Ogdensburg, N. Y., and was awarded a Diploma as master of Dental Surgery, by a State board of censors at Albany. He was for a time in Gouverneur, then in Newton, Jasper Co., Iowa. James is now settled in practice in Monmouth, Ill.

### CHILDREN.

Dan Everett and Leslie Andrew, b. in Gouverneur, N. Y., Lillian Emeline and Jay Lincoln, b. in Newton, Iowa.

VIII. KEYES, MITTIE M. (27), m. in Napolean, Henry Co. O., Dec. 21, 1865, Edward Pearce. Res. Howard city, Mich.

### CHILDREN.

William H., Joseph N., Andrew E., Adelbert E., Cora May, L. Arvilla, Lewis E.

VIII. KEYES, ELIZABETH A. (28), m. in Napolean, O., Dec. 24, 1866, Jacob Brubaker. Res. Breckenridge, Mo.

### CHILDREN.

Henry E., Freddie, dec. Rosanna M., Lillian M., Harvey L.

VIII. KEYES, EVERETT A. (29), enlisted as private in the late war, in Co. H., 106 Reg. N. Y. State Vols., was promoted from time to time, and at the close of the war was about to be made Captain, but did not get his papers. He m. in Napolean, O., Feb. 7, 1869, Jemima Rafferty, res. Dalas, Wis. Farmer and Justice of the Peace.

### CHILDREN.

35. Newton E., b. Mar. 26, 1870.
36. Mary A., b. July 21, 1871.
37. Walter W., b. Feb. 20, 1873.
38. Bertha J., b. Sept. 16, 1874.
39. George E., b. May 4, 1876.
40. William K., b. Jan. 28, 1878.
41. Rosanna H., b. May 16, 1879.

VIII. LUCIUS J., (30), was in the late war. He m. Oct. 4, 1873, Harriet A. Fawver. Res. Napolean, Henry Co., Ohio.

### CHILDREN.

42. Weslie Vincent, b. July 20, 1874.
43. Elnora Idell, b. Jan. 11, 1876.
44. Olive, b. July 1, 1878.

VIII. KEYES, BENJ. F. (33), m. Lilla Hale. Res. Howard City, Mich.  son

45. Dennis, b. Dec. 22, 1877.

VII. KEYES, NATHAN (9), s. of Nathan, m. 1st, Mrs. Almira Moore, and lived in the vicinity of De Kalb, N. Y., where his children were born and raised. After the death of his wife, about 1873, he removed to Atlanta, Logan Co. Ill., and m. Miss Zarina Farr. Res. Atlanta.

### CHILDREN.

Dorville, Martha, Amelia and Angelia.

VII. KEYES, SAMUEL (10), s. of Nathan, m. Dency Johnson, in De Kalb. He removed to Sycamore, De Kalb Co. Ill., between 1850 and 1855. Res. for a time in Mo., last heard from in Osage, Bourbon Co., Kan.

### CHILDREN.

46. Milan, who m. and dec. early. Had one dau.

## LATEST REPORTS.

VI. KEYES, DAVID (643 of Gen., 1st part), s. of Cyprian, Jr., was a Farmer and m. Ruby Adams of Milford, N. Y. David d. Mar. 27, 1857, aged 76. Ruby his wife, d. Feb. 6, 1837, aged 68. Both d. in West Windsor, N. Y.

### CHILDREN.

1. Israel, b, in the Spring of 1800.
2. Ezra, b. Aug. 1804.
3. Evaline, m. Emery Blatchley. Children now living, Ruby, Electa, David.
4. Ashley.
5. Levi, b. 1811, in Milford, N. Y.
6. Nelson, d. in the Spring of 1867, unm.
7. Gilson, b. Jan. 31, 1816.

8. Harriet, m. Harvey Travis. Three children.

    · Lewis, William, George.

9. Hannah, m. Stenard Humiston. She d. Sept. 1878.

### CHILDREN.

Jane, Adelbert, Ruby, William, Harriet, Eva and Ella.

10. John.

VII. KEYES, ISRAEL (1), s. of David, m. Celestia Shay, and had 8 children, 6 now living. He was a Farmer as are his two sons. He d. Dec. 1, 1869, in Kirkwood, N. Y.

### CHILDREN.

George, Stallam, Eleanor, Ruby, Almira, Verona.

VII. KEYES, EZRA (2), s. of David, m. Eliza J. Gilman, in West Windsor, N. Y. He was a Farmer and Sheriff, and d. Sept. 3, 1843.

### CHILDREN.

Sarah J., David E.

VII. KEYES, ASHLEY (4), s. of David, m. Maria Shay.

### CHILDREN.

Henry, Edgar, Melissa, James, Lucius, Arvilla, Sarah and Nellie.

VII. KEYES, LEVI (5), s. of David, m. Sarah Piper, a Teacher, in 1832. Levi was a Mechanic, and lived in Binghamton, until after the death of his mother, when he bought a farm in West Windsor, where he has since resided.

### CHILDREN.

11. Jerusha, b. 1835, m. Mar. 21, 1859, d. May 15, 1875, in Little Valley, N. S.

12. Asa, b. Feb. 22, 1837, d. Feb. 1843.

13. Cyprian, b. Feb. 13, 1841, m. Dec. 1866. Farmer, res. in Kirkwood.

14. Logenia, b. Mar. 16, 1844, educated for a Teacher, m. ——— Soule, Apr. 11, 1867. We are indebted to Mrs. Soule for the record of David Keyes' descendants. Res. West Windsor, Yew York.

15. Adelbert, b. May 15, 1847, m. May 26, 1874. Lives on the homestead in West Windsor.

16. Isaac, b. Oct. 27, 1849, m. Apr. 14, 1872. Res. Kirkwood, New York.

17. Sarah, b. Oct. 18, 1853, m. July 4, 1874.

VII. KEYES, GILSON (7), s. of David, m. 1st, Adeline Harding, who dec. No chil. He m. 2d, Cornelia McCollister, and had one son. He m. 3d, Sept. 22, 1856, Anna Toban, by whom he had two sons.

### CHILDREN.

18. David Henry, b. Dec. 25, 1848, s. of the 2d marriage, m. Nellie Lester in Binghamton, N. Y.

19. Frank Reginald, b. Mar. 6, 1858. Clerk in Binghamton, unmarried.

20. George Gilson, b. May 5, 1862. Cigar maker, unm.

VII. KEYES, JOHN (10), s. of David, m. Jane Stevens. They had two chil. Edwin F., and Myron. Mrs. Keyes, dec. many years ago, and John married again. Res. in Iowa.

VII. KEYES, THOMAS SUMNER (603 of Gen. 1st part), b. Sept. 21, 1819, m. Dec. 31, 1843, Catharine Lathrop. Farmer, res. in Richford, Tioga Co., N. Y.

### CHILDREN.

21. Sarah Elizabeth, b. June 27, 1845.

22. Horace Henry, b. Feb. 22, 1847, d. Aug. 7, 1849.

23. William Sumner, b. May 16, 1852, m. Elmira Gee, Sept. 16, 1877.

24. Benjamin Thomas, b. Aug. 22, 1857.

IX. KYES, SARAH M. (668 of Gen. 1st part), dau. of W. B. Kyes, m. Oct. 25, 1864, Geo. W. Hazelett.

### CHILDREN.

25. Nellie Kyes, b. Feb. 16, 1867.

26. Alice Bell, b. May 4, 1871.

27. Clara Lee, b. Oct. 8, 1875.

IX. KYES, SEVELLON C. (669 of Gen. 1st part), m. Mar. 10, 1878, Gertrude Blatchley.

IX. KYES, BELL (670 of Gen. 1st part), m. Aug. 10, 1869, W. Hazelett.

### CHILDREN.

28. Claude Kyes, b. Aug. 23, 1870.
29. Fred William, b. Jan. 26, 1873.
30. Lynn Brooks, b. Oct. 24, 1874.

The two youngest sons of Thomas N. Keyes of Bellows Falls, Vt., (720 of part 2d), were in the late war. Alfred G., (738), was at Winchester, and in the hottest of the fight, while raising his gun to shoot, a shell burst in front of him, a portion of which struck the gun, severing it in two. One part fell to the ground and the other he brought off the field as a trophy. At the same time he received a wound that nearly severed his thumb from his hand. Upon applying to the surgeon, he was informed "he should soon be relieved of his thumb." Anxious to save it, he applied to another surgeon and had it dressed, and although crippled, it is better than none, and another trophy of that field. He now draws a pension.

V. KEYES, ELIZABETH (100 of Gen. 1st part), who m. Joshua Blanchard and had a son,

31. Amos, b. 1773, in Wilton, N. H., pupil in Phillips Academy, afterwards a prominent citizen of Andover, Mass. Cashier, &c.

32. A John Keyes was living in Springfield, Mass., from 1669, to 1671. Name on the town records. Nothing farther known of him.

33. Aaron Keyes, was among the first settlers of Watertown, N. Y. About 1802, he erected a Coopers shop, near what is now the centre of the town. His son,

34. Kimball, lives in Oswego Co., N. Y.

35. Thomas, s. of Kimball, still carries on the trade in Watertown.

36. An Abel Keyes, died a few years since in Algonquin, Ill. His widow still lives there, also a son,

37. Henry.

38. J. L. Keyes, another son of Abel now resides in Des Moines, Iowa. Is clerk of the County Court, and a prominent man.

39. Rev. W. S. H. Keys, D. D., res. at Parsons Ranche, Lewisburg, Penn.

40. Lewis Keyes resides in Wells, Me. His store was burned to the ground during the year, 1878 or '9. His sons and other members of his family res. in Wells.

41. Isaac Keyes was living in Springfield, Ill., within a few years.

42. Sol. Keyes of Cambridge, and Sally Newhall of Leicester, Mass., were published, Jan. 23, 1798, in Leicester.

43. John D. Keyes. This name found on a gravestone in Dixon, Ill.

44. Asenath Keyes and John Ashley were married, date uncertain.

45 Henry Keese was married to Elizabeth Parry, Sept. 5, 1721, by Rev. Nath'l Rogers, Portsmouth, N. H. "This man was a substantial citizen of Portsmouth, paying in 1727, a tax of 22 dollars.

46. Samuel Keese, Town Clerk of Portsmouth, was also a man much respected, as is shown by his seat in the pulpit with the minister."

47. A Samuel Keais m. Widow Mary Hoddy, 1695. Mention is also made in early records of one,

48. Peter Keais. There is no proof that either of the four last mentioned individuals belong to our genealogy.

Keyes, in 307, 311 and 312, of Gen. 1st part, pages 29 and 32, should be spelled Kyes.

Cypron, (282 of 1st part), should have been spelled Cyprian, which is undoubtedly the original method of spelling the name. Descendants spell it, Cyprian, Cyprien, Cypron and Cypren.

On page 253, 16th line, for Samuel, read William.

**VI. KEYES, ASHLEY** (31 Gen. 1st part), s. of Elisha, and great grandson of Dea. John Keyes. The following is from "The Independant Press," of Greenville, Pa., of Jan. 1853.

## OBITUARY.

Ashley Keyes was born Nov. 29th, 1765, at Shrewsbury, Mass., where he spent the first twenty-five years of his life. Thence he went to Vermont and settled at Newfane, in Windham Co., when that country was quite new. There he resided until he was nearly seventy years old, when he removed to Bristol, Ohio. About three years since he came to this borough with his son Benjamin L. Keyes, at whose house he had a comfortable home and received those kind attentions which are so peculiarly needful and agreeable to one weighed down by the infirmities of old age, and where he died on the 27th day of January, (1853), aged 87 years and two months.

It is said that he was a man of remarkably mild and peaceable disposition, and that he never failed to secure the confidence and esteem of those who became acquainted with him. It is believed that he never had an enemy. He was strictly moral during his whole life, and it is thought by his friends that he experienced a change of heart after he had passed his three score years and ten. E. J.

The following notice of the death of Naham Keyes, (45 Gen. 1st part), s. of Ashley, is from "The Lake Superior News," of Marquette, Mich., April 10, 1862.

## ANOTHER OLD RESIDENT GONE.

We have to announce the loss of another one of our oldest inhabitants—Mr. Naham Keyes, who departed this life April 5th, (1862), of Pulmonary disease, aged fifty two years. Mr. Keyes came to Marquette about fifteen years ago, and was among the first who came with the intention of making it their abiding place. He was a quiet, law abiding citizen, and probably without an enemy in the world, which can be said of few others. Peace to his Ashes.

VIII. KEYES, CHARLES W. (55 Gen. 1st part,) grand s. of Ashley, after his graduation at Williams Coll., travelled a year in Europe, and has since held a prominent and influential position in his native city, Quincy, Ill. "Attorney at Law."

Ella L., (84 Gen. 1st part), only dau. of Emerson W. Keyes of Brooklyn, N. Y., d. Sept. 10, 1879.

A later account of the family of Charles Keyes, page 276, omits the dau. Hannah, in the list of his children. John Banker, 2d son, m. Jane Allaire.

Eleazer W. Keyes, graduated at the Coll. of New Jersey, 1795. Probably the Eleazer W., mentioned in Miss Hemenway's Vt. Gazetteer, page 567, and the Eliezer, (278, Gen. 2d part), recorded at Pomfret, Conn., in which record the W. is omitted.

On page 299, 6th line, for James, read **Dr. Waid.**

VII. COL. JOHN K. PAIGE (319 Gen. 2d part), grad. probably at Williams College. He had three sons,

49. J. C. T. Paige. Grad. at Williams College.

50. John K. Paige. Grad. at Union, Schenectady.

51. Aldigo C. Paige. Grad. at Union.

52. Leonard, s. of J. C. T. Paige, (49 above), **grad. at** Union Coll. 1878.

VII. ALDIGO C. PAIGE (325 Gen. 2d part), grad. at Williams Coll. His son,

53. Edward Winslow, grad. at Union, and at Cambridge Law School. Res. Schenectady, N. Y.

Three sons of Mrs. Diana C. (Paige) Jackson, (326 Gen. 2d part), grad. at Union Coll, Schenectady.

# INDEX.

## A

Aaron, 149, 154, 159, 200, 212, 213, 303. Aaron W., 159.
Abbie F., 214, 241. Abbie L., 50.
Abbie M., 179. Abbie R., 297.
Abbie S., 199.
Abby, 20, 84. Abby S., 189.
Abel, 166, 181, 183, 184, 186, 187, 196, 200, 288, 289, 303. Abel J., 27, 28. Abel K., 182.
Abi, 74.
Abial, 154.
Abigail, 12, 16, 19, 49, 83, 88, 89, 98, 99, 166, 178, 183, 190, 200, 203, 240, 267, 282, 288. Abig. C., 297, 298. Abig. H., 247. Abig. J., 65. Abg. P., 184, 189. Abig. T., 196.
Abijah, 163, 237, 267, 268. Abijah W., 268.
Abner, 77, 190, 198. Abner H., 16.
Abraham, 236.
A. C. Paige, 93.
Ada, 9, 78, 181, 303. Adah, 36.
Adda, 275. Ada M., 52.
Addison, 10, 18, 52. Addison A., 10, 11.
Adaline, 133, 138, 246. Adeline, 33, 272.
Adaliza M., 102.
Adam C., 67.
Adela G., 74. Adella C., 213.
Adelaide A., 270, 271.
Adelbert, 301, 302. Adel. E., 299.
Aditia M., 1382.
Adna, 79.
Adson D., 79.
Agnes G., 117. Agnes J., 99.
Agnes L., 40. Agnes W., 177.
Ahira K., 182. Ahira Z., 246.
Alanson, 40. Alanson H., 287.
Albert, 12, 40, 99, 100, 109, 243, 270, 284. Albert A., 239, 284.
Albert B., 198, 199. Albert C., 270. Albert F., 30, 31. Albert G., 226. Albert H., 9, 201, Albert L., 278. Albert M., 173.
Albert N., 255. Albert P., 145.
Albert R., 43, 263, 297.
Alberta, 31.
Alcey E., 10.
Aldtigo C., 91.
Alexander D., 117, 251. Alex. H., 122. Alex. S. B., 122. Alex. S. S., 122.
Alfred, 198, 241. Alfred A., 15.
Alfred De F., 277. Alfred E., 127.
Alfred G., 142, 303. Alfred P., 141, 199.
Alford B., 65.
Alice, 158, 194, 215, 220. Alice A., 36, 124. Alice B., 146, 210, 302. Alice M., 28, 136, 246. Alice R., 47.
Alicia M., 156.
Allen C., 5.
Almira, 77, 193, 194, 201, 246, 290, 301. Almira C., 91, 94. Almira E., 189. Almira J., 201.
Almond, 55. Almon, 72.
Alonzo, 14, 76. Alonzo A., 214.
Alonzo B., 214.
Alphens, 221, 246.
Alston, 73.
Alta D., 289.
Alvan, 169. Alvah, 206. Alvah E., 194, 250. Alvin C., 22. Alvin L., 241.
Ama, 249.
Amasa, 47, 77, 78, 79, 83, 84, 105, 110. Amasa W., 81.
Amanda, 252. Amanda E., 284.
Amanda S., 135.
Ambrose, 73, 246.
Amelia, 69, 76, 218, 300.
Amial, 213.
Amory, 52, 54.
Amos, 12, 13, 17, 63, 77, 81, 82, 98, 101, 303. Amos E., 17, 271.

Amos H., 17.
Amy A., 126. Amy L., 40, 278.
Amy S., 248.
Andre, 252.
Andrew, 64, 69, 72, 73, 74, 280.
And. A., 272. And. E., 299.
And. F., 127, 129. And. J., 32,
101, 193, 259. And. R., 252,
255. And S., 106, 263.
Angelia, 300.
Angelica, 39.
Angeline, 192, 244, 276. Angeline
A., 102. Angeline C., 81.
Angie M., 80.
Ann, 75, 152, 288. Ann A., 154.
Ann M., 41, 202, 219, 220.
Anna, 4, 88, 89, 111, 132, 137,
158, 150, 191, 200, 212, 213, 285,
286, 263, 285. Anna E., 241.
Anna F., 134. Anna G., 125.
Anna J., 73. Anna R., 31.
Annah, 98.
Anne, 78. Anne S., 199.
Annette, 52. Annette N., 99.
Annette S., 81.
Annice, 47. Annis J., 275.
Annie, 293. Annie L., 273. Annie
R., 11. Annie S., 156.
Anson, 41, 79. Anson L., 80.
Antoinette, 91, 226, 282.
Antonia, C. A., 127.
Arabella, 292.
Arad, 197.
Araminta, 275, 293.
Archibald, 64, 67, 245.
Artemus, 47, 101.
Arthur, 54, 73, 93, 101. Arthur C.,
188. Ar. F., 157. Ar. G., 141.
Ar. H., 124, 134. Ar. K., 32.
Ar. L., 278. Ar. N., 31. Ar.
P., 244. Ar. R., 170. Ar. S., 11.
Ar. T., 83.
Arvilla, 301, 206. L. Arvilla, 299.
Asa, 24, 42, 43, 44, 78, 131,
132, 133, 165, 166, 173, 176, 180,
288, 301. Asa G., 99. Asa K.,
44. Asa L., 180.
Asahel, 214. Asahel, Jr., 214.
Asenath, 51, 72.
Ashley, 3, 300, 301, 305. Ash. Jr. 4.
Atwood B., 271.
Augusta, 11, 272, 290. Augusta
A., 14. Augusta J., 15.
Augustus S., 134.
Aurilla S., 30.

Austin O., 52.
Ave, 69.
Avis, 76, 88, 282.
Azubah, 3, 64, 240, 241.
Azuba, 274.

B

Bathsheba, 264.
Bayley, 260.
Bell, 52, 303. Bella, 227. Belle,
197. Belle W., 125.
Benjamin, 24, 46, 47, 182, 196, 250,
251, 252, 256, 257, 259, 289. Benj.
F., 42, 43, 159, 160, 161, 191, 297,
298, 300. Benj. L., 4. Benj. S.,
250. Benj. T., 302.
Benton D., 101, 283.
Berenice M., 122.
Bertha, 168, 170, 224. Bertha
A., 153. Bertha J., 299,
Berton, 248.
Bessie, 69, 100, 284. Bessie A.,
191. Bessie, L., 14. Bessie M.
C., 117. Bessie Van M., 157.
Betsey, 4, 13, 20, 40, 42, 82,
159, 182, 193, 200, 206, 208, 250,
251, 252, 255, 293. Betsey
C., 45. Betsey H., 296, 297.
Bettie, 220, 226, 227, 292.
Betty, 38, 48, 49.
Beulah, 209.
Beverly W., 75.
Bigar, 12.
Blanche, 182.
Breighton, 46.
Buran, 222.
Burton, 241, 275.

C

Caleb H., 44. Caleb T., 44.
Calista, 72.
Calvin, 28, 206, 207, 237, 252, 253,
290. Calvin A., 268. Calvin D.,
170. Calvin F., 167. Calvin Jr.,
238. Calvin W., 169, 170, 197.
Campbell, 221.
Carleton, 161.
Carlos K., 135.
Caroline, 54, 122, 123, 152, 178,
203, 248, 284, 289. Car. E., 145.
Car. F., 75, 121. Car. H., 41.
Car. M., 117. Car. W., 100, 195.
Carpenter, 196.
Carrie, 82, 181, 186, 187. Carrie
E., 19, 66, 125. Carrie J., 108.
Carrie M., 68, 127, 179, 196.

Carroll, 9.
Casper, 197.
Cassius C., 212.
Cate, 38.
Catharine. 24, 93. 97, 178, 192, 248, 292. Cath. E., 263. Cath. B., 160. Cath. F., 27. Cath. S., 14, 15. Cath. W., 184, 195.
Cautious M., 298.
Cella I., 297.
Chandler, 54.
Charles, 21, 23, 50, 53, 64, 66, 67, 85, 93, 134, 177, 179, 182, 183, 190, 239, 242, 243, 244, 256, 262, 270, 276, 284, 286, 291, 292, 297. Cha. A., 82, 103, 104, 186, 202. Cha. B., 44, 189. Cha. C., 16, 35, 276, 277. Chas D., 19, 124, 127, 145, 146, 174, 177, 207. Chas. E., 33, 46, 65, 102 208, 210, 241, 256, 272, 273, 291. Chas. F., 5, 14, 67, 144 Chas. G., 18, 19, 176, 277, Chas. H., 16, 17,65, 127, 162, 163 173, 257, 272, 273, 278. Chas. J., 259.
Cha. K., 5, 213. Chas. L., 95, 156, 159, 192, 288. Chas. M., 135, 258. Chas. N., 17, 272. Cha. O., 203. Chas. P., 173. Cha. R., 66, 170. Chas. S., 195. Cha. T., 44. Chas. U., 50. Cha. W., 5, 22, 80, 144, 206, 207, 268, 306.
Charlotte. 84, 92, 159, 180, 196, 219, 283, 292. Char. A., 96. Char. E., 15, 93, 146, 284, 292. Char. L., 108.
Chauncey, 250.
Chester, 28, 84, 87. Chester D., 272.
Chitty C., 192.
Christopher. 23. Chris. C., 239.
Cincinnatus, 36.
Clara, 40, 97, 197, 247, 248. Clara A., 203, 211. Clara B., 199.
Clara G., 203. Clara J., 141.
Clara L., 302. Clara M., 32, 291.
Clara S., 163.
Clarence E., 16, 187. Clar. R., 9.
Clarissa, 4, 40, 91, 98, 238, 243, 247, 248.
Claude K., 303.
Clemantine, 161, 162.
Cliffe M., 298.
Clinton, 124. Clinton W., 277.

Clotilda, 275.
Clyde, 124. Clyde B., 298.
Columbus, 27, 28.
Conrad S., 11.
Cora H., 28. Cora M, 299.
Corinna. 78.
Cornelia, 5, 72, 220, 249. Cor. R, 50. Cor. C., 284. Cor. L., 192.
Cornie P., 285.
Cornelius. 93, 198. Corn. A., 270.
Corn. F., 158.
Corydon D., 198.
Cotton, 40.
Curtis, 103.
Cynthia. 53, 74, 184. Cyn. B., 270. Cyn. C., 71. Cyn. E., 52. Cyn. I., 255. Cyn. L., 55. Cyn. M., 189.
Cyprian, 24, 48, 49, 53, 301, 304.
Cyril, 105.
Cyrus, 100, 101. Cyrus H., 203, 221. Cyrus J. 283.

**D**

Daisy. 239. Daisy M. R., 272.
Dana W., 199.
Danforth, 111, 122, 123, 124, 131, 136, 146, 231, 286 Dan. D., 140, Dan. K., 286.
Daniel, 64, 73, 74, 152, 147, 164, 165, 166, 167, 183, 206, 212, 215, 240, 241, 242, 246 247, 248, 287. Dan. A., 212, 213. Dau. B., 194. Dan. E., 299. Dan. H., 218. Dan. M., 82. Dan. W., 270.
Dapheria, 77.
Daphney, 75.
Darwin, 125. Dar. P., 152, 153.
Dassy, 41.
David, 13, 18, 20, 21, 24, 40, 48, 49, 52, 56, 105, 111, 129, 131, 132, 137, 138, 142, 145, 148, 164, 192, 273, 276, 277, 292, 300. Dav. A., 270, 278. Dav. B, 53. Dav. C., 14, 270. Dav. D., 50. Dav. E., 55, 123. Dav. H, 275, 302. Dav. L., 129, 251. Dav. R., 183.
Deau W., 83.
Deborah. 191.
Delia, 68, 177, 238. Della A., 30, 31, 263.
Deliverance, 21.
Della M., 50.
Delocia, 41. Deiotia, 129.
Delora, 258.
Dennis, 49, 50, 300.

Dennison N., 243, 244.
Denslia, 293.
Dent, 285.
Diadama, 21.
Diana C., 91.
Diantha, 208, 281.
Dick, 177.
Dinah, 24, 25.
Docia, 82.
Dodd N., 218.
Donald, Mc D., 254
Dolly, 213. Dolly B., 34, 37.
Dolly M., 35. Dolly T., 49.
Dora M., 104.
Dorcas, 213. Dorcas C., 35.
Dorothea 23. Dor. 276. Dor. G. 47.
Dorothea B., 214.
Douglas, 258.
Dwight N., 240. Dwight B., 248.
D. Dwight, 270. Dwight, W. 127

E

Earl F., 142.
Earnest M., 15. Earnest N., 32.
Earnest V., 28.
Ebenezer, 2, 3, 25, 26, 27, 30, 32, 54,
85, 164, 190, 196, 240, 245. Eben.
Jr., 27 29, 197. Eben S., 27, 28.
191. Eben W., 161.
Eber, 3, 4, 10, 267.
Edee B., 296.
Edgar, 243, 301. Edgar D., 141.
Edgar E., 50. Edgar G., 192.
Edgar M., 81. Edgar W., 145.
Edith, 175, 189. Edith J., 40.
Edith M., 281.
Edna, 79. Edna L., 55, 153.
Edward, 27, 28, 29, 40, 62, 77, 103,
105, 110, 111, 158, 181, 209, 268.
Ed. A., 11, 208, 269. Ed. C.,
5, 297. Ed. D., 125, 127. Ed. E.,
77, 186, 187. Ed. F., 67, 125, 125.
Ed. G., 208, 278. Ed. H., 158.
Ed. J., 50. Ed. Jr., 126, 285.
Ed. L., 112, 117, 119, 120, 122,
142. Ed. M., 14, 140. Ed. P., 114.
199, 299. Ed. S., 93, 96, 105, 209,
228. Ed. W., 5, 29, 97. Ed. Z. 24.
Edwin, 54, 167, 181, 201, 202, 203.
Edwin A., 36, 211. Edwin E.,
127. Edwin K., 17. Edwin L.,
41. Edwin R., 75, 106, 107, 123,
125, 173. Edwin S., 41. Edwin
W., 17, 45, 256.
Effie L., 17.
Egbert Le Roi, 127, 128.

Elbert M., 39.
Elbridge, 290, 291.
Eldon R., 225. Eldon W., 138.
Eldora, 209.
Eleanor, 120, 301. El. E., 278.
El. F., 117.
Eleazur, 84. Ellezur, 84. El. F.,
191. Eleizer T., 245.
Electa, 38, 179, 238, 288, 300.
Electa S., 167, 168, 288.
Elexa, 262.
Eli, 240. Eli Jr., 240.
Elias, 1, 2, 20, 21, 60, 61, 73, 75,
105, 110. Elias A., 22. Elias
F., 39. Elias H., 126. Judge
Elias, 109, 285. Elias S., 39.
Elihu, 262.
Elijah, 264. Elijah C, 276, 277.
Elina E., 275.
Eliphalet, 102.
Elisha, 3, 27, 248, 264. Elisha Jr.,
27, 28. Elisha D., 247. Elisha
W., 184. E. W. Jr., 187.
Eliza, 39, 41, 54, 84, 181, 186,
203, 218, 230, 246, 278.
Eliza A., 100, 208, 247. Eliza C.,
92, 93. Eliza F., 248. Eliza G.,
175. Eliza J., 191. Eliza K.,
283. Eliza M., 101.
Elizabeth, 3, 9, 12, 20, 64, 66,
77, 78, 86, 87, 88, 103, 105, 106,
111, 129, 130, 148, 149, 150, 163,
164, 182, 183, 191, 217, 219, 221,
231, 237, 249, 253, 264, 273, 274,
275, 276, 280, 282, 303. Eliz. A.,
64, 67, 74, 298, 299. Eliz. E., 55.
Eliz. G., 201. Eliz. H., 16. Eliz.
J., 195. Eliz. M., 212. Eliz. P.,
149. Eliz. S., 87, 281.
Elkanah, 2.
Ella, 33, 194, 229, 301. Ella F., 211.
Ella J., 41. Ella L., 11, 103, 305.
Ella M., 195, 210. Ella N., 289.
Ella S., 27, 259.
Ellen, 9, 30, 171, 180, 220, 283, 290.
Ellen A., 65, 211. Ellen D.,
175, 176. Ellen E, 65, 205.
Ellen F., 9, 28. Ellen G., 10. Ellen
L, 18, 103, 126, 173. Ellen M.,
114, 159, 172, 204, 212, 246.
Ellen R., 199, 224.
Ellsworth 69.
Elmer A., 50.
Elmira, 238.
Elmore LeRoy, 275.
Elnathan, 84, 87, 88, 91, 282.

**Elnora** l., 300.
**Elton**, 171.
**Elvina**, 275, 293.
**Elvira**, 191, 274.
**Ely**, 38, 40.
**Emerson**, 11. Em. W., 10.
**Emily**, 4, 32, 40, 64, 73, 75, 184, 285.
  Em. A., 139. Em. H., 126. Em.
  M., 16. Em. S., 272.
**Emma**, 79, 145, 194, 220, 238. Em.
  A , 17. 50. Emma D., 272. Em.
  F., 199. Emma J , 32. 276 Em.
  L , 28. Emma O., 125. Emma
  S., 197. Emma T., 68.
**Emmeline**, 158, 181, 274. Emm.
  E., 144. Emm. M., 196. Emm.
  S., 243.
**Emory** C., 32.
**Eurilla**, 209.
**Ephraim**, 12, 19, 61, 62, 64, 69, 72,
  73, 79, 190, 193, 198.
**Eph.** A., 77. Eph. W., 291.
**Erasmus** D., 112.
**Erastus**, 98, 100, 283.
**Ervin** B., 31.
**Esther**, 1, 78, 106, 108, 111, 126, 147,
  196, 197, 237, 255, 285, 290.
**Esther** A., 74. Est. C., 123. Est.
  M., 211.
**Ethel**, 170, 175.
**Etta** 239. Etta A., 81.
**Eugene**, 39.
**Eugenia**, 11.
**Eunice**, 60, 130, 285.
**Eva**, 301. Eva M., 43. Eva I., 37.
**Evaline**, 300.
**Eve**, 69.
**Eveline**, 180, 181. Eveline M., 43.
**Everette**, 54. Everett, 240, 296,
  298. Everett A., 298, 299.
**Ezekiel**, 163, 190, 197.
**Ezra**, 49, 240, 243, 248, 267, 300, 301.
  Ezra B., 49, 50. Ezra H., 247.
  Ezra, Jr., 241. Ezra S., 12, 271.
  Ezra W., 12.

**F**

**Fannie**, 170. Fan. A., 272. Fán-
  nie C., 142. Fan. E., 291.
**Fanny**, 138, 206, 291. Fan. F., 75.
**Ferrando** C., 46.
**Fidella**, 239.
**Fielding**, 75, 76.
**Fletcher** D., 192.
**Flora** A., 33, 179, 208. Flo E., 16,
  211. Flo. M., 198, 290.

**Florence**, 156, 157, 170, 177, 271.
  Flor. A., 117, 187. Flor E., 32.
  Flor. G., 43. Flor. J., 207.
**Frances**, 29, 217. Fran. F., 196.
  Fran. G., 149, 163. Fran. J., 80.
  Fran. O., 36.
**Francis**, 18, 25, 30, 31, 33, 34, 38,
  39, 42, 45, 67, 103, 218, 219, 250.
  Fran. A., 196. Fran. B., 45.
  Fran. E , 37, 288, 291. Fran. H.,
  291. Fran. W., 117, 226, 227, 228.
**Frank**, 14, 30, 73, 75, 88, 99, 108,
  125, 186, 198, 242, 218, 219,
  243, 255, 290. Frank A., 186.
  Frank E., 80, 179, 182, 189.
  Frank F., 141, 211. Frank G.,
  127. Frank H , 75, 256. Frank
  J. B., 202. Frank K , 72. Frank
  P., 41, 206. Frank R., 302.
  Frank W , 281.
**Franklin**, 72, 99, 196, 204, 205, 283,
  290. Frank B , 161. Frank D.,
  37. Frank W , 145, 281.
**Frederic**, 63, 6, 37, 72, 77, 145, 258.
  Frederic A., 5, 211. Frederic
  K , 45, 179. Frederic P., 186.
**Fred**, 89, 134, 177, 189. Fred A.,
  17. Fred. C., 136, 196. Fred. E.,
  104 Fred. H., 40, 168. Fred. L.,
  41, 82. Fred W., 241, 303.
**Freddie**, 19, 299. Freddie H., 272.
  Freddie O., 83.
**Freelon** E., 37. Freelon K., 37.
**Freeman**, 143.

**G**

**Gayton** H., 31.
**Geneva** May, 66.
**George**, 20, 33, 40, 53, 74, 93, 154,
  157, 160, 183, 193, 219, 222, 244,
  250, 252, 262, 272, 281, 288, 293,
  301. Geo. A., 33, 41, 82, 125, 199,
  222, 277. Geo. B., 140, 111, 175,
  176, 251. Geo. C., 101. Geo. D.,
  37. Geo. E., 28, 53, 162, 194, 286.
  Geo. F., 14, 43, 76, 167, 194, 197,
  204. Geo. G., 9, 116, 147, 228,
  302. Geo. H., 19, 32, 43, 44, 69,
  96, 124, 141, 158, 186, 187, 211.
  288, 291. Geo. L , 168, 288. Geo.
  M., 195. Geo. P., 66, 222, 224,
  225. Geo. R., 168, 204, 211. Geo.
  S., 122, 157. Geo. S. W., 204.
  Geo. T., 144, 225. Geo. W., 50,
  81, 93, 102, 123, 138, 201, 203, 212,
  228, 246.

Georgia, 9. Georgia M.. 13.
Georgianna, 15. Geor. F., 37.
Gerrish, 237.
Gersham, 215, 216, 217, 218, 228, 292, 293.
Gertrude E., 136, 175. Ger H , 281.
Giddings W., 111, 127.
Gilbert S., 277. Gilbert W., 277.
Gilman M., 195.
Gilson, 300, 302.
G. N., 255.
Gould D., 136.
Grace, 93, 212. Grace B., 157. Grace L., 291.
Graham, 81.
Grosvenor, 46.
Grove W., 298.
Gustavus, 27, 28.

**H**

Hale L., 167, 168.
Hamilton A., 120. Ham. M., 173.
Hamlin W., 127, 128.
Haney M., 40.
Hannah, 3, 20, 23, 34, 37, 60, 63, 64, 67, 77, 80, 149, 164, 196, 213, 215, 240, 247, 264, 267, 273, 276, 291, 292, 301. Hann. B., 287. Hann. E., 181, 241. Hann. J., 192. Hann. M., 106. Hann. P., 291, 292. Hann. T., 210. Hann. V., 196. Hann. W., 91.
Harden, 245.
Harland, 78. Harlan P., 248.
Harley L., 39, 275.
Harlow W., 66.
Harman. 73.
Harold F., 124.
Harriet, 9, 38, 47, 52, 73, 133, 140, 181, 208, 246, 257, 274, 290, 301. Harriet A., 74, 249. Harriet C., 275. Harriet E., 139, 144. Harriet L., 228, 269. Harriet N., 53, 143. Harriet S., 139.
Harry, 82, 258, 284, 297. Harry D., 147. Harry K., 5. Harry R., 36. Harry T., 93.
Hartwell C., 191.
Harvey, 219. Harvey L., 299. Harvey R., 178, 179. Harvey S., 218.
Hasme, 200.
Hattie, 275. Hattie A., 162. Hattie E., 142. Hattie J., 66. Hattie L., 128. Hattie W., 37.

Hazen, 198.
Heiress, 62.
Helen, 31, 54, 170, 175, 244, 282. Helen A., 128. Helen C., 269. Helen E , 127. Helen F., 55. Helen M., 41, 210, 286.
Heman, 241.
Henrietta L., 37.
Henry, 21, 22, 40, 60, 63, 92, 93, 99, 104, 129, 130, 143, 144, 193, 244, 246, 256, 263, 280, 289, 301, 304. Henry A., 146, 147, 208. Hen. B., 254. Hen. C., 170, 224, 284. Henry E., 299. Henry F , 18, 199, 273. Henry H., 249. Henry J., 194. Henry K., 201, 284. Henry L., 233. Henry M., 199. Henry O., 158. Henry P., 22, 33. Henry S., 39, 92, 199. Henry W., 39, 127, 194.
Hepsibah, 3, 48, 49, 132. Hepcy H., 55.
Herbert D., 68. Her. E., 45. Her. F., 40. Her. L., 271. Her. W., 127, 128, 241, 291.
Hetty M., 87, 88, 256.
Hezekiah, 47.
Hillie H., 297.
Hiram, 21, 54, 69, 77, 82, 180, 221, 262, 263, 274. Hiram A., 81. Hiram E., 247. Hiram P., 180.
Homer, 214. Homer E., 11, 108. Homer J., 39.
Horace, 40, 53, 54, 138. Hor. A., 28, 213. Hor. H , 297, 302. Hor. N., 218. Hor. T., 143, 144. Hor. W., 198, 199.
Horatio, 263. Hor. A., 37. Hor. A. B., 30. Hor. N., 247.
Hortense E., 161.
Howard F., 29. How. L., 244. How. M., 9.
Hugh, 264. Hugh Y., 253.
Huldah, 2, 3, 63, 64, 105, 179, 201, 244. Huldah B., 14.
Humphrey, 228, 229, 292, 293. Capt. Hum. 217, 218.

**I**

Ida E., 167, 195. Ida F., 241. Ida M., 179, 289. Ida S., 50.
Imla, 150, 157.
Ira 18, 196, 214. Ira H., 284. Ira S., 255.
Irene, 39, 271.
Irving J., 108.

**I**

Isaac, 130, 183, 193, 195, 292, 302, 304. Isaac B., 275.
Isaac H., 172.
Isabel, 9. Isabella, 41, 285. Isabella F., 144.
Isaiah, 105, 108.
Isidora F., 212.
Israel, 48, 77, 165, 166, 167, 168, 300, 301. Israel N., 50.
Issacher, 200, 290.
Ivory, 204.
Ivy, 271.

**J**

Jacob, 165, 181, 183, 214, 231, 293.
James, 2, 12, 20, 23, 88, 98, 100, 158, 166, 167, 177, 183, 192, 193, 200, 203, 204, 249, 250, 251, 253, 255, 260, 280, 283, 286, 289, 293, 296, 297, 301. James A., 81, 297. James B., 102. James D., 170. James E., 73. James H, 39, 45, 99, 106, 219, 220. James, Jr., 204. James K., 203. James M., 139, 253, 254. James P., 193, 194, 220. James, Sen., 97. James W., 161, 228.
Jane, 60, 67, 163, 179, 220, 252, 273, 301. Jane A., 254. Jane C., 222, 224. Jane L., 123. Jane S., 248. Jane W., 259, 276.
Janette, 79, 177.
Jared, 167. Jared B., 258.
Jasper H., 254.
Jay G., 298.
Jennie M., 205.
Jeduthan, 12, 13, 267, 269.
Jemima, 19, 27, 32. Jemima K., 32. Jemima W., 30.
Jenievieve, 182.
Jennie, 145, 186, 283. Jennie A., 105. Jennie C., 41. Jennie K., 128, 224. Jennie M., 82.
Jeptha, 201.
Jeremiah, 105, 109. Jer. J., 106, 108, 109.
Jerome, 106.
Jerusha, 83, 84, 301.
Jesse, 191, 262. Jesse G., 276, 278. Jesse S., 278.
Jessie, 187, 212. Jessie E., 33. Jessie R., 65. Jessie W., 298.
Joann E., 241.
Joanna, 19, 148, 149, 200, 237.
Joash, 200, 211.
Joel, 47, 150, 152, 166, 170, 238, 239.

Joel E., 201. Joel P., 172, 288.
John, 2, 12, 13, 60, 62, 64, 72, 75, 77, 88, 92, 104, 123, 125, 147, 150, 154, 156, 164, 178, 180, 192, 197, 203, 216, 219, 220, 228, 231, 242, 245, 246, 249, 250, 251, 252, 253, 256, 257, 258, 262, 264, 267, 273, 276, 277, 280, 282, 284, 285, 287, 292, 293, 301, 302, 303. John A., 13, 14, 41, 88, 89, 135, 201, 206, 278. John B., 66, 228, 262, 270, 276, 278, 306. John C., 68, 76, 204, 268. J. C P., 95. John D., 304. Des. John, 2. John E., 67, 125, 277. John F., 15, 18, 19, 30, 39, 144, 211, 260. Gen. John 89. John H, 4, 17, 94, 159, 214, 215, 284. John H. F., 96 John K., 15, 91, 93, 220, 224, 306. John K. Jr., 220. John L., 50, 144. John M., 73, 106, 157, 173, 222, 253, 255. Maj. John, 211. John N., 15, 270. John P., 125. John Q., 43. John S., 154, 156, 189, 214. John Sen., 218. John W., 52, 92, 93, 112, 222, 224. John T., 221. John T. G., 194. J. L., 304.
Jonas, 23, 38, 49, 62, 77, 99, 150, 154, 165, 178, 190, 191, 197, 200, 209, 211, 288. Jonas C., 274. Jonas F., 202. Jonas, Jr., 178.
Jonathan, 19, 20, 24, 34, 42, 132, 148, 149, 158, 182, 191, 234, 288. Jon. F., 198, 199, 280. Jon. H., 159. Jon. Jr., 25, 159. Jon. M., 43. Jon. O, 30, 31. Jon. V., 163. Jon. W.,
Joseph, 23, 60, 62, 123, 126, 148, 149, 159, 159, 160, 163, 184, 185, 219, 220, 252, 262, 272, 292, 293. Jos. A., 23. Jos. B., 154, 157. Jos. C., 196, 221. Jos. D., 284. Jos. E., 160. Jos. F., 111, 129, 210. Jos. H., 16, 17, 160, 273. Jos. Jr., 118, 288. Jos. K., 189. Jos. L., 245. Jos. N., 299. Jos. S., 187. Jos. W., 55, 152, 153, 157.
Josephine, 54, 161, 293. Jos. A., 163. Jos. B., 74, 75. J. Jos., 298, 299.
Josephus, 202.
Joshua, 193, 195, 212.
Josiah, 31, 36, 202, 213, 240, 262. Josiah R., 296.

41

Josie A., 271.
Jotham, 13, 49, 52, 53. Jotham, Jr., 55.
Judith, 60, 76.
Judson, 55.
Julia. 74, 84, 257, 258. Julia A., 41, 208. Julia B., 272. Julia E., 47, 48, 269. Julia M., 270. Julia R., 83. Julia S., 192.
Julian, 194. Julian V., 160.
Juliette, 54. Julietta, 246. Ju. E., 83. Ju. G., 11.
Julius, 122, 123, 257, 258.
July A., 275.
Justin, 38, 74. Justin E., 40. Justin H., 189.
Justus, 105, 110, 111.
J. Dwight, 39.

### K
Karl D., 123. Karl S., 281.
Kate, 212, 254. Kate K., 128. Kate L., 67. Kate W., 96.
Katie, 187, 203. Katie L., 281.
Kendall G., 272.
Kent O., 192.
Keyes, 128, 138.
Keziah, 21.
Kimball, 303.
Knight, 245.
Kittie, 186. Kittie Bell, 113.
Kitty, 248.

### L
Laban, 191, 289. Laban J., 192.
Laertes J., 226.
Lal, 220.
Larned, 78, 281.
Laura, 55, 91, 133, 201, 220, 238. Laura A., 66, 179. Laura B., 71, 175, 282. Laura E., 65, 189, 207. Laura L., 192. Laura M., 136.
Lauren K., 93.
Lauretta, 82.
Laurinda, 159. Laurin. M., 214.
Lauriston, 75, 76.
Lavina, 217.
Lavinia, 276, 285.
Leles, 23.
Llewellyn T., 37.
Lemuel, 38, 40, 41, 264.
Lena C., 213. Lena M., 142. Lena J., 101.
Leonard, 12, 284. Leonard A., 208.
L. Leon, 134.
Leslie A., 299. Leslie G., 28. Lesley L., 46. Leslie W., 298.
Lester, 243.

Letitia, 222.
Leverett, 283.
Levi, 38, 40, 47, 200, 213, 238, 300, 301.
Levinah, 48, 49, 215, 237.
Lewis, 3, 11, 85, 193, 196, 275, 289, 301. Lewis E., 299. Lewis H., 238.
Lewis L., 46.
Libby A., 192.
Liberty, 158.
Lillian E., 299. Lillian M., 125, 299.
Lillie, 125, 227. Lillie C., 145.
Linn, 78, 79.
Linda, 61, 79.
Linsey W., 210.
Lisle, 73.
Lizzie A., 125. Lizzie E., 29, 128. Lizzie F., 29. Lizzie L., 134.
Logenia, 301.
Loren, 73. Loren A., 74. Loren B., 74. Loren P., 244.
Lorenzo, 27, 106. Lo. D., 238, 239. Lo. M., 32.
Louis P., 228. Louis R., 187. Louis W., 168.
Louisa, 140, 163, 228, 274. Louisa A., 196. Louisa B., 223. Louisa N., 83.
Louise D., 14. Louise E., 127. Louise H., 50. Louise I., 128.
Lovisa, 275.
Luce, 83.
Lucinda, 78, 80, 134, 183, 208, 236, 243. Lucinda B., 134.
Lucia, 285. Lucia W., 282.
Lucius, 243, 244, 301. Lucius J., 298, 299. Lucius M., 171.
Lucretia, 217, 236, 292.
Lucy, 13, 33, 41, 42, 44, 45, 49, 83, 98, 140, 149, 154, 166, 167, 178, 181, 182, 183, 236, 245, 267, 284, 295. Lucy B., 122. Lucy J., 27. Lucy M., 214, 29.
Luke, 4.
Lulu E., 182. Lulu F., 204.
Luna F., 271.
Lusilla F., 203.
Luther, 42, 46, 238, 296. Luther F., 197. Luther H., 14, 15, 197.
Luther M., 16.
Luthera, 77.
Luvica, 218.
Lydia, 12, 20, 34, 37, 50, 148, 149, 157, 158, 159, 200, 213, 237, 259,

264. Lydia A., 10, 67. Lydia B., 74. Lydia E., 43, 73 Lydia K., 10, 197. Lydia M., 246.
Lydia B., 75.
Lyman, 245, 257, 274. Lyman B., 211.
Lynn B., 303.

M

Mabel, 170. Mabel F., 104, 187.
Mabelle A., 271.
Mae A., 134. Mack R., 169.
Mahala, 256, 257.
Malcolm S., 108.
Mamie A., 186.
Marcella, 218.
Marcus, 101, 209, 210. Mar. B., 22. Mar. C., 207, 290. Mar. M., 204 Mar. W., 210.
Margaret, 229, 250, 283. Mar. B., 66. Mar. J., 228.
Margaretta C., 277.
Marguerite E., 40, 55.
Maria, 83, 87, 88, 212, 258. Maria A., 162, 210. Maria C., 91.
Maria H., 201. Maria M., 209.
Mariam, 191.
Marian 5, 274.
Marion B., 157. Marion C., 15. Marion I., 146. Marion S., 135.
Marietta, 35, 83, 246, 248. Marietta B., 248. Marietta W., 71. Mariette, 54.
Marium H., 101.
Marsdin, 65.
Marshall, 244. Marshall M., 171, 172. Marshall S., 142.
Martha, 5, 21, 28, 55, 77, 131, 158, 221, 236, 242, 243, 252, 255, 270, 300. Mar. A., 194, 204. Mar. B., 53, 224. Mar. C., 50. Mar. E., 76, 222, 259, 297. Mar. G., 144. Mar. J., 270. Mar. L., 222, 223. Mar. M., 76, 158, 193. Mar. P., 33. Mar. R., 291. Mar. S., 160.
Marther, 41.
Martin B., 22. Martin K., 44. Martin L., 80.
Marvin, 245, 246.
Mary, 1, 3, 9, 14, 17, 20, 38, 39, 44, 51, 53, 55, 56, 60, 61, 67, 74, 79, 82, 84, 88, 99, 111, 129, 131, 132, 140, 147, 152, 154, 164, 167, 169, 179, 180, 196, 206, 215, 219, 228, 236, 240, 242, 243, 249, 270, 274, 282, 283, 284, 285.

Mary A., 4, 45, 46, 54, 68, 93, 108, 112, 134, 145, 173, 187, 212, 244, 275, 278, 291, 292, 299.
Mary B., 72, 126. Mary C., 22, 271. Mary D., 191. Mary E., 11, 32, 43, 66, 69, 124, 168, 191, 195, 199, 209, 210, 269, 291. Mary F., 29, 33, 44, 93, 209. Mary G., 28, 172. Mary H., 52. Mary J., 15, 18, 19, 47, 192, 193, 195, 211, 255, 271. Mary K., 9, 46, 124. Mary L., 32, 72, 108, 157, 170, 212, 214, 277, 278. Mary O., 13, 125, 207, 290. Mary P., 29, 170. Mary R., 16. Mary S., 136. Mary V., 221. Mary W., 92, 93, 123, 153, 223.
Massa, 21.
Mathew P., 76.
Mathias, 23.
Mattie, 220. Mattie B., 204, 298. Mattie E., 297.
Matilda, 219.
Maxwell, 122.
May 212.
Mazelda, 77, 78, 79.
Mehitable W., 80.
Mehumen, 77.
Meliscent, 23.
Melissa, 52, 301. Melissa A., 179. Mel. M., 9. Mel. W., 55.
Mellen E., 37.
Melville B., 17. Melville W., 272.
Melvina E., 135.
Mercey, 218. Mercey A., 80.
Merlin H., 15. Merlin, 270.
Merton J., 16.
Milon, 300. Milon C., 211.
Miles, 73. Miles G., 67.
Milford, 280.
Milo, 77. Milo O., 22.
Milton, 248, 253, 257.
Mina, 135.
Minette F., 292.
Minnie B., 136. Minnie E., 167. Minnie F., 126. Minnie H., 32. Minnie M., 179.
Miranda J., 289.
Miriam, 24, 64, 71, 72, 99, 100, 149, 163.
Mittie M., 298, 299.
Molly, 18.
Monroe, J., 275.
Moody, 191.
Moors, 30.
Morris O., 39.
Morses, 78, 80.

Moses, 13, 21, 60, 163, 212. Moses, Jr., 163. Moses W., 17.
Myra C., 171.
Myrta, 275.

**N**

Nahum, 3, 4, 159, 160, 163, 178, 179, 183, 201, 203, 119.
Nancy, 71, 133, 159, 160, 163, 178, 179, 183, 201, 203, 219. Nancy B., 235. Nancy E., 159, 209. Nancy F., 75, 76. Nancy H., 201. Nancy L., 106.
Naomi, 27, 30, 33. Naomi K., 32. Naomi S., 30.
Nathan, 16, 240, 242, 296, 300. Nathan A., 255. Nathaniel, 240, 245, 256, 264. Nath. A., 268.
Nehemiah, 85.
Nella E., 179.
Nellie, 28, 301. Nellie D., 83. Nellie E., 81. Nellie G., 298. Nellie K., 302. Nellie L., 80, 83. Nellie R., 228. Nellie S., 194.
Nelson W., 93, 195, 300.
Neta, 81.
Nettie E., 80. Nettie R., 27.
Newell, 53, 55.
Newton, 274. Newton E., 299.
Nicholas, 221.
Norman, 187. Norman D., 186. Norman L., 92.
Norris D., 35.
Nye P., 103.

**O**

Ogden, 14. Ogden B., 139.
Olive, 16, 78, 88, 130, 196, 200. Olive C., 256. Olive E., 17. Olive F., 29. Olive S., 189.
Olivia, 182.
Oliver, 236, 244, 259, 260. Oliver A., 184, 188. Oliver G., 27, 28.
Oren, 38, 262. Orin, 214, 237. Oren D., 38.
Orenza, 78.
Orison, 79, 80.
Orlando, 257, 258, 259. Orlando W., 199.
Orpha, 81.
Orson H., 83.
Oscar, 238. Oscar D., 256.
Otis, 158, 286.
Ozander A., 134.

**P**

Paphyrus B, 248.
Pardon, 133, 134, 137, 146, 247, 248.

Parmella, 40. Parmella E., 55.
Patience, 38.
Patrick H., 35.
Patty, 48, 49, 149, 150, 164. Patty W., 64.
Paul, 21. Paul M., 29.
Paulina, 243.
Payne, 180.
Peabody, 48, 51, 83, 87.
Penelope, 104.
Peggy, 83, 85.
Percey, 84.
Percy, 105.
Perley, 64, 69, 76. Perley G., 65, 68, 71. Perley M., 74.
Perry A., 192.
Persis, 19, 20, 45, 48. Persis B., 50.
Peter, 1, 249, 304. Peter K., 17, 271.
Phebe, 1, 2, 12, 13, 16, 19, 132, 180, 181, 235, 236, 273, 285, 292. Phebe A., 22. Phebe H., 180.
Phidelia, 134.
Philharma, 63, 64, 75.
Philinda, 4. Philinda A., 10.
Phile, 78. Phila, 237, 245.
Philemon D., 180.
Philip K., 157.
Phinehas, 53. Phin. C., 52, 53. Phin. D., 178, 179.
Polly, 34, 36, 42, 89, 150, 163, 178, 184, 213, 240.
Prentice, 98, 99. Capt. Prentice, 102.
Prentiss, 245. Prentiss M., 36.
Prescott, 156.
Preston, 29.
Priscilla, 129, 202, 203, 290.
Prudentia, 109.

**R**

Rachel, 163. Rachel N., 67.
Raleigh, 10.
Ralph, 82, 258. Ralph C., 188.
Rawdon, 40.
Raymond, 178.
Rebecca, 1, 99, 131, 150, 190, 247.
Reliance, 237.
Renewa E., 74.
Rensslaer, 138, 287.
Reuben, 129, 130, 213.
Rex, 78.
Rhoda, 12, 21, 238, 257. Rhoda N., 30.
Richard, 260. Richard A., 207. Richard F., 91. Richard G., 71.

**R**

Richard M., 14.  Richard W., 261.
Rina, 15.
R. Kimball, 268.
Robert, 1, 20, 87, 228, 235, 251, 252, 273, 274, 280.  Rob. D., 141.  Rob. L., 256.  Rob. S., 274, 275.  Rob. W., 251.  Rob. Y., 224.
Robison, 221.
Roderic, 258.
Roger, 157, 250.
Rollin H., 283.  Rollin K., 170.  Rollin W., 169.
Rosamond A., 30.
Roscoe, 73.
Roseltha L., 81.
Rosie M., 126.
Rosina, 55.  Rosine T., 158.
Rouitoma, 245.
Roswell, 98, 102.  Roswell K., 171.
Roxana, 51.  Roxanna, 110, 111.
Roxa, 204.
Roxy, 204.  Roxy E., 126.
Royal, 4, 9, 135.  Royal P., 171, 173.
Ruby E., 173.
Ruel, 240, 241.
Rufus, 158.
Russell M., 22.
Ruth, 13, 16, 18, 60, 77, 129, 130, 150, 164, 198.  Ruth H., 134, 197.  Ruth S., 206.
Rutillus W., 30, 31, 32.
Ruthven S., 126.

**S**

Sabiana B., 221.
Salla, 150.
Sallie E., 211.
Sally, 34, 38, 42, 62, 64, 72, 78, 133, 137, 142, 143, 159, 166, 178, 181, 183, 190, 193, 201, 213, 240, 286.  Sally C., 286.  Sally K., 138.
Salma, 25, 27, 279.
Salmon G., 243, 270.
Samas, 12.
Samuel, 87, 101, 164, 190, 193, 194, 231, 250, 251, 252, 253, 255, 262, 263, 264, 278, 283, 296, 300.  Sam. A., 253.  Sam. B., 261.  Sam. H., 194, 251, 265.  Sam. J., 64, 66, 262, 263.  Sam. K., 87.  Sam. P., 161, 283.  Sam. T., 191.  Sam. W., 86, 281.
Sampson, 61, 88, 89, 98, 103, 110, 200, 205, 206.  Samp. Jr., 104.  Samp. Sen., 282.
Sarah, 1, 2, 12, 19, 20, 23, 44, 45, 59, 60, 67, 77, 87, 102, 105, 109, 111, 131, 132, 134, 140, 148, 200, 201, 209, 216, 218, 231, 237, 243, 285.  Sarah A., 36, 67, 68, 69, 145, 162, 182.  Sarah B., 86, 87, 283.  Sarah D., 274, Sarah E., 55, 127, 221.  Sarah F., 5.  Sarah G., 196.  Sarah J., 68, 79.  Sarah M., 36, 52, 73, 129, 134.  Sarah P., 85, 127, 128.  Sarah S., 272.  Sarah T., 210.  Sarah, V., 35.
Sarepta, 134.
Seth, 238, 262, 263.  Seth Q., 51.  Seth C., 278, 279.
Sevellon C., 52, 303.
Sewall, 181, 182, 196, 290.
Shepherd, 242.
Sherburn, 289.
Shubael, 247, 248, 249.
Sidney W., 243, 249.
Silas, 12, 19, 20, 272.  Silas D., 248.  Silas P., 225.
Simeon, 150, 285.  Simeon P., 239.
Simon, 12, 267.  Simon, Jr., 267.  Simon S., 184, 186.
Sir Isaac N., 298.
Smyrna S., 46.
Solomon, 25, 27, 30, 60, 61, 105, 106, 131, 132, 133, 135, 137, 140, 117, 200, 201, 215, 236, 242, 267, 268, 287, 304.  Sol. A., 31.  Sol. M., 134, 135.  Capt. Sol. 130.  Sol. N., 30, 31.
Solon, 71, 72.  Solon A., 36.  Solon T., 36.
Sophia, 40, 133, 181, 182.  Sophia A., 123.  Sophia J., 106.  Sophia M., 160.  Sophia P., 39.
Sophronia C., 145.
Spencer K., 93.
S. P. Everett, 296.
Stacy C., 101.
Starr, 211.
Stebbens, 77.
Stella A., 104.  Stella E., 104.
Stephen, 61, 69, 72, 83, 87, 92, 93, 104, 149, 150, 190, 196, 204, 206, 209, 235, 236, 237, 274, 275, 281, 282, 283, 289, 296.  Steph. A., 159.  Col. Steph. 85.  Steph. F., 210.  Steph. K., 85, 171, 173, 202.  Steph. P., 65, 84, 92, 102.  Rev

**S**

Steph., 68.   Steph S., 86, 220,
  281.   Steph. T., 210, 211.
Stillman, 214.
Submit, 12, 23.
Sumner, 46.   Sumner W., 162.
Susan, 238.   Susan A., 17.   Susan
  B., 80.   Susan C., 134.   Susan
  J., 145, 172.   Susan L., 47.
  Susan M., 44.   Susan W., 229.
Susanna, 13, 17, 164.
Sybil, 191, 200.
Sylvanus H., 36.
Sylvester, 145, 289.   Sylvester P.,
  240.   Sylvester W., 239.

**T**

Tabitha, 130, 164.
Tamar, 3.
Tamsia, 253.
Tennison E., 198.
Thaddeus, 21, 242, 243.
Thama, 135.
Thankful, 45, 200, 215.
Theda, 79.
Theodore, 253.   Theo. A., 95.
  Theo. E., 127.   Theo. L., 17.
  Theo. S., 87, 95.
Theora B., 221.
Thirza, 68.
Thomas, 2, 12, 18, 21, 42, 89, 137,
  138, 143, 218, 229, 231, 265, 267,
  280, 292.   Thom. B., 292, 293.
  Thom. C., 144.   Thom. E., 45.
  Thom. G., 208.   Thom. J., 49.
  Thom. K., 45.   Dea. Thom., 23.
  Thom. L., 221.   Thom. N., 43,
  140, 142.   Thom. S., 43.   Thom.
  W., 229.
Thurston T., 210.
Timothy, 24, 38, 212.
Titus, 237.
Tolman, 274.
Trueworthy, 159, 161.
Tryphena, 3, 264.
Tylar, 52, 53.

**U**

Uriah, 200, 213.

**V**

Veranus, 198.
Verona, 301.
Victor S., 27.
Vine, 78, 81.
Viola, 239.   Viola A., 275.
Virgie D., 177.

**W**

Wade, 135, 222.   Wade K., 224.
Wallace B., 141.   Wallace L., 207.
Walter, 163, 201, 204.   Walter H.,
  201.   Walter P., 168.   Walter W.,
  187, 299.
Ward, 211.
Washington, 133, 136, 137, 142, 144,
  146, 219, 221, 225, 287, 292.
  Wash. F., 103.
Warren, 19, 29, 75, 137, 145.   War-
  ren C., 241.   Warren S., 106, 108,
  145.   S. Warren, 207.
Wealthy R., 239.
Welcome, 246.
Weslie V., 300.
Willard, 4, 5, 154.   Willard C., 5.
  Willard E., 11.
William, 46, 51, 62, 64, 69, 72, 73,
  85, 86, 87, 140, 142, 154, 156, 161,
  165, 180, 181, 183, 186, 191, 193,
  195, 198, 213, 219, 242, 243, 252,
  253, 256, 259, 271, 280, 282, 301.
  William A., 47, 278.   Will. B., 51.
  Will. C., 274.   Will. D., 39, 249,
  255.   Will. E., 101, 195, 276, 277,
  278, 283, 297.   Will. F., 17, 211.
  Will. G., 221.   Will. H., 14, 35,
  74, 76, 128, 199, 255, 270, 272, 284,
  299.   Will. J., 139, 228.   Will. Jr.,
  181.   Will. K., 246, 299.   Will. L.,
  16, 39, 194, 253, 254.   Will. M.,
  14, 201.   Will. Mc C., 226.   Will.
  P., 103, 221.   Will. R., 64.   Will.
  S., 224, 286, 302.   Will. S. P.,
  228, 255, 260.   Will. T., 37, 87.
  Will. V., 14.   Will. W., 35, 43,
  45, 64, 65, 97, 135, 245.   Rev. W.,
  S. H., 304.
Williams, 99.
Willis, 38, 39, 161, 182, 239, 242,
  243.   Willis S., 182, 291.
Wilson, 245.   Wilson, Jr., 245.
  Wilson K., 275.
Winfield, S., 117, 118, 211.
Winnifred, 9.   Winn. P., 29.
Winona, 31.
Winthrop B., 211.   Win. S., 34.
Worthy, 258.
Wright S., 159, 162.
Wynn. H., 39.

## Z

Zachariah, 91, 92, 93.
Zachary, 88.
Zama, 79.
Zealy, 76.
Zebadiah, 288, 290.   Zebediah, 60,
  147, 287.
Zechariah, 61, 104.
Zenas, 21, 48, 80.
Ziba, 18.
Zoa, 205.   Zoa A., 212.